Responsible and Sustainable Business

Liangrong Zu

Responsible and Sustainable Business

The Taoism's Perspective

Springer

Liangrong Zu
Founder of Global Youth Leadership
Academy (GYLA), Taoist Leadership Academy
for Sustainability & Excellence (TLASE), Partner
Expert on HR Strategy of UNIDO
Vinovo, Italy

ISBN 978-3-030-91115-7 ISBN 978-3-030-91117-1 (eBook)
https://doi.org/10.1007/978-3-030-91117-1

This Springer imprint is published by the registered company Springer Nature Switzerland AG.
The registered company address is: Gewerbestrasse 11, 6330 Cham, Switzerland

Preface

Those who learn from the ancient Tao
Are able to guide the present world.
Those who follow the law of Nature
Are able to know the source of the universe.
—Laozi, Tao Te Ching, Ch. 14

I have been living this book since 2013 when I signed the publishing agreement with Springer and finally sat down to complete my writing when the COVID-19 pandemic disrupted our lives and changed our perceptions of the VUCA era (volatility, uncertainty, complexity and ambiguity) in 2020. It was the pandemic crisis that awakened and led me back to Chinese classical wisdom in an uncertain world:

"Good fortune leans on misfortune,
Misfortune lurks behind good fortune.
Who knows when one shall change to another?
No paradigm can be followed.
Normal can change to abnormal,
Good can change to evil.
People have been deluded for a long time."
—Laozi, Tao Te Ching, Ch. 58[1]

Life is like a wood chip floating on the surface of water,
It runs with the flow, and stops on the river islets.
Thus, committing your life to fate with selflessness.
Valuing not the breath of life, but emptying yourself,

[1]The English version of *Tao Te Ching* that author cited in this book was translated by the author. The translation was built on the author's comprehensive study and review of hundreds of the existing English translations and interpretations, combining his knowledge and understanding of Chinese philosophy, literature and history, and his years of research on modern management and leadership. The purpose of this translation is to endeavour to unlock the secret of *Tao Te Ching* and embark on a quest to deepen spiritual understanding of thoughts and wisdom of Laozi, so that it can effectively serve today's world.

You can have freedom.
Detaching yourself from the outer world,
You can comprehend fate and be free of sorrow.
—Jia Yi (201–169 B.C.) "The Owl"

The ancient Chinese sages teach us that uncertainty is the only certainty there is, and knowing how to live with insecurity is the only security. The sages inspire us to do more meaningful things in times of crisis because they always believe that crisis does not bring us only threats and dangers but opportunities and hopes. In times of uncertainty, if we run with the flow, we can stop on the river islets (security); if we commit ourselves to fate with selflessness, we can have freedom; if we do not value the breath of life, but empty ourselves, and detach ourselves from the outer world, we can comprehend our fate and be free of sorrow.

The crisis offers me the opportunity of pursuing something meaningful, one of which is to work hard to offer Taoism's wisdom through writing this book to those who are interested in the Chinese traditions, especially to great leaders who are able to respond to the challenges and take responsible decision for the post-pandemic development.

Laozi is an ancient Chinese sage, author of the *Tao Te Ching* (the Book of the Way and Virtue) and the founder of philosophical Taoism. His wisdom on how to identify, disentangle, interpret and solve important issues that had confronted him in ancient times still sustain deep and lasting influence over our modern mind. Laozi's wisdom has the unfailing function to empower, enlighten and guide us through complexity, adversity and uncertainty and to address timely and important practical issues in our today's world.

I have learnt on the years' study journey into Chinese classical traditions that how powerful Laozi's wisdom is in directing and guiding us to live a meaningful and successful life. The treasures of Tao are unexhausted and significant. The Tao is just like what we know about the forest—there is no ready-made timber in the forest, but we can take advantage of the forest to produce timber. Laozi says in *Tao Te Ching*, Ch. 28, that *the Tao is like a block of wood; those who are good at carving it into pieces, and making whatever they want, can become a great leader*. The Tao cannot prevent the world from disaster, but it can refine everything in the universe. The Tao is abstruse and mysterious, and cannot be seen, heard and touched, but Tao dominates and creates everything in the universe. Thus, if we understand and master the principles of Tao, and apply them in our life and work, there is nothing we cannot do well.

I fell in love with Chinese classical traditions, particularly with the wisdom of Taoism about ten years ago when I received a call for paper from Conference Committee on Practical Wisdom for Management from the Chinese Classical Traditions. The conference was organized in Shanghai, China, in June 2010. I did not submit the paper to the conference, because I did not have any knowledge about Chinese classical wisdom. However, the call inspired me to begin the long journey into the study of Chinese traditions. Since 2010, I have dedicated most of my time and effort to immersing myself in the philosophy of Taoism and Confucianism, and endeavouring to integrate the Chinese classical philosophy into teaching and research in management and leadership. I believe that Chinese traditional wisdom will play an important role in changing people's thinking, behaviours and the world as a whole through enriching, inspiring and enhancing the present and future generations.

Since the late 1990s, when I began to develop and organize educational and training programmes for business executives and government officials, when I embarked on teaching in the areas of corporate social responsibility (CSR) and sustainable development for academic institutions, and when I undertook PhD research on CSR in Nottingham University Business School, I have always learned and promoted the new ideas and best practices of Western management to the organizations I have worked with. I was dreaming one day that I would be able to introduce Chinese wisdom and values from our ancient sages to the Western world.

On the journey to search for practical wisdom of Chinese classical traditions, I found that a growing number of civil societies, academics, public intellectuals and business practitioners have consistently been searching for values, ideas and practices from Eastern wisdom. They would expect that the practical wisdom from our ancient ancestors could inspire and guide a new generation of leaders to make wise decisions in response to climate change and other wicked problems in the world. The researches and findings have offered me food for thought and shed light on modern management and leadership. However, I have discovered that the more I studied it, the more I was confused with the findings and outcomes that some of the academic researchers have produced in terms of interpretations and commentaries on the wisdom of Taoism.

I was so curious about what it is going on with the current study of Taoism. I did some searches at the beginning of 2021 for Laozi's book *Tao Te Ching* and got about six million of results, and with the title *Dao De Jing*, about ten million of results. What does this mean? It implies that today we have immersed ourselves in the enormous information on Taoism, and might lead us astray from the true wisdom of Taoism if *Tao Te Ching* is misinterpreted.

The wisdom of Chinese traditions can serve as a guide to address timely and important practical issues in the real world. But I found that there is a missing link between what academic researchers or philosophers have translated, interpreted and commented on the bible of Taoism, and what business practitioners have applied and practised in the real world. In other words, on one hand, those who undertake researches on or interpretation of the Chinese classical wisdom and philosophy have no or less knowledge of management and leadership science. On the other hand, those practitioners who try to draw on and apply the principles and wisdom of Taoism in their work lack the knowledge of Chinese classical traditions; they substantially depend on the interpretations, translations and commentaries which are done by researchers and philosophers. This leads to confusion and misunderstanding or misinterpretation of Chinese traditional wisdom, particularly when wisdom and principles are applied in the practices of business and management. I will further discuss the missing link issue in Chap. 1.

The purpose of this book is to bridge the gap or build the link between the wisdom of Taoism and practices of business and management built on my academic background on management, practical experience and understanding of Chinese classical traditions. The book intends to provide practitioners and business leaders with the easy-to-understand and easy-to-practice approach. The approach I developed is called "3C Model", which is based on Taoism's wisdom, specifically Laozi's "the three treasures": *compassion (empathy, courage, charity, etc.), conservation (moderation, prudence, effectiveness, etc.) and compliance (humility, integrity, accountability, etc.).*" The "three treasures" are the essence and core virtues of Taoism for human survival. The emergence and survival to our times of several old civilizations is one good testimony to the remarkable resourcefulness and resilience of Taoism.

3C model of Taoism provides a new holistic approach to sustainable business development and responsible leadership because, at its core, is the dialectic study of changing phenomena. It complements the Western positivist approach that is good at analytical investigation of an isolated subject in a stable context. With a combination of 3C model of Taoism and Western scientific methodologies, realities are more likely to be discovered in a more accurate way. I am confident that through the study of the existing problems of management and leadership, and 3C model thinking, you will discover that traditional Taoism, recovered by contemporary thinkers and leaders, complements the inadequacies of modern philosophies. The ancient wisdom of Taoism allows for holistic observation, systems thinking and synthesis, while modern science is good at positivism, reductionism and analysis. A combination of the two will provide a powerful new platform and paradigm of thinking for enhancing our understanding of the nature and practice of adaptive management and leadership, in the complex and uncertain world.

The book discusses 3C model of Taoism and its implications for sustainable business development, containing stories and reflections of inspiring and compassionate business leaders who care about what is truly important in life. Leaders who search for meaning, purpose and fulfilment in the external world of business and in the internal world of consciousness and conscience should embrace the 3C model. I hope that leaders lead the 3C model of Taoism where their external actions and internal reflections are mutually supportive so that their spirituality and rationality can go hand in hand, rather than being each other's competitor.

In this book, business leaders at every level, as well as MBA students, professors and consultants, will discover for themselves the new thinking paradigm of 3C model, the true wisdom and principles of Taoism; experience of Taoist leadership in business; new insights into business practices when traditional success criteria are supplemented and reshaped by the Taoism's perspective; and opportunities for spiritual growth through Taoist leadership and Tao of management.

I have learnt from the unlimited resources which I collected for writing this book over the past few decades; some of the pioneer practitioners and business leaders have done well in this spiritual area; I am expecting that this book could be a powerful confirmation, validating what you have already known and practised. I hope when you are moving in this direction, this book can give you inspiration and strength to continue your journey. If you are searching for more fulfilment in your work, this book can be a much-needed source of wisdom and guidance, and also as to how to deal with the challenges that pop up when one conscientiously attempts to make spirituality the foundation for responsible leadership and sustainable business development.

This book provides rapid and easy access to ancient ideas and current practices in sustainable business development. Drawing on concepts and findings from a range of different disciplines and using authentic examples of responsible and sustainable business to illustrate the key principles and wisdom of Taoism, it offers a wealth of insights into the process of and pathway to sustainable business development. I hope that this broad interdisciplinary approach in this book is well-suited to effectively address the multifaceted issues faced by modern organizations and leaders. It is also my hope that you find the journey through this book as helpful and as inspiring as I found writing it.

Thank you sincerely for your willingness to explore with me the wisdom of Taoism in your life and work.

Vinovo, Italy Liangrong Zu

About Global Youth Leadership Academy (GYLA)

GYLA
Of the youth,
By the youth, and
For the youth
Is flourishing in the Earth.
—Liangrong Zu, Founder of GYLA

Youth means a temperamental predominance
Of courage over timidity,
Of the appetite for adventure over the love of ease.
Nobody grows old merely by a number of years.
We grow old by deserting our ideals.
—Samuel Ullman

Global Youth Leadership Academy (GYLA) was founded in 2016. GYLA combines creativity, leadership and entrepreneurship to tackle major social and environmental issues. GYLA works on many different levels to achieve positive social change—including advocacy, research and policy influence as well as developing some innovative learning and training programmes for young people. GYLA benefits from Dr. Liangrong Zu's thirty years' expertise and experience in education and training in the central government and United Nations. The purpose of GYLA is to inspire and empower youth as future leaders for social change and global engagement in achieving the UN 2030 Agenda for Sustainable Development.

GYLA is a unique platform where young people can dialogue with and learn from global successful leaders; it is a cradle where young people can be nurtured to grow and become future leaders, and it also aims to unleash young people's inner sources of new growth potential and achieve new levels of personal fulfilment.

GYLA is a perfect programme for young people, who are ambitious and conscientious to be globally responsible leaders and entrepreneurs in the future. The programme offers young people an exciting opportunity to explore the practical side of developing their successful career path by providing interdisciplinary studies and the UN's expertise while allowing them to expand their knowledge they have gained in their universities, and have the chance to research real-life case studies and success stories. Upon completing the GYLA programme, young people are expected to be able to put all of their new skills and knowledge to good use in their study and work.

Go with You, GYLA
I have imagined countless times,
What you look like when I meet you
I finally knew
That is the beauty of the moon meeting the stars,
That is the vast expanse of the sky embraced by the sun.
In the countless morning light, bright moon and clear breeze,
You watched the youth tenderly pursuing their big dreams
You said wherever I came from,
As long as I work hard and have talent.
You said the desire to protect peace
Is not far away.
This is our GYLA,
My youth is blooming in your embrace
My future will become brilliant because of you.
Poem by Jiaoyue Li, GYLAer, from Huazhong University of Science and Technology, February 2021

GYLA: In Support of SDGs

Since it was founded, GYLA shares the purpose and vision of the United Nations on youth development and youth engagement, which are cross-cutting issues in the 2030 Agenda for Sustainable Development. GYLA finds itself an intrinsic link to the United Nations. GYLA was launched at a historical juncture as the UN 2030 Agenda for Sustainable Development was adopted in 2015, and the UN 2030 Youth Strategy was developed in 2017. The purpose and values of GYLA correspond to the UN's mission on youth development that António Guterres, UN Secretary-General, empathized:

> All our hopes for a better world rest on young people. Sustainable development, human rights, peace and security can only be achieved if we empower these young people as leaders. The United Nations must empower young people, increase their participation in society and their access to education, training and jobs.

Guy Ryder, Director General of International Labour Organization (ILO), further voiced the urgency of youth empowerment:

> The time has come to unleash the potential of today's youth to become leaders, entrepreneurs, citizens and agents of change. Opening up opportunities for young people is a priority on the policy agenda in all regions of the world and for the ILO's tripartite constituency.

The global leaders are calling for members of state to equip young people with the skills and technology required now and anticipate future needs through strong education and training systems, in order to amplify youth voice, support and empower youth participation in public life and organizations and keep up with technological change and meet the UN 2030 Agenda for Sustainable Development.

YOUTH2030

WORKING WITH AND FOR YOUNG PEOPLE

GYLA was born for empowering young people as future leaders to engage in the movement of social change, because she is aware that the active engagement of youth in sustainable development efforts is central to achieving sustainable, inclusive and stable societies by the target date, and to averting the worst threats and challenges to sustainable development. As the United Nations turned 75 in 2020, and with only 10 years remaining to make the 2030 Agenda a reality for all, it is very important for institutions at the local, national and global levels to engage young people in global action for SDGs. GYLA is a powerful knowledge sharing and learning platform where young people are equipped with frontier expertise and new technology, and empowered to become systems thinkers, change makers, social innovators, green entrepreneurs and future leaders for a better world.

> *"We cannot always build the future for our youth,*
> *But we can build our youth for the future"*
> —Franklin D. Roosevelt

For this purpose, GYLA endeavours to be a leader in working with young people: in understanding their needs and in helping to put their ideas into action. In so doing, GYLA integrates SDGs and UN 2030 Youth Strategy in her curricula and activities to empower young people to realize their full potential and to stand up for their rights, and to engage themselves in the efforts to contribute to the achievement of SDGs.

Principles of GYLA

GYLA was established *"**of the youth, by the youth, and for the youth**"* with the purpose of inspiring and empowering youth as future leaders for social change. In times of pandemic crisis, GYLA has played a more important role in supporting and amplifying youth voices and actions by boosting the quality and delivery of different programmes and activities, and outreaching and helping more young people to mitigate the negative impact, particularly in the developing countries.

GYLA *of the Youth*

GYLA is a unique platform built for young people to learn from global successful leaders, and exchange information and knowledge with their peers. Young people are encouraged to take ownership of GYLA: in other words, to take the initiative to bring about positive results of GYLA and also change the world for a better future. Taking ownership means caring about and improving the quality and outcome of GYLA programme much as an owner of GYLA. When they take ownership, young people are able to show others that they can trust them to do the right things right. GYLA's core values are at the heart of creating an environment where young people feel empowered to act and bring about social change. GYLA *of the youth* is to nurture a culture that fosters and values ownership. Young people have an obligation to GYLA in terms of results and to act on the GYLA programmes that impact those results. Young people are also empowered to be accountable for their own results of their actions.

Memorable Encounter with GYLA
Encountering GYLA in 2021 winter,
I was impressed by it at first sight.
GYLA is like a ray of enchanting light,
Leading my way to the future that may be bright.
Participating in GYLA in 2021 winter,
I met scholars of great knowledge and fame,
I met classmates with a clear lifelong aim.
I can feel in my heart there's hope that flames.
Sometimes learning a concept brand new,
I kept wondering and felt so confused.
Knowing this is essential to get mind fuelled,
I held a firm belief I would finally get used.

(continued)

I've also learnt about
I should be brave to speak out,
Even though not too loud.
It is still worthwhile to be proud.
Now I may try to see with a global view,
And try to achieve more in my youth.
Poem by Xinyi Zhu, GYLAer from China Labour Relations University. February 2021

GYLA *by the Youth*

Young people are the owners of GYLA; therefore, they have the right and power to govern and manage GYLA, and responsible for the quality and future of GYLA growth. Since the foundation, GYLA programme has been managed, prepared, organized, implemented and evaluated by the GYLA dream team and GYLAers. The GYLA dream team is the leader of overall GYLA operations. It consists of three sub-teams respectively responsible for social medial, multimedia design and production and news and reporting. The members of the dream team are recruited from the outstanding GYLAers who graduated from GYLA activities. They are talented and highly qualified with good character, and humble to serve others. What is more, the dream team also encourages and involves participants to work for GYLA during the implementation of activities.

GYLA *for the Youth*

The mission of GYLA is to inspire youth to dream more, learn more and do more. Achieve more and become more. Young people have the creativity, the potential and the capacity to make change happen—for themselves, for their communities and for the rest of the world. GYLA is also a dreamer like the youth; therefore, GYLA can promise youth to be the guiding light of the youth, and the stepping stone of the youth, to realize the dreams and goals. Goals give purpose, purpose gives faith, faith gives courage, courage gives enthusiasm, enthusiasm gives energy, energy gives life and life lifts us over the bar. The ambitious goal of GYLA is to engage with millions of young people, particularly in impoverished areas and lower-income countries, to create change through participation in different types of learning programmes and social events that GYLA will organize, build solid youth networks and reach young people to work on peacebuilding and sustainable development, and is committed to empowering underprivileged youth by providing them with space to participate by offering them with various accessible resources and activities.

Impact of GYLA

Since 2016, GYLA has organized seven editions of offline and online learning programmes; over 1200 outstanding college students from about fifty top universities have participated in the activities. Many of the outstanding participants have been successfully worked as interns and volunteers in the United Nations agencies, some have continued to study in the well-known universities in the world, some have found jobs in the multinational companies and some started up their own social and green enterprises.

"In GYLA, you will learn more about yourself, know more about the world-how it works, and know more about how to develop yourself to make contribution to the world."

Naiqian Zhang GYLAer in 2019 from Harbin Institute of Technology. Worked as an Intern at International Telecommunication Union in Geneva, Switzerland.

GYLA has become a well-known brand and flagship programme, and greatly influential in academic institutions, United Nations Agencies and young people. Some GYLAers use a feast as the metaphor to describe GYLA's impact:

"if we are fortunate enough to meet GYLA when we are young,
wherever we go and whatever we do,
GYLA always lives in our heart.
In our heart, GYLA is just like a moving feast:
a feast of knowledge,
a feast of culture, and
a feast of friendship."

Some GYLAers regard GYLA as the Pandora's Box in which GYLA brings them some new and unexpected gifts and sources which they cannot learn in their universities. Some see GYLA as a grand opera; they compared GYLA to a Chinese opera. GYLA is composed of profound knowledge and focuses on youth education. Following the trend of the times, GYLA aims to help young people take the opportunity and adapt to the challenges in the new era. The charm of this audio-visual feast lies in the convergence of Eastern wisdom and Western science, which enables the youth to step out of the ivory tower, realize their mission and adapt themselves in the fast-changing world. GYLA is a gorgeous opera with lingering tunes and enduring images. GYLA is a big stage for ideas and exchanges. GYLA helps the youth to develop their broad vision and global leadership, and encourages the youth to think more about social issues and fulfil the social mission of youth in a complex environment. On the stage of GYLA, we are committed to playing our roles. The curtain of this stage never falls, and GYLA will for sure continue to impact future generations.

"GYLA was a turning point in my life. It was this precious opportunity that enabled me

to get a deep understanding of the Sustainable Development Goals, which are in urgent need

to be realized, and I think it's our job to take the responsibility."

Wenrui Li, GYLAer in 2019 from Nanjing University, currently studying in Oxford University

"In GYLA, we broadened our horizons, learned about problems and challenges faced by all mankind, and understood the responsibility and mission that we youth should bear."

Kaiqiang Tang, GYLAer in 2019 from Nanjing University. Founder of Nanjing Spiderman Intelligent Robot Co., Ltd.

I would like to end up with the comments from Professor Xiaocheng Wu, vice-president of Zhejiang University. Zhejiang University was the pioneer university that collaborated and jointly launched GYLA programme in 2016. Dr. Wu described the impact of GYLA from four areas which pertinently conclude the structure of GYLA programme:

- *GYLA is created with Height.* GYLA aims to cultivate global young talents for their role in the UN Sustainable Development Goals.
- *GYLA has curricula in Depth.* GYLA's curricula focus on 3Q (development of youth talent: IQ: intellectual knowledge, EQ: emotional intelligence and CQ: cross-cultural intelligence), 3C (development of leadership: character, competence, connection) and 3H (development of entrepreneurship: heart, head, hand). GYLA empowers young people to pursue innovation and aspiration with inclusive, deep and diversified force of culture in curricula.
- *GYLA is scholastic in Breadth.* GYLA has broad and in-depth cooperation with Zhejiang University and other top universities in China, facilitating their resources to serve the basic education of international talents.
- *GYLA is nourishing in Warmth.* With the philosophy of "education for all without exclusion", GYLA is nourishing the abilities, dreams and ideals of young people with individualized and diversified teaching and multiple opportunities; thus, GYLA is a warm and friendly family for all.

"Looking back into GYLA activities, I wonder what makes GYLA so charming, given that the knowledge shared by the professionals is already the invaluable treasure for the participants. It comes to me that GYLA is made by a group of people with great love to serve the participants, their career and life, and this world. They are always willing to share everything they have with others. I believe the participants have also been touched by their warming hearts. Hope more youth leaders will be able to learn from GYLA about how to serve the world in the future. GYLA gives the youth a light in their way all around."

– The comments from Chunliang Zha, tutor of Tianjin University

Acknowledgements

Laozi concludes his ideas and thoughts in the last verse of *Tao Te Ching*:

> *"The more you give of yourself, the more you find of yourself;*
> *The more you give to others, the more you receive from others."*
> —Laozi Tao Te Ching, Ch. 81

Since 2010 when I started my long journey into the study of Taoism, I have received support and assistance. Therefore, I am determined to write a good quality of the book to give back to those who have supported me. I tried to decode and explain the concepts and principles of Tao and all the related ideas that have guided us in our thinking over the years. The process has been a true labour of love and has given me profound insight into the world of Taoism.

I am deeply indebted to all those who have helped me along the journey to the world of Taoism. In addition to the prestigious academic scholars from China and other countries, especially Professor Samuel Idowu, London Metropolitan University, and Professor René Schmidpeter, Founder of M3trix, and Cologne Business School, who have inspired and supported me to engage in the research of combining Taoism's wisdom with management science.

I am grateful to Professor Qingxia Xia, a specialist in Chinese traditional philosophy, for dedicating her time to exchanging, discussing and reviewing my work and providing me with a lot of valuable advice and comments.

I would like to thank the team at Springer, particularly, Christian Rauscher, Senior Editor, Business, Operations Research & Information System, Barbara Bethke and Parthiban Gujilan Kannan, for their support and encouragement to bring the book to a broader audience.

Great admiration, gratitude and credit go to my family who supports and encourages me to carry on with my work.

Finally, many thanks also go to GYLA team members who have worked with me and the outstanding college students who have participated in Global Youth Leadership Academy (GYLA) over the past few years, with whom I have shared wisdom and ideas of Taoism in the class. The feedback they have provided helps me to improve my work.

Contents

About the Author

Dr. Liangrong Zu is a specialist in corporate social responsibility (CSR), business ethics, systems thinking for sustainable development, social innovation and social entrepreneurship, Taoist leadership and management, etc.

He has been working for the central government and the United Nations for about 30 years. He is the founder of Global Youth Leadership Academy (GYLA), and founder of Taoist Leadership Academy for Sustainability and Excellence. Dr. Zu is currently working as a Partner Expert on HR Strategy in the United Nations Industrial Development Organization (UNIDO)

Dr. Zu holds PhD in business and management at the Nottingham University Business School, United Kingdom, specialized in the areas of CSR, business ethics, corporate restructuring, and governance. He received his master's degree in economics of education from Beijing Normal University.

Dr. Zu has been responsible for developing, organizing, and teaching educational and training programs for government officials, business executives, academic professionals, and young leaders since joining United Nations. The programs he has developed focus on CSR, socially responsible restructuring, sustainable business development, sustainable leadership, sustainable supply chain management, responsible management education, social innovation, green entrepreneurship, youth leadership for Sustainable Development Goals, etc.

Dr. Zu was and is the member of several Academic Committees and Boards: IMD-Syngenta Advisory Board (Lausanne, Switzerland); Jury Member of Sustainable Entrepreneurship Award (Vienna, Austria); Board of Trustees of Cologne Business School (Cologne, Germany); Organizational Committee for International Conference on CSR, Sustainability, Ethics & Governance; Member of Springer Board for the Series Books on CSR, Sustainability, and Ethics & Governance. Dr. Zu is also the visiting professor at many top Chinese universities.

Dr. Zu is the author of many books: "Corporate Social Responsibility, Corporate Restructuring and Firm's Performance," "Responsible and Sustainable Business: Perspectives from Taoism's Wisdom," "Responsible Management and Taoism: Overcoming Challenges in the VUCA Era," "Global Youth Leadership for SDGs: Empower Youth as Future Leaders for Social Change." Dr. Zu is also co-editor of "Encyclopedia of CSR," "Dictionary of CSR"; "The Future of the UN Sustainable Development Goals: Business Perspective of Global Development" and "Encyclopedia of Sustainable Management; and the Future of the UN Sustainable Development Goals: Business perspectives Global Development in 2030." He has also authored many articles published in *Journal of Business Ethics* and other national and international journals. He has coordinated with prestigious universities and United Nations professionals in developing two business textbooks on *Labor Dimensions of CSR* and *Sustainable Supply Chains Management*.

Over the past decades, Dr. Zu has dedicated himself to study of the Chinese classical wisdom, with a focus on Taoism, Confucianism philosophy, and I Ching (the Book of Change), combining his research areas of CSR, sustainability, management, and leadership. Recently, Dr. Zu initiated a Trilogy of Taoist Leadership for Sustainability & Excellence: *Responsible business, responsible management and responsible leadership* in collaboration with some of the well-known international publishers. The Trilogy will be published in the upcoming years.

List of Figures

List of Tables

Part I
Introduction: "Silent Spring": Man Proposes, Tao Disposes

Tao creates all creatures,
Te (virtue) nurtures them,
Matter shapes them,
Circumstances completes them.
—Tao Te Ching, Ch. 51

Man proposes, Tao disposes.
(Whatever man does shall hold to Tao.)
—Tao Te Ching, Ch. 59

Since 2020, all of us in the world have lived in the "silent spring" in a time of COVID-19. The pandemic has led to a dramatic loss of human life worldwide and presents an unprecedented challenge to public health, food systems and the world of work. The economic and social disruption caused by the pandemic is devastating: tens of millions of people are at risk of falling into extreme poverty, while the number of undernourished people, currently estimated at nearly 690 million, could increase by up to 132 million by the end of 2020. Nearly half of the world's 3.3 billion global workforce are at risk of losing their livelihoods. Informal economy workers are particularly vulnerable because the majority lack social protection and access to quality health care and have lost access to productive assets (Chriscaden 2020).

This phenomenon reminds me of the seminal book, "Silent Spring" published in 1962. "Silent Spring" is an environmental science book by Rachel Carson, documenting the adverse environmental effects caused by the indiscriminate use of pesticides. The book of Silent Spring began with a "fable for tomorrow"—a true story using a composite of examples drawn from many real communities where the use of DDT had caused damage to wildlife, birds, bees, agricultural animals, domestic pets, and even humans. The book has been celebrated as the catalyst that sparked our consciousness of ecological crises.

Carson's passionate concern in Silent Spring is with the future of the planet and all life on Earth. She calls for humans to act responsibly, carefully, and as stewards of the living earth. Carson identified human hubris and financial self-interest as the crux of the problem and asked if we could master ourselves and our appetites to live as though we humans are an equal part of the earth's systems and not the master of them.

The advent of industrial manufacturing, modern technology and COVID-19 have transformed our lives, we came to recognize interconnection, interdependence and interaction between human beings and nature, specially, the connections between economic exploitation, social inequality, and environmental problems. Therefore, the prevailing notion of the conquest of nature—as if nature were a foreign territory to be subjected at will, and as if humanity did not exist in the midst of the earth's metabolism—could only lead to what Frederick Engels referred to, metaphorically, as the "revenge" of nature.

Engels warned human beings of unintended consequences of human's conquest over nature in the past hundred years. He said that "Let us not, however, flatter ourselves overmuch on account of our human conquest over nature. For each such conquest takes its revenge on us. Each of them, it is true, has in the first place the consequences on which we counted, but in the second and third places it has quite different, unforeseen effects which only too often cancel out the first." Engels further explained the unintended consequences by illustrating a few real-life stories in the history. One of them is the people who, in Mesopotamia, Greece, Asia Minor, and elsewhere, destroyed the forests to obtain cultivable land, never dreamed that they were laying the basis for the present devastated condition of these countries, by removing along with the forests the collecting centers and reservoirs of moisture. When, on the southern slopes of the mountains, the Italians of the Alps used up the pine forests so carefully cherished on the northern slopes, they had no inkling that by doing so they were cutting at the roots of the dairy industry in their region; they had still less inkling that they were thereby depriving their mountain springs of water for the greater part of the year, with the effect that these would be able to pour still more furious flood torrents on the plains during the rainy seasons. Those who spread the potato in Europe were not aware that they were at the same time spreading the disease of scrofula.

Thus, at every step we are reminded that we by no means rule over nature like a conqueror over a foreign people, like someone standing outside nature—but that we, with flesh, blood, and brain, belong to nature, and exist in its midst, and that all our mastery of it consists in the fact that we have the advantage over all other beings of being able to know and correctly apply its laws.

And in fact, with every day that passes we are acquiring a better understanding of these laws and getting to perceive both the more immediate and the more remote consequences of our interference with the traditional course of nature. In particular, after the mighty advances made by the natural sciences in the present century, we are more than ever in a position to realize, and hence to control, also the more remote natural consequences of at least our day-to-day production activities. But the more this progress, the more will men not only feel, but also know their oneness with nature, the more impossible will become the senseless and unnatural idea of a contrast between mind and matter, man and nature, soul and body, such as arose after the decline of classical antiquity in Europe and obtained its highest elaboration in Christianity." (Engels 2012).

Engels pointed out the important dimensions of the inseparable oneness of humanity with nature, the inherent destructiveness of capitalism, and the necessity of socialism for the survival of earth, and the complete interdependence of human social relations and human relations to nature, which have a significant impact on building a sustainable world in the future. His wisdom and belief are reflected in Taoism's wisdom in terms of unity of man and nature, oneness, wholeness and holism, etc.

Martin Heidegger claimed that modern technology, with its violent metaphysics, destroys Being (Heidegger 1977). However, it is not modern technology itself that is dangerous but its careless and wide-scale implementation by modern-day business. With its exclusive focus on profit-making, modern-day businesses tend to violate the integrity and diversity of natural ecosystems, the autonomy and culture of local communities and the chance that future generations will lead a decent life. The metaphysics of modern-day business can be described by the following statements: (i) *'to be' is to be a marketable resource;* (ii) *'to be' involves being either an object available for productive activity on the market, or else a subject who makes use of such objects;* and, (iii) *the only mode of thinking is calculative thinking; the consideration and measurement of every being as a marketable resource* (Young 2001).

With the deepening world environmental crisis, more and more people have come to realize that the problem of the environment not only is brought about by modern industry and technology, but also has a deep connection with people's world outlook, with their sense of value, and with the way they structure knowledge. Some people's ways of thinking have, in certain ways, unbalanced the harmonious relationship between human beings and nature, and overstressed the power and influence of the human will. People think that nature can be rapaciously exploited.

This philosophy is the ideological root of the current serious environmental and ecological crisis. On the one hand, it brings about high productivity; on the other hand, it brings about an exaggerated sense of one's own importance. Confronted with the destruction of the Earth, we have to conduct a thorough self-examination on this way of thinking. I believe that Taoism has teachings that can be used to counteract the shortcomings of currently prevailing values. Taoism looks upon humanity as the most intelligent and creative entity in the universe, which is seen as encompassing humanity, Heaven, and Earth within the Tao.

Part I will discuss the missing link between spiritual world of Taoism and business world, and how we change our thinking to build a sustainable society.

References

Chriscaden, K. (2020, 13 October 2020). *Impact of COVID-19 on people's livelihoods, their health and our food systems: Joint Statement by ILO, FAO, IFAD and WHO*. WHO. Retrieved December 13, 2020, from https://www.who.int/

news/item/13-10-2020-impact-of-covid-19-on-people%27s-livelihoods-their-health-and-our-food-systems

Engels, F. (2012). *Dialectics of nature*. Wellred.

Heidegger, M. (1977). The question concerning technology and other essays. Garland Publishing.

Young, J. (2001). *Heidegger's later philosophy*. Cambridge University Press, Cambridge.

Chapter 1
The Missing Link: Spiritual World of Taoism and Business World

Everything affects and is
Affected by every other thing.
– Frederick Engels

In the Preface, I touched on the problem of the missing link between the spiritual world and business world. I found that some of the business executives and spiritual scholars or philosophers are also aware of the problem. In recent years, I have seen some of business practitioners and philosophy scholars and researchers work together to unlock the secret of the Eastern classical wisdom by complementing the knowledge they don't have in areas of Taoism and management science.

The Case of Joint Work on "Real Power"

James A. Autry, a former Fortune 500 executive, an award-winning business author and one of the most popular and influential consultants in the business community, worked with Stephen Mitchell, a bestselling author and translator of the Chinese classical traditions. His recent translation of Tao Te Ching has been called "definitive for our time". They worked together and published a book, "Real Power: Business Lessons from the Tao Te Ching" in 1998. I like the compact book, and very much appreciate the comments that James made:

> The Tao Te Ching, perhaps the world's most profound book of leadership wisdom, talks about the principles that underlie all truly fulfilling enterprise. It is a way that many powerful business leaders already practice but call by other names, such 'servant leadership' or 'value-based leadership' or 'leadership from the heart'. Each of these phrases describes aspects of the wisdom in this ancient text. It supersedes all systems yet brings fulfilment, both personal and organizational. (Autry & Mitchell, 1998).

James has quoted the wisdom and principles from Tao Te Ching for years as a senior corporate executive and as a consultant, in speeches and management seminars. In his book, "Real Power", James worked with Stephen to interpret and apply 41 verses or chapters of Tao Te Ching as management principles in business

L. Zu, *Responsible and Sustainable Business*,
https://doi.org/10.1007/978-3-030-91117-1_1

operations. However, they missed two important chapters: 8 and 67. The passage 8 is about the great qualities of water-like leadership, which implies great leaders shall develop qualities of servant leadership. Water is one of the most important metaphors that Laozi loves to use in his work, because of the qualities of water, such as modest and humble to serve, being receptive and inclusive, being honest and trustworthy to all creatures, being transparent and justice, being adaptive and flexible, etc. The verse 67 is about the "three treasures" Laozi always cherishes, which I call it 3C in my book: *compassion (empathy, courage and charity, etc.), conservation (moderation, prudence, effectiveness, etc.), and compliance (humility, integrity, accountability, etc.)*. This verse is the cornerstone of Tao Te Ching, and also seen as the essence of all Laozi's thoughts. As a matter of fact, 3C Model of Taoism in my book is built on the principles of the "three treasures", if you are interested in knowing, please continue your reading journey.

I'd like to take one verse that James and Stephen selected and adapted to business in their book to illustrate how important for researchers and practitioners to really understand profoundly the essence of Laozi's wisdom so that it can be effectively applied in our life and work. Let's take a look at the verse one in Tao Te Ching. The verse one is one of the most popular verses and also the most difficult one to understand. I have found hundreds of the different versions of the translations, interpretations and commentaries, but up to now, people are still debating which translation or interpretation is correct. I don't want to argue who is wrong or right, what I value the wisdom of Taoism is how to apply it in our life and work, otherwise, we discount the values of Tao Te Ching.

> The Tao that can be worded is not the eternal Tao,
> The name that can be named is not the eternal name.
> The un-named is origin of Heaven and Earth,
> The named is manifestation of myriad things.
> Observing the wonder usually through non-being.
> Observing the manifestation usually through being.
> ...
> – Laozi, Tao Te Ching, Ch. 1

That is my translation. This is Stephen's translation in 1991:

> The Tao that can be told is not the eternal Tao,
> The name that can be named is not the eternal name.
> The unnamable is the eternally real,
> Naming is the origin of all particular things.
> Free from desire, you realize the mystery,
> Caught in desire, you see only the manifestations.
> – Laozi, Tao Te Ching, Ch. 1

In the verse one, it is very important to understand the six concepts: Tao, name, eternal Tao, eternal name, being and non-being. They are the key to interpret the verse correctly. It is also important to understand the Chinese culture and history. I think that the key question here is why Laozi put this verse at the beginning of Tao Te Ching, and what messages he wants to convey to our creatures, and what wisdom we can learn from the verse. Laozi was not playing word game with us. In China, we have a tradition, which is, we always place the most important thing at the beginning and in the end. It is true of Tao Te Ching, Laozi placed the two important verses at the beginning and the end: "*heavenly Tao is to benefit, but yet never do harm; sage's Tao is to do good, but yet never contend.*" (Tao Te Ching, Ch.81).

Let's take a look how Autry and Mitchell (1998) interpret and apply the first verse in modern management.

> What is most valuable doesn't have a name. The wise leader is comfortable with the mystery of that and doesn't waste energy trying to figure it out. She doesn't need to label everything and doesn't let herself be limited by the desire for any particular result. She knows that their job is to bring people together in the workplace and, through training as well as through personal encouragement, to assure that they understand how their individual jobs connect with the greater purpose of the business. Once that's done, she trusts that committed people working together in a community of effort will produce more than she could ever have prescribed through ta formal strategic planning process. This is the basis for real power. (Autry & Mitchell, 1998, p.4).

This is the wisdom and principles that Autry draws on from the verse one and adapted it in the business management. I am sorry to say that I cannot figure it out the relationship between the wisdom of verse one and management ideas. I am afraid that the secret and essence of the first verse is not unlocked, therefore it is not fully understood.

Laozi's Mental Model: 3W Thinking Tool for Decoding the Bible of Taoism

Built on the information and knowledge I collected after reviewing hundreds of documents, translations and commentaries on Tao Te Ching and, expertise on management, leadership, economics, philosophy, psychology, history, and Chinese literatures over the past decades, I have tried very hard to decode and unlock the secret of Tao Te Ching through the infographics and mind maps to discover and understand what Laozi's mental model is to write the book of Tao Te Ching.

Let's explain briefly mental models. Mental models are how we understand the world. Not only do they shape what we think and how we understand, but they shape the connections and opportunities that we see. Mental models are how we simplify complexity, why we consider some things more relevant than others, and how we reason. Mental models also guide your perception and behaviour. They are the thinking tools that we can use to understand life, make decisions, and solve problems. Mental models are imperfect, but useful. There is no single mental model from physics or engineering, for example, that provides a flawless explanation of the entire universe, but the best mental models from those disciplines have allowed us to build bridges and roads, develop new technologies, and even travel to outer space. As historian Yuval Noah Harari puts it, "Scientists generally agree that no theory is 100 percent correct. Thus, the real test of knowledge is not truth, but utility." The best mental models are the ideas with the most utility. They are broadly useful in daily life. Understanding these concepts will help us make wiser choices and take better actions.

This is why we need to understand what Laozi's mental model was. When we know Laozi's mental model well, we are able to understand the way he saw the world. I discovered that Laozi's mental model is probably, I called, 3W Model: *what, why and how: observing what it is; discovering why it happens, and advising how to do it*. I also found out that 3W mental model was also the approach that Confucius used to inspect and appraise the qualities of people. Confucius said, "*Inspect what he does, observe how he does, and discover why he does.*" In the book of Tao Te Ching, in most of the verses, Laozi began with "WHAT": describing a phenomenon or a symptom or an event, then, he told us "WHY": the causes, and then he generated some principles from WHAT and WHY, gave us advice of "HOW": principles or methodology. I'd like to use the verse 7 as an example.

WHAT
Heaven is eternal and earth is everlasting.
WHY
Why Heaven and Earth exist forever is
Because they do not live for themselves.
(author's note: they complement each other to become a whole).
Thus, they are sustainable.
HOW
(author's note: Laozi generated the virtue from the relationship between Heaven and Earth in the universe, and can be applied it in society)
Therefore, great leaders
Place themselves behind; and find themselves ahead.
Lay down their lives, and find themselves thrive.
Give no thought to themselves, and find themselves fulfilled.

The 3W mental model reminds us that Laozi was very good at methods of logic and induction. This is beyond people's imagination, because most of the western philosophers thought that the Chinese philosophers were not good at these methods, particularly in the ancient China. I believe that is why so many people don't understand or misinterpret the book of Tao Te Ching. Because simple logical errors in the early interpretation of Tao philosophy have now become big issues between the Eastern and Western philosophies.

Aristotle said, "*The least initial deviation from the truth is multiplied later a thousand fold.*" Therefore, the errors in Tao philosophy were not committed by Laozi, but by early historical interpreters. Many early interpretation errors are due to simple logical errors in what Alder classified as the "fallacy of reductionism." This kind logical errors is to "assign much greater reality to the parts of an organized whole than to the whole self; or even worse, maintaining that only the ultimate component parts have reality and that the whole they constitute are mere appearances, or even illusionary." (Adler, 1997). American anthropologist and generalist Gregory Bateson said that a person committing logical errors of this kind may 1 day eat the menu instead of the meal (Grof & Valier, 1984).

Two Paradigms of Thinking for Observing the World

Now, let's come back to the verse one of Tao Te Ching. Laozi uses the terms of two opposites or more appropriately, two complements to describe WHT, i.e., the nature of the myriad things (Tao and name; eternal Tao and eternal name), then, he explains why there are differences between them, because worded Tao and named name are parts of the whole nature, thus, they are not eternal. Finally, Laozi suggested two paradigms of thinking to observe the known and unknown world. Figure 1.1 is one of the infographics I devised to have a better understanding of the verse one.

Laozi provides us in the first chapter of Tao Te Ching with the paradigm of thinking, in other words, how to see and understand the world. We live in the world which is both unknown (that cannot be worded and named) and known (that can be worded and named). But both of the worlds are always governed and disciplined by the eternal Tao (law of nature) and eternal Name (the wholeness).

We must understand what paradigm is and how we can use it if we want to know the known and unknown world. The concept of a paradigm is extremely useful. Coined by the American physicist and historian of science Thomas Kuhn, author of the ground-breaking book "*The Structure of Scientific Revolutions*", the term paradigm describes conceptual systems that dominate the thinking of scientific communities during certain specific periods of the evolution of science (Kuhn, 2012). Initially each new paradigm has a positive and progressive role. It identifies legitimate scientific problems, offers methodology for conducting scientific experiments, and describes criteria for evaluating the data. A paradigm clearly defines not only what reality is, but also what it is not and cannot possibly be. Once the paradigm is accepted, its basic philosophical assumptions are not questioned and scientists focus their attention and efforts on its further elaboration and articulation.

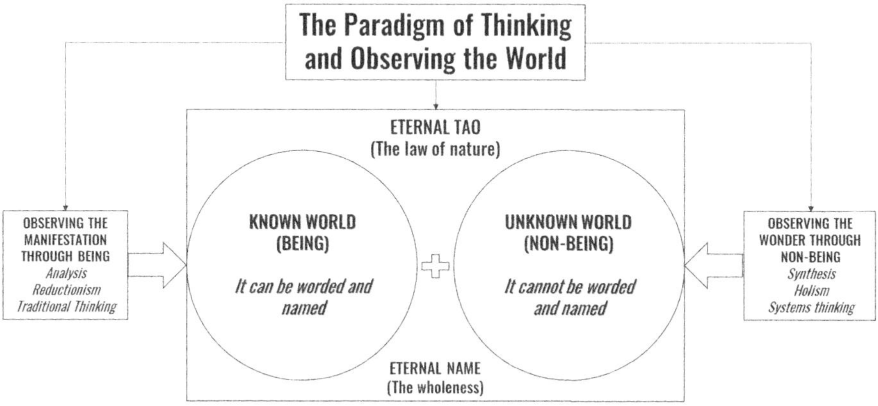

Fig. 1.1 The wisdom of Tao Te Ching: the paradigm of thinking. Source: the author devised based on Tao Te Ching, Ch. 1

A paradigm is the foundations that shape our way of seeing and understanding the world, it is the assumptions and methods out of which we build our theories. Laozi provides us with two fundamental paradigms: synthesis or systems thinking and analysis or reductionism. Analysis is the traditional method of reasoning taken within modern science whereby we try to gain an understanding of a system by breaking it down into its constituent elements. Synthesis is the foundations to systems thinking, works in the reverse direction trying to gain an understanding of an entity through the context of its relations within a whole that it is part of. Syntheses means the combination of components or elements to form a connected whole: It is a process of reasoning that describes an entity through the context of its relations and functioning within the whole system that it is a part of.

Systems thinking is this process of reasoning called syntheses and it is referred to as being what is called holistic, meaning that it is characterized by the belief that the parts of something are intimately interconnected and explicable only by reference to the whole. Syntheses focus on the relations between the elements, i.e., the way those elements are put together or arranged into a functioning entirety and like with analyses we can also identify a few key stages in this process of reasoning.

We can explain the two paradigms of Taoism's thinking from the perspective analysis and synthesis. Laozi says that "Observing the wonder usually through non-being; observing the manifestation usually through being." "*Observing the wonder usually through non-being*" means we can observe and understand the unknown world (wonder like heaven and earth) by applying the paradigm of synthesis or systems thinking (non-being); "*observing the manifestation usually through being*" implies that we can observe and understand the known world (manifestation like all creatures and objects) by adopting the paradigm of analysis or reductionism (being) (see Fig. 1.1).

In his book of Tao Te Ching, Laozi mentioned the concept of "*observation*" many times. *Observation* is an important approach that Laozi and other ancient philosophers employed to see and understand the world. Because in ancient times, people didn't have any scientific instruments and equipment to conduct the scientific experiment and analysis. Even today, the observation approach is still very important and helpful for people to probe the natural world and gain knowledge, just as Albert Einstein says, "*knowledge can't draw from experience, but only from the discovery and observation of reason to the fact that the comparison of the two.*"

The paradigm of thinking Laozi described in the first verse reflects the Chinese way of thinking: synthetic, intuition, historical and practical (Soo, 1981). The first characteristic of the Chinese way of thinking is 'synthetic', or we call it systems thinking. This approach places its emphasis on the whole rather than its parts, harmony rather than opposition. This synthetic emphasis is manifested first in the Chinese view of the universe, society and man. While being dynamic, all constituents of the universe form a harmonious whole, a unity of nature and man, a synthesis of all existences and non-existences.

That is why in Chinese philosophy there is no dichotomy between nature and man, or between supernatural and natural. Furthermore, society, which is part of the universe is also conceived of as a moral whole consisting of a large number of families, which in turn consist of individuals. Man, as part of society and thereby of the universe, is conceived of as a harmony of feelings, desires and reason. In short, the Chinese conception of the universe, society and man is synthetic and as such, it emphasizes the whole rather than its parts though the parts are always considered in relation to the whole.

As we discussed, this synthetic perspective should not be interpreted as meaning that the Chinese mind denies the value of analysis. For any type of synthesis at all, one needs data to ground judgements and inferences. Analysis is involved here. Thus, the Chinese way of thinking does not deny the value of analysis, because it is viewed not as opposed to, but complementary to, synthesis. Indeed, without analysis, no synthesis is possible. Similarly, the Chinese mind does not consider that 'the parts', 'conflict', 'opposition', 'either-or', etc., are purely negative; they are also positive in the sense that together with their counterparts they form a whole, balanced perspective of reality.

"Intuition" is conceived of "non-being" as the way of thinking. Intuition is not understood as a primitive or instinctive hunch, that is, as irrational or anti-scientific thinking. Laozi also empathizes the importance of intuition in probing and understanding the natural world in the last part of the passage:

> The source of being and non-being all comes from Tao,
> But they are different in name.
> Both of being and non-being are the mystery.
> The mysteries hide in the mystery,
> But they are the doors to probe the world trough intuition.
> – Laozi, Tao Te Ching, Ch. 1

The mystic says, "*whatever you do, something in the very foundation of existence will remain unknowable—a mystery*." And if the mystics are not right, then I think that science is going to destroy the whole meaning of life. If there is no mystery, the whole meaning of life is destroyed and the whole beauty is destroyed. Intuition is our consciousness, our being. Intuition is the mystic rose that will lead us to the ultimate ecstasy and to immortal life. Albert Einstein claims that "*the intuitive mind is a sacred gift and the rational mind is a faithful servant. We have created a society that honours the servant and has forgotten the gift*".

Intuition refers to a direct, immediate apprehension of the totality of the thing or situation concerned, resulting from observation and reflection upon life experience. Intuition has three distinctive features. The first is its "immediacy" or "directness". Faced with a thing or situation, we tend to apprehend its meaning immediately and directly, without the explicit aid of any reasoning process according to formal logic. But this does not mean that the concept of intuition denies the value of reason or logic; in fact, our mind is very 'rationalistic'. Another feature is its "oneness" or "wholeness". What is intuited is always single whole or oneness which is a multi-faceted synthesis of immediate, direct experiences. Intuition has an all-embracing character that includes all aspects of the thing or situation involved, though all these aspects may not be explicit. The content of oneness or wholeness of intuition contains what is known or determinate, as well as what is unknown or indeterminate. But what is important and emphasized in intuition is the apprehension of this manifold whole rather than its various constituent parts. Thus, the oneness or wholeness is synthesized from its various parts has priority; and the parts are always seen within their oneness or wholeness.

The third is that intuition is reflective and dynamic. It is reflective because intuition, insofar as it is a direct, immediate apprehension, is not a definitive single act of understanding, but rather the result of a process of reflection based on long, lived experience. In this sense, intuition can be considered to be experiential. The quality of intuition depends on a person's living experience as well as his ability to reflect. This point is exemplified by practically all Chinese philosophical writings, which are often in the form of conclusions or sayings, resulting from long and profound observations and reflections on personal experiences.

The way of thinking is always important for those who want to see and understand the world, and lead the world. Buddha says, "*The thought manifests as the word. The word manifests as the deed. The deed develops into habit. And the habit hardens into character. So, watch the thought and its ways with care. And let it spring from love, born out of concern for all beings.*" If we want to understand well what Tao Te Ching is about, we must understand the paradigm of thinking in Tao Te Ching. The paradigm can guide us to discover the treasures, and unlock the secrets which are hidden in Tao Te Ching.

When I explained what I have discovered and learned from Taoism's wisdom, my intention is not to criticize or deny any ideas and findings that other scholars have produced and shared with us. It is absolutely normal that all of us have the right and different ideas and methods to discover and interpret the Taoism's wisdom, it is unwise to ignore the great achievements and contributions others have made to the promotion and dissemination of Chinese classical traditions and wisdom.

I have dedicated most of my time and effort to studying Taoism's wisdom from perspective of management and leadership. In other words, I try to integrate Chinese philosophy and spiritual wisdom in the Western management and leadership science, I also try to identify the evidence and research findings from the Western science to validate the principles and ideas of Chinese traditions. Chinese needs science, and the Western needs Eastern wisdom, particularly in an era of VUCA. I do hope that I will be able to share with those who are eager to know Chinese classical wisdom that is easy to understand, easy and simple to practice and apply it in life and work.

References

Adler, M. J. (1997). *Ten philosophical mistakes*. Simon & Schuster.

Autry, J., & Mitchell, S. (1998). *Real power: Business lessons from the Tao Te Ching*. Nicholas Brealey Publishing.

Grof, S., & Valier, M. L. (1984). *Ancient wisdom and modern science*. State University of New York Press.

Kuhn, T. S. (2012). *The structure of scientific revolutions, 50th anniversary edition*. The University of Chicago Press.

Soo, F. Y. K. (1981). *Mao Thse Tung's theory of Dialectic*. D. Reidel Publishing Company.

Chapter 2
The Future We Choose: From 3D World and 3C World

In the cautionary but optimistic book: "The Future we Choose: Surviving the Climate Crisis", Figueres and Rivett-Carnac (2020)—the architects of the 2015 Paris Climate Change Agreement—tackle arguably the most urgent and consequential challenge humankind has ever faced: the world's changing climate and the fate of humanity. The authors outline two possible scenarios for the planet. In one world that we are creating, they describe what life on Earth will be like by 2050 if we fail to meet the Paris targets for carbon dioxide emission reduction, and the world will lead to warming of more than 3 degrees. The authors warn us that if governments, corporations, and individuals make no further efforts than those registered in 2015, we will go to a warming of at least 3.7 °C by 2100. Worse yet, if they do not fulfil even the registered commitments, we can expect warming of 4 or 5 degrees. Another world is the one we must create. Figueres and Rivett-Carnac describe what it will take to create and live in a carbon neutral, regenerative world. They argue for confronting the climate crisis head on, with determination and optimism. The world we must create, limiting warming to no more than 1.5 °C. We cannot turn back the clock on past emissions. However, even at this late stage, we can strive for and achieve a better world in which nature and the human family will not only survive but thrive together (Figueres & Rivett-Carnac, 2020)

As early as 2500 years ago, Laozi, our Chinese sage, and founder of philosophical Taoism also describes the two worlds that human beings created or would create: the harmonious and sustainable world where man and nature become one (eco-system), and the destructive and unsustainable world where man and nature become divided (ego-system).

Harmonious and Sustainable World (Eco-System)

This is the universe we live with consciousness of oneness:
Earth that stays aligned with oneness becomes stable.
The valley that stays aligned with oneness becomes full.
Heaven that stays aligned with oneness becomes clear.
The divinity that stays aligned with oneness become efficacy.
All creatures that stay aligned with oneness thrive.

L. Zu, *Responsible and Sustainable Business*,
https://doi.org/10.1007/978-3-030-91117-1_2

The rulers who stay aligned with oneness govern with justice.

Destructive and Unsustainable World (Ego-system)

Conversely, this is the universe where we live without consciousness of oneness:
Earth that loses stability shall quake.
The valley that is not kept full shall dry up.
Heaven that loses clarity shall crack.
The divinity that loses efficacy shall vanish.
The creatures that lose energy shall die out.
The rulers who govern with injustice shall perish.

This is the most important characteristic of the Taoism's world view or wisdom: the awareness of the unity and mutual interrelation of all things and events, the experience of all phenomena in the world as manifestations of a basic oneness. All things are seen as interdependent and inseparable parts of this cosmic whole; as different manifestations of the same ultimate reality.

Albert Einstein had a good understanding of humans as an inseparable part of the one, as he writes:

> A human being is part of the whole called by us universe ... We experience ourselves, our thoughts and feelings as something separate from the rest. A kind of optical delusion of consciousness. This delusion is a kind of prison for us, restricting us to our personal desires and to affection for a few persons nearest to us. Our task must be to free ourselves from the prison by widening our circle of compassion to embrace all living creatures and the whole of nature in its beauty. The true value of a human being is determined by the measure and the sense in which they have obtained liberation from the self. We shall require a substantially new manner of thinking if humanity is to survive.

The wisdom we learn from Taoism is that the consciousness of oneness is a remarkable tool for identifying and solving problems in the past, present and future. In today's fast-paced, forward-looking, achievement-oriented world, many of us keep turning away from what we have in the hope of something better. There's nothing wrong with looking ahead, except that so often it includes ignoring what's already available. Those aligned with the consciousness of oneness are capable of looking in both directions—towards what's ahead and what's here. And often they look forward out of curiosity, interest, and engagement, not out of a sense of lack. They do not disregard the resources available right now.

We also learn that the consciousness of oneness is critical as we strive toward sustainability. It reflects back to us our own completeness—that we have enough, that we do not need to indulge, over-spend, or over-consume. And it attunes us to how our actions impact others, the earth, and even our sense of who we are. It does not let us ignore the consequences of how we treat others or life. In fact, it uses that information to inspire and build more sustainable approaches. When we examine sustainable practices, we see the consciousness of oneness at work reassuring entire communities that resources are at hand, that sharing does not deplete, that trust is both natural and necessary. And we see how what we have now can be the best starting point for the future, because with the power of human attention, sometimes the smallest resource can prove infinitely helpful. This is the scenario or the world Laozi expected us to live that is harmonious and sustainable.

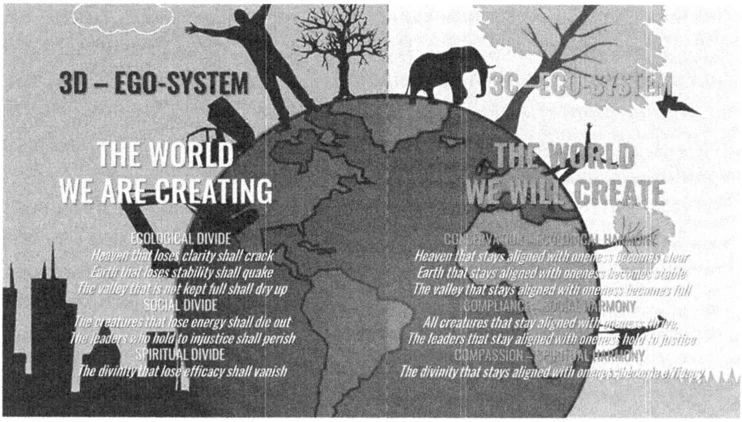

Fig. 2.1 From 3D to 3C: the world we are creating and the world we will create

Figure 2.1 shows that another world that Laozi described manifests in the form of three major divides: the ecological, the social, and the spiritual. The symptoms were validated by the findings of the researches that Otto Scharmer has done in recent years. Scharmer called the three divides 3D (Scharmer & Kaufer, 2013).

The ecological divide: Earth that loses stability shall quake, and the valley that is not kept full shall dry up (Laozi). Today, we are depleting and degrading our natural resources on a massive scale, using up more non-renewable precious resources every year. Although we have only one planet, we leave an ecological footprint of 1.5 planets; that is, we are currently using 50% more resources than our planet can regenerate to meet our current consumption needs. As a consequence, one-third of our agricultural land has disappeared over the past 40 years. Rapidly falling water tables are taking us on a path toward food riots. Food prices are expected to double by 2030 (Scharmer & Kaufer, 2013).

The social divide: All creatures that lose energy shall die out, and rulers who govern with injustice shall perish (Laozi). Two and a half billion people on our planet subsist on less than US$2 per day. Although there have been many successful attempts to lift people out of poverty, this number has not changed much over the past several decades. In addition, we see an increasing polarization in society in which, in the case of the United States, the top 1% has a greater collective worth than the entire bottom 90% (Scharmer & Kaufer, 2013).

The spiritual-cultural divide: Heaven that loses clarity shall crack; the divinity that lose efficacy shall vanish (Laozi). While the ecological divide is based on a disconnect between self and nature, and the social divide on a disconnect between self and other, the spiritual-cultural divide reflects a disconnect between self and Self—that is, between one's current "self" and the emerging future "Self" that represents one's greatest potential. This divide is manifest in rapidly growing figures on burnout and depression, which represent the growing gap between our actions and who we really are.

Our human being's survival requires among others: the "three treasures" cherished by Laozi in Tao Te Ching. Building on the "three treasures", I developed 3C Model of Taoism: *compassion (empathy, courage, charity, etc.), conservation (prudence, moderation, effectiveness), and compliance (humility, integrity, accountability, etc.).* 3C Model can effectively respond to 3D challenges, and is the blueprint for us to build a sustainable world.

Compassion-spiritual harmony: compassion is about empathy, courage and charity and kind toward all creatures in the world. The whole idea of compassion is based on a keen awareness of the interdependence of all these living beings, which are all part of one another and all involved in one another. (Merton, 2008). Compassion is feeling with intelligence, it is about the feeling that arises when you are confronted with another's suffering and feel motivated to relieve that suffering. Much of the wisdom we need in order to live more in tune with life around us presents itself through our feeling intelligence. For example, people feel good when they recycle, feel empowered through volunteering in their community, feel they are part of a community when purchasing local goods. And many are saddened by the meaninglessness of their lives, enraged over the injustices of the world, and shocked by the destruction of the environment. Compassion requires business leaders to do well by doing good for development of human society, and to provide opportunity for all people to grow and thrive in the universe.

Conservation-ecological harmony: conservation is about moderation, prudence and effectiveness—deliberating, planned and thoughtful preserving and protecting resources; wise utilization of a natural product to prevent waste and ensure future use of resources that have been depleted; caring about your body, knowing when and how to avoid wasting one's time and energy, and direct them in a meaningful way, in accordance with one's purpose in life. Conservation requires business leaders to care and protect the natural resources and environment, to enhance human well-being in economically efficient way, and to make the planet a better place for all creatures to live sustainably.

Compliance-social harmony: compliance is about humility, integrity, and accountability—not daring to take the lead in the world, keeping oneself within one's own bounds, not reaching out to things above one, but submitting to one's superior. Compliance is about the awareness that seeing oneself as being above or ahead of other people can only lead to failure. In terms of social and economic responsibility, compliance means adherence to, or conformance with, rules, laws, standards, and policies. It also implies a sense of accountability and an obligation to uphold pertinent codes of conduct. From a more legalistic perspective, business compliance entails devising a formal internal system of policies, procedures, controls, and actions to detect and prevent violations of laws, regulations, rules, standards, and policies. Ethics forms the foundation for a company's program and the code of ethics/conduct. While the code of conduct helps set the overall corporate tone toward compliance expectations, a company's program should be a series of integrated mechanisms designed to address all aspects of compliance breaches.

These qualities of compassion, conservation and compliance are innate human capacities (individual and collective), and values that can be called forth, nurtured, and developed in the crucible of daily practice. We must understand that when we are conscious of oneness, we are able to distance ourselves from many of the limitations that shape and define much of our lives. We can feel a powerful peace and even joy as psychological, emotional, and even physical dynamics that would otherwise limit or define our experience are let go, put aside or transcended. Through accessing this consciousness, we can stay cool under fire, find objectivity when we are overwhelmed and stay focused in thought and action despite turmoil around us. The experiences open us into a realm called by different spiritual traditions: pure consciousness. We become one with the vast creative forces within existence. By cultivating the 3C mindsets, we give clearer, stronger direction to our lives and to our world, setting the necessary foundation for us to collectively co-create the world we want.

I will further elaborate 3C model of Taoism in Chap. 8.

References

Figueres, C., & Rivett-Carnac, T. (2020). *The future we choose: Surviving the climate crisis*. Alfred A. Knopf.

Merton, T. (2008). *Choosing to love the world: On contemplation*. Sounds True.

Scharmer, O., & Kaufer, K. (2013). *Leading from the emerging future: From ego-system to eco-system economies* (2nd ed.). Berrett-Koehler Publishers.

Chapter 3
Changing Your System, Changing the World: From Ego-system to Eco-system

We understood from what we discussed in Chap. 2 what we do is shaped by what we think, how our future become will be shaped by who we choose to be now. We are what we think. Our thoughts are the tools with which we carve our life story on the substance of the universe. When we rule our mind, we rule our world. When we choose our thoughts, we choose results (Shanklin, 1929). Laozi says,

> I am what I think,
> I think the Tao, the Tao is released in me,
> And I become wise
> I think the Virtue, the Virtue is released in me,
> And I become virtuous.
> I think the loss, the loss is released in me,
> And I become failure.
> – Laozi, Tao Te Ching, Ch. 23

This passage also implies that if we plant wheat, we get wheat; if we plant flax, we get flax. Flax does not produce wheat; wheat does not produce flax-the seeds are different. What we realize as we observe this is the Tao of cause and effect in action. If people's thought is good, their actions and deeds are good, so they will surely receive blessings. If people's thought is bad, their actions and deeds are also bad, so they will surely bring on misfortune. Good and bad thought are the cause of events, receiving blessings and bringing on misfortune are the effect of events. When there is a cause, it will surely have an effect. It cannot be that the fruit of good seed is not good, nor can it be that the fruit of bad seed is not bad. The consequences of good and bad are like shadows following forms, certain and invariable. It is all a matter of choosing between planting good and planting evil, distinguishing what is good and what is bad. Therefore, great leaders consider the beginning when they do things; being careful about things in the beginning, they are able to complete them in the end.

If we want to transform from ego-system to eco-system, we must change our paradigm of thinking. Figueres and Rivett-Carnac (2020) claim that if we cannot control the complex landscape of a challenge, the most powerful thing we can do is

L. Zu, *Responsible and Sustainable Business*,
https://doi.org/10.1007/978-3-030-91117-1_3

change how we behave in that landscape. All too often in the face of a task, we move quickly to "doing" without first reflecting on "being"—what we personally bring to the task, as well as what others might. And the most important thing we can bring is our state of mind. The actions we pursue are largely defined by the mindset we cultivate in advance of the doing. When we're faced with an urgent task, it may feel counterintuitive to first look inside ourselves, but it is essential. Today's thinking shapes how we enact tomorrow's reality. Our current crisis requires a total shift in our thinking. To survive and thrive, we must understand ourselves to be inextricably connected to all of nature. We need to cultivate a deep and abiding sense of stewardship. This transformation begins with the individual. Who we are and how we show up in the world defines how we work with others, how we interact with our surroundings, and ultimately the future we co-create.

Attempting change while we are informed by the same state of mind that has been predominant in the past will lead to insufficient incremental advances. In order to open the space for transformation, we have to change how we think and fundamentally who we perceive ourselves to be. After all, if what's at stake is nothing less than the quality of human life for centuries to come, it is worth digging down to the roots of who we understand ourselves to be. Systemic change is a deeply personal endeavour. Our social and economic structures are a product of our way of thinking.

Scharmer and Kaufer (2013) argue that addressing the 3D requires a new consciousness and collective leadership capacity. We must see the world in new ways, only in so doing, do we discover a revolutionary approach to learning and leadership. In most large systems today, we collectively create results that no one wants. The reason why stuck in the patterns of the past is that our lack of awareness of the inner place from which our attention and intention originate. Scharmer and Kaufer (2013) explain that although our world is interconnected in ways unimaginable even a decade ago, in many cases, our awareness—whether as individuals, organizations or nations—is still limited and local. To use an analogy from biology, even though our actions affect the larger ecosystem of which we are a part—in fact the multiple interacting economic, social, political and environmental ecosystems—we still behave as though our actions are narrow in scope and impact. We see ourselves as part of a far smaller, more isolated ego-system. Scharmer and Kaufer (2013) further explain why actions based on this "ego-system" awareness not only result in recurring crises, but doom any attempt to resolve them—we are trying to meet new challenges with an obsolete mindset. To show the shape of the emerging future they bring this ecosystem awareness to bear on areas such as labour, capital, production, technology, leadership, ownership and many others, offering a blueprint for a new society based on a profound understanding of how the actions of each affects the many.

As Albert Einstein put it so eloquently: "*we cannot solve problems with the same kind of thinking that created them.*" Thinking creates the world. The structures of yesterday's economic thought manifest in the structures of today's institutions and actions. If we want to upgrade our global economic operating system, we need to start by updating the thinking that underlies it; we need to update the essence of economic logic and thought. The findings of Scharmer's study reveal that the 3D symptoms were caused by today's system which does exactly what it is designed to do. It is a system that features a number of significant structural disconnects: a disconnect between the financial and the real economy; a disconnect between the infinite growth imperative and the finite resources of Planet Earth; a disconnect between the Haves and the Have Nots; a disconnect between institutional leadership and people; a disconnect between gross domestic product (GDP) and well-being; a disconnect between governance and the voiceless in our systems; a disconnect between actual ownership forms and best societal use of property and a disconnect between technology and real societal needs.

The disconnects represent a decoupling of two worlds: a decoupling of the structure of societal reality from the structure of economic thought. We could also say that they're a decoupling of the structures of eco-system reality from the structures of ego-system awareness. Today's economic reality is embedded in a global eco-system of environmental, social, political, and cultural contexts that are highly intertwined and that evolve in uncertain, complex, and volatile ways. These conditions require a mindset on the part of decision-makers that is more open, attentive, adaptive, and tuned in to emerging changes. Instead, what we often observe in current reality is a disconnect between reality and awareness; that is, between an eco-system-centric global economy and an ego-system-centric awareness of institutional decision-makers. The result is a war of the parts against the whole. We see the impact of this disconnect, for example, in the dramatic overuse of scarce resources, which is often spoken of as "the tragedy of the commons."

Scharmer and Kaufer (2013) proposed the journey from ego-system to eco-system awareness, or from "me" to "we," has three dimensions: *(1) better relating to others; (2) better relating to the whole system; and (3) better relating to oneself.* These three dimensions require participants to explore the edges of the system and the self. Exploring the edges of the system means going to the place of most potential: for example, walking in the shoes of some of the most marginalized people, such as residents of remote villages in Africa or immigrants in a developed country. It is our experience that the new in any system shows up first at the periphery. That's where you see the problems and the opportunities as if through a magnifying glass. Diverse stakeholder groups can use their shared experiences to become aware, to make sense of what is actually going on. Exploring the edges of the self means shifting the inner place from which one operates. It means opening the mind, the heart, and the will. It means suspending old habits of judgment. It means empathizing. And it means letting go of what wants to die in oneself and letting come what is waiting to be born.

The findings and results of Scharmer's researches have validated Laozi's wisdom:

> The humble is the foundation of the noble,
> The lower is the foundation of the higher,
> Thus, ancient rulers treated themselves as
> the orphaned, the lonely and the unworthy.
> Are they really low and mean? No, they are not.
> – Laozi, Tao Te Ching, Ch.39

The wisdom of Laozi teaches us that great leaders must change their mindset or thinking paradigm, particularly, develop their opposite thinking through consciousness of oneness or the whole system in which we are interconnected and interdependent. The oneness can dissolve many of the boundaries that we thought were important. Boundaries between the sacred (noble, high) and the ordinary (humble, low), between humans and earth, earth and heaven, between heart and mind, and between 'you', and 'me' are weakened in the simplicity and beauty of oneness, and great leaders must understand that true nobility comes not from being superior to others, but, rather, from being superior to our previous selves.

From the perspective of spiritual world to natural world, natural scientists have provided ample evidence that we have reached several planetary boundaries, beyond which Earth's bio-systems cannot sustain life. Soon there will be little left to extract and exploit. Concerned social scientists are clear on what we need to do: we must move toward a regenerative economy, an economy that operates in harmony with nature, repurposing used resources, minimizing waste, and replenishing depleted resources. We must return to the innate wisdom of nature herself, the ultimate regenerator and recycler of all resources. Less understood but just as important is the fact that we have reached the limits of our individualistic competitive approach. For a long time, Western societies have tended to prize self-interest over the well-being of the whole. We need to enlarge our understanding of ourselves and our relationships with others, and certainly with the natural systems that enable human life on Earth.

The practices and guidance we learn from Taoism's wisdom can assist us in the realization of divine unity. But how does spiritual practice work? Laozi points out that one of the first steps includes distinguishing between a "higher" or more "real" part of our self from a "lower" or "false" self. The words "Self" or "higher Self," "soul," "eternal," or "divine quality" are used to describe the part of us that is real or near to the absolute truth. In contrast, the "lower" self is our "ego," our self-interest, or our vices, ruled by our desires—most notably our physical desires—that get in the way of our realization.

Taoism's wisdom helps us to realize oneness in part through cultivating or "waking up" the aspects of consciousness that are already attuned to the hidden truth of unity, like detachment, clarity, generosity, openness, compassion, and devotion. We use practices like meditation, contemplation, service, and remembrance to align our consciousness with what is already present and true. This path guides us through a process that strengthens our higher and deeper qualities, while destroying our pettiness or erotic qualities. The wisdom of Laozi also inspires and empowers us to serve all beings as a way to realize the truth of oneness.

References

Figueres, C., & Rivett-Carnac, T. (2020). *The future we choose: Surviving the climate crisis*. Alfred A. Knopf.

Scharmer, O., & Kaufer, K. (2013). *Leading from the emerging future: From ego-system to eco-system economies* (2nd ed.). Berrett-Koehler Publishers.

Shanklin, I. O. (1929). *What are you?* Unity School of Christianity.

Chapter 4
The Purpose and Structure of the Book

There are people who make things happen,
There are people who watch things happen, and
There are people who wonder what happened.
To be successful, you need to be a person
Who makes things happen.
—Jim Lovell

My ideas are easy to understand, and
Easy to practice, but
Nobody in the world
Understands and practices them.
My ideas have a source, and
My actions have a purpose, but
Nobody understands them, because
They don't know me.
The less people know me,
The rarer those who follow me.
This is why the sages
Always wear coarse clothes, and
Keep the jade inside.
—Laozi, Tao Te Ching, Ch. 70

Laozi left with the world only one book in his life, "*Tao Te Ching*". It is cherished as the bible of Tao, it contains only 5000 words, full of Laozi's ideas and principles that we cannot exhaust. But unfortunately, over the past 2500 years, few of us can understand the essence of Tao Te Ching. That is why Laozi voiced his concerns in Tao Te Ching.

What Laozi says and acts is obviously one and the same: Tao, the Way. Those who don't understand Tao have little chance of understanding what Laozi says, or why he acts the way he does. Reading his book, we can understand the difficulty people might have to grasp its essence of Tao. That difficulty must have been as great in his own time, among his own people. Although they were familiar with the language and the context in which Laozi spoke, his ideas must have seemed odd,

L. Zu, *Responsible and Sustainable Business*,
https://doi.org/10.1007/978-3-030-91117-1_4

even mysterious. We still struggle with his words, although science and learning have in some ways taken us closer to his worldview.

Laozi's ideas in Tao Te Ching are straightforward. One might even call his words simple. But there's jade inside. The words reveal the treasure of Tao to those who can study and understand them properly. They may be few, even fewer if we just count those who are certain of understanding his ideas correctly. That would be only those who are already familiar with Tao. Anyone else is not likely to figure it out.

You might wonder: for whom was the Tao Te Ching written, if those who can understand it already know what it says, and the others are unlikely to learn it by studying Tao Te Ching? Laozi cannot have been very optimistic about the reception of his ideas in his book. He probably didn't care too much, since he is supposed to have written it when leaving China for good.

Who are the people with Laozi's wisdom? They are those who really understand and act upon in accordance with Laozi's thoughts and principles. Those who lead with Laozi's wisdom excel quietly, invisibly, unknown to most and misunderstood by those around them. This is what Laozi called who wear the plain clothes while keeping jade inside. In other words, they assume an unremarkable external appearance and hold spiritual treasures deep in the heart. As Laozi says that the wise leaders hold and cherish three treasures: compassion, conversation and compliance, which are natural principles and easiest things to practice. But unfortunately, most people adore only splendid exteriors and cannot see the sage's heart of jade.

Laozi expects that the ideas and principles of Tao should be the guidelines and compass for organizations to create a sustainable and harmony society. However, in reality, particularly in modern world, few of his ideas and principles are understood and put into practice. This is because most people are deluded by greed, self-interest, short-sightedness, self-indulgence, and competition. Most of us allow our lives to be shaped and defined by models that stress scarcity, competition, and individualism. Similarly, the restrictions—cognitive, financial, social, and political—that limit our capacity to know the abundance of life put up roadblocks to our giving and receiving of resources, and contribute to a deep inner malaise and feeling of lack. It's a vicious circle. Our original and genuine nature is befuddled by greed in the outer world, that's why we cannot understand the ideas and principles of Tao.

However, Laozi also realizes that we do have a few of people understand and practice his ideas and principles, they are rare birds. Laozi describes three kind of people who demonstrate their attitudes toward Tao. Some people initially feel very positive and open. Some are hesitant, and others are like to be threatened and put off.

> *Those who have high wisdom hear of Tao, they diligently practice it.*
> *Those who have low wisdom hear of Tao, they doubt it.*
> *Those who have no wisdom hear of Tao, they laugh loudly at it.*
> *Laughing at Tao means the Tao is not easy to know*
> —Laozi, Tao Te Ching, Ch. 41

This implies that to be able to fully apply Taoism's wisdom and principles in the business world requires prudent and honest scholarship that is equipped with diligence, understanding, rigor and critical spirit. Because as Laozi describes:

The Tao that is bright seems dark,
The Tao that goes forward seems fall backward
The Tao that is even seems rough
High virtue seems like a valley
Great purity seems tarnished
Expansive virtue seems lacking
Vigorous virtue seems idle
Pure and simple virtue seems turbid.
The largest square has no corners
The great vessel is slow to complete
The great sound seems soundless
The great form seems formless
The Tao is too subtle to be described.
Yet it is only the Tao that develops and perfects all things.
—Laozi, Tao Te Ching, Ch. 41

Those who have high wisdom make things happen, those who have low wisdom watch things happen, and those who have no wisdom wonder what happened. The purpose of the book is to offer a delightful, practical, and digestible approach for business leaders to make good things happen for a better future in an uncertain world. Through inspiring examples and unique insight, the book will outline ideas and principles of Tao for responsible leaders to develop sustainable business. The central aim of the book is to update the very old and often forgotten "excellence" of Taoism—to see why Taoism's thought as the master virtue that allows individuals, organizations, and society as a whole to survive and thrive. Recognizing the enduring effect of Taoism's wisdom, the book takes a practical turn to seek to understand how the practical wisdom may help to shed light on modern management and leadership.

This book endeavours to simplify and unlock the secrets of Laozi's ideas and principles so that business leaders can understand them easily and apply them in their business strategy and operations.

In this book, the discussions and analysis are organized around 3C Model of Taoism (compassion, conversation and compliance). The book combines 3C Model of Taoism with the modern management, especially the concept of 3P model of sustainability to guide business leaders to embark on a path toward sustainable business development.

The book examines the role that organizations play in developing a more sustainable business environment in the future by applying Taoism's wisdom. The focus is on the philosophical and spiritual aspects of sustainable business development in relation to modern management practices. The book includes examples of how leading global corporations are leading change using the principles, strategies, processes, and practices of sustainable development. The examples highlight innovative approaches for achieving sustainable success.

The book is intended to assist executives, managers, and professionals in formulating, implementing, and evaluating business strategies and decision-making processes concerning sustainable business development. It provides insights into what leading global corporations have done and are doing to create extraordinary value and provide benefits for their customers, stakeholders, and constituents. It studies the implications of these changes for executives, managers, and professionals and explores the next generation of strategic and environmental management methodologies.

The book is divided into four parts:

Part I starts with a call to Taoism's wisdom in today's uncertain world, examining why there is missing link between the spiritual world and business world in the case of Taoism's wisdom and practices of business and management. Part I also discusses the challenges and wicked problems our society is facing: 3D—The ecological divide the social divide, and the spiritual-cultural divide, and how 3C—compassion, conservation and compliance can tackle the 3D challenges for a better world and bright future we want.

Part II investigates the concepts of corporate social responsibility and sustainability from perspectives of management science and Taoism's wisdom, and discusses why business needs philosophy, particularly the Eastern wisdom. Part III provides an overview of 3C model of Taoism and the implications for 3P (people, planet, and prosperity) of sustainability. It describes integrated framework of Taoism's wisdom and sustainability, and finally analyses how to do business responsibly with compassion, conservation and compliance.

Part IV explores the wise strategies for creating responsible and sustainable solutions. It especially examines the power and importance of purpose-driven leadership from the perspectives of Taoism's wisdom for sustainable business development. It also discusses the new concepts and instruments of sustainability risk and crisis management in today's uncertain world. Part V discuss the relationships between Taoism's wisdom and sustainable development from the international perspective, particularly it focuses on the UN 2030 Agenda for Sustainable Development. By holding firm to the principle of "no one is left behind", this section also discusses the importance of youth development in achievement of SDGs. Part V concludes the book by offering some guidelines for successful integrating Taoism's wisdom in sustainable business development.

I expect those who endeavor to learn and apply ancient wisdom of Taoism for sustainable business development will be able to take up one idea of Laozi, make that one idea of your life—think of it, dream of it, live on that idea. Let the brain, muscles, nerves, every part of your body, be full of that idea, and just leave every other idea alone. This is the way to success.

Part II
Taoism's Wisdom Matters to Modern Management

Heaven is eternal and Earth everlasting
Why Heaven and Earth exist forever is
Because they do not live for themselves.
Thus, they are sustainable.
—Laozi, Tao Te Ching, Ch. 7

The relevance of the Chinese classical traditions has drawn much discussion not only within Chinese society and Chinese business, but also in the global community and business. Beyond the internal relevance, the evolution of the Chinese variant of the market economy and its moral and philosophical framing has global significance, and other parts of the world may need to take notice. The crisis has accelerated shifts in global geopolitics and global economics, with deep implications for global culture, management culture included. Chinese culture increasingly will permeate international culture and move from peripheral to mainstream status. To ignore this in management education would be a grave oversight.

Ancient Chinese philosophy may be a valuable source of inspiration for modern management. Ideas from Confucian and Taoist wisdom may not directly offer us better management techniques or organization models, but they do help us discover the limits of the theory and practice of management, rooted in Western philosophical and ethical traditions, and broaden our view of management (Blomme and Hoof 2014).

The Chinese classical traditions, particularly Taoism's wisdom, provide a rich legacy that may shed light on modern management. However, they also pose considerable challenges for modern scholars and researchers. Critical questions to be asked are: how could these grand ideas and wisdom, developed in the far away ancient times, still be relevant to the twenty-first century? In what way are these practical wisdoms applicable to modern management? Could these wisdoms guide us to make wise decisions in response to social and environmental issues in today's world, and whether could the wisdoms provide practical principles for sustainable business development?

The book will answer the questions. I have dedicated the decades years of my research in identifying and defining the linkage between practical wisdom of

Chinese classical traditions and modern management. The book will also identify well-defined terms what the meanings and contents of the practical wisdoms in specific modes of management, and explain in rigorous terms, how these wisdoms are applied and their implications. This generic set of issues can be applicable to a broad range of management concerns, including leadership, strategy, corporate social responsibility, business ethics, sustainable development, stakeholder relationships, and among others.

I understand that it is not easy for me to achieve that goal, because to be able to fully apply ancient wisdoms for today's management requires a prudent and honest scholarship that is equipped with diligence, understanding, rigor and critical spirit. Practical wisdom has to address timely and important practical issues in the real world. Like all true wisdoms, Taoism's wisdom has the unfailing function to inspire, enlighten, and guide people through complexity, adversity and uncertainty.

Reference

Blomme, R. J., & Hoof, B. v. (2014). *Another state of mind perspectives from wisdom traditions on management and business*. Palgrave Macmillan.

Chapter 5
Integrating Eastern Thoughts in Modern Management

Werner Heisenberg, the founder of quantum mechanics, once said, "*it is probably true quite generally that in the history of human thinking the most fruitful developments frequently take place at those points where two different lines of thought meet. These lines may have their roots in quite different parts of human culture, in different times or different cultural environments or different religious traditions: hence if they meet, that is, if they are at least so much related to each other that a real interaction can take place, then one may hope that new and interesting developments may follow*" (Werner Heisenberg 1989). Taking into consideration of Heisenberg's observation of what can happen when lines of thought meet rather than diverge, I intend to incorporate cutting-edge management science in the West and ancient mystical knowledge and wisdom in the East. We have seen more and more research on the philosophy and wisdom of Taoism in order to understand it more and more deeply. It might be better to undertake comparative study of two thinkers of two different cultures. The book is the attempt of reinterpreting management and sustainable business development from the perspective of Taoism by exploring parallels from management science.

Management is a Western invention that combines scientific thinking with practical solutions to business problems (Locke 1984, 1989). It arose in the Second Industrial Revolution at the beginning of the twentieth century and its basic ideas have not changed greatly since. The rational design of organizational structures, procedures and control instruments is combined with the management of individual employees. The separation of execution and control has resulted in the existence of a group of managers charged with the translation of organizational goals into performance, with general knowledge-based principles of management guiding the work of managers. There are increasing signs of the limits of this twentieth-century management approach in the changing conditions of today's global economy, with managers and management theories receiving the blame. The crisis phenomena in business and finance of the early years of the new millennium have reinforced this tendency toward self-doubt in the field of management. In such a situation, it makes sense to reflect on the basic assumptions of the field. One way of doing this is to

L. Zu, *Responsible and Sustainable Business*,
https://doi.org/10.1007/978-3-030-91117-1_5

examine the culturally specific assumptions in management. How does management limit itself by exclusively building on a 'Western' set of assumptions? Do other cultures offer different sets of assumptions that enable us to think of different approaches to management?

What would new practical and theoretical possibilities this create? This chapter will discuss and share the Chinese classical wisdom. In ancient Chinese philosophy, a world that makes sense to us, far removed from the assumptions of modern management. Management shares the Western conception of a world consisting of objects with stable attributes governed by unchanging laws about which we can gather objective knowledge. Human beings are seen as distinct individuals with needs and wants, who make free choices on the basis of their goals and values (Nisbett 2003). Managers create, control and change organizations on the basis of proven models and methods. This world is very different from that presented in the ancient Chinese texts: an interconnected, ever-changing world, without stable objects and attributes, in which people find their way by harmonizing with a context that is beyond their control.

Classical Chinese philosophy consists of different schools and ideas, so speaking of 'the Chinese worldview' implies simplification and a risk of stereotyping. However, in comparison to the equally diverse Western culture, the Chinese tradition has some recognizable distinctions with which we will deal here. We will focus on Taoism especially on texts attributed to Taoism, with the Tao Te Ching of Laozi as the central text.

It is not only the content of Chinese philosophy that is different from the Western tradition; the texts are also very different in style and presentation. Western in contrast to the Greek tradition of public debate, in which logic was seen as the road to the truth and arguments as legitimate instruments to win a debate, Chinese wisdom avoids logical argument and debate (Nisbett 2003). The texts are poetic and ambiguous and contain few statements of problems, logical arguments, or conclusions. Wise people in ancient China were not engaged in a quest for the truth, but tried to show the 'way,' that is, how people can live their lives productively. Anecdotes, poems and sayings make up the core of their texts.

The studies have proved that sages and philosophers, after all, are reality seekers, scientists are reality seekers too. Both groups are interested in what is, and both groups comment on it—yet the two groups have historically described the same reality differently. Science and philosophy approach reality with different aims, and with different questions in mind. The two groups do deal with the same reality, but they don't get the same answers because they don't ask the same questions. They subject the data to different interpretive frameworks, and this results in different—though not necessarily incompatible—descriptions of reality (Macdonald 2001).

Chinese traditional Taoism provides a powerful new holistic approach to leadership studies, because, at its core, is the dialectic study of changing phenomena. It therefore complements the western positivist approach that is good at analytical investigation of an isolated subject in a stable context. With a combination of Taoism and western scientific methodologies, realities are more likely to be discovered in a more accurate way. Through the study of the existing problems of leadership studies and the establishment of a Taoist model of leadership, we discovered that traditional Taoism, recovered by contemporary thinkers and leaders, complements the inadequacies of modern philosophies; ancient wisdom of Taoism allows for holistic observation and integration while modern science is good at positivism and analysis; a combination of the two provides a powerful new platform for enhancing our understanding of leadership as well as the nature and practice of adaptive leadership, in the rapid and complex changes of the global twenty-first century, and through a combination of Taoism and modern leadership theories, a brand-new leadership model or theory is likely to be developed to account for real organizational outcomes.

How Chinese and Western Thinking Differ?

In Chap. 1, I touched on the paradigm of Chinese thinking: synthetic, intuition, historical and practical. The first characteristic of the Chinese way of thinking is 'synthetic', it is also called systems thinking. This approach places its emphasis on the whole rather than its parts, harmony rather than opposition. This synthetic emphasis is manifested first in the Chinese view of the universe, society and man. While being dynamic, all constituents of the universe form a harmonious whole, a unity of nature and man, a synthesis of all existences and non-existences. Another important approach is intuition, which refers to a direct, immediate apprehension of the totality of the thing or situation concerned, resulting from observation and reflection upon life experience. Intuition has three distinctive features.

However, in Laozi's book of Tao Te Ching, we find one of the most important thinking paradigms is opposite thinking. For example, Laozi says,

> *Those who intend to contract it must first expand it.*
> *Those who intend to weaken it must first strengthen it.*
> *Those who intend to abolish it must first establish it*
> *Those who intend to receive must first give*
> *This is the subtle wisdom:*
> *The soft and the weak triumph over the hard and the strong.*
> —Laozi, Tao Te Ching, Ch. 36

Laozi observes that "all things that connote Yin and Yang" contradictions are universal. The two opposite sides are by no means isolated but are mutually interdependent. A lot of contradictory concepts in pairs thus frequently appear in Tao Te Ching: big and small, high and low, advance and retreat, beautiful and ugly, new and old, strong and weak, rigid and supple, having and having-not, honour and disgrace, gain and loss, Yin and Yang, difficulty and easy, etc. Several concepts are cited in Tao Te Ching, Ch. 2, for example, "*The whole world knows the beautiful as beautiful, hence, the existence of the ugly; the whole world knows the good as good, hence, the existence of the bad...*".

The above contrarian insights exemplify the process of "thinking opposite," an age-old strategy deeply embedded in the arts and sciences, as well as in management.

If you want to better understand an object or concept, conceive of the opposite. If you want to understand how a machine was put together, disassemble it. If you want to achieve a particular result, define the end goal and then fashion a line of development leading back to the beginning. The practical advantages of oppositional thinking are at least four: first, it allows us to see solutions to problems that we would otherwise not see; second, it makes us more mentally flexible and imaginative; third, it teaches us to be comfortable with ambiguity and paradox; and finally, it often makes us laugh, a sure sign of happiness (Wright 2020). Therefore, from the notion that the movements of the Tao are a continuous interplay between opposites, the Taoists deduced the basic rule for human conduct. Whenever you want to achieve anything, they said, you should start with its opposite.

Let's illustrate the opposite thinking with the yin and yang. Classical Chinese philosophy emphasizes processes of change: the rhythm of the seasons, the rise and fall of empires and emperors, the alternation of poverty and affluence in society, the phases in human life from birth to death (Blomme and Hoof 2014). Everything is in constant flux. Yin and yang form the fundamental opposition in Chinese thought, based on which other oppositions can be constructed. Yin and yang are opposites, but each concept implies its opposite. Yang stands for light, initiative, force, and clarity. Yin represents darkness, passivity, flexibility, and hidden qualities. The heavens are pure yang, the earth is pure yin. The male is yang, the female is yin. The human body is organized in terms of yin–yang oppositions: the (rigid, solid) back is yang in relation to the soft belly, which is yin. Fat is yin as opposed to the muscles that are yang. Too much of either of them results in disease. Curing the disease means restoring the harmony between yin and yang (Blomme and Hoof 2014).

Change is the result of yin–yang interaction. This idea was elaborated in the Book of Changes, the Yi Jing, which offers a method of understanding situations and thinking about the future. The basic logic of this method of divination is based on the assumption that extreme situations eventually turn into their opposite: what is extremely yang will become yin and vice versa. In a period of high trust, we sow the seeds of conflict, in excellent leadership lies the beginning of moral decay. The Yi Jing teaches us to read situations, not in terms of their fixed attributes, but in terms of their potential, in the dispositions present in the situation. The new is always hidden in the old (and vice versa): understanding this can help us to act productively. This dialectical way of thinking—thinking in pairs of mutually opposing concepts—differs from Western logic. It accepts that something is the case and that the opposite is also the case. This acceptance of contradiction is related to the pragmatic emphasis in Chinese thinking: understanding that there are different opposing tendencies is more practical than deciding on a unique truth (Nisbett 2003), as dealt with in the subsection 'the unity of knowing and doing' in greater detail.

Table 5.1 summarizes ancient Chinese thinking in comparison to Western thinking. The right-hand column represents Western thinking, which lies at the basis of current management theory and practice. Most of these assumptions are taken for granted in management. Most change-management approaches, for example, assume that we move from one well-defined situation to another. We see people in

Table 5.1 Chinese thinking vs. western thinking

Theme	Chinese thinking	Western thinking
Logic of creation	From the inside, on the basis of processes of self-organization	From the outside, on the basis of goals and plans
Human relationships	People who are the product of relationships and produce these relationships	Relationships between autonomous individuals on the basis of individual rights and duties
Harmony/ conflict	Dynamic adaption of parts on the basis of differences and complementarities	Absence of conflict and equality between individuals; conflict resolution through debate and argument
Change	Creative processes on the basis of dispositions that exist in the situation, driven by the dynamics between specific persons and conditions	Movement from static situation A to static situation B, driven by external goals and plans
Knowledge	Specific, situational knowledge, which is closely tied to the observer, their intentions and actions	General knowledge about objective reality which is independent of the superficial appearance of things and of the practical relevance to those involved

Source: Blomme and Hoof (2014), another state of mind perspectives from wisdom traditions on management and business

organizations as individuals with given needs and goals. When we think of the creation of organizations, we assume a design based on fixed principles. The centre column suggests that we can think differently, also in management. This implies, for example, that we can see change differently, in terms of self-organizing processes, or that we can see people not as individuals but as playing a part in a particular social context. This could lead to different views of management.

I will further discuss the paradigm of Chinese thinking in Chap. 8 from the perspective of 3C Model thinking.

Why Business Need Philosophy?

In today's business world, the rise and fall of organizations, sometimes, depends on fortunate timing, sometimes, on economic factors beyond their control. Debi Ghate (2011) claim that the most common cause of organizational success or failure is the fundamental principles on which the leader of the business acts. Businesses largely succeed or fail based on basic ideas—i.e., their philosophy—not complex strategies or esoteric activities. Sometimes these concepts are held implicitly rather than explicitly, but the leader's actions are driven by his beliefs.

In the wake of the financial crisis, an era of severe turbulence, rapid changes and increasing complexity has emerged. A black cloud hangs over the past decade's economic prosperity and global consumption habits, which fundamentally challenges the purpose of business. All too often the approach to business practices has been one-dimensional, lacking in richness and depth. This goes for both the cheerleaders and the critics of the current business practices (Poulsen 2013). In these times, it is important to be able to view the world in different shades—one of possibilities, rather than constraints. While the discipline of philosophy can help pave the way forward, it remains to be widely regarded as irrelevant to formal education programs in business schools. But they might think differently, if they take a closer look.

"Once hired, philosophy majors advance more rapidly than their colleagues who possess only business degrees" writes Thomas Hurka (1990), Professor of Philosophy at the University of Calgary. He strongly advises the younger generation to consider majoring in philosophy, if they want to be successful in business. This is supported by a recent study by Payscale, which shows that while starting salaries of philosophy graduates might be less than those with business degrees, by mid-career, the salaries of philosophy graduates surpass those of marketing, communications, accounting and business management. Taking this into consideration, it appears that having the right business degree from a prestigious business school does not guarantee a successful career in business.

Following this line of thought, Matthew Stewart, former management consultant of the Mitchell Madison Group tells, "If you want to succeed in business, don't get an MBA, study philosophy instead" (Stewart 2006). In his experience, MBA programs basically involved, "taking two years out of your life and going deeply into debt, all for the sake of learning how to keep a straight face while using phrases like "out-of-the-box thinking," "win-win situation," and "core competencies." Even though this is arguably an exaggeration of the current state of business education, it is hard to neglect the verity: the concept of 'business as usual' in management education is swiftly becoming old-fashioned, while the socio-economic challenges of globalization only mature. In many countries, labour market conditions are deteriorating with unemployment rates worsened to an unprecedented level. For the younger generation, the prospects of employment are declining, as they are often the 'last ones in' and the 'first ones out' of a bleak job market.

"The world of work is currently out of sync with the world of education—meaning young people don't have the skills needed to get jobs," says Dominic Barton (2012), Global Managing Director of McKinsey & Company, calling for urgent action. Instead of focusing on the lack of jobs out there, he argues that the available openings require skills that the younger generation simply do not possess. They face a distinctively new normal, as the operational capacities of business leaders are fundamentally changing. In order to successfully navigate in an uncertain, volatile and increasingly complex business environment, a supplementary approach to rational problem-solving and optimal decision-making is required.

The rising demand for both creative and concrete problem-solving as well as abstract and strategic thinking indicates the necessity to broaden the reflectivity-horizon of the narrow business perspective that future business leaders will determine their decisions within. Business tends to seek one rationalised conclusion at the expense of others. This closes opportunities, rather than opens them. Philosophy, on the other hand, can through critical reasoning continually question and rethink the assumed certainties and its basic premises. In this sense, business and philosophy might seem poles apart at first glance and their interdisciplinary potential has for long been largely unrecognized on traditional business schools, but this is about to change.

Rethinking Business Education

In the book *Rethinking Undergraduate Business Education*, the renowned Carnegie Foundation for Advancement of Teaching took the lead in transforming the preparation of future business leaders. In the US, business is the most popular field of undergraduate study, reflecting the growing centrality of business in society today (Colby et al. 2011). According to the authors, it is therefore of utter importance that future business leaders' function both productively and responsibly in a highly demanding and increasingly complex business environment. However, the results of the nationwide study of undergraduate business education cited in the book showed that "*it is too often narrow, fails to challenge students to question assumptions, think creatively, or to understand the place of business in larger institutional contexts*." The implications of their observations suggest that business education neither guarantees success, nor prevents failures in business. So, what is to be done? In confronting the challenge, the authors argue for an integrative approach that combines the business disciplines with liberal arts and social sciences in order to help future business leaders have a better understanding of the other institutional sectors, the pluralism of values and operating logics that businesses depend on. This could prove to play a decisive role in the future business environment, when adapting to change is not enough.

Following the movement, Per Holten-Andersen, President of Copenhagen Business School, took action. "The market forces are so strong that they force us to go in a direction that some of us actually don't favour," he says. At the 2012 Academy of Management Annual Meeting in Boston, he delivered a provocative speech to the gathering of scholars and business leaders in the management discipline. In the wake-up call, he advocates that we must be willing to constantly challenge our traditional beliefs and perceptions in order to engage in the discussion of where we are heading, and where we want to head. The call to confront our habitual mindset is not grounded in the common anti-capitalistic bias, where business is evil and cannot be trusted, but in an assessment of the long-term socio-economic impact of short-term decision-making. He explains: "I am not an anti-capitalist. I should say that I am actually a great believer in the merits of capitalism myself. But I am certainly more in favour of democracy than the very raw capitalism that we are seeing at the moment changing Europe and also parts of America." These thoughts might not be new, but it is certainly a remarkable statement bearing in mind his influential position and the crowd of business-enthusiasts he was addressing.

Why Are Philosophy Useful?

What does all this have to do with philosophy? For too long, philosophy- bashing has been keen to follow the mantra of '*too much talk, not enough action*' in the field of business. This is not, however, surprising if you approach philosophy with the same instrumentality that dominates business. Philosophy pursues questions rather than answers them. In this sense, the responsibility of philosophy is not so much to answer our questions, but to question our given answers. This raises the question: What is philosophy? Just to be clear, philosophy is not some kind of recipe or precept. You do not become a moral subject by studying Immanuel Kant or a good citizen by reading Plato's The Republic.

Nevertheless, the placement of the concept of morality or justice under an investigative lens can help us move beyond the confinements of prevailing knowledge. This is the essence of the discipline of philosophy—it teaches not what to think, but how to think. It examines the enduring fundamental questions concerning human life, society, ethics and knowledge, just to name a few. Whereas, the business discipline represents a definite ordering of the world through the fabrication of concepts, methods and models as a way to reduce complexity, philosophy explores its conceptual framework and developments. It goes without saying that Porter's Five Forces and almost every other generic framework for problem-solving are heuristics: they can speed up the process of finding a solution, but it is at the expense of autonomous thinking. In this way, philosophy can help articulate the blind-spots of business by looking behind its assumed certainties and theoretical preconditions. By pondering the questions which are beyond the scope of business, philosophy can broaden the reflectivity-horizon of future business leaders to help them manage complexity and make sound decisions, not only in the purview of good business, but also in accordance with the needs of society.

This, however, does not point to a future of philosopher-leaders, as Plato encouraged. This is because the pragmatic judgement and technical expertise of business is still very much needed to direct the philosophical reflections towards practical decisions and concrete actions. In this regard, business models, concepts and strategies are certainly still a necessity. But in order to keep improving them, philosophy demands attention. This is the interdisciplinary potential of business and philosophy.

The Case in Point: Eastern Thoughts in Management Philosophy of Haier

Haier is one of the successful Chinese companies in the global business. It is one of the world's largest producers of household appliances. I'd like to discuss the case of Haier to illustrate the impact and influence of Taoism's wisdom on Haier's business strategy and management philosophy. The name of Haier means a sea. The sea, river or water are the favourite metaphors that Laozi frequently used to describe the qualities of great leaders and organizations.

> *Why sea and river become leaders of hundreds of valleys*
> *Is that they stay below them.*
> *Therefore,*
> *If great leaders want to stand above people,*
> *They shall speak to them from below.*
> *If they want to stand ahead of people,*
> *They shall place themselves behind.*
> —Laozi, Tao Te Ching, Ch. 66

The metaphor of river and sea refers to good qualities of great leaders: humility and magnanimity. Sea and river are receptive to receiving waters from streams. It is as if they were the rulers of all these streams and valleys. Why river and sea are able to dominate over valleys? Because their nature drives them to be humble to stay in the lowest position, so that all streams and rivulets of valleys can flow into them naturally. Observing the qualities of river and sea, Laozi found that the principles can apply equally well to leaders. Great leaders must emulate nature of rivers and seas to be humble to lead and serve people. If they wish to have influence over people, leaders must always stay in the lowest position like river and sea. In other words, they must be humble to what they do and what they say to people. If they wish to guide or direct people to reach their purpose, leaders must place other interests above their own. These are the qualities that great leaders must develop and embrace.

This is a very different concept from the conventional "might makes right" paradigm, where one seizes power by force, and bullies others with it. Great leaders are the exact opposite. They have no need to seize anything or fight against anyone. Because of this, no one fights with them. Instead, people support great leaders from the heart.

I believe that the management philosophy of Ruimin Zhang, CEO of Haier, has been influenced by Taoism's wisdom. He describes his company as "the great sea into which rivers of all origin, size and path flow. Be it a brook of no name, a running river that travels through mountains and plains, or just a torrent of muddy water, the sea takes them all, and turns them into an immense body of water. The sea is indiscriminate and accommodating, as if it has limitless capacity, to rivers of all kinds. The Yangtze River, the Yellow River and the hundreds of streams along the way are all rushing persistently to it in spite of the long journey and the zigzag caused by the terrain. Where rivers end, the sea's immense presence begins. Its everlasting waves are magnificent. It is eternally unrivalled" (Blomme and Hoof 2014).

In Ruimin Zhang's leadership style, we found that he integrates Chinese wisdom, American management, and German technology in his management. His eagerness to learn through reading and self-study compensated for the lack of formal education in that period. Working in a state-owned company in the field of household equipment from 1968, he climbed the hierarchy from the lowest levels up to management, which gave him a sharp eye for the motivations and needs of people on the shop floor. In 1982, he was appointed general manager of the Qingdao refrigerator plant, which was in a very bad state at that time. One in five refrigerators had defects at the end of the production line. From 1984 to 1990, the company cooperated with the German firm Liebherr. This joint venture provided Haier with the necessary technical know-how. In 1990, the 'Haier' brand was launched, which sounded German but also contained the Chinese character for 'sea'. In combination, the brand stood for German quality and international orientation.

Peter Drucker was one of the great models for Zhang, who read the former's work in the 1980s. He was especially impressed by the book "The Effective Executive". Zhang applied Drucker's principles of result-oriented management in Haier in a tight system of performance control. Haier combined this American style of management with inspiration from ancient Chinese wisdom. In numerous interviews and articles, he has expressed his Chinese view of business. The family is a model for the business organization and the five Confucian virtues are central to attaining harmony. Paternalism is not eschewed: father—son and teacher—pupil relationships are central to the development and transfer of knowledge.

Taoism has provided Zhang with a language to probe into the dynamics that give life to an organization. Talking about soft, invisible and silent aspects of organization, Zhang likes to use quotes from the Tao Te Ching, such as

> *All creatures in the world are born of being,*
> *And the being is born of non-being*
> —Laozi, Tao Te Ching, Ch. 40

The harmony in organizations is brought about by organizational culture, which Zhang interprets in a Taoist way: a unity that arises from a play of opposites:

> *The Tao is one,*
> *One gave birth to two,*
> *Two gave birth to three,*
> *And three created all creatures.*
> —Laozi, Tao Te Ching, Ch. 42

Soft aspects of organization are often more important than hard structures and systems, according to the CEO, who quotes the Tao Te Ching (Ch. 36) to support his view: "*What is soft and supple conquers the rigid and strong*". The Taoist perspective is also apparent in the way Zhang thinks about the leadership role: 'Perhaps I have not achieved what Laozi described – a populace unaware of the presence of their ruler. But that brilliance may be within my successor's reach' (Zhang 2007). Sun Zi's military thinking has particularly inspired Haier's CEO in relation to marketing strategies. Try to find your enemy's—in this case the foreign competitor's—weak points. Haier has often been successful, although the European market has been rather difficult to crack. However, in the United States, Haier avoided the market for large refrigerators, where competition was strong, and was successful in the selling of smaller products.

The Haier story illustrates how Chinese wisdom can play a role in practical management and leadership; however, the ancient wisdom is not likely to replace the techniques of modern management. Even in a completely Chinese company, management is primarily based on a Western scientific paradigm, as we can see in the application of American performance management at Haier. German technology is another essential ingredient of the story and this technology is rooted in Western science. However, Ruimin Zhang adds essential traditional Chinese elements. He broadens his attention to aspects of management and leadership that are often overlooked in the Western management paradigm and which have some relevance beyond this case.

Zhang is aware of the importance of the invisible, silent and soft aspects of organization that are often not paid any attention. He uses poetic language and metaphor to deal with the 'unspeakable,' where management often emphasizes measurement and precision. The importance of invisibility extends to his role as a leader. In contrast to dominant ideals of visibility and transparency, the ideal leader is seen as a person whose contribution is implicit, of which the followers are unaware.

As the case of Haier suggests, ancient Chinese wisdom is not likely to replace the dominant Western paradigm of management, just as Chinese medicine is not a serious alternative to science-based Western medicine. However, as the medical example also suggests, old Chinese wisdom may contribute to loosening the dominant approaches to management issues, by widening the attention of management to elements that are often neglected, such as the organization as a community, the importance of the invisible, unspeakable and soft aspects of organization, and the contextual nature of processes. Individual leaders and managers can find inspiration in the ancient texts of Taoism, Confucianism and the writings of Sun Zi, and come to understand their humble contribution to the processes of organization, which cannot be grasped using the predominant concepts and models of management.

References

Barton, D. (2012, 7 November 2012). *Young people don't possess the right skills for jobs*. Telegraph.co.uk. Retrieved November 12, 2020, from https://www.telegraph.co.uk/finance/jobs/youth-unemployment-competition/9659515/Young-people-dont-possess-the-right-skills-for-jobs.html

Blomme, R. J., & Hoof, B. v. (2014). *Another state of mind perspectives from wisdom traditions on management and business*. Palgrave Macmillan.

Colby, A., Ehrlich, T., Sullivan, W. M., & Dolle, J. R. (2011). *Rethinking undergraduate business education: Liberal learning for the profession* (1st ed.). Jossey-Bass.

Debi Ghate, R. E. R. (2011). *Why businessmen need philosophy: The capitalist's guide to the ideas behind Ayn Rand's Atlas shrugged*.

Heisenberg, W.. (1989). *Physics and philosophy: The revolution in modern science, Harper perennial modern classics*. Harper & Row Publishers.

Hurka, T. (1990). *How to get to the top – Study philosophy*. Retrieved December 16, 2020, from https://thereitis.org/how-to-get-to-the-top-study-philosophy/

Locke, R. R. (1984). *The end of the practical man: Entrepreneurship and higher education in Germany, France and Great Britain, 1880–1940*. JAI Press.

Locke, R. R. (1989). *Management and higher education since 1940: The influence of America and Japan on West Germany, Great Britain and France*. Cambridge University Press.

Macdonald, C. (2001). *Toward Wisdom: Finding our way to inner peace, love & happiness.* .
Nisbett, R. E. (2003). *The geography of thought: How Asians and Westerners think differently and why*. Nicholas Brealy Publishing.
Poulsen, A. (2013, 26 July). *Why future business leaders need philosophy*. Retrieved June 20, 2020, from http://bigthink.com/experts-corner/why-future-business-leaders-need-philosophy
Stewart, M. (2006, June 2006). *The management myth*. The Atlantic. Retrieved November 20, 2020, from https://www.theatlantic.com/magazine/archive/2006/06/the-management-myth/304883/
Wright, C. M. (2020). *The hidden habits of genius: Beyond talent, IQ, and Grit—Unlocking the secrets of greatness*. Dey Street Books.
Zhang, R. (2007). Raising Haier. *Harvard Business Review, 85*, 141–146+157.

Chapter 6
Laozi and Tao Te Ching: The Source of Taoism's Wisdom

The classical Taoism began with the Chinese philosopher Laozi. The set of philosophical teachings and religious practices of Taoism rooted in the understanding of the Chinese character *Tao*, or "The Way" was founded by Laozi in the 600 B.C. in his work *Tao Te Ching* (*The Book of the Way and Virtue*). Tao Te Ching laid the philosophical foundation for the religion's beliefs, and also offers ideational principles and practical guidelines for today's business, leadership and government. The philosophical system with the core principles of Tao has a deep effect on the traditional culture of China and the world as a whole.

Laozi and Tao Te Ching

Today, Laozi is well known as an ancient Chinese philosopher, author of Tao Te Ching, and founder of philosophical Taoism. Laozi, in Chinese, means older (*Lao*) master (*zi*). I think since the ancient times, we, Chinese people think that age equals wisdom, when you are getting old, your wisdom is also added substantially, although it is not the case today. "*Zi*" means master who are experienced and learned. His real personal name is called Dan Li.

Laozi is absolutely a unique sage who accumulated his wisdom and thoughts beyond our imaginations, and gains the prestige of being of older origin. While studying his legend and history, we couldn't find too much information about him, I think that Laozi in the context of lack of scientific facilities in his time, he was able to develop his philosophy and gained wisdom, probably from two channels, one was from the books he read. The legends says that Laozi worked as the head of national library in Dynasty of Zhou, where he could access much more information and knowledge that others couldn't. The second channel is that he learned by observation, particularly by observing universe, natural world, and society during the Warring States period. The wisdom and thoughts he learned and developed by observation are clearly reflected in his book of Tao Te Ching.

L. Zu, *Responsible and Sustainable Business*,
https://doi.org/10.1007/978-3-030-91117-1_6

Learning by observation was the most important and effective way for all sages in ancient times to understand the knowledge and law of universe. We can find full of the examples in Tao Te Ching. One of the examples is that Laozi used the metaphors of water, earth, heaven, maintain, valley, river, sea, baby, woman, etc. to illustrate the principles of the Tao and Te. In the verse 54, Laozi encouraged great leaders and rulers to learn by observing others: "*individual learns virtue by observing other individual; family learns virtue by observing other family; community learns virtue by observing other community*...". This view of point has been validated by two well-known scientists, Joseph Needham, British biochemist, historian and sinologist, and Albert Bandura, Canadian-American psychologist and Professor Emeritus of Social Science in Psychology at Stanford University.

Joseph Needham is known for his scientific research and writing on the history of Chinese science and technology. In his book "*Science and Civilization in China, Vol. 2*" reveals that: As Maspero (II) has reminded us, there is much significance in the fact that throughout the centuries Taoist temples have been known as *kuan* (observation); and other terms, such as *ssu* (mosque) or *miao* (temple), which have been applied to temples of other religions, have not been used for those of the Taoists. Now the original meaning of *kuan* was 'to look'. Already, in the Tso Chuan, *kuan* has acquired the meaning of a watch-tower, and is the regular word used for the observation of natural phenomena for divination. Embodied therefore in the common present-day name for a Taoist temple is the ancient significance of the observation of nature, and since in their beginnings magic, divination and science were inseparable, we cannot be surprised that it is among the Taoists that we have to look for most of the roots of Chinese scientific thought. What benefits the ancient Taoist philosophers hoped might be derived from the observation of natural phenomena, wider than the satisfaction of the desire of rulers and feudal lords to know what the future held for them, will shortly appear (Needham 1995).

Albert Bandura has been responsible for contributions to the field of education and to several fields of psychology, including social cognitive theory, therapy, and personality psychology, and was also of influence in the transition between behaviourism and cognitive psychology. He is known as the originator of social learning theory and the theoretical construct of self-efficacy, and is also responsible for the influential 1961 Bobo doll experiment. This Bobo doll experiment demonstrated the concept of observational learning. In his book of "Social Learning Theory" published in 1997, he claims that "*most of human behaviour is learned observationally through modelling: from observing others one forms an idea of how new behaviours are performed, and on later occasions this coded information serves as a guide for action. Because people can learn from example what to do, at least in approximate form, before performing any behaviour, they are spared needless errors.*" (Bandura 1977).

I believe it very important for us to know how Laozi's thoughts was developed in his life and history so that we can have a better understanding of the principles and wisdom that Tao Te Ching embodies and will be able to apply it in our life and work today.

We know that Laozi didn't leave us with so many books, but only the text of Tao Te Ching with about five thousand words. The bible of Taoism was divided into two parts. The first one started with the word Tao, the Way, and the second with the word Te, Virtue. The word Ching refers to a book or cannon that has become a classic, a scripture revered as sacred, transmitting wisdom of old, fundamental to Chinese culture and philosophy. Many researches argues that the division into 81 chapters is a later invention, probably made in the first century BC. The number of chapters is chosen to create the symmetry of 9×9, which has distinctive symbolic meaning in Chinese tradition.

Laozi excelled in wisdom, and his wisdom reflected in the bible of Taoism is inexhaustible. We do not receive wisdom, we must discover it for ourselves, after a journey through the wilderness which no one else can make for us, which no one can spare us, for our wisdom is the point of view from which we come at last to regard the world. Tao Te Ching offers ideational principles and practical guidelines for today's business, government, and leadership. The philosophical system with the core of Tao has a deep effect on the traditional culture of China and the world. Nowadays, when the human community is facing the heightened contemporary fears about increasingly fractured relations between humanity and natural world, from resource depletion and species extinction to pollution overload and toxic surplus, the classical wisdoms of Taoism provide new insights and values for human community to be in search of the solutions to social and environmental crisis and new and sustainable relationships to the earth.

The great influence of Laozi's wisdom has been exercised on every aspect of people's life, work and organizations in China and beyond. No other book except the Bible has been translated into English and other languages as often as the Tao Te Ching. Yet this treasure of Chinese philosophy is little known to the general public in the Western world, much less to students and practitioners of management. But I am hoping that this book can prove as relevant and fresh today as it must have been over two thousand years ago. To make the material accessible to the hurried executive, business student, or admirer of Eastern ways, this book can set the ideas in the context of the modern business world.

The Core Concepts of Taoism

Taoism is organized around several key principles and, like any philosophical outlook, presents a way of seeing and understanding reality.

Tao (Way): The Law of Universe

The Laozi's work, "Tao Te Ching"—"*The Power of the Tao (Way) and Te (Virtue)*" embraces the two central concepts: "*Tao (Way) and Te (Virtue)*". The word "Tao" has several meanings and many applications. Primarily, Tao refers to the eternal, life-giving force of the universe, the universal law of nature. It is also the process by which the universe governs itself. It is all-inclusive. There is nothing outside Tao. It is, in Laozi's words, "the mother of myriad things". Everything that takes form is an expression of the Tao. According to Laozi, Tao is without beginning, without end." It "exists by and through itself. It existed prior to Heaven and Earth and indeed for all eternity."

Tao, The Way

There is something that evolved from chaos,
Exists before Heaven and Earth
Silent and formless
Independent and changeless
Circulating and ceaseless
It is the mother of the universe
I do not know its name, call it "Tao".
—Tao Te Ching, Ch. 25

Not only are all forms latent in Tao, but all forms and everything that exists has Tao, a "way" to fulfil and each is in its own "way" unique and constantly changing, growing, developing. Humans, being part of the Tao, could lead lives that would be characterized by the balanced, harmonious flow found in nature simply by following the same principles that governed the functioning of the universe. They also realized that this process of alignment would be natural to us, would allow our true nature to emerge. In this way we would achieve our true birth-right, experiencing ourselves as an integral, rather than separate, element of creation. We would enter and become the Circle of Tao. In this way, Taoism offers a practical wisdom dedicated to personal well-being, social accord, and the accelerated evolution of individual consciousness. Its purpose has always been to assist humans in experiencing their essential nature as inseparable from that of the cosmos. As such the concepts of Taoism function as a guide to spiritual growth and transformation and are directly applicable to daily life.

Te (Virtue): Manifestation of Tao and Inner Nature of Myriad Things

Te, usually translated as *"Virtue"*, is the "uprightness" symbolized by a straight line indicating the Tao, or Way, which is conformity to principles and which also symbolizes the axis mundi. Te is, in a sense, Tao made manifest, the revelation of the true nature of the Tao. Although occasionally employed to signify conventional is the quality of natural goodness which is the result of enlightenment and of the manifestation and function of the Tao in man and all that exists in the universe. The word "Te" is used in Taoist literature to indicate power or strength (as the Latin root, virtus, indicates). Virtue refers to the fact that all things contain an inherent power or strength that comes from their own essential being or true inner nature. This power derives from the fact that our true self is an expression of the Tao, because it is intrinsically connected with the power of the Universe. However, the idea of Virtue is that of power exercised without the use of force and without inappropriate interference in the existing order of things.

Te, The Virtue

This "Virtue" has no moral overtones; it is an inward quality in man and all creatures, a potentiality and latent natural power arising from and dependent on the Tao, from which it is an emanation. Zhuangzi defines it as "the perfect attainment of harmony", and says that "there is nothing more fatal than intentional virtue, when the mind looks outward". Virtue is an inward quality and state. To do right is to obey the laws of Nature, of Virtue, and to live in conformity and harmony with them. Failure to do so brings automatic and equally natural retribution, disharmony, disruption, and consequent misery. Heaven is just as bound by these ordinances as is man, in view of the mutual interdependence of all things.

Yin-yang: Harmony and Balance

Taoism's central organizing principle is the interconnectedness of all life with its flow of continuous change. Nowhere is this idea expressed in such a unique and exquisite manner as in the concept of yin-yang, which describes the underlying unity of life through the interplay of opposites. Yin-yang is also known as the *Di and Tian,* Earth and Heaven, the principle of dualism in the manifest world. It indicates that all things and all processes contain two primal energies or forces. These two basic aspects of manifestation often are described as masculine and feminine, light and dark, negative and positive, creative and receptive. The original meaning of the term signified the light and dark sides of a mountain. From a Taoist point of view, however, these two polar opposites are not

Yin - Yang

seen as distinctly separate or in conflict, but rather as interdependent and complementary.

Yin-yang became the cosmic symbol of primordial unity and harmony and manifest phenomenal duality, or, as Zhuangzi calls it, the symbol of "The Two Powers of Nature", the two great regulating forces of cosmic order in the phenomenal world. The yin-yang diagram shows the two great forces of the universe, the dark and light, negative and positive, female and male, to be held in complete balance and equality of power; together they control everything in the realm of manifestation. The two forces are mutually interdependent and neither can stand alone nor be complete in itself. The two completely balanced powers are held together in the all-embracing circle of unity and the whole figure symbolizes the primordium.

It is a realm of relationships and it is this essentially creative duality of the yin-yang that gives rise to this state and all the balance of opposites and complementary qualities of the phenomenal world. It is necessary to have a pair for any form of relationship and creation. These give rise to further forms of life, again whether physical, mental, or spiritual. For anything to be able to be conceived or thought or perceived in the manifest world there must be a relationship. It is of this that Zhuangzi says, "*The perfect negative principle is majestically passive. The perfect positive is powerfully active.... The interaction of the two results in that harmony by which all things are produced.*" Yin-yang are at one and the same time a division and a reunion, and if they are spoken of as contending forces, they are also co-operating powers and the tension in which they are held is that of harmony, of the mutual play of creation, not of conflict. There is no Creator in Taoism, but the operation of the Tao brings about a spontaneous creation through the interaction of the yin and the yang.

So deeply does the yin-yang symbolism penetrate that it is carried into all forms of life and the entire setting of man. It must be appreciated at all different levels, from the vastness of the universe to the close intimacy of the home and to all the ramifications of the plant and animal kingdoms. The yin is the mother aspect, mercy and wisdom, extending from the lowest and humblest peasant to the serene and all-embracing compassion and motherhood of the Moon Mother, the Queen of Heaven, represented, in China, by Kwan-yin. The yang, the father aspect, is justice and method and the power of the Sun. Man's nature must also be held in the yin-yang balance of intellect and feeling. "There must be human-heartedness as well as wisdom." The feminine is the passive, receptive, and soft, and in the body is represented by the flesh, while the masculine is the active, aggressive, and hard, and in the body is the bone.

The Perfect Man, or Sage, so frequently referred to in both Taoist and Confucianist writings, was in himself a perfect yin-yang harmony. "In repose he shares the passivity of the yin, in action the energy of the yang" (Zhangzi 1989). He possessed a balance of head and heart, mind and emotions, intelligence and instinct. He is neither negative nor positive, but the happy mean, the central axis, the pole. By itself, the critical, rational, analysing mind is prone to hubris, its names, defines, and limits, and mistaking the naming of a thing for the understanding of it, sees itself as all-powerful and all-wise. The feelings, uncontrolled by mind, tend to dispersal and dissipation, while mind, unmodified by feeling, produces hardness and petrifaction. Today we have examples of this disastrous divorce between mind and emotions in the arid intellectualism of a so-called intelligentsia on the one hand and the morbid over-interest in sensation and sexualism on the other.

As feeling and mind the yin-yang is also being and thought. The feminine, instinctive, intuitional, and emotional is also depth, as the masculine, intelligence, rational is height. Each should inform and reconcile the other. The yin principle rises from rest, the yang is generated by motion. Another name for the yin-yang is "The Two Essences". The essences emerge from the First Principle, the Tao, which, working in and through all things, is responsible for change, mutations, and all transformation. It is essentially concerned with the rhythms of life; it is the "perfectly balanced union" which establishes an inner harmony in man and the universe, so that man becomes at peace with himself and the world about him, with the world within and the world without. It renders him harmless both to others and himself. It produces the Perfect Man of Confucianism and the Sage of Taoism.

One of the outstanding teachings of Taoism is the strength of weakness. The yin power of passivity is more enduring than the yang force of direct action; the one has a controlled, sustained power, the other is quickly spent and dissipated. This strength-in-weakness is also connected with the symbolism of the valley and the womb. It is that which receives and accepts all things, but from which, in turn, all things emerge. It is because it is the lowest, humblest place that the valley receives the full force of the waters which fall into it from the high, yang places. Majestic waterfalls and turbulent mountain torrents, for all their power, come down to the lowly and are absorbed by it and converted into the deep-flowing, broad, quiet and irresistible forces of the rivers, lakes, and oceans, the yin principle.

Opposed to the yin-water principle is the yang-fire, but both these powers are ambivalent as the forces of either destruction or creation. This dual role is also found in Nature herself, who can be ruthlessly destructive or benevolent in giving unstintingly of life, like the Great Mother, of whom Kwan-yin is the Chinese manifestation in her two aspects of creator and destroyer, life and death, holding within herself the tension of opposites which is the process of transformation through Wisdom (yin) and Method (yang) into the ultimate unity, the Tao.

If the two forces are working in perfect balance, a unity is achieved which becomes a power in itself and has a controlled force behind it. On the other hand, imbalance and disharmony have no power, but disintegrate into total ineffectiveness. Anything out of harmony, wrong, or maladjusted, either physically, mentally, or spiritually in the individual in particular, or the world in general, is to be regarded as a failure in, or disturbance of, the balance of the yin-yang forces. This applies not only to human beings but to all life in the maintenance of its health and wellbeing. "If the equilibrium of the positive and negative is disturbed ... man himself suffers physically thereby" (Zhangzi 1989).

The two great powers at work in the world can be beneficent or hostile according to the conduct of the individual or the state in either maintaining or disturbing the equilibrium. When the balance is disrupted the masculine and feminine are in conflict and then they, instead of being creative and harmonious, become malign and destructive, each striving for dominance and thereby producing inflation of the personal ego, developing it out of proportion, and from that arises discord and violence. Neither should usurp the function of the other. Each, in its normal working, corrects the inadequacies or excesses of the other. But the yin-yang is not only perfect duality and relationship in manifestation; the whole symbol is also contained within the circle of unity, the Tao, so that the whole is at once the symbol of duality and non-duality. (Cooper 2010).

Ziran Wu Wei (Spontaneity and Non-action): Going with the Flow

Taoism is the philosophy of the art of living and relationships; it deals with the whole of nature and man's place in it. It is the philosophy of the rhythm of life and simplicity of mind and spirit together with the absence of calculated activity, as expressed in the doctrine of *wu wei,* and the presence of *spontaneity*, *balance and harmony* (Cooper 2010).

"Ziran" & "wu wei" are an important value and principle in Laozi's philosophy. *Ziran* is the core or highest value that Laozi embraces and advocates in his Taoist philosophy. *Wu wei* is a core or universal principle of Tao that Laozi upholds for human beings to realize the value of *ziran*, and their oneness with Tao. The value of "*ziran*" and principle of "*wu wei*" are the cornerstone of Laozi's political idea and philosophy of "governing and leading with non-action". *Ziran & wu wei* are correlated and interdependent, and provide a unifying philosophical framework for understanding the Laozi's thought and wisdom of Tao Te Ching.

There are two interpretations of *ziran*, the first, the dominant one is interpreted as nature, as primordial and pristine natural "reality". For example, Wang Bi (226–249 C.E.) proposes a naturalistic understanding of *ziran*. From his perspective, nature has normative content: humanity is ultimately to take nature as its model. Wang Bi also advocates a "*go with the flow*" conception of *ziran*: model after the natural environment so as to inform human ethical ideals. The second meaning of *ziran* is concerned with self-so-ness or in human terms, pertaining to an individual's spontaneity. The appropriate response to spontaneity of individuals is to avoid, insofar as possible, imposing or using restrictive norms and methods, that is, *wu wei*. The power of "*ziran*" reflects in Tao Te Ching:

> *Man models himself on Earth.*
> *Earth models itself on Heaven.*
> *Heaven models itself on Tao.*
> *Tao functions on her own spontaneously (ziran)*
> —Laozi, Tao Te Ching, Ch. 25

Laozi puts *ziran* in the highest position of all things. Using this highest concept, Laozi wants people to understand and be able to pursue the ideal state of the world through his idea that Tao is the model for man, earth, and Heaven.

Ziran & Wu wei offer an account of ethics. If *ziran* is understood as spontaneity and we are to foster it, we must, in simple terms, refrain interference; allowing for the spontaneity of an individual requires us not to impose unnecessary constraints on this individual. In other words, it is to practice *wu wei* (Lai 2007). *Wu wei* means refraining from activity contrary to Nature, i.e. from insisting on going against the grain of things, from trying to make materials perform functions for which they are unsuitable, from exerting force in human affairs when the man of insight could see that it would be doomed to failure, and that subtler methods of persuasion, or simply letting things alone to take their own course, would bring about the desired result (Needham 1995).

Wu wei was letting things work out their destinies in accordance with their intrinsic principles. To be able to practise *wu wei* implied learning from Nature by observations essentially scientific (Needham 1995). Needham's interpretation of *"wu wei"* focuses on refraining from coercive policies and practices. However, *wu wei* may also be conceived more proactively, in terms of the sage's implementation of policies and institutions that foster participation of the common people. *Wu wei* may also include acting against existing norms and practices (Lai 2007). *Wu wei* refers to behaviour that arises from a sense of oneself as connected to others and to one's environment. It is not motivated by a sense of separateness. It is action that is spontaneous and effortless. At the same time, it is not to be considered inertia, laziness, or mere passivity. Rather, it is the experience of going with the grain or swimming with the current. Our contemporary expression, "*going with the flow*," is a direct expression of this fundamental Taoist principle, which in its most basic form refers to behaviour occurring in response to the flow of the Tao.

The principle of *wu wei* contains certain implications. Foremost among these is the need to consciously experience ourselves as part of the unity of life that is the Tao. Laozi advises us to be quiet and watchful, learning to listen to both our own inner voices and to the voices of our environment in a non-interfering, receptive manner. In this way we also learn to rely on more than just our intellect and logical mind to gather and assess information. We develop and trust our intuition as our direct connection to the Tao. We heed the intelligence of our whole body, not only our brain. And we learn through our own experience. All of this allows us to respond readily to the needs of the environment, which of course includes ourselves. And just as the Tao functions in a manner to promote harmony and balance, our own actions, performed in the spirit of *wu wei,* produce the same result.

I will further elaborate the concepts of Tao with some examples so that they can be understood well in the next chapters.

Taoism's Wisdom: Implications for Management and Leadership

Laozi's Tao Te Ching has been studied over the past decades from different perspective of philosophy, religion, medical, war, psychology, etc. Since the twentieth century, an increasing number of studies have turned their attention to management thinking of Laozi by drawing on the classical wisdom to guide modern management. Most of the studies concentrate on Tao of business, management, leadership and organization.

Heider (1997) in his book of *The Tao of Leadership* interpret the text of Laozi's Tao Te Ching from a leadership perspective, with a view to providing the guidance for anyone in a position of leadership. He interpreted each of 81 chapters in Tao Te Ching and analysed the implications for managing people at workplace. For example, being a wise and successful leader, he/she must be conscious of what is happening in the group, but not coercive. They do not impose a personal agenda or value system on the group. The leader follows the group's lead and is open and to whatever emerges. The leader judges no one and is attentive to both "good" and "bad" people. His book also explains the principles of the Tao. The natural process exists, without judgement, when everything is what it's meant to be and does what it needs to do. He provides the simplest and clearest advice on how to be the very best kind of leader: be faithful, trust the process, pay attention, and inspire others to become their own leaders. Heider's book is a blend of practical insight and profound wisdom, offering inspiration and advice (Heider 1997).

Some of the researches also touch on this subject. Dreher (2002) argues that leading with the Tao, the power of respect should be energized based on the Tao's principle of "those who would lead wisely must first respect life". Thus claims that a major principle of Tao is respect: for ourselves, one another, and the life process. Respect transforms reality, turning fragmented interactions into living relationship, conflicts into creative communication, and lifeless, mechanical systems into learning organizations.

Pheng (1994) analyses Tao Te Ching and its relevance to project leadership in construction. He concludes that the desirable leadership style advocated by Laozi is basically that of being gracious and non-competitive. In the context of construction industry, he argues that there are many ideas from the Tao Te Ching which are at odds with modern project management principles. Therefore, the extent to which Laozi's teachings can be applied to enhance the leadership qualities of project managers in the construction industry will depend very much on a good understanding of Tao Te Ching.

Gerstner's research (2011) focuses on the strategic aspects that can be found in Tao Te Ching, and his findings offers interesting perspectives on the relationship between personal development and sustainability. Personal development and leadership personality are seen as the driving forces behind the development of true sustainability in operational processes and interactions, whether the context be business, political, or social governance. He defines sustainability in his study as something that must originate with self-cultivation through individual practice before it can extend into leadership and guidance of organizational processes and patterns. According to the Tao Te Ching, if a leader's personal attitudes and behaviour are not imbued with sustainable patterns, it is difficult to organically "re-" produce them in the outside world. Such concepts of sustainability are as valuable today as over before (Gerstner 2011).

Some studies are interested in examining and adapting the teachings of Taoism to the world of the modern manager from the perspective of personal development, human resource management, team-building, workplace management, partnership, competitiveness advantage, and business strategy, etc. For example, (Messing 1989) argued that the Tao enables the manager to tap his inner resources on the way to real success, human accomplishment and satisfaction, and based on that, he developed a time-tested framework within which to improve manager's awareness, understanding and skills.

Chang (1988) regards Tao of management as a water-style management, which contains three features: the top principle is "Tao follows its course", in other word, no leadership is in charge; the best model is "I do nothing but people enrich themselves", in other word, interference should be avoided or reduced, and soft management is the strategy and approach. He claims that combining Tao's wisdom with modern knowledge and high output techniques can obtain position and promotion, win and win any negotiation, build up positive attitudes, creativity, achievement skills, and gain true power happiness, power, riches, status, and fame, promoting genuine success.

In Japan, top Japanese executives have studied and applied the principles of the Analects of Confucius to their effort to build a modern state since the Meiji Restoration just after the opening of Japan and in the early post-World War II era. But more recently, Japan's industrial revitalization has been realized as the result of the strenuous restructuring efforts by Japan's top executives inspired by Western-style management approaches. However, many Japanese business leaders believe that they have benefited from the principles of Tao Te Ching, Laozi's powerful philosophy (Taguchi 2006).

How to build a team by coaching? Some authors have applying the wisdom of Tao to unlock the potential of people by applying the techniques of coaching. Coaching is used by manger to realise the potential of his employees, his organisation and himself, but to become a great coach requires nurturing a few simple skills and habits. Landsberg's study on the Tao of Coaching can help manager to boost his effectiveness at work by inspiring and developing those around him. He takes us through the stages needed to implement coaching to maximum effect, and provides the techniques and tools of coaching that are vital for anyone who wants to develop a team of people who will perform effectively and who will relish working with us (Landsberg 2009).

As I mentioned, many practitioners now have been inspired by Chinese classical wisdoms and apply in their business strategy and management. James Autry is one of them. He has applied Laozi's Tao in a meaningful way to the world of business. He is an award-winning author and his new book *Real Power: Business Lessons from the Tao Te Ching* offers a stimulating interpretation of this ancient classic that provide the guidance and inspiration missing from most modern management texts, and addresses contemporary business situations with the wise paradoxes that are the hallmark of Laozi's work. He proposes an ageless approach to the workplace that deals uniquely with various issues of our time like compensation, competition, training, and downsizing (Autry and Mitchell 1999).

References

Autry, J., & Mitchell, S. (1999). *Real power: Business lessons from the Tao Te Ching*. Nicholas Brealey Publishing; New e. edition.

Bandura, A. (1977). *Social learning theory*. Englewood Cliffs.

Chang, S. T. (1988). *Integral management of Tao: Complete achievement*. Atlantic Books.

Cooper, J. C. (2010). *An illustrated introduction to Taoism: The wisdom of the sages*. World Wisdom.

Dreher, D. E. (2002). Leading with the Tao: the energizing power of respect. *The Learning Organization, 9*(5), 206–213. https://doi.org/10.1108/09696470210442150

Gerstner, A. (2011). Leadership and organizational patterns in the Daodejing. *Journal of Management Development, 30*(7/8), 675–684. https://doi.org/10.1108/02621711111150191

Heider, J. (1997). *The Tao of leadership: Lao Tzu's Tao Te Ching adapted for a new age*. Humanics New Age.

Lai, K. (2007). Ziran and Wuwei in the Daodejing: An Ethical Assessment. *Dao, 6*(4), 325–337. https://doi.org/10.1007/s11712-007-9019-8

Landsberg, M. (2009). *The Tao of coaching: Boost your effectiveness at work by inspiring and developing those around you*. Profile Books.

Messing, B. (1989). *The Tao of management: An age old study for new age managers* (1st ed.). Gower Publishing.

Needham, J. (1995). *Science and civilization in China* (Vol. 2). Cambridge University Press.

Pheng, L. S. (1994). Lessons from Lao Tzu's Tao Te Ching for the Facilities Manager. *Facilities, 12*(12), 6–14. https://doi.org/10.1108/02632779410071704

Taguchi, Y. (2006). *Tao management: Japanese management philosophy based on the Tao Te Ching*. .

Zhangzi. (1989). *Chuang Tzu: Mystic, moralist and social reformer* (H. A. Giles, Trans.). Bernard Quaritch.

Part III
3C Model of Taoism and Sustainability: An Integrated Framework

Heaven is eternal and Earth everlasting
Why Heaven and Earth exist forever is
Because they do not live for themselves,
They are sustainable.
—Laozi, Tao Te Ching, Ch. 7

The Chinese have discovered, and have practised for many centuries, a way of life which, if it could be adopted by all the world, would make all the world happy.
—Bertrand Russell, British philosopher

When we look at human civilization in the future from the perspective of modern scientific development, we are greatly worried by the crisis of civilization that lies in the near future. The crisis in modern civilization has long been recognized by Russell, Toynbee, Beucha, Daisaku Ikeda and other wise scholars in the East and West. As Daisaku Ikeda said, this crisis is a cultural crisis, created by the cultural activities of people. The crisis is mainly manifested in two aspects: first, the serious destruction of the harmonious relationship between man and nature and the danger of retaliation by nature; second, the desolation of man's own spiritual realm, psychological disorders, moral degradation, etc. Both of these crises are caused by Western civilization's unilateral development of material things and conquest of nature to satisfy human desires.

The development of modern Western civilization has destroyed the harmonious relationship between man and nature and caused mankind to suffer the unintended consequences of nature's merciless retaliation. Today, this situation has deteriorated. The desperate economic exploitation and fierce competition have driven people to ignore all consequences, and the interests of future generations, and also exert much more pressure on nature. The conflict between economic development and nature threatened the sustainable development of society.

In times of uncertainty and crisis, some Westerners have placed their hope in the ancient Eastern civilization and classical wisdom. As early as the 1920s, Bertrand Russell, British philosopher, said that *East and West are likely to be fruitful to both parties. They may learn from us the indispensable minimum of practical efficiency, and we may learn from them something of that contemplative wisdom which has enabled them to persist while all the other nations of antiquity have perished* (Russell 1966). He also warned Westerners that if they did not learn from Eastern civilization, the West would surely be headed for the destruction of civilization. *"The Chinese have discovered, and have practised for many centuries, a way of life which, if it could be adopted by all the world, would make all the world happy."* In the introduction to his book "Jesus Lived in India", the contemporary German scholar Holger Kersten expressed the West's longing for Eastern wisdom: "*The most forceful impetus for promoting such an internationalization of religion has always come, and continues to come, from the East. Western Man must now reorient himself in the most literal sense of the word-turn towards the eastern dawn. The Orient is the origin and source of our experience of the inner realm*" (Kersten 2011).

The traditional cultures of the East, such as Taoism and Confucianism all hold a holistic view of the unity of nature and man, focusing on the perfection of spiritual life, the harmony of nature and human relationships, and on intuition. They are very different from the Western traditions of subject-object dichotomy and focus on material life and rationality. As early as 2500 years ago, Laozi was already aware of the negative impact of indulgence in material life. The profound wisdom of Taoism is more like the efficacy medicine and the light in the crossroad for promoting civilizational self-awareness and saving civilizational crisis.

In Part II, I will start with some of the scandal cases which can illustrate the crisis of our modern civilization. I will also discuss the integrated framework built on Taoism's wisdom and modern sustainability science. The framework serves as the principles of sustainable business development.

References

Kersten, H. (2011). *Jesus lived in India*. Penguin.

Russell, B. (1966). *The problem of China*. George Allen & Unwin Ltd.

Chapter 7
The Crisis of Leadership: Failure of Business Ethics

Success in almost any field depends more on
Energy and drive than it does on intelligence.
This explains why we have so many stupid leaders.
—Sloan Wilson

There is no calamity greater than greed,
No trouble greater than avarice.
—Laozi, Tao Te Ching, Ch. 46

Those who lead a nation with Tao in ancient times,
Did not motivate people to be intelligent,
But inspire them to be genuine and honest.
Those who lead with intelligence bring nation to calamity.
Those who lead with noble character bring nation to prosperity.
—Laozi, Tao Te Ching, Ch. 65

To have a better understanding of this verse, I'd like to illustrate wisdom of Laozi with the metaphor of lamplight. When lamplight shines inside a room, then the room is light while outside is dark. When the lamp is moved outside, then outside is light while inside the room is dark. This is the Tao of proper use of illumination (Liu 2013). People's intellect and knowledge are like the light of a lamp. If that light is mistakenly used outside, in a contentious and aggressive manner, aiming for fame and gain, scheming and conniving day and night, thinking a thousand thoughts, imagining ten thousand imaginings, chasing artificial objects and losing the original source, light on the outside but dark inside, this will go on until the body is injured and life is lost. If people give up artificiality and return to the real, dismiss intellectuality and cleverness, consider essential life the one matter of importance, practice inner awareness, refine the self and master the mind, observe all things with detachment so all that exists is empty of absoluteness, are not moved by external things and are not influenced by sensory experiences, being light inside and dark outside, they can thereby aspire to wisdom and become enlightened. Light that does

L. Zu, *Responsible and Sustainable Business*,
https://doi.org/10.1007/978-3-030-91117-1_7

not dazzle progresses to lofty illumination. Therefore, a classic says, "the great sage appears ignorant, the great adept seems inept."

Now let's discuss some business scandals which run counter to Laozi's wisdom.

We have been shocked by the increasing numbers of scandals in the business world in recent years. Let me just take the three business scandals which were mired within one month in September 2015. The three world-wide and well-known companies were typically representatives of irresponsible businesses in terms of environmental pollution, human rights violation (particularly workers' rights and interests), and social exclusion. The leaders of the three companies have been a massive public and media outcry about their reprehensive and irresponsible behaviours. These companies are the cheating scandal of German car manufacturer Volkswagen; sweatshop scandal of 7-Eleven in Australia, and social exclusion scandal of Turing Pharmaceuticals in America.

Volkswagen were investigated and found that Volkswagen engineers intentionally manipulated internal software to rig emissions-test for their diesel vehicles. It was reported that 11 million diesel-powered cars owned by consumers around the world were rigged with the software to cheat emission testing. Aside from openly flouting environmental law, reports revealed that the issue have attributed the rigged software to hundreds of thousands of tons of previously unknown air pollution. The pollution involved, smog-including Nitrogen Oxides (NOx), can contribute to respiratory ailments and premature deaths that have been linked to breathing contaminated air. The emission cheating scandal of Volkswagen reveals fundamental flaws in environmental standards for large companies.

American corporation Turing Pharmaceuticals was publicly vilified for its predatory pricing when it raised the price of the drug Daraprim by over 5000%. This is a drug used to treat infections associated with HIV and AIDS. The drastic price increase has had a direct impact on patients' ability to purchase their needed medications. Therefore, Martin Shkreli, CEO of Turing helped turn himself into a true lightning rod for criticism with his brand of brash, pugnacious, insulting behaviour. He was described by the Washington Post as "the most hated man in America". When he joined Turing, Shkreli set a business strategy for Turing: to obtain licenses on out-of-patent medicines and re-evaluate the pricing of each in pursuit of windfall profits for the new company, without the need to develop and bring its own drugs to market (James Surowiecki 2015). Maximization of profitability for the company, particularly for himself is his ultimate goal, without taking the social responsibility into the business strategies. Consequently, it led him to be arrested in December 2015 by the FBI after being indicted on federal charges of securities fraud. Shkreli's behaviour may seem egregious, he is far from alone: using F.D.A. restrictions meant to protect consumers in order to hike prices of drugs has become a well-known and highly profitable business strategy.

The scandal of convenience store chain 7-Eleven in Australia was revealed by ABC as its use of exploitative and illegal work practices to reduce its labour costs. Employees were being paid less than half the legal minimum wage. Young and foreign workers were especially targeted. Institutionalized wage fraud and labour exploitation at 7-Eleven kept store costs down, increased profits both for franchisees and especially for the parent company. That's highly illegal and goes against the Australian tenet of giving people living in this country a "fair go". The South Morning Herald reports that 7-Eleven head office deliberately ignoring systemic wage fraud throughout the franchise system. Wage fraud is systemic across almost all franchises in Australia. Because the US Head office of 7-Eleven is not just turning a blind eye, it's a fundamental part of their business. The US head office has a well-documented history of fostering similar problems. The US authorities have taken a much harder line on franchisees caught exploiting migrant workers with several prosecuted and sent to jail. The scandal saw the resignations of 7-Eleven's chairman Russ Withers, and its CEO Warren Wilmot (Ferguson and Danckert 2015).

What do the three companies have in common? First one is that they are all big companies. We might wonder whether big companies are bad and villains. It is obvious that big business has resources and power to abuse the planet and people. The perceived value of big business to society in the public consciousness has been low for some time. The perception can be consolidated by the evidences from the scandals of Enron and Worldcom in the last decade. Big business has consistently come near the bottom in the 'most trusted institution' rankings of various global surveys, in sharp contrast with non-governmental organizations (NGOs), who usually come top. The second is that each company suggests there was an ethos in place in these corporations that held that "bad ethics is good business". For example, seven years of highly orchestrated cheating at VW meant increased sales. In 2009 VW became the world's biggest car manufacturer. Institutionalised wage fraud and labour exploitation at 7-Eleven kept store costs down, increasing profits both for franchisees and (especially) for the parent company. 7-Eleven has twice been names Australia's "franchisor of the year". Price gouging at Turing meant a drug listed on The World Health Organization's essential medicines list could bolster the company's profits by exploiting the sick and vulnerable. The third one would be the ethical failure of leadership. All of them did not authentically embrace environmental sustainability and social responsibility in their personal beliefs and behaviours even though sustainability and responsibility were shown in their office or websites or in their business strategies. They behaved like mercenaries—by mortgaging the future to inflate short-term earnings, by putting career ahead of company, by exploiting vulnerable employees, by preying on customer ignorance, or by manipulating the political system in ways that reduce competition (Hamel 2012). Specifically, they were lack of credibility. A leader's credibility depends upon two qualities: what he or she does (competency) and who he or she is (character). Because of their deficiencies in either created an integrity problem. The highest principle of leadership is integrity. Martin Winterkorn, former Volkswagen CEO says "I personally am deeply sorry that we have broken the trust of our customer and the public.", However, he also said that "I am doing this in the interests of the company even though I am not aware of any wrongdoing on my part"; "I have always been driven by my desire to serve this company". The Executive Committee of Volkswagen is aware that coming to terms with the crisis of trust will be a long-term task that requires a high degree of consistency and thoroughness.

Martin Shkreli, the 32-year-old hedge-fund manager turned pharmaceutical-company CEO, who achieved instantaneous notoriety last fall when he acquired the U.S. rights to a lifesaving drug and promptly boosted its price over 5000 percent, from $13.50 a tablet to $750. He likens himself to the robber barons, and was seen as a perfect villain. He is an avid user of social media, where he relishes portraying himself as a wealthy young hedge-fund guy. He tweets obnoxious snapshots of labels of $1000-plus bottles of wine like 1982 Lafite-Rothschild, along with selfies inside a helicopter buzzing over Manhattan or posed next to a life-size chess set by a pool in the Hamptons. He's such a perfect villain when viewed from afar that it's almost impossible not to like him more up close. He swerves seamlessly among obnoxious bravado, old-world politeness, purposeful displays of powerful intelligence, and even flashes of sweetness. He defends his actions as both irrelevant in the larger scheme of things and in keeping with the American tradition. But it's hard to know which manifestation of Martin is authentic. What muddles the picture even more is the arena in which he operates: small biotech companies, some of which thrive thanks to loopholes, legal frauds, pipe dreams, and stock promoters—and a smattering of real science, just enough to ignite fantasies of fame and fortune. Shkreli was driven to attain these roles because of his thirst for power or lust for riches. His successes were inevitably short-lived, because his actions continually sowed the seeds of the next upheaval, the next rebellion, the emergence of the next ruthless leader.

The scandals and crises in these companies highlighted the paradox: more ethics management does not imply a consistent and integral commitment to ethics. Ethics may be reduced to being applied in a selective and market-driven way. The scandals also revealed that limits of business ethics as the practice of moral self-regulation. Although they were also committed to corporate social responsibility (CSR) programs and had integrated CSR and sustainability in their business strategies, this did not help them to anticipate and avoid the crisis.

The three cases also show that they are all greedy and self-interested. It is greedy, ill-intentioned individuals who contribute to the crisis. As President Obama notes, self-interested actors engaged in clearly illegal behaviour that helped bring about the crisis, and these criminals should be sent to jail.

We also observed from the cases and other pervasive phenomena over the past years that the corporations and business leaders have consistently favoured the material over the spiritual, competition over cooperation, exploitation of natural resources over conservation, science and technology over religion, rational knowledge over intuitive wisdom and so on. This has led to a profound cultural imbalance which lies at the very root of our current economic and financial crisis—an imbalance in our thoughts and feelings, our values and attitudes, and our social and political structures. The health of the planet, and the social systems that guide and maintain our relationships to each other and to the earth have been degraded by our imbalance towards self-interest and individual success.

The Chinese former Prime Minister Jiabao Wen claims that the loss of morality is an underlying cause for the current crisis. Some people have sacrificed principle and sought profits at the expense of public interests. They have crossed the moral baseline. We should call on all enterprises to take up their social responsibilities. Within the body of every businessman should flow the blood of morality.

Jeffrey Sachs (2011) claims in his book of The Price of Civilization, "*A society of markets, laws, and elections is not enough if the rich and powerful fail to behave with respect, honesty, and compassion toward the rest of society and toward the world.... Without restoring an ethos of social responsibility, there can be no meaningful and sustained economic recovery*". And Hamel (2012) calls for values which matter now more than ever. Because he found that in recent years, rapacious bankers and unprincipled CEOs have seemed hell-bent on setting new records for egocentric irresponsibility. In a just world, they would be sued for slandering capitalism. Large corporations are now among society's least trusted institutions. As trust has waned, the regulatory burden on business has grown. Reversing these trends will require nothing less than a moral renaissance in business. The interests of stakeholders are not always aligned, but on one point they seem unanimous: the challenges of today's global era require a new, more responsible and sustainable approach than conventional concepts suggest. We need the leaders like Dale Partridge, the Sevenly founder. In his book "People over Profit", he uncovers the seven core beliefs shared by consumers, starters, and leaders behind this transformation. These beliefs have enabled Dale to build a multimillion-dollar company that is revolutionizing the marketplace. He believes the core beliefs are the secret to creating a sustainable world that values honesty over deception, transparency over secrecy, authenticity over hype, and ultimately, people over profit (Partridge 2015).

If the business ethics paradigm of moral self-regulation through stakeholder management and CSR programs is not sufficient to overcome the contradictions in our economic system, what can business ethics offer in this context of uncertainty and distrust? Instead of founding business ethics in the grand rational theories of modernity, such as utilitarianism, Kantianism and social constructivism, László Zsolnai (2015) claims that we could find inspiration in the older spirit-driven philosophies of life and community, because they can be very helpful with rediscovering the difference between the ratio and the spirit as faculties of the human mind. He believes that it is time to restore the balance between rationality and spirituality and to re-vitalize our faculty of 'spiritual intelligence' as a source of wisdom in management and leadership (Zsolnai 2015).

We need such an ideal leader who possesses the perfect marriage of a philosophic mind and an ability to lead. The leaders need an infusion of wisdom to help guide them to a more balanced and effective approach to living and leading that goes beyond their previous professional knowledge and skills in leadership management. The rising concern with ecological ethical and social issues call for the wisdom of Taoism, which counteracts the overemphasis of rational, masculine attitudes and values, and regains a balance between the masculine and feminine sides of human nature. The awareness of the profound harmony between the world view of modern science and the views of Taoism appears as an integral part of a much larger cultural transformation, leading to the emergence of a new vision of reality that will require a fundamental change in our thoughts, perceptions and values.

Taoism advocates a balance and harmony to develop and sustain social solidarity that represents a dynamic, harmonious and integral balance between "individual" values and "collective" values; the human integrity - that represents a dynamic, harmonious and integral balance between "material" values and "spiritual" values; the societal continuity that represents a dynamic, harmonious and integral balance between "progressive" values and "traditional" values; and the relational mutuality that represents a dynamic, harmonious and integral balance between the "own personal and societal" values and the "other's personal and societal" values.

Sustainable business performance was only possible when leaders and their organizations acted in concert with certain core universal principles, including integrity, responsibility, compassion, and forgiveness (Lennick and Kiel 2011) . The principles of Tao is the core universal principles that can empower business leaders to achieve sustainable business development.

References

Ferguson, A., & Danckert, S. (2015). Revealed: How 7 eleven is ripping off its workers. *Sydney Morning Herald*. Retrieved November 12, 2015, from http://www.smh.com.au/interactive/2015/7-eleven-revealed/

Hamel, G. (2012). *What matters now: How to win in a world of relentless change, ferocious competition, and unstoppable innovation* (1st ed.). Jossey-Bass.

Lennick, D., & Kiel, F. (2011). *Moral intelligence 2.0*. Prentice Hall.

Liu, I.-m. (2013). *Awakening to the Tao* (T. Cleary, Trans.). Shambhala Publications.

Partridge, D. (2015). *People over profit: Break the system, live with purpose, be more successful)*. Nelson Books.

Sachs, J. (2011). *The price of civilization: Reawakening American virtue and prosperity*. Random House.

James Surowiecki. (2015, 12 October 2015). The Financial Page: Taking on the Drug Profiteers. *The New Yorker*. https://www.newyorker.com/magazine/2015/10/12/taking-on-the-drug-profiteersv.

Zsolnai, L. (2015). *The spiritual dimension of business ethics and sustainability management*. Springer.

Chapter 8
Changing Thinking for Sustainable Business: 3C Model Thinking

To become wise, you've got to have models in your head.
And you've got to array your experience –
Both vicarious and direct—on this latticework of models.
– Charlie Munger

Model Thinking: Unpacking the Wise Decisions for High Performance

We live in a complex world with diverse people, firms, and governments whose behaviours aggregate to produce novel, unexpected phenomena. We see political uprisings, market crashes, and a never ending array of social trends. How do we make sense of it? Models. Evidence shows that people who think with models consistently outperform those who don't. And, moreover people who think with lots of models outperform people who use only one. Why do models make us better thinkers? Models help us to better organize information—to make sense of that fire hose or hairball of data (choose your metaphor) available on the internet. Models improve our abilities to make accurate forecasts. They help us make better decisions and adopt more effective strategies. They even can improve our ability to design institutions and procedures.

Models can embed multiple disciplines and leverage more knowledge. Models can be tested, calibrated, and compared. And models do not commit logical errors. Models do not suffer from cognitive biases. Models can help us to understand better the world. Mastery of models improves our ability to reason, explain, design, communicate, act, predict, and explore.

We need to learn different thinking models from great and successful people. One of them is Charlie Munger. Charlie Munger is the business partner of Warren Buffett, but he is not as well-known as Buffett, however, he is famous for his wisdom, business philosophy, particularly his mental models. We can learn his wisdom from his multiple speeches, and his books. For example, in the book "Poor Charlie's Almanack: The Wit and Wisdom of Charles Munger", we learn "worldly wisdom" which consists of a set of mental models framed as a latticework to help solve critical business problems. He explains, "*What is elementary, worldly*

L. Zu, *Responsible and Sustainable Business*,
https://doi.org/10.1007/978-3-030-91117-1_8

wisdom? The first rule is that you can't really know anything if you just remember isolated facts and try and bang'em back. If the facts don't hang together on a latticework of theory, you don't have them in a usable form. You've got to have models in your head. And you've got to array your experience—both vicarious and direct—on this latticework of models." (Munger, 2007)

Charles Munger's wisdom and experiences teach us the lesson that many-model thinkers can make better decision. Scott E. Page's research also supports the wisdom. Many-model thinking has tremendous practical value. Practice it, and you will better understand complex phenomena. You will reason better. Thinking with models will do more than improve your performance at work. It will make you a better citizen and a more thoughtful contributor to civic life. It will make you more adept at evaluating economic and political events. You will be able to identify flaws in your logic and in that of others. You will learn to identify when you are allowing ideology to supplant reason and have richer, more layered insights into the implications of policy initiatives, whether they be proposed greenbelts or mandatory drug tests (Page, 2018).

Page (2018) claims that with many models, we avoid the narrowness inherent in each individual model. A many-models approach illuminates each component model's blind spots. Policy choices made based on single models may ignore important features of the world such as income disparity, identity diversity, and interdependencies with other systems. With many models, we build logical understandings of multiple processes. We see how causal processes overlap and interact. We create the possibility of making sense of the complexity that characterizes our economic, political, and social worlds. And, we do so without abandoning rigor - model thinking ensures logical coherence. That logic can be then be grounded in evidence by taking models to data to test, refine, and improve them. In sum, when our thinking is informed by diverse logically consistent, empirically validated frames, we are more likely to make wise choices. I think this reflects Albert Einstein's wisdom, "*We cannot solve our problems with the same thinking we used when we created them. The more things change, the less we can rely on our habitual ways of doing things. The more things change, the more we need to be able to think 'outside of our boxes'*."

Therefore, in an era of VUCA world, we need many models to make sense of complex systems. Complex systems like politics, the economy, international relations, or the brain exhibit ever-changing emergent structures and patterns that lie between ordered and random. If we hope to understand the spread of diseases, variation in educational performance, the variety of flora and fauna, the effect of artificial intelligence on job markets, the impact of humans on the earth's climate, or the likelihood of social uprisings, we must come at them with different mental models such as machine learning models, systems dynamics models, game theory models, and agent-based models.

Laozi's "Three Treasures" for 3C Model Thinking

> I have three treasures to hold and cherish,
> The first one is compassion,
> The second is conservation,
> The third is compliance.
> – Laozi, Tao Te Ching, Ch.67

The "three treasures" as Laozi describes in the verse 67 is the essence of Tao Te Ching, and core virtues and principles of the Tao. Figure 8.1 illustrates the "three treasures": *compassion, conservation and compliance*. Laozi says that compassion (empathy, courage, charity, etc.) leads to courage, conservation (moderation, prudence and effectiveness, etc.) to generosity, and compliance (humility, integrity, accountability, etc.) to leadership. They contain the seeds to what are practically their opposites, therefore, Laozi warns human beings the unintended consequences that is resulted from the opposites in dire need of the three treasures, for example, those who are courageous without compassion, generous without conservation, and leading without humility shall suffer calamity. Courage without compassion is what can be seen in soldiers with no care for the lives they take, or self-appointed heroes who bully people around them for no other reason than that they can. Inconsiderate courage is indeed disastrous, sooner or later also to the ones expressing it. Generosity without moderation and prudence leads to meaningless waste. It's gluttony, and no fortune is so great that it will not be spent, eventually. It's also provocative. Even those who benefit from such generosity are offended by it. Whatever they get from it, they are at the same time reminded of their own lack of resources. Generosity without moderation and prudence is flaunting one's fortune. It's perceived as vulgar, almost obscene. Such gifts are bitterly received, not only

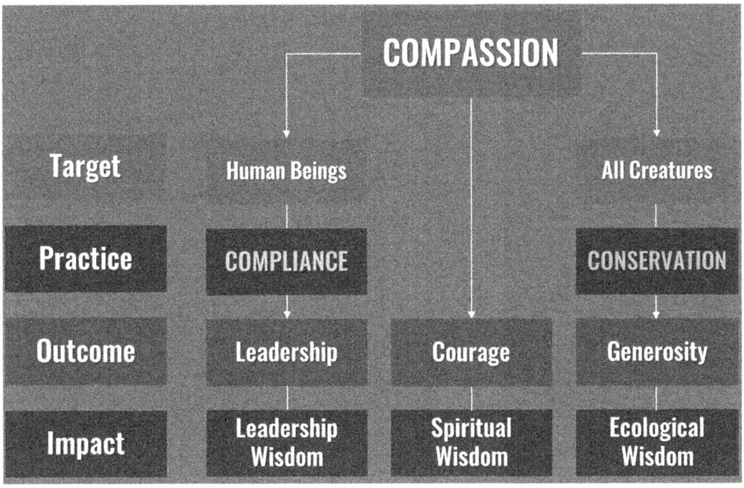

Fig. 8.1 Laozi's three treasure

because they seem to mean nothing to the donor. They are insults to the receiver. Worst by far is to lead without humility. The leader who wants to be superhero in the world might cause widespread destruction. Through history, we have had the misfortune of experiencing plenty of them. There are some such leaders and rulers today, as well.

We need to beware, because those who have the desire to lead without humility in the world will spare no efforts to get there. Once they do, it's extremely difficult and costly to get rid of them. So, we have to consider very carefully what persons we allow to be our leaders. A golden rule is to avoid giving power to people who want it, or loudly claim to be best fit for it. The best leaders we can find are usually those who are reluctant to shoulder the responsibility. They take it seriously. Those we need to convince to take the job are the ones we should get for it. But those who jump at the opportunity should be stopped at the entrance. Responsible leaders must learn Laozi's wisdom. The survival of the world depends on it, now that we have such enormous resources and so terrible weapons at the disposal of our leaders.

Laozi emphasizes that compassion is the most important quality of the three treasures. Those who remain compassionate will be successful and avoid blame. Even when they must go to war, if they still remain compassionate, they will be victorious and the enemy will not grieve it. That's a mighty power, surpassing most weaponry. When they defend themselves, remaining compassionate, they will not be conquered, because they have something so fine to protect. The enemy will congratulate them, out of respect for their nobility. In a sharp conflict, it's necessary to see the adversary as evil and oneself as good. Otherwise, it's very difficult to muster up the necessary resolve to fight until winning. The one who remains compassionate is certainly good, and therefore has the most splendid advantage. The enemy will find it hard to hate him. Even Heaven agrees on this. So, fate seems to work in favour of those who remain compassionate. That is because compassion is a trait of the Tao. The compassionate is treated the same by the Tao. Compassion breeds compassion. So, there's no reason to deviate from it.

Tao of Model Thinking: From Knowledge to Wisdom

> Keeping learning increases knowledge day by day
> Keeping practicing the Tao decreases (knowledge) day by day
> Keeping decreasing (knowledge) leads to non-action (wisdom).
> – Laozi, Tao Te Ching, Ch.48

> Where is the wisdom we have lost in knowledge?
> Where is the knowledge we have lost in information?
> – Opening Stanza of T. S. Eliot's Choruses from the Rock, 1936

Laozi's and Eliot's wisdom reveals the relationship between knowledge and wisdom. If we add another message of "*where is the formation we have lost in data?*", then we are able to develop DIKW Model or pyramid (data, information,

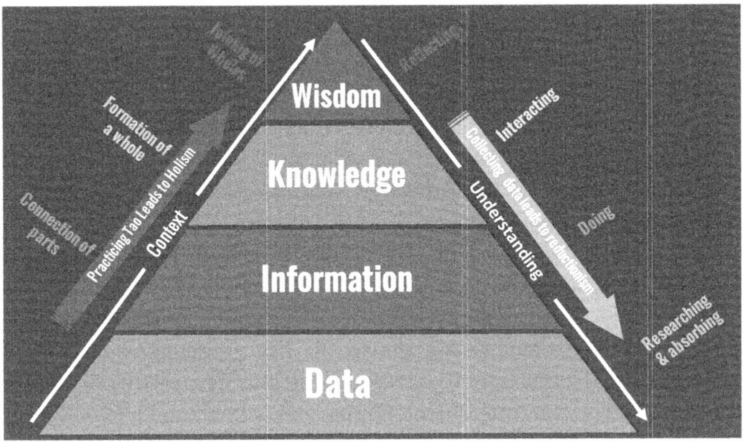

Fig. 8.2 Tao of mental models: transforming from knowledge to wisdom

knowledge and wisdom). Figure 8.2 shows the Tao of mental models which transform data to wisdom.

DIKW model describes a hierarchical relationship between data, information, knowledge and wisdom. In DIKW pyramid, wisdom is on the top of the pyramid, and data and information on the bottom. Going up the hierarchy means increasing abstraction, context, human input, meaning, and value. From the perspectives of systems thinking and holism of Taoism, as we move up the levels we go through a synthetic reasoning, synthesizing process, where we are combining or putting together the building blocks or parts to create something new or generic patterns or the whole. As we put things together it requires choosing how things are put together and thus the increase in the importance of context, human agency, and meaning as we go up the hierarchy. This is the systems thinking or holism approach, and also the mental model of Taoist. Going down means breaking things down into constituent parts (whole to parts)—what is called analysis, analytical reasoning—and a reduction in meaning, context and an increase in automation—reductionism approach.

From perspective of model thinking, pursuit of wisdom which is on the top of DIKW pyramid requires many-model thinking. Sometimes, wisdom consists of selecting the best model, as if drawing from a quiver of arrows. In Taoism's wisdom, "*wu wei (non-action)*" is the best model of living and working. Other times, wisdom can be achieved by averaging models; this is common when making predictions. When taking actions, wise people apply multiple models like a doctor's set of diagnostic tests. They use models to rule out some actions and privilege others. Wise people and teams construct a dialogue across models, exploring their overlaps and differences.

3C Model Thinking of Taoism

Building on Laozi's "three treasures", I developed 3C Model approach. 3C model thinking is a systems thinking and also sustainability thinking. We know that the universe is a big system, an intricate web of interdependent relationships spanning past, present and future. In the universe, society, planet, and economy are also subsystem. Sustainable development is also a system. All the parts of system are interdependent and interconnected. Key environmental issues demonstrate their relationship to socioeconomic aspects of development, in the light of increased climate threats and environmental disasters. Systems thinking is a process for understanding the interrelationships among the key components of a system. For example, in planet, systems thinking examples include ecosystems in which various elements such as air, water, movement, plants, and animals work together to survive or else they perish. In society, systems consist of people, structures, and processes that work together to make an organization "healthy" or "unhealthy". In economy, sustainability concepts should be incorporated into strategy, planning, policy, and implementation. We can take advantage of "systems thinking approach" to have a better understanding of the qualitative and quantitative aspects of development trends for sustainability.

As we discussed that the Tao is oneness, wholeness, and a system. In Taoism, the seeker aims to become one with the Tao which flows through all parts and dimensions of life, preceding and encompassing the entire universe. Systems thinking is defined as a discipline for seeing wholes, as a framework for seeing interrelationship rather things, for seeing patterns of change rather than static snapshots. 3C Model thinking is seen as a systems thinking and synthesis approach to understand interconnections, interactions, and interdependencies among social, environmental and economic issues. 3C Model thinking is a way of seeing the connections, links, or relationships among different disciplines or sectors. Instead of seeing parts and pieces of how things happen, it allows the interdependent whole to be appreciated. 3C Model thinking requires business leaders to focus on how the thing interacts with the other constituents of the system instead of isolating smaller parts. It is about interdependence and interrelationships with connections. In systems of greater complexity, the system as a whole may have properties and organization that cannot be understood by studying its parts in isolation.

In the 3C Model, compassion is more concerned with our interconnection with people and planet. The whole idea of compassion is based on a keen awareness of the interdependence of all these living beings, which are all part of one another and all involved in one another. Being compassionate is to be conscious that all creatures in the universe are interconnected and interdependent, our smallest, least significant thought, word, and action have real consequences throughout the universe.

Compassion is feeling with intelligence, it is about the feeling that arises when you are confronted with another's suffering and feel motivated to relieve that suffering. Much of the wisdom we need in order to live more in tune with life around us presents itself through our feeling intelligence. For example, people feel good when they recycle, feel empowered through volunteering in their community, feel they are part of a community when purchasing local goods. And many are saddened by the meaninglessness of their lives, enraged over the injustices of the world, and shocked by the destruction of the environment.

When we feel compassion or deep connection with another person, and it's behind much of our efforts to protect the environment, upon which we are dependent. By recycling, for example, we recognize that we are connected to the earth and have responsibilities to reduce waste and be good stewards. Our freedom makes us fearless in thoughts and actions; our compassion for others compels us to search for more powerful inner resources in order to serve others.

Conservation is the principle of valuing and using efficiently the outer resources like human and natural resources, as well as the inner resources like the time, energy, mind and spirit. Those who are compassionate can hold on to the principle of conservation by being moderate and saving their own energy and resources to help others. When human beings hold to the principle of compassion, we become less focused on boundaries and hierarchies, we open ourselves to the direct experience of beauty, timeless, and sacredness with life itself. A lack of awareness of life's sacredness keeps us from distant, and allows us to use the earth's resources for our own ends. But the more we see and know through the principle of compassion, the less likely we are to shield ourselves from the natural and powerful reverence for the earth and the morality likely we'll recognize the sanctity of life.

Gratitude and reverence are integrated into the principle of conservation. Such attitudes can help us enter into a direct relationship with life—a relationship of respect in which we are not higher or lower, but equal. And they help us relate to life with conscious recognition of how we are provided for by this planet and by the many people who have worked to feed us. Such attitudes keep us from felling distant from the many ways that life sustains us and bring closer to the real nourishment of life.

Conservation is more concerned with planet and profit, because conservation have much to do with resources or capital. When people discuss sustainability and act in sustainable ways, it's usually in the context of environmental conservation and care for our planet. Conservation is at the heart of the planet portion of any sustainability framework, or diagram. Sustainability origins are within environmental science and environmental conservation. The concerns about the planet came first, then as sustainability was refined, the definition incorporated people, and profit in later iterations of the concept of sustainability. The planet part of the sustainability in diagram reminds us that the essential part of the balance is to care for the earth. Sustainability guidelines help lead decisions towards choices that lessen the detrimental impact of economic activity across the planet. To help shape decision-making processes, businesses often rely on subject matter experts to help inform them of the impact that their economic activities impose on the earth.

Conservation requires business leaders to care and protect the natural resources and environment, to enhance human well-being in economically efficient way, and to make the planet a better place for all creatures to live sustainably.

Compliance is about humility, integrity, self-control and accountability—not daring to take the lead in the world, keeping oneself within one's own bounds, not reaching out to things above one, but submitting to one's superior. Compliance is about the awareness that seeing oneself as being above or ahead of other people can only lead to failure. In terms of social and economic responsibility, compliance means adherence to, or conformance with, rules, laws, standards, and policies. It also implies a sense of accountability and an obligation to uphold pertinent codes of conduct. From a more legalistic perspective, business compliance entails devising a formal internal system of policies, procedures, controls, and actions to detect and prevent violations of laws, regulations, rules, standards, and policies. Ethics forms the foundation for a company's Program and the code of ethics/conduct. While the code of conduct helps set the overall corporate tone toward compliance expectations, a company's program should be a series of integrated mechanisms designed to address all aspects of compliance breaches. A company's program can only emerge when basic operational components of a program are in place. These key components of a program include: top management commitment; compliance organization (structure, function, and assigned responsibilities); standards and procedures to detect and prevent fraud; and effective mechanisms for communication, training, auditing, control, evaluation, reporting, and corrective action (Nitish Singh & Busse, 2015).

Compliance requires business leaders to comply with rules, standards, ethics and code of conduct so that people can live in harmony with each other, and to avoid the crisis, conflicts and disasters in the process of social and economic development. Managing compliance is not just a functional necessity—it's a critical component needed to successfully navigate the turbulent global environment and deliver against the business strategy—especially in the wake of high-profile cases and recent events around the world.

The 3C Model thinking shall be employed to develop collaborative consciousness and systems thinking for generating a cooperative spirit and an amicable dialogue of civilization in the universe. The collaborative consciousness is characterized by a propensity of an individual to relate to other humans and cooperate with them in order to survive, to meet his needs and to build a better future for himself, for his family, for his business and for society at large.

The 3C Model are the building blocks for sustainable business and responsible leadership, because the principles of 3C are more in tune with who we are and what we need, and they are creative forces that bind us to life and to each other in a deeply sustainable way. The 3C Model is able to be applied in organizations for guiding leaders to achieve sustainable goal by making the most of their resources, transcend conflict, transform problems, adapt to change, and enrich their business, environment, community and society.

3C Model of Taoism vs. 3P Model of Sustainability

3P Model: People, Planet and Profit

Sustainability has many definitions, but one of the most common definitions used today is from the 1987 Brundtland Commission: "*Sustainable development is development that meets the needs of the present without compromising the ability of future generations to meet their own needs.*" Sustainability is also described by the triple bottom line (3BL)—People, Planet, and Profit (3P). This approach requires businesses and institutions to give a full accounting of all their practices—financial, environmental, and social—in an effort to measure total cost, not just financial profit or loss. These three words of "People, Planet and Profit" that all start with a P, describe how the goal of sustainability is within the sweet spot of all of these different values. "3P" succinctly describes the triple bottom lines and the goal of sustainability.

"People" (social capital) pertains to fair and beneficial business practices toward labour and the community and region in which a corporation conducts its business. A 3BL company conceives a reciprocal social structure in which the well-being of corporate, labour and other stakeholder interests is interdependent. An enterprise dedicated to 3BL seeks to provide benefit to many constituencies and not to exploit or endanger any group of them. The "upstreaming" of a portion of profit from the marketing of finished goods back to the original producer of raw materials, for example, a farmer in fair trade agricultural practice, is a common feature. In concrete terms, a 3BL business would not use child labour and monitor all contracted companies for child labour exploitation, would pay fair salaries to its workers, would maintain a safe work environment and tolerable working hours, and would not otherwise exploit a community or its labour force. A 3BL business also typically seeks to "give back" by contributing to the strength and growth of its community with such things as health care and education. Quantifying this bottom line is relatively new, problematic and often subjective. The Global Reporting Initiative (GRI) has developed guidelines to enable corporations and NGOs alike to comparably report on the social impact of a business.

"Planet" (natural capital) refers to sustainable environmental practices. A 3BL company endeavours to benefit the natural order as much as possible or at the least do no harm and minimise environmental impact. A 3BL endeavour reduces its ecological footprint by, among other things, carefully managing its consumption of energy and non-renewables and reducing manufacturing waste as well as rendering waste less toxic before disposing of it in a safe and legal manner. "Cradle to grave" is uppermost in the thoughts of 3BL manufacturing businesses, which typically conduct a life cycle assessment of products to determine what the true environmental cost is from the growth and harvesting of raw materials to manufacture to distribution to eventual disposal by the end user.

Currently, the cost of disposing of non-degradable or toxic products is borne financially by governments and environmentally by the residents near the disposal site and elsewhere. In 3BL thinking, an enterprise which produces and markets a product which will create a waste problem should not be given a free ride by society. It would be more equitable for the business which manufactures and sells a problematic product to bear part of the cost of its ultimate disposal. Ecologically destructive practices, such as overfishing or other endangering depletions of resources are avoided by 3BL companies. Often environmental sustainability is the more profitable course for a business in the long run. Arguments that it costs more to be environmentally sound are often specious when the course of the business is analysed over a period of time.

Sustainability Redefined: From the Parts to the Whole

In recent years, an increasing number of researches have tried to interpret sustainability from the lens of systems thinking in the complex environment. We understand that sustainability is not a property of a thing, things in isolation cannot be sustainable. Sustainability is more what we call an emergent feature of whole systems, it is not so much about the parts as how the parts work together to enable effective overall outcomes. For example, an electric car is not sustainable if the power system it is running on imports coal from the other side of the planet to provide it with electricity. Or likewise, if we build an eco-home in the middle of suburbia where the inhabitants have to drive a long distance to do shopping or take their kids to the park, this again will not achieve sustainable outcomes. It is precisely because sustainability is about a relationship between a whole system and its environment that it cannot be achieved through changing the properties of parts but instead requires us to look at how whole systems work; how all the parts are interrelated to enable the emergence of an efficient whole system and thus sustainable results. This is to a large extent why sustainability presents such an intractable challenge to our existing institutional framework. Traditionally we take a very analytical approach to management, we break systems down into their parts, analyze the parts and try to optimize them assuming that if all the parts are working then the whole will be working.

From the perspective of systems thinking, sustainability in practice can be seen as the art of doing business in an interdependent world. Sustainability respects the interdependence of living beings on one another and on their natural environment. Sustainability means operating a business in a way that causes minimal harm to living creatures and that does not deplete but rather restores and enriches the environment. Although most people think first of the environment when they hear the term of sustainability, sustainability also respects the interdependence of various elements in society on one another and on the social fabric. Sustainability means operating a business in a way that acknowledges the needs and interests of other parties (community groups, educational and religious institutions, the workforce, the public) and that does not fray but rather reinforces the network of relationships that ties them all together.

Sustainability also respects the interdependence of differing aspects of human existence. Economic growth and financial success are important and provide significant benefits to individuals and society as a whole. But other human values are also important, including family life, intellectual growth, artistic expression, and moral and spiritual development. Sustainability means operating a business so as to grow and earn profit while recognizing and supporting the economic and noneconomic aspirations of people both inside and outside the organization on whom the corporation depends. The only way to succeed in today's interdependent world is to embrace sustainability. Doing so requires companies to identify a wide range of stakeholders to whom they may be accountable, develop open relationships with them, and find ways to work with them for mutual benefit. In the long run, this will create more profit for the company and more social, economic, and environmental prosperity for society.

3C Model of Taoism for Sustainability

As I described in the preceding section, the 3C Model fits well in the arena of sustainable development, and even much broader and profound than the concept of sustainability in terms of connotation and significance. The 3C Model is more comprehensive and inclusive and covers social, environmental, economic and spiritual realms.

In the 3C Model, these three fundamental pillars (compassion, conservation and compliance) are interconnected that the actions in one area can reinforce the goals of another. Thus, this indicates the importance and overall goal of achieving integration and a balance between the three pillars of sustainable development. Accordingly, in striving for a balance between the pillars, we are in essence trying to achieve sustainability, endeavouring to be embrace the principles of 3C model.

Figure 8.3 shows that compassion lies in the intersection between people (society) and planet (environment): *bearable*, whereby society works towards life style adjustments. In that, we are cognisant of our impact and thereafter contribute towards a healthier environment and well-being. Compliance is in the intersection between planet (environment) and profit (economic): *equitable*, which fully attains an equal and fair share of resources to people. Thus, by having equitable distribution, we help to eradicate poverty, social inequality and raise the standard of living of the society. Conservation lies in the intersection between profit (economic) and planet (environment), *viable,* where we strive to meet economic growth and development, while operations are pursued with environmental protection in mind. Therefore, investments must be feasible to sustain itself, create jobs, contribute to the GDP, and protect the environment from harm. Thus, to achieve sustainability, we must find a balance between the three pillars in relation to being viable, equitable, and bearable. Thereby fostering through sustainable development, poverty alleviation, gender equality, capacity building, clean technology, clear institutional framework, economic growth and development, sustained biodiversity (protection &

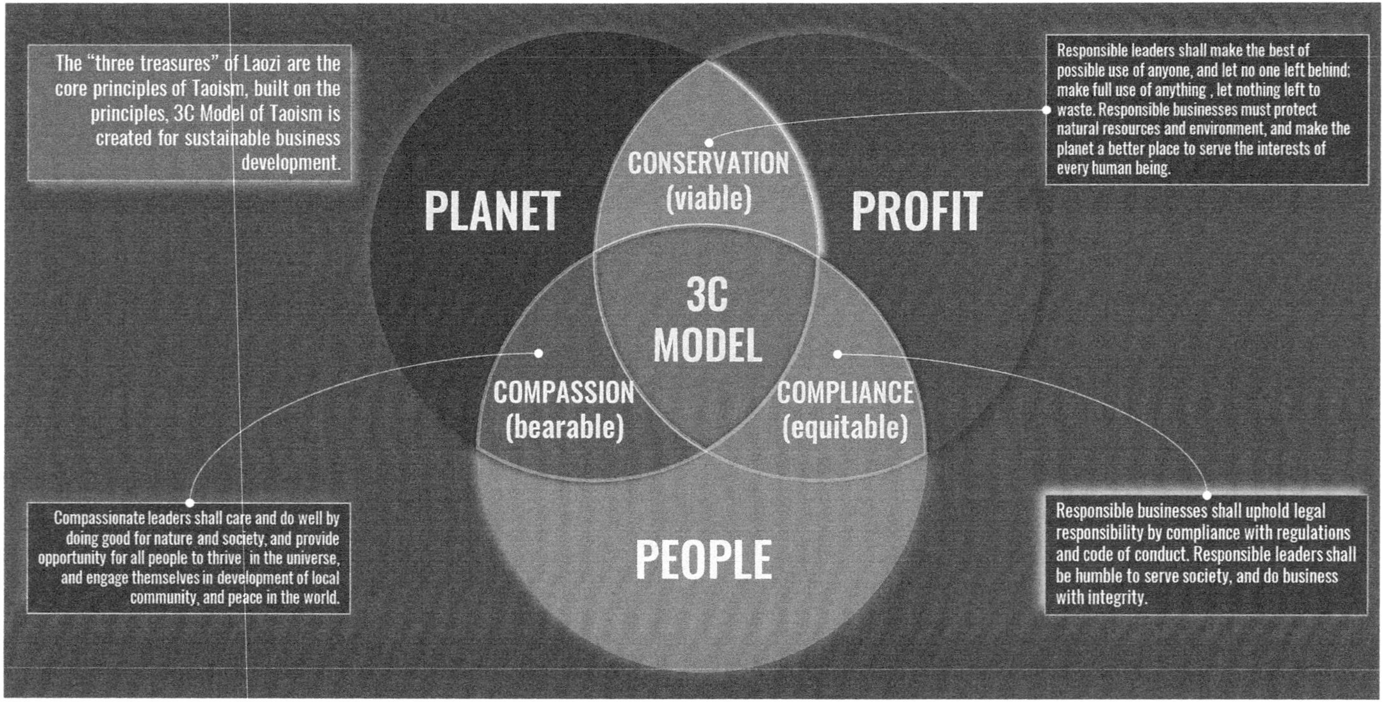

Fig. 8.3 3C Model of Taoism vs. 3P Model of sustainability

conservation of ecological services). This in turn helps to develop and meet short-term horizons, with long-term vision.

References

Munger, C. T. (2007). *Poor Charlie's Almanack: The wit and wisdom of Charles T. Munger* (3rd, expanded ed.). Walsworth Publishing.

Page, S. E. (2018). *The model thinker: What you need to know to make data work for you*. Basic Books.

Nitish Singh, & Busse, T. J. (2015). *Compliance management: A how-to guide for executives*. Praeger.

Chapter 9
3C Model for Sustainable Business Development

Integrated Framework: Taoism's Wisdom, Responsible Leadership and Sustainable Development

This Chapter will examine the impact of Taoism's wisdom on corporate social responsibility, sustainability and propose an integrated framework for sustainable business development based on the principles of 3C (compassion, conservation and compliance).

In this chapter, I propose a comprehensive and integrated framework of the three constructs in the context of sustainable business development (SBD), contending that Taoism's wisdom and responsible leadership are the two principal antecedents of SBD. The integrated framework includes the four dimensions of the Tao of sustainable business and its relationship (see Fig. 9.1):

- *Wisdom of Taoism: the foundation of SBD*
- *3C Model of Taoism-compassion, conservation and compliance: the principles of responsible leadership*
- *Responsible leadership: the driving force for SBD*
- *SBD: the goal of an organization*

Taoism's Wisdom

Wisdom is a defining attribute of the responsible leadership. Wisdom involves the righteousness of a leader who organizes his life properly and who takes his place in a helpful way within the community, who does justice to the claims of others. This is an implication of "practical wisdom". Business leaders need an infusion of wisdom to help guide them to a more balanced and effective approach to living and leading that goes beyond your previous professional training and education.

L. Zu, *Responsible and Sustainable Business*,
https://doi.org/10.1007/978-3-030-91117-1_9

Fig. 9.1 3C Model of Taoism for SBD: an integrated framework. Source: Author developed based on Laozi Tao Te Ching

As I discussed in Chap. 6, in Taoism, "*wu wei*" is one of the core notions or principles, it refers to non-action or non-doing. *Wu wei* has been variously translated as 'effortlessness,' 'spontaneous action,' 'non-aggression' and 'non-meddlesome action'. The principle can be understood as behaviour that arises from a sense of one's connections to others and the environment: we do the natural thing rather than what we think we should do. That is, we follow nature. Following nature refers to both the orientation of the relationships between human beings and between humans and the natural world.

Wu wei does not refer to passivity, or does nothing. The distinguished sinologist Joseph Needham defines *wu wei* as "refraining from action contrary to nature" and justifies his translation with a quotation from *Chuang Tzu: "Non-action does not mean doing nothing and keeping silent.* Let everything be allowed to do what it naturally does, so that its nature will be satisfied." If one refrains from acting contrary to nature or, as Needham says, from *"going against the grain of things,"* one is in harmony with the Tao and thus one's actions will be successful. "*wu wei*" is practical wisdom, which means "figuring out the right way to do the right thing in a particular circumstance, with a particular person, at a particular time" (Schwartz and Sharpe 2011).

Practical wisdom combines will with skill. Skill without will—without the desire to achieve the proper aims of an activity—can lead to ruthless manipulation of others, to serve one's own interests, not theirs. And will without skill can lead to ineffectual fumbling around—the sort of thing we see in people who "mean well" but leave situations in worse shape than they found them. Skills are learned through experience, and so is the commitment to the aims of a practice. That's why we associate wisdom with experience. But not just any experience will do. Some experiences nurture and teach practical wisdom; others corrode it. Aristotle emphasized two capacities that were particularly important for such practical moral skill—the ability to deliberate about such choices and the ability to perceive what was relevant in a particular circumstance. Good deliberation and discernment were at the heart of practical wisdom.

A leader with Taoism's wisdom has the moral will to do the right thing and the moral skill to figure out what the right thing is in any particular situation. Being a leader with Taoism's wisdom needs to figure out the right way to do the right thing in a particular circumstance with a particular person at a particular time. In doing this, you need to learn certain character traits like loyalty, self-control, courage, fairness, generosity, gentleness, friendliness, truthfulness, perseverance, integrity, open-mindedness, thoroughness and kindness. Aristotle called these traits "*excellences*" (arete)—often translated as "*virtues*". None of these other traits could be exercised well without it. All the traits and virtues are embodied in Laozi's "three treasures": *compassion, conversation and compliance*, in the book, I call it 3C Model of Taoism. The 3C Model is very much concerned with the classical human virtues most essential to leadership and sustainability—empathy, courage, charity, moderation, prudence, effectiveness, humility, integrity, self-awareness and accountability, etc. The Taoism's wisdom is for those who want to become wise and highly effective leaders. It focuses on a uniquely constructive and compassionate approach to leadership based on positive spiritual principles contained in the teachings of Taoism. It addresses priceless wisdom for leading ourselves and others. The wisdom will appeal to those who are concerned with moral and humanitarian issues in work and human relationships. It draws on wisdom that blazes an effective leadership path consisting of such ingredients as compassion, conservation and compliance of three treasures of Tao. The Taoism's wisdom not only has a place in the complex dynamic, contemporary business world, but can be a key part of realizing more meaningful, fulfilling, and even more successful careers and organizations.

What relevance does wisdom—more specifically wisdom from Taoism—hold for responsible leaders? Human beings have pursued wisdom since time immemorial. Moberg (2007) has emphasized human being's natural curiosity in the search for wisdom. In Aristotelian fashion, Moberg argues that wisdom can be compared with a two-sided coin. One side holds the answers to the profound mysteries of life, while the other holds the answers to the everyday judgments and decisions we have to make. The latter is often described as practical wisdom (Schwartz 2011; Chandler 2013; Marker 2013). Human beings are also spiritual beings (Fry 2003), looking for 'wise' ideas on how to cope with daily problems. This emergent need for 'wise' ideas has been triggered by the tendency of management and behavioural scientists to focus on the development of instruments and to search for causality in human behaviour (Pyszczynski et al. 2004).

Wisdom and leadership and management practices are not topics that are frequently discussed together. When they are, the perspective is usually philosophical or psychological. Theories on how notions and ideas from wisdom traditions can contribute to leadership and management practice are thin on the ground and most of the scholarly and management publications address wisdom in relation to the concept of leadership (Kriger and Seng 2005; Yang 2011; Ben-Hur and Jonsen 2012; Gottlieb 2012; Kaipa and Radjou 2013; Hoof and Blomme 2013). One important reason for this omission is that wisdom traditions are often associated with dogmas and enduring convictions. However, the ideas and notions from wisdom traditions can themselves be a highly inspirational and powerful force when these dogmas and convictions are omitted. When we flesh out the texts of these wisdom traditions and transpose them to a modern setting, they can cause shifts in perspective and serve as input for further reflection. The human being who is grappling with life and work may find that these wisdom traditions can offer him insight into the subtle changes taking place in his outer and inner world, and help him to develop self-awareness so that he can help others to address their own grappling (Kriger and Seng 2005).

Now what most of us might be concerned about how we can make the concept of wisdom more accessible to leaders and managers, and what relevance the concept of wisdom holds for leaders and managers who are grappling with problems and ambiguities on a daily basis. Let me start with what the dimensions that wisdom actually entails and what the implications for leadership and management are.

I found that the academic scholars have identified four dimensions of wisdom which could be included in moral will and moral skills as I discussed. Moberg (2007) refers to the concept of wise responses to the surrounding environment, which is related to the psychological components of wisdom and includes knowledge, thinking, emotions and motivation. Other authors also refer to the psychological condition of a wise attitude and the corresponding behaviour (Kriger and Seng 2005; Izak 2013). These psychological conditions point to a certain state of mind that makes people act wisely.

Blomme et al. (2013) argue that, as a first dimension, wisdom is a competence. One important aspect of a competence is whether it can translate ideas or notions into practice and into action. In the psychology of learning this process is commonly known as ‘transfer’ (Blomme 2012). An important condition for transfer is an ability and willingness to put knowledge and wisdom into practice.

The second dimension is leadership—not only leadership of others but also leadership from within. Kriger and Seng (2005) note that a ‘wise’ leader notices subtle changes in his outer and his inner world. By reflecting upon these and by being morally disposed to prevent harm to the social environment, a leader can arrive at ‘wise’ leadership. Acting in an unpredictable and chaotic world awash with ambiguities and inadequate and distorted information, Moberg (2007) calls for skilful manoeuvring and cautious behaviour. When they discharge their responsibilities for the well-being of the people they lead, leaders must act cautiously in trying to understand the changes in the environment and in themselves (Kriger and Seng 2005). Wise leadership is often reflected in its relational accomplishments.

McNamee (1998) stresses the importance of the role of the leader in dialogues which generate wisdom through a process of interaction. This also holds for the leader's role in the establishment and maintenance of communities aimed at sharing and collective activities (Blomme 2012). Hence, putting wisdom into practice calls for 'wise' leadership.

The third dimension concerns the question of how we can support engagement and innovation in others and ourselves, and how we stay engaged and innovative as leaders and managers. Engagement does much more than influence the corporate performance; it is a much broader concept that also addresses the possibilities for individuals to decide when and where to translate their cognitive, affective and physical energy into activities (Kahn 1990; Rich et al. 2010). Although, on the one hand, work engagement may seem specific to the individual (one either does or does not have a positive attitude to life), various studies have shown that it is positively influenced by personal and external resources (Schaufeli and Salanova 2006; Rich et al. 2010). When it comes to state of mind, one may suggest that the individual state of mind is an important precondition for engagement. Having already defined state of mind as the first dimension, what I want to emphasize here is that we can learn lessons from wisdom traditions that will enable us to use external resources to enhance engagement and thus increase creativity and innovation.

Wisdom traditions have demonstrated beyond doubt that their value patterns have retained their influence over time; but this could be attributable, to some extent, to an inbuilt flexibility and an ability to adapt to the spirit of the time. Hence, wisdom traditions may be sources of creativity and inspire people to make optimal use of external conditions to become engaged and innovative. Consequently, putting wisdom into practice calls for the right state of mind, and an effective use of external resources, to become engaged, creative and innovative.

For the fourth dimension, we want to stress the importance of communities. Every wisdom tradition has a strong moral dimension, which includes the prevention and alleviation of human suffering and a debt to the community to which one belongs. The insights of wisdom traditions give directions on how to work and live together in a setting where people can develop and flourish. Hence, in business also, this idea, in which communal sharing and significance are prevalent, can enhance mutual trust and collaboration (Sims and Sauser 2013). This seems to be in line with the seminal work of Fiske, and Blomme, Van der Veen and Venugopal, who argue that community building and sharing increase trust and reduce bureaucracy. The preconception that you must take care of the members of your community so that they can take care of you has a moral dimension. The maintenance of communities is therefore an important condition for trust, learning, creation and innovation. Also, although leaders have a moral responsibility toward the community members, they should be aware that it is the community who brings about the conditions for 'wise leadership,' including legitimacy and obedience. Hence, putting wisdom into practice calls for the building and maintenance of communities.

As the last dimension, I want to address the subject of empathy and sensitivity to different cultures. Whether you realize it or not, we are consciously or subconsciously influenced by wisdom traditions that uphold similar values and perspectives to our own. Having been raised with certain preconceptions, we might find people from another wisdom tradition strange and incomprehensible. In that sense, we might refer to a right state of mind in which we are open to cultures with which we are not familiar. Often the differences between the wisdom traditions of the West and the East are exaggerated. This attitude fails to do justice to the rich kaleidoscope of the different wisdom traditions which emerged in different places and in different periods with specific economic, social and societal questions that were in need of answers. There are big differences between wisdom traditions, especially between those founded in Western Europe, the Middle East, Africa, Asia-Pacific and India, which invite misinterpretations and complicate collaboration and business. Spanning bridges between the various regions call for 'wise' behaviour with strong elements of cautiousness and sensitivity. In sum, putting wisdom into practice calls for a willingness to associate with people raised in another wisdom tradition and insight into other cultures (Blomme and Hoof 2014).

In recent years, I found that the rise of a global wisdom society has embraced Taoism's wisdom, for example, global wisdom embodies a system perspective and has a deep respect for natural systems, human needs, and future generations. It requires that people trust the dynamics of self-organization, learn from the new sciences, and serve society ethically. A global wisdom society with global wisdom organizations values all cultures and traditions and skilfully utilizes multiple ways of knowing for the greater benefit of all life. Institute of Noetic Sciences research suggests that a global wisdom society will be marked by the following (Davis et al. 1997):

- *A profound recognition of universal interconnectedness among all peoples and all life*
- *A commitment to right action for the benefit of all, guided by the mysterious intelligence of the whole*
- *Valuing learning and openness above certainty and closure, and embracing multiple ways of knowing*
- *Living in ecological balance*
- *Acknowledging that humans exist in a universe alive with consciousness and spirit.*

A global wisdom organization embraces the following:

- *Holding a systemic perspective and always looking at the wholeness, interrelatedness, and harmony and balance of living systems and the universe.*
- *Operating from a deep understanding of and respect for natural systems and cycles, human needs, and future generations.*
- *Trusting the dynamics of self-organizing and collective consciousness as well as co-intelligence; that is, having the capacity to evoke creative responses and initiatives that integrate each person's diverse gifts for the benefit of all.*
- *Learning from the new sciences.*

- *Ethically serving society and Earth in life-affirming, sustainable ways, including those that are in harmony with natural ecological and global environmental systems; being in stewardship of the whole.*

In a global wisdom culture, everyone is both leader and follower. The essence of leadership is co-creating and holding the space for people to talk and act with each other about what is important to them, their organization, their community, and the world. Rather than physical space, this is energy space for reflection and deep inquiry whereby a deeper source of meaning can arise. One function of a leader is to help people discover the expertise and wisdom in them and in others (Wheatley et al. 2003).

As we become more conscious of our interdependence and more valuing of the experiences and responsibilities that arise in relationships to others, we empower Taoism's wisdom in our own lives and in the world.

Responsible Leadership

Leadership is the action of leading people in an organization towards achieving goals. Leaders do this by influencing their people and follower behaviours in several ways. A leader sets a clear vision for the organization, motivates people, guides them through the work process and builds morale. Leadership is the timeless practice of guiding others in pursuit of a goal, destination or desired outcome. At the most fundamental level, a leader is someone who motivates, inspires and guides others toward pre-established goals. Responsible leadership is a process of interaction with all stakeholders integrating around a common good and shared goal, taking place in organization and outside and based on values and principles of ethics.

From the perspective of Taoism's wisdom as illustrated in Fig. 9.2, fundamental to being a responsible leader in action is thinking holistically and systemically. Leaders are agents of change in a bigger system and that they have the power to impact that system—positively or negatively. Their organizations give them the tools to do this through the provision of their services and product offering. When leaders acknowledge that they are playing a part within a wider system and that their agency can—indeed will inevitably—impact this system, they become powerful. Such realization can lead to a negative or a positive engagement. Irresponsible leaders set out to manipulate the system for their own ends, their company's goals at the expense of the other members of the system. They tend to have a narrow view of their relationships, seeing them as predominantly transactional in nature. Typically, their belief in a wider system is short term and predicated on a utilization mindset. On the other hand, responsible leaders begin to realize that their agency can be intentional. They see that it is possible for the wider whole to benefit from the interactions and the interdependencies. They have a deep-seated belief in a generative mindset based on what is possible, while being acutely aware of the inherent

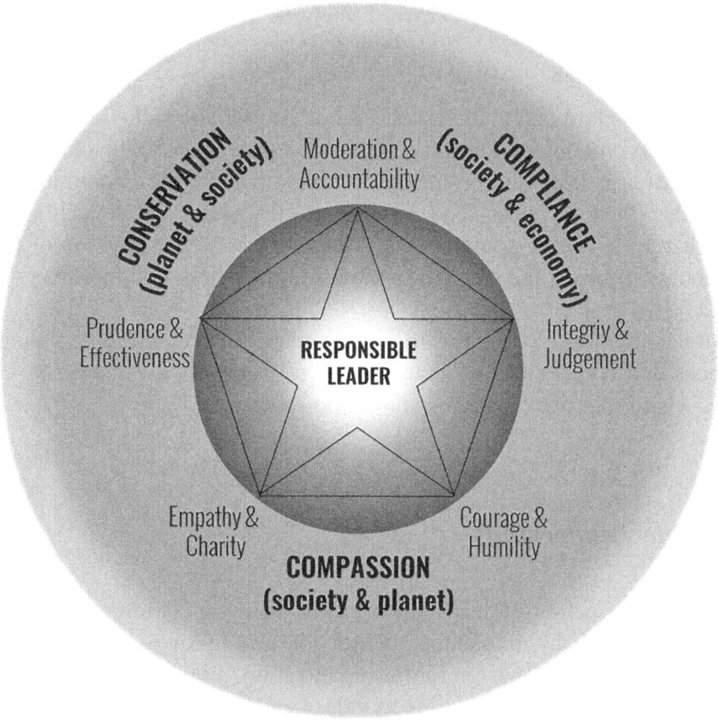

Fig. 9.2 Ten character strengths for responsible leadership. Source: the author developed based on 3C Model of Taoism

tensions within the system. Responsible leaders tend to focus on embracing the uncertainties and paradoxes rather than trying to fix them.

Responsible Leadership can be defined as having ability to practice moral will and skills to do right things right for the interests of multi-stakeholders like society, environment and economy, and future generations. More specifically, in Taoism's wisdom, I identified ten character strengths for developing responsible leadership from the 3C Model of Taoism. Each character strength falls under one of these three broad virtue categories (3C), which are universal across cultures and nations. See the full character strengths list in Fig. 9.2. The ten character strengths will be further elaborated in Chaps. 11, 12 and 13.

- *Empathy and charity:* know yourself and others: being able to be compassionate to care and serve others;
- *Prudence and effectiveness:* engaging in systems thinking and purpose-driven leadership for a sustainable future;
- *Judgement, integrity and moderation:* being able to make informed ethical judgments about existing norms and rules;

- *Courage, humility and accountability:* displaying moral courage and accountability to make a positive change in an uncertain world;

Adding a responsibility dimension to the concept of leadership that extends beyond mere liability means that leaders will be expected to assume a position on local societal or organizational conditions. They also have to be prepared to take a stand wherever ethics, laws and regulations are flawed or non-existent. This entails speaking up where unethical practices are concerned. Responsible leadership offers the possibility of uncovering mutually beneficial solutions for all stakeholders engaged in the problem-solving process.

What can we learn from Taoism's wisdom about responsible leadership? The Taoism's wisdom requires responsible leaders to anticipate the consequences of their decisions, orient their thinking to the long-term and consider the potentially negative impact that businesses have on people, society, and the planet. As Fig. 9.2 demonstrates that

- *The responsible leader sees things as interconnected and interdependent in the complex world.*
- *The responsible leader is both future focused and grounded firmly in the present, the here and now, and the practical on-the-ground impact of actions.*
- *Responsible leadership is about connecting at a deeper level with stakeholders—at the soul, story and heritage level that provides meaning for staff teams, communities and customers.*
- *The narrative is aligned with the vision across the wider organizational system through a culture that the leader role models wholeheartedly and authentically, often at considerable personal risk.*

Responsible leaders know who they are, what they stand for, and are not afraid to step forward, even at personal risk. They are passionate and can inspire others through their personal energy, commitment and sense of purpose.

Sustainable Business Development (SBD)

In this book, from the perspective of Taoism's wisdom, sustainable business is defined as a business that strives to meet the principles of 3P and 3C, specially, incorporates principles of sustainability and Tao into each of its business decisions and strategy; supplies environmentally friendly products or services that replaces demand for non-green products and services; is more social and greener than traditional competition, and has made an enduring commitment to environmental principles in its business operations.

Figure 9.1 shows that sustainable business development (SBD) requires responsible leaders to integrate sustainability in business strategy and operations. In other words, sustainable business development is about keeping the balance between social, economic, and environmental concerns in corporate decision-making; taking care of the natural resources the company uses, recompensing the communities in which companies work and promoting long-term value-creation for shareholders. But it is important to understand that, next to increasing environmental and social pressures, there are foremost solid economic reasons behind the sustainable business trend.

Sustainable business development can bring many benefits to the environment and society, such as less pollution, healthy ecosystems, advanced public health and happy consumers, however, the elemental driver is company profit. Without profit, companies cannot survive and thrive. As we discussed in preceding section, John Elkington, founder of Sustainability, a British consultancy, came up with the concept of the ‘triple bottom line’. Elkington stated that companies should adhere to three specific measures of performance: (1) profits and losses; (2) the organisation’s impact on people; and (3) pollution and resource depletion (Elkington 1994). The 3C model of Taoism forms the basis of sustainable business development.

On a company level, sustainability has become key to staying competitive through measures such as waste management, improved resources, operational efficiency and especially improved brand equity and reputational benefits. According to the Harvard Business Review (Nidumolu et al. 2013), sustainability is now the main driver of business innovation. Sanders and Wood (2015) have identified two types of companies who invest in sustainability: embracers who have adopted sustainability-driven strategies; and cautious adopters who have taken sustainability initiatives and are starting to make sustainability part of their business strategy. The difference between these two categories is their level of commitment to sustainability.

SBD requires a holistic and systems view of the business environment taking social, economic and environmental considerations as well as the more conventional concerns of customers, markets and competition. SBD involves defining, assessing, and improving the whole business enterprise to achieve superior and sustainable performance that exceeds the challenges of the present and the expectations for the future. It integrates business purpose, strategies, leadership and capabilities, and needs and expectations into an effective management system for creating innovative solutions for customers, stakeholders, and shareholders of global corporations. SBD is a way for corporations to improve the present and create a better future.

SBD depends on the leadership of executive management and its vision of harmony between the enterprise, human activities, and the natural world. SBD and the 3C Model thinking are naturally linked, since both focus on the whole system as their platform for making dramatic improvements to the quality of life, the business and natural environments, and social, economic, and environmental concerns. 3C Model thinking allows leaders to successfully integrate the corporate and strategic management systems of the corporation, including activities related to customers, stakeholders, supply networks, strategic partners, and related industries.

SBD involves the convergence of separate management systems that focus on specific opportunities and challenges into a management framework that can respond to the business environment and create sustainable success through effective strategies and exceptional leadership. Its centerpiece is the integration of all of the internal capabilities and resources of the corporation with all of the external contributors to exceed the needs, requirements, and mandates of the external business environment. Attaining this integration depends on a comprehensive understanding of all of the forces (internal and external) that drive change and responding to them in ways that enhance the positive attributes of the enterprise and mitigate the negative impacts and consequences. Responsible leadership, technological and innovation, and organizational capabilities are critical to this task.

CSR and Sustainability: Business View vs. The Taoism's View

I discussed the concepts of sustainable development, corporate social responsibility, triple bottom-line, etc. in the preceding chapters. This section will further elaborate the concepts and definitions from the perspectives of business and Taoism.

CSR and Sustainability: Business View

Corporate social responsibility (CSR) is about what and how companies do good to society and environment and respond to and meet the various needs of stakeholders while doing business and making profitability. Carroll (1991) demonstrates that corporate social responsibility is made up of four responsibilities (economic, legal, ethical and philanthropic) that are interrelated and argues that corporate social responsibility cannot be achieved without meeting the four responsibilities sequentially namely economic, legal, ethical and philanthropic responsibilities.

Why do companies have to do business in a socially responsible way? Because we are all interdependent in the universe, interconnected and interacted with each other. We live with and relate to each other and the earth. Our smallest, least significant thought, word, and action have real consequences throughout the universe. Thus, each of us has a role to play in sustaining the whole. We come to realize we are responsible for everything we do, say, or thing, responsible for ourselves, everyone and everything else, and the entire universe. In today's highly interdependent world, individuals, governments, and international communities can no longer resolve many of their problems by themselves. We need one another. We must therefore develop a sense of universal responsibility. It is our collective and individual responsibility to protect and nurture the global family, to support its weaker members, and to preserve and tend to the environment in which we all live. We need to create the new social-political, economic, and even cognitive structures with the enduring, universal, and unifying powers of peace, compassion, empathy, and reverence.

However, the principles and value of CSR haven't been recognised by most of business leaders although it is so obvious and important. The debate over whether a firm should exist solely for making profits or whether it should pay heed to the social and environmental concerns that accompany the practice of CSR has never been ended.

As Martha Nussbaum contends, "If our world is to be a decent world in the future, we must acknowledge right now that we are citizens of one interdependent world, held together by mutual fellowship as well as the pursuit of mutual advantage, by compassion as well as self-interest, by a love of human dignity in all people, even when there is nothing that we have to gain from cooperating with them". Thus, in this interconnected and flat world there is a need for concerted action by the businesses to take steps that would alleviate the pressing issues of the day (Nussbaum 2007). As we move through the twenty-first century coming to terms with the wide-scale loss of resources and the impending challenges of energy scarcity, it can help to ground ourselves in the often—untapped human capacity for generosity. This means fully acknowledging real-world limitations while at the same time strengthening our capacity to give.

As simple as it sounds, a great deal of change can take place with just a small shift awareness. But this shift requires not only that we give up some things, but we accept others—including a greater degree of responsibility. Responsibility is how we are moved and challenged. Without feelings of responsibility, we often stay concerned mostly with what we need and what we want. Accepting responsibility opens a door to life that is dynamic and changing, that draws us into deeper relationships and even reveals more of who we are by forcing us to discover qualities and resources we didn't know we had.

The concept of sustainable development or sustainability has been interpreted and defined in different time and circumstances since it emerged. As I explained it in Chap. 8 from the perspective of triple bottom line or 3P, sustainability is concerned with social responsibility, environmental and economic (or business) sustainability. This requires that a company's responsibility should lie with stakeholders rather than shareholders. Environmental sustainability describes the capacity of the environment to continue indefinitely to provide a healthy place for us to live and work and the resources necessary to sustain a healthy economy and businesses. Business sustainability can be defined as the capacity of a business enterprise to continue to operate successfully, i.e. to generate sufficient and appropriate economic activity to meet stakeholders' requirements on an ongoing basis. Of course, we believe that business sustainability is the most critical long-term objective of most business enterprises. While these two types of sustainability are different, they are also, in today's world, inextricably linked. If the environment ceases to be sustainable, enterprises that depend on it for resources and on healthy consumers for purchases of their products will cease to be economically sustainable. The gradual reduction in the sustainability of our global environment will result in the consequent reduction in the ability of business enterprises to sustain themselves economically and remain viable. At the same time, enterprises that are not economically sustainable—those that require more and more energy and non-renewable resources and that pollute the environment—will ultimately contribute to environmental unsustainability as well.

A sustainable business is any organization that participates in environmentally friendly or green activities to ensure that all processes, products, and manufacturing activities adequately address current environmental concerns while maintaining a profit. It is the process of assessing how to design products that will take advantage of the current environmental situation and how well a company's products perform with renewable resources (Rennie 2008).

Most people think of sustainability in the context of the rising environmental awareness and corporate social responsibility efforts, which focus on ways to make better use of limited, shrinking, and in some cases already scarce raw planetary resources. But this is simply one application of the sustainability principle. Sustainability can be defined broadly as the ability to maintain something at a certain level, indefinitely. While the definition is easy to grasp, more subtle are two important implications. The first is that to be sustainable, any given asset, no matter what it is, must be kept whole, without making significant trade-offs that undermine the capital used to generate and maintain it. The second follows from the first: sustainability hinges on the ability to see finite resources as the very source of innovation. This insight brings to the fore the creative tension at the center of elegance: achieving the maximum effect with the minimum effort (May 2010).

CSR and Sustainability: The Taoism's View

The values and ideas of corporate social responsibility (CSR) and sustainability are embedded in the principles of Taoism. Laozi says,

> *Heaven is eternal and earth everlasting*
> *Why heaven and earth can endure forever*
> *Is because they do not live for themselves*
> *Thus they are sustainable.*
> —Laozi, Tao Te Ching, Ch. 7

The passage defines the concept of CSR and its relationship with sustainability by using the metaphor of Heaven and Earth. What a socially responsible business does should like the Heaven and Earth does, are utterly free from self-interest. The selflessness and altruism allow them to carry on their mutual giving and taking without harming each. They do businesses in accordance with the principle of Tao and Te (Virtue):

> *Giving birth without possession.*
> *Serving without claiming any credits.*
> *Leading without domination.*
> *This is called the profound virtue.*
> —Laozi, Tao Te Ching, Ch. 51

The principle of the Tao in the passage illustrates the relationship between social responsibility and sustainability. It reflects the core elements of corporate social responsibility: voluntary contribution to community and society beyond the self-interest. By doing it in a socially responsible manner, business can be sustainable socially and economically:

The sage places his self-interest behind, but becomes a leader;
Puts himself away, but yet finds himself protected.
Is it not because he lives only for himself?
That's why his self-interests can be accomplished
—Laozi, Tao Te Ching, Ch. 7

The more they help others, the more they possess.
The more they give to others, the more they gain
—Laozi, Tao Te Ching, Ch. 81

In Laozi's Tao Te Ching, many passages touch on the concept of sustainable development. One of important definitions of sustainability is about concept of life cycle and its impact:

All creatures come into being,
I thereby observe their life cycle:
All things grow and flourish, but
Each ends up returning to its origin.
Everything rises and falls, but
Ends up returning to its root.
Returning to the root, one shall attain tranquillity;
Attaining tranquillity, one shall return to its nature;
Returning to one's nature, one shall understand the universal law.
Understanding the universal law leads to enlightenment,
Not understanding the universal law leads to calamity.
Understanding the universal law, one shall be inclusive,
Being inclusive, one shall be fair,
Being fair, one shall become the stewardship,
Being the stewardship, one shall act in accord with law of nature,
Acting in accord with law of nature is
In line with the principle of Tao.
Holding to the principle of Tao,
One shall be sustainable, and free from danger in life.
—Laozi, Tao Te Ching, Ch. 16

This passage demonstrates that Taoist sustainability is closely related to sustainability of natural processes or "cycles" of production and reproduction. This is most obvious in regard to four seasons, which are a basic pattern of regulation in an agrarian society. The sustainability course of the four season orders human activity and labour. The regular return of the seasons, the renewed growth of life in spring, is a cornerstone of human and cosmic survival—the sustainability of the productive course of time is fundamental for sustaining both nature and culture.

The "new birth" of life in the course of time is not entirely a new birth; it is rather the seamless continuation of a process of reproduction, and of life and death, which is never essentially interrupted. However, in order to sustain the life cycle, all creatures must act in accordance with the law of nature, which is unchanging and universal principle. All creatures in the universe can grow and develop sustainably only by complying with the law of nature. Otherwise, they end up disaster and calamity. In this view, sustainability is the endurance of systems and processes in the universe, and is about how biological and ecological systems remain diverse and productive.

If we take nature itself as our today's model, Laozi's wisdom implies that sustainability should become a cradle-to-cradle process and a powerful growth engine. In order to guarantee more sustainable business practices into the future, businesses must reduce their company's ecological footprint and increase their resource efficiency and productivity so that resources are not unnecessarily depleted or permanently damaged, and still ensure a sufficient profit and the creation of social value.

Laozi's life cycle thinking is related to product life cycle management and assessment in today's business world, which is a new approach to sustainability emerging as companies consider their total environmental impact—from growing raw materials to the consumer's disposal of their product. The United Nations Environment Programme (UNEP) and the Society for Environmental Toxicology and Chemistry (SETAC) launched in 2002 an International Life Cycle Partnership, known as the Life Cycle Initiative (LCI), to enable users around the world to put life cycle thinking into effective practice. Life Cycle Thinking (LCT) is about going beyond the traditional focus and production site and manufacturing processes to include environmental, social and economic impacts of a product over its entire life cycle. The main goals of LCT are to reduce a products resource use and emissions to the environment as well as improve its socio-economic performance through its life cycle. This may facilitate links between the economic, social and environmental dimensions within an organization and through its entire value chain.

Life cycle thinking is made operational through Life Cycle Management (LCM). LCM is a management approach that puts the tools and methodologies in the life cycle thinking basket into practice. It is a product management system that helps enterprises to minimize the environmental and social burdens associated with their product or product portfolio during its entire life cycle (UNEP 2007).

From the social and environmental perspective, this passage says "*Understanding the universal law, one shall be inclusive, being inclusive, one shall be fair.*" Inclusion and fairness entail not only the distribution of resources within nature and society at a point of time, but also the distribution of resources across generation. This concept of sustainability is exactly in line with the one defined in the Brundtland Commission Report: "*development that meets the needs of the present without compromising the ability of future generations to meet their own needs.*"

Laozi calls upon us to keep to fairness so that we can take on the stewardship which is the idea that the living generation must be stewards of the earth's resources for the generations that will come later. We must defend the interests of those whom we've never met and never will, those are our descendants and our fellow humanity. What qualities and responsibilities should a steward embrace? (Hamel 2012) elaborates well the concept of steward. Hamel claims that if you are a leader at any level in any organization, you are a steward—of careers, capabilities, resources, the environment, and organizational values. What matters now, more than ever, is that managers embrace the responsibilities of stewardship. He suggests that stewardship imply five things:

- *Fealty: A propensity to view the talents and treasure at one's command as a trust rather than as the means for personal gain.*
- *Charity: A willingness to put the interests of others ahead of one's own.*
- *Prudence: A commitment to safeguard the future even as one takes advantage of the present.*
- *Accountability: A sense of responsibility for the systemic consequences of one's actions.*
- *Equity: A desire to ensure that rewards are distributed in a way that corresponds to contribution rather than power.*

Hamel's five qualities of stewardship reflect in the 3C Model of Taoism as we discussed previously. When we apply the 3C model to business, it requires a business to care for the humanity and quality of life, and engage in actions that appear to further some social good beyond the interests of the firm. Conservation is about being frugal of and protecting the natural resources and environment. (Chen 1989) believes *jian* ("conservation") is "organically connected" with the Taoist metaphor *pu* ("uncarved wood; simplicity"), and "stands for the economy of nature that does not waste anything. When applied to the moral life, it stands for the simplicity of desire." When we apply to business, it requires that business should protect nature and environment by increasing resources efficiency and productivity. Compliance is about being prudent in acting consistently with principles, values and beliefs to avoid the crisis, conflicts and disasters in the process of survival and development of human societies. It implies that being a responsible and sustainable business should not be to reach the minimum requirements of stakeholders but to exceed them in complying with social and environmental rules and standards. It requires a business to monitor and ensure its active compliance with the spirit of the law, ethical standards and international norms. The 3C model of Taoism could be also called "farmer values", which are the virtues that Hamel described his parents-in-laws, Ferne and Eldon Findley who built Findley farm successfully and sustainably: *prudence, thrift, self-discipline, and sacrifice* (Hamel 2012).

As a working definition, sustainability can be defined as the practice of maintaining processes of productivity indefinitely—natural or human made—by replacing resources used with resources of equal or greater value without degrading or endangering natural biotic systems (Hendrix 2014). Broadly defined, sustainable development is a systems approach to growth and development and to manage natural, produced, and social capital for the welfare of their own and future generations.

From the perspective of Taoism's view, *sustainability can be defined broadly as the ability to maintain something at a certain level, indefinitely*. The definition is more subtle with two important implications.

- *The first is that to be sustainable, any given asset, no matter what it is, must be kept oneness or wholeness, without making significant trade-offs that undermine the capital used to generate and maintain it.*
- *The second follows from the first: sustainability hinges on the ability to see finite resources as the very source of innovation. If we hold on to the Tao, we will find our self in a world as whole as it is holy. This is not a world that sustains our models of economic growth and consumer desires. This is rather a world of wonder and magic and a world that needs our attention—that needs to be sustained as much as it sustains us.*

Therefore, Laozi encourages business leaders to make the shift in consciousness, to see the universe with new eyes. Just as the Canadian environmentalist David Suzuki says,

> *The way we see the world shapes the way we treat it.*
> *If a mountain is a deity, not a pile of ore;*
> *If a river is one of the veins of the land, not potential irrigation water;*
> *If a forest is a sacred grove, not timber;*
> *If other species are biological kin, not resources; or*
> *If the planet is our mother, not an opportunity—then,*
> *We will treat each other with greater respect.*
> *Thus is the challenge, to look at the world from a different perspective.*

The Tao is the central principle at the core of everything between Heaven and Earth. "Oneness or wholeness" is where the Tao resides. This oneness manifests itself in many different ways: clarity, tranquillity, divinity, life, and more. Oneness manifests clarity in Heaven, tranquillity on Earth, divinity in gods, and abundant life in all living things. In the same way, when we connect with the Tao described by Laozi, we gain clarity in the mind, tranquillity in the heart, divine power in spirituality, and abundant energy to live life to the fullest. Those who wish to lead must have this oneness in order to establish the standard of leadership. Conversely, when we lack that connection, our experience is quite the opposite. We struggle with confusion in the mind; we feel unsettled and ill at ease; the spiritual strength we enjoyed before has become an empty void; we are tired, listless, and unable to stir ourselves into action. Whatever leadership we may want to establish collapses with nothing to hold it up.

From the perspective of sustainability, "oneness" is the core value of the concept of sustainability which refers to the unity of universe, environment and society without being damaged and disturbed externally. Oneness implies that sustainability is seen as closed systems that maintain processes of productivity indefinitely by replacing resources used by actions of humans with resources of equal or greater value by those same humans without degrading or endangering natural biotic systems. To maintain "oneness", or sustainability, the responsible and proactive decision-making and innovation need to minimize negative impact and maintains balance between ecological resilience, economic prosperity, political justice and cultural vibrancy to ensure a desirable planet for all species now and in the future (Magee et al. 2013).

Taoism's Wisdom and Business Success

The book of Rpuzan and Pruzan-Mikkelsen (2006), "Leading with Wisdom" offers us full of real-life stories about the successful and responsible leaders who led with spiritual purpose and wisdom. I found that all of them have embraced the similar wisdom of 3C model of Taoism. For example, Janiece Webb, senior vice president of Motorola in USA was one of the responsible leaders who were interviewed. Janiece Webb was famous for being tough in her business decisions and heartful in her support for each employee. She has long held a spiritual view of life that starts with "getting in touch with the essence of God inside of me—finding God inside myself," and that she lovingly extends to seeing "God in everyone...we're all connected". This expression of her love as the interconnectedness of all human beings impacts on her view of her role and responsibility as a leader. She said, "I believe that you can create giants out of ordinary people when you act in balance and harmony with people. Sometimes this requires tough love and that can be done within proper bounds. And it can be hard to see God in everyone. I have worked with so many incredible teams of people, and I have seen parts of life that I never thought I would see. To me this is what success is all about.' "I believe that a corporation has a soul and what that means to me is that, yes, you do perform in a capitalistic mode, but you do it with integrity, with absolute deep respect for people - not hollow words, but really treating them with dignity. A company that has soul has compassion. It doesn't mean they can't be tough and it doesn't mean they can't strive for big goals. You can be competitive with compassion, but if you are competitive without compassion you will lose your soul."

Multiple studies have shown that shows of compassion, as well as acts of kindness and generosity, create a ripple effect that stems from those who do the act, to those who observe the act, and the ripple continues expanding, impacting numerous others who are all benefited as a result of just one single show of compassion. At the conclusion of one particular study performed by James Fowler of UC San Diego and Nicolas Christakis of Harvard they shared, "The results suggest that each additional contribution a subject makes to the public good in the first period is tripled over the course of the experiment by other subjects who are directly or indirectly influenced to contribute more as a consequence. These results show experimentally that cooperative behaviour cascades in human social networks." They go on to say that "as a result, each person in a network can influence dozens or even hundreds of people, some of whom he or she does not know and has not met" (Anderson 2015).

If one single show of compassion can have that far reaching of an impact, just imagine the enormous impact an entire company of people showing compassion can have. All it takes is one person to be willing to take the lead. When a leader creates a "ripple" it has the power to affect the greatest number of people in their organization. Research performed at Stanford University has revealed that our relationship with a direct manager is probably the primary influence on the quality of our workplace experience, yet many managers still overlook the centrality of compassion to their role. Emma Seppala, associate Director of the Center for Compassion and Altruism Research and Education explained why compassion in business makes sense, and how compassionate workplaces are good for employee health and the corporate bottom line. She further shared with us the new research findings with us, "when organizations promote an ethic of compassion rather than a culture of stress, they may not only see a happier workplace but also an improved bottom line. Happy employees also make for a more congenial workplace and improved customer service. Employees in positive moods are more willing to help peers and to provide customer service on their own accord. What's more, compassionate, friendly, and supportive co-workers tend to build higher-quality relationships with others at work. In doing so, they boost co-workers' productivity levels and increase co-workers' feeling of social connection, as well as their commitment to the workplace and their levels of engagement with their job. Given the costs of health care, employee turnover, and poor customer service, we can understand how compassion might very well have a positive impact not only on employee health and well-being but also on the overall financial success of a workplace" (Seppala 2013). Therefore, a leader who desires to succeed cannot afford to overlook the importance of showing compassion, nor can they discount the impact their example will be on the entire organization of people they lead.

Case in Point: Successful business in British Small Firm

I'd like to describe a successful small business in UK to illustrate how the efficacy of Tao can transform a company. I came across the news one day about the impact of Taoism's wisdom on the business culture in a small firm in Britain when I tried to collect some case studies for the Chinese classic philosophy of *Tao Te Ching* for this book (Gascoigne 2005). The firm is called Farrelly Facilities and Engineering, based in the UK's West Midlands, provides the services covering installation of ventilation systems, building refurbishment and mechanical and electrical maintenance. Back in the middle of 1990s, the company suffered from staff turnover running at about a third every year, despite a good package of pay and benefits, because the employees saw their jobs as a grim, dogged struggles. Gerry Farrelly, Director of Farrelly Facilities and Engineering scrutinized the workings of his firm as he prepared it for Investor in People accreditation and realised his employees were not a happy bunch. In pursuit of a new direction, Farrelly began to search for the one great book that can inspire him to chart a course to personal fulfilment and business success. He read many management books, and from the book called *The Servant Leader*, he found the Chinese classical wisdom, Tao Te Ching, which interprets the principles of the Tao to suit a business environment. He discovered that he needs management from the bottom if there is a problem with his business, it will be at the top with the people who run it. Having decided that the problem of the staff's negative approach to work was the result of his management style, which was to lead aggressively in order to survive in construction or else people would take advantage. Farrelly took a year out from running the company to consider his strategy.

One of the sources that inspired Gerry Farrelly to transform his management style and business culture is the ancient Chinese classical philosophy of *Tao Te Ching*. One of the principles of Tao they applied in his leadership is

> *Giving birth without possession.*
> *Serving without claiming any credits.*
> *Leading without domination.*
> *This is called the profound virtue.*
> —Laozi, Tao Te Ching, Ch. 51

Built on this principle, they made a conscious decision to steer away from macho management to water-like or compassionate management. For instance, since 1998, the managers introduced the new 'worker-friendly' policies and created a new culture of the fun, enjoyment, empowerment, leadership from the bottom, particularly, the Six Basic Rules of Heroes such as empathy, social skills, motivation, self-regulation, self-awareness and emotional skills were practiced throughout the company. As a result, the company turned into a so-called '*Happiness Centred Business*', the firm's turnover doubled in three years, profits tripled. Farrelly employees now describe themselves in the company literature, which they write themselves as 'among the happiest on this planet' (Dourado 2007). As a result of the firm's outstanding business performance, significant contribution or have achieved noteworthy success through investors in people, Farrelly was awarded "Achievers 2000" in 2000, and a prestigious National Award in 2001 by Investors in People UK (Evening Mail 2001).

I could call the style the servant leadership, the sea-like leadership. They lead and manage employees with respect, honesty, love, and spirituality. All employees enjoy full autonomy, no "telling off" as there must be a blame-free culture. The leaders help staff set up their own businesses and provide advice and support to those wanting to set up their own business. The leaders with this style lead their people should like the sea: to be humble, to be grateful, and to be reverent. Laozi says,

> *Why sea and river become leader of hundreds of valleys*
> *Is because they stay in low position.*
> *Thus, great leaders who*
> *Want to stand above people, must speak to them from below;*
> *Want to stand ahead of people, must place themselves behind.*
> *Therefore, when great leaders*
> *Lead from above, people do not feel burdened;*
> *Lead from behind, people do not feel obstructed.*
> —Laozi, Tao Te Ching, Ch. 66

The result is that the firm becomes a more productive, successful, and happier organization, and a more meaningful life for the leader and employees. The success of Farrelly Facilities and Engineering further validates that Taoism's wisdom can make great change in business leadership and management in the modern world.

References

Anderson, A. R. (2015). *Can compassion contribute to success?* Retrieved November 15, 2020, from https://www.forbes.com/sites/amyanderson/2015/12/06/can-compassion-contribute-to-success/#7a80aa854da8.

Ben-Hur, S., & Jonsen, K. (2012). Ethical leadership: Lessons from Moses. *The Journal of Management Development, 31*, 962–973. https://doi.org/10.1108/02621711211259901

Blomme, R. J. (2012). Leadership, Complex adaptive systems, and equivocality: The role of managers in emergent change. *Organization Management Journal, 9*(1), 4–19. https://doi.org/10.1080/15416518.2012.666946

Blomme, R. J., & Hoof, B. v. (2014). *Another state of mind perspectives from wisdom traditions on management and business*. Palgrave Macmillan.

Blomme, R. J., Veen, J. V. D., & Venugopal, V. (2013). *The silver lining of a dark cloud: Using social innovation to make the supply chain a crisis buster.*

Carroll, A. (1991). The pyramid of corporate social responsibility: Toward the moral management of organizational stakeholders. *Business Horizons, 34*, 39–48. https://doi.org/10.1016/0007-6813(91)90005-G

Chandler, J. (2013). Seven Pillars of Wisdom: The idea of qualitative market research. *International Journal of Market Research, 55*(5), 627–650. https://doi.org/10.2501/IJMR-2013-042

Chen, E. M. (1989). *Tao Te Ching: A new translation with commentary*. Paragon House.

Davis, J., Schoorman, F., & Donaldson, L. (1997). Toward a stewardship theory of management. *The Academy of Management Review, 22*, 20. https://doi.org/10.2307/259223

Dourado, P. (2007). *The 60 second leader: Everything you need to know about leadership, in 60 second bites*. Capstone Publishing

Elkington, J. (1994). Towards the sustainable corporation: Win-win-win business strategies for sustainable development. *California Management Review, 36*(2), 90–100. https://doi.org/10.2307/41165746

Evening Mail. (2001, 28 March 2001). *Farrelly facilities: Prestigious award.* https://search.proquest.com/docview/323417695?accountid=41835.

Fry, L. (2003). Toward a theory of spiritual leadership. *The Leadership Quarterly, 14*, 693–727. https://doi.org/10.1016/j.leaqua.2003.09.001

Gascoigne, C. (2005, 20 March 2005). Happy workers make profits. *Sunday Times*. http://search.proquest.com/docview/316718484?accountid=41835.

Gottlieb, E. (2012). Mosaic leadership: Charisma and bureaucracy in Exodus 18. *The Journal of Management Development, 31*. https://doi.org/10.1108/02621711211259910.

Hamel, G. (2012). *What matters now: How to win in a world of relentless change, ferocious competition, and unstoppable innovation* (1st ed.). Jossey-Bass.

Hendrix, M. K. (2014). *Sustainable backyard polyculture: Designing for ecological resiliency.* Library of Congress Cataloging-in-Publication Data.

Izak, M. (2013). The foolishness of wisdom: Towards an inclusive approach to wisdom in organization. *Scandinavian Journal of Management, 29*(1), 108–115. https://doi.org/10.1016/j.scaman.2012.07.002

Kahn, W. A. (1990). Psychological conditions of personal engagement and disengagement at work. *Academy of Management Journal, 33*(4), 692–724. https://doi.org/10.5465/256287

Kaipa, P., & Radjou, N. (2013). *From smart to wise: Acting and leading with wisdom*. Jossey-Bass.

Kriger, M., & Seng, Y. (2005). Leadership with inner meaning: A contingency theory of leadership based on the worldviews of five religions. *The Leadership Quarterly, 16*(5), 771–806. https://doi.org/10.1016/j.leaqua.2005.07.007

Magee, L., Scerri, A., James, P., Thom, J., Padgham, L., Hickmott, S., Deng, H., & Cahill, F. (2013). Reframing social sustainability reporting: Towards an engaged approach. *Environment, Development and Sustainability, 15*. https://doi.org/10.1007/s10668-012-9384-2

Marker, A. (2013). The development of practical wisdom: Its critical role in sustainable performance. *Performance Improvement, 52*, 11–21. https://doi.org/10.1002/pfi.21343

May, M. E. (2010). *In pursuit of elegance: Why the best ideas have something missing*. Broadway Books.

McNamee, S. (1998). Reinscribing organizational wisdom and courage: The relationally engaged organization. In S. Srivastva & D. L. Cooperrider (Eds.), *Organizational wisdom and executive courage*. New Lexington Press.

Moberg, D. J. (2007). Practical wisdom and business ethics. *Business Ethics Quarterly, 17*(03), 535–561. https://doi.org/10.5840/beq200717336

Nidumolu, R., Prahalad, C. K., & Rangaswami, M. R. (2013). Why sustainability is now the key driver of innovation. *Engineering Management Review, IEEE, 41*, 30–37. https://doi.org/10.1109/EMR.2013.6601104

Nussbaum, M. (2007). *Frontiers of justice: Disability, nationality, species membership*. Belknap Press of Harvard University Press.

Pyszczynski, T., Greenberg, J., & Koole, S. L. (2004). Experimental existential psychology: Exploring the human confrontation with reality. In: *Handbook of experimental existential psychology* (pp. 3–9). Guilford Press.

Rennie, E. (2008). Growing Green, Boosting the bottom line with sustainable business practices. *APICS Magazine, 18*(2).

Rich, B. L., Lepine, J. A., & Crawford, E. R. (2010). Job engagement: Antecedents and effects on job performance. *Academy of Management Journal, 53*(3), 617–635. https://doi.org/10.5465/amj.2010.51468988

Rpuzan, P., & Pruzan-Mikkelsen, K. (2006). *Leading with wisdom: Spiritual-based leadership in business*. Routledge Taylor & Francis Group.

Schaufeli, W., & Salanova, M. (2006). Work engagement. An emerging psychological concept and its implications for organizations. *Research in social issues in management (volume 5): Managing social and ethical issues in organizations*, 135–177.

Schwartz, B. (2011). Practical wisdom and organizations. *Research in Organizational Behavior, 31*. https://doi.org/10.1016/j.riob.2011.09.001.

Schwartz, B., & Sharpe, K. (2011). *Practical wisdom: The right way to do the right thing*. Riverhead Books.

Seppala, E. (2013, April 15, 2013). Why compassion in business makes sense. *Greater Good Magazine*. https://greatergood.berkeley.edu/article/item/why_compassion_in_business_makes_sense.

Sims, R. R., & Sauser, W. I. (2013). Toward a Better Understanding of the Relationships among ReceivedWisdom, Groupthink and Organizational Ethical Behavior. *Journal of Management Policy and Practice, 14*(4).

UNEP. (2007). *Life cycle management: A business guide to sustainability*. U. N. E. Program.

Wheatley, M., Tannenbaum, R., Griffin, P. Y., & Quade, K. (2003). *Organization development at work: Conversations on the values, applications, and future of OD*. John Wiley.

Yang, S.-y. (2011). Wisdom displayed through leadership: Exploring leadership-related wisdom. *The Leadership Quarterly, 22*(4), 616–632. https://doi.org/10.1016/j.leaqua.2011.05.004

Chapter 10
Doing Business with Compassion: Social Responsibility

Power of Compassion

> Those who act with compassion win in the offense,
> Those who act with compassion stand their ground in the defence.
> It is Heaven that rescues and protects them with compassion.
> – Laozi, Tao Te Ching, Ch. 67

This is the power of compassion as Laozi experienced in the ancient times. Those who act with compassion will achieve victory in the offensive, because love gives them the courage and strength they need. If they defend their loved ones or a cherished cause, they achieve security and protection. Because they follow the Tao, Heaven itself will come to their aid, events will seem to conspire in rendering assistance at just the right time, as if they are safeguarded by divine powers. All manners of resources and allies will appear and rally to their cause, in unexpected ways that no one could foresee. Anyone who witnesses this process at work will know that, indeed, the Tao is great beyond compare.

Why compassion is powerful is because compassion is a holistic understanding of a problem or the suffering of another with a commitment to act to solve the problem or alleviate the suffering. Thomas Merton, American writer and theologian said "*The whole idea of compassion is based on a keen awareness of the interdependence of all these living beings, which are all part of one another and all involved in one another.*" It is very important to understand that all creatures are part of the universe and are interconnected and interpedently with each. The more we recognize hidden connections in life, the more likely we will see and work with the forces—like compassion, courage, or kindness—that respect and strengthen those connections. Conversely, the less we recognize our mutual interdependence, the more likely we will perpetuate having experiences that accentuate our fear, selfishness, and even isolation

The findings of the researches today have justified the power of compassion that Laozi claims. For example, Christopher Kukk (2017) in his book, "*The*

L. Zu, *Responsible and Sustainable Business*,
https://doi.org/10.1007/978-3-030-91117-1_10

Compassionate Achiever: How Helping Others Fuels Success" call people who achieve success by helping others compassionate achiever. He noticed that compassion has been one of the most underappreciated but consistent characteristics of successful people across a wide range of occupations (Kukk, 2017). Klein and Dollenmayer (2014) also provides some sampling of the research about the power of compassion:

- *Compassion fosters greater self-esteem and health.* Rachel Piferi, of Johns Hopkins University, and Kathleen Lawler, of the University of Tennessee, demonstrated that people who were compassionate toward others lowered their blood pressure and reported "greater self-esteem, less depression, and less stress."
- *Compassion strengthens resilience.* Practicing compassion is one path to building resilience, which is the ability to respond to adversity and despair. As the late Jerilyn Ross, president and CEO of the Anxiety Disorders Association of America for 30 years, showed: "Doing things for other people, thinking about other people, is like giving your brain a break from despair. . . It creates a sense of satisfaction that increases endorphins and therefore a sense of well-being." Meredith Maran calls it the "activism cure."
- *Compassion creates a happier workplace, boosts productivity, and improves the bottom line.* Sigal Barsade, of the Wharton School at the University of Pennsylvania, and Olivia O'Neill, of George Mason University School of Business, found "a clear, positive correlation between compassionate behaviour, work satisfaction, and company success." As they've seen, compassion brings meaning to work and, when employees find meaning in their work, they are three times as likely to stay with their company.
- *Compassion improves academic performance.* A 2011 landmark study of 213 social and emotional learning programs (SEL), programs that help students understand and manage emotions) with a combined sample of more than 270,000 K-12 students clearly demonstrated that students participating in SEL programs make larger improvements with respect to academic, attitudinal, and behavioural measurements than their peers without SEL programs. SEL-taught children, for instance, had an 11-percentile-point gain in their academic achievement over their non-SEL counterparts. In a 2015 Columbia University study titled "The Economic Value of Social and Emotional Learning," the authors found that SEL programs produce an $11 return on every $1 spent. Why such an amazing return on investment? SEL- taught students develop the intellectual and social-emotional skills not only to increase academic success, but also to avoid problem behaviours such as alcohol and drug abuse, violence, truancy, and bullying, which reduces costs to the community via lower crime (from misdemeanors to felonies), hospitalization (mental health and addiction services), and school dropout rates.
- *Compassion strengthens the political, civic, and economic health of communities.* Paul Zak, the founding director of the Center for Neuroeconomic Studies at Claremont Graduate University, uncovered oxytocin's role in nurturing the political and economic health of a community. Because compassion activates

oxytocin in the brain and oxytocin fosters trust between people, where "trust is high," according to a study by the Pew Research Center, "crime and corruption are low."

Many scientists believe that compassion may even be vital to the survival of our species, and they're finding that its advantages can be increased through targeted exercises and practice. Here are some of the most exciting findings from this research so far (Keltner et al., 2010).

Compassion makes us feel good. Compassionate action (e.g., giving to charity) activates pleasure circuits in the brain, and compassion training programs, even very brief ones, strengthen brain circuits for pleasure and reward and lead to lasting increases in self-reported happiness. Feeling compassion for one person makes us less vindictive toward others. Restraining feelings of compassion chips away at our commitment to moral principles. Employees who receive more compassion in their workplace see themselves, their co-workers, and their organization in a more positive light, report feeling more positive emotions like joy and contentment, and are more committed to their jobs. More compassionate societies—those that take care of their most vulnerable members, assist other nations in need, and have children who perform more acts of kindness—are the happier ones. Compassionate people are more socially adept, making them less vulnerable to loneliness; loneliness has been shown to cause stress and harm the immune system.

Matthew Fox (1999) claims that compassion may be a passionate way of living born of an awareness of the interconnectedness of all creatures by reason of their common Creator. To be compassionate is to incorporate one's own fullest energies with cosmic ones into the twin tasks of (1) relieving the pain of fellow creatures by way of justice-making, and (2) celebrating the existence, time and space that all creatures share as a gift from the only One who is fully Compassion. Compassion is our kinship with the universe and the universe's Maker; it is the action we take because of that kinship (Fox, 1999).

Multiple studies show there is a positive relationship between compassion and firm performance. According to (Poorkavoos, 2016) a 2016 Roffey Park study, leadership that shows an awareness of the suffering of others and is non-judgmental, tolerant of personal distress, empathic and able to determine and activate appropriate action provides a better workplace than leaders who fail to create a compassionate workplace culture. Compassion in the workplace provides many benefits, improving workplace culture and creating an environment that is welcoming and supportive of employees. According to a 2018 Glassdoor roundup of 20 companies where employees are happiest, a top priority for workers is a company that provides support for work/life balance and personal as well as professional growth (Grassdoor, 2018).

Even more noticeable is employee reaction to a workplace that takes stress seriously and strives to limit employee stress and burnout. According to the Wellness Council of America, symptoms of stress at work manifest in missed work days, lower productivity, higher medical costs and a higher incidence of employee turnover. A compassionate workplace can provide support for stress management and improve employee health, both physically, mentally and emotionally. A simple way to foster stress management is to permit employee socialization—a few minutes at the water cooler chatting can send employees back to work with renewed focus and lower stress levels, after connecting with colleagues who have the same challenges and stressors they do. Decreased stress means employees are less likely to burn out and more likely to be productive.

Compassion matters for six types of strategic advantage that affect firm performance: innovation, service quality, collaboration, retaining talented people, employee and customer engagement, and adaptability to change (Worline & Dutton, 2017). Armenteros (2018) explores those relationships using Structural Equation Modelling with data from 250 innovative organizations, and found that that both variables—compassion and innovativeness—contribute positively to firm performance. Moreover, this article empirically demonstrates the key role played by innovativeness, which explains the positive relationship between compassion and firm performance, and also directly enhances firm performance.

Empathy, Leadership and Empowerment

> Great leaders have no self-interest,
> But always put other interests above their own.
> They are good to those who are good,
> They are also good to those who are not good,
> Thus, it leads to genuine goodness.
> They trust those who are trustworthy,
> They also trust those who are untrustworthy,
> Thus, it leads to genuine trust.
> – Laozi, Tao Te Ching, Ch.49

The 3C Model of Taoism reveals that compassion is a multipart process that involves a felt and enacted desire to alleviate suffering. Specifically, compassion is defined as a four-part human experience that unfolds in relation to suffering. The first part of the process involves noticing other's pain. The second part involves interpreting suffering in ways that lead us to understand those who are suffering as worthy of our compassion. The third part of the process involves feeling empathic concern—this is the emotional aspect of the process. And the fourth part is acting to alleviate suffering in some way (Dutton et al., 2014). In this verse of Tao Te Ching, Laozi interpreted empathy as the intellectual identification with or vicarious experiencing of the feelings, thoughts, or attitudes of another, and defined it as the desire to increase another person's personal welfare before consideration of one's own. To increase another person's welfare before one's own is a matter of a true desire to help another based on the occurrence of empathy experienced for the individual in need. This passage also indicates that leadership is about empathy. It is about having the ability to relate to and connect with people for the purpose of inspiring and empowering their lives. Great leaders with empathy are able to attune to a wide range of emotional signals, letting them sense the felt, but unspoken, emotions in a person or group.

Empathy is one of the core parts of compassion. Empathy refers more generally to our ability to take the perspective of and feel the emotions of another person, compassion is when those feelings and thoughts include the desire to help. Altruism, in turn, is the kind, selfless behaviour often prompted by feelings of compassion. Compassion and empathy—our ability to truly feel for others—are some of the most powerful manifestations of the consciousness of Taoism's wisdom. When we are really touched by a person in need, our concern draws us into his or her world so quickly it's as though we were never separate. Empathy extends well beyond feeling to understanding, and it extends beyond individuals to groups, communities, peoples, even species. Empathy is at the heart of real rationality, because it goes to the heart of our values, which are the basis of our sense of justice (Lakoff, 2011). Just as Laozi says,

> A grudge is reconciled, but cannot be gotten rid of.
> Requiting ill will with goodwill is not solution.
> Thus, though the sage keeps the receipt of a loan,
> Never claims payback.
> Those who are virtuous are empathetic like a creditor.
> Those who are not virtuous are un-empathetic like a tax collector.
> The Tao of Heaven is impartial, and always helps those who are empathetic.
> – Laozi, Tao Te Ching, Ch.79

Laozi's wisdom teaches us that empathy is also about the feeling state of another. Carl Rogers, a humanistic psychologist, describes: to sense the client's private world as if it were your own, but without ever losing the "as if" quality... To sense the client's anger or fear, as if it were your own, yet without your own anger, fear, or confusion getting bound up in it (Kirschenbaum & Henderson, 1989).

Michael Ventura, entrepreneur and CEO of award-winning strategy and design firm Sub Rosa, shares how empathy—the ability to see the world through someone else's eyes—could be what your business needs to innovate, connect, and grow. He claims that empathy is not just about being nice. It's not about pity or sympathy either. It's about understanding—your consumers, your colleagues, and yourself—and it's a direct path to powerful leadership. Employing empathy in your business decisions can also help you avoid potentially devastating pitfalls in full view of the whole world (Ventura, 2018). With the prevalence of social media, we have to be more conscious and careful than ever to dodge a misstep that will land you as a defendant in the court of public opinion.

Empathy and Empowerment: Toward to Common Good

Empathy is a critical aspect of our future—if we are to have one. The recent advances in science suggest empathy and connectivity have a lot to offer the future: *biologists and cognitive neuroscientists are discovering mirror-neurons—the so-called empathy neurons—that allow human beings and other species to feel and experience another's situation as if it were one's own. We are, it appears, the most social of animals and seek intimate participation and companionship with our fellows* (Rifkin, 2009). Social scientists, in turn, are beginning to re-examine human history from an empathic lens and, in the process, discovering previously hidden strands of the human narrative which suggests that human evolution is measured not only by the expansion of power over nature, but also by the intensification and extension of empathy to more diverse others across broader temporal and spatial domains. The growing scientific evidence that we are a fundamentally empathic species has profound and far-reaching consequences for society, and may well determine our fate as a species. Rifkin (2009) holds that developing our empathic consciousness is what's needed in order to deal with peak oil, climate change, and other global challenges. This isn't an impossible task—we only need to look and see what's really taking place in the world, allow ourselves to care, and articulate our feelings through behaviour and policy changes. We need to acknowledge that life actually matters to us.

Empathy, empowerment and envisioning are the three key components of Charismatic leadership. These key components stimulate followers' need for achievement, need for affiliation, and need for power. These motivational effects of charismatic leadership then act to improve followers' role perceptions, task performance, job satisfaction, sense of collective identity, group cohesiveness, organizational citizenship behavior, and self-leadership (Choi, 2006).

Charismatic leaders engage in empathic behavior by being sensitive to their followers' needs and emotions, sharing their emotions, and helping them realize their objectives. Followers with a high need for affiliation which is enhanced by the empathic behavior of a charismatic leader perceive strong collective identity and show organizational citizenship behavior directed toward the leader and co-workers. Their groups will thus be highly cohesive.

Charismatic leaders empower their followers by enhancing their perceptions of self-efficacy and their confidence in their ability to overcome obstacles, by using verbal persuasion and verbal recognition, and by functioning as a role model. Followers with a high need for power which is enhanced by the empowering behavior of a charismatic leader are motivated to develop and exercise self-leadership.

Empowerment is a feeling, a quiet dignity and belief that every individual has value and a determination to base one's life actions on that belief. Martin Luther King, Jr. and Mahatma Gandhi demonstrate empowerment, as does contemporary activist Shannon Galpin (Mountain to Mountain) who empowered women in Afghanistan to ride bicycles when it was forbidden. Empowered individuals move societies forward. Empowerment can result when someone else bestows responsibility or faith in us.

The findings of Cousineau (2018) shows that in the practice of kindness, there is a slippery point at which showing empathic concern and enacting kind deeds could go one way or the other: toward discomfort and distress or toward ease and joy. The direction depends on a sense of safety and your balance of empathic concern with

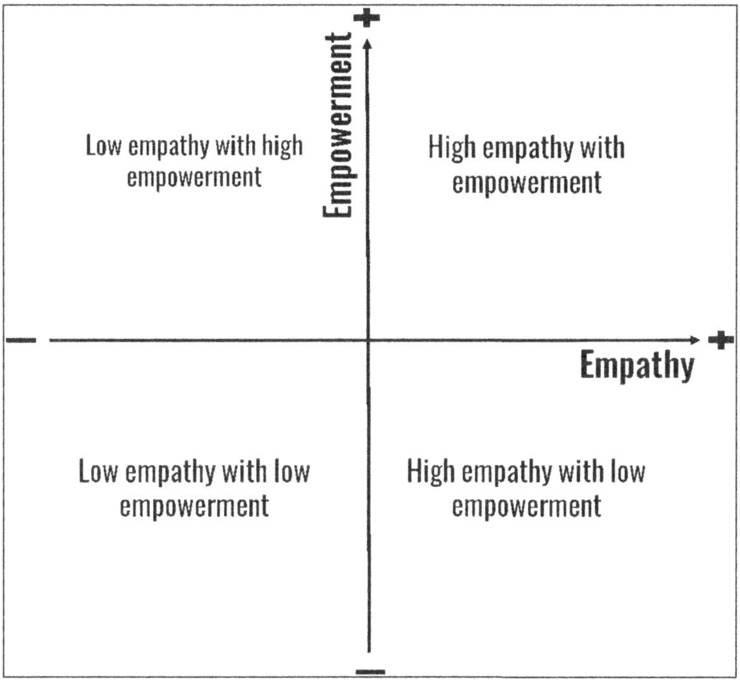

Fig. 10.1 Empathy and empowerment. Source: Tara Cousineau (2018), The kindness cure: how the science of compassion can heal your heart and your world

how empowered you feel. Cousineau developed empathy-empowerment grid which can help us reflect more deeply about what might help or hinder kindness in us (Fig. 10.1).

High empathy with high empowerment is a state of caring that results in kind behaviours and a personal commitment to the well-being of others. It is a feeling of empathic concern that is followed by acting in alignment with that feeling to offer things such as a caring presence, affection, or relief. This generosity becomes contagious, the circles of care widen, and social justice is valued. This orientation brings a healthy striving for both the personal and collective good.

High empathy with low empowerment is being under a self-protective empathy lethargy. The caring impulse toward yourself or others is present, but the ability to be of help and service, or to affect positive change, is short-circuited by real obstacles or personal discomfort, fear, exhaustion, or disillusionment. You are more likely to be in a state of empathic distress or compassion fatigue, which is the inability to tolerate the pain or suffering of others.

Low empathy with high empowerment is a position of power and confidence. You are motivated by selfish goals, act at the expense of others, harbour a disregard for the well-being of others, and view others as outsiders.

Low empathy with low empowerment is a state of apathy and isolation. This may happen when faced with a real or perceived threat to survival, pervasive trauma, disengagement from others, or an ingrained sense of learned helplessness. You feel numb, so you can't act.

Therefore, charismatic leaders need to develop their high empathy, and the ability to empower their followers.

Charity and Giving: Transforming the World Through Doing Good

> Great leaders do not hoard,
> The more they give of themselves, the more they find of themselves.
> The more they give to others, the more they receive from others.
> – Laozi, Tao Te Ching, Ch.81

Laozi stresses the importance of the law of giving and receiving. The more you help and live for others, the more you feel happy and satisfied because you are returned with the great honour and respect from others. No person was ever honoured for what he received. Honour has been the reward for what he gave. The more you give, the more you will receive. It is more blessed to give than to receive because you keep the abundance of the universe circulating in your life. In fact, anything that is of value in life only multiplies when it is given. That which doesn't multiply through giving is neither worth giving nor worth receiving. If, through the act of giving, you feel you have lost something, then the gift is not truly given and will not cause increase. If you give grudgingly, there is no energy behind that giving.

Tagore (2014) says in his poem of Gitanjali, "*The universe operates through dynamic exchange...giving and receiving are different aspects of the flow of energy in the universe. And in our willingness to give that which we seek, we keep the abundance of the universe circulating in our lives.*" In his book, The Power of Kindness, Piero Ferrucci, a transpersonal psychologist from Florence, Italy, articulates the ways oneness is expressed through the heart: for the generous person, borders are permeable. What is yours—your suffering, your problems—is also mine: This is compassion. What is mine—my possessions, my body, my knowledge and abilities, my time and resources, my energy—is also yours: This is generosity. The true benefit of generosity, for the giver, is not a material advantage but an inner revolution. We become more fluid, more willing to risk. We place less store on possession and more on people. And the boundaries between us and others become less drastic, so that we feel part of a whole in which it is possible to share resources, emotions, and ourselves (Ferrucci, 2006).

Charity and giving is one of the great virtues or qualities that great leaders always embody in the community. Tadao Yoshida, the Japanese YKK's founder says, "*No one prospers without rendering benefit to others.*" Great inner joy comes from helping others to better their lives. Truly giving from the heart fills your life with joy and nourishes your soul. Giving provides an intrinsic reward that's far more valuable than the gift. As Mahatma Gandhi said, "To find yourself, lose yourself in the service of others." Brian Tracy, a Canadian-American motivational public speaker and self-development author also says, "Love only grows by sharing. You can only have more for yourself by giving it away to others"

The act of giving is always the cornerstone for abundance. Most people believe when you give something away, you actually lose it; but that couldn't be further from the truth. When you give, it seems like the universe is pleased with that action and in return, you're blessed with more. Giving is such a natural act that after you do it, you get a rush of endorphins and other good feeling natural chemicals that flood the body. If you give what you have, you will never go without.

Giving and Servant Leadership

> Great leaders
> Act on it without action, teach it without words.
> Let all things flourish without meddling in their affairs.
> Give birth to them without possession.
> Serve them without presuming upon reward.
> Accomplish them without claiming credit.
> – Laozi, Tao Te Ching, Ch.2

Giving is one of the key elements of servant leadership. John Hope Bryant (2009) in his book of Love Leadership: The New Way to Lead in a Fear-Based World reveals the fifth law of love leadership: giving is getting (Bryant, 2009). The fifth law of love leadership translates into a long-term commitment to serving others, starting with serving those who work in your organization and expanding out to serving your partners, vendors, and customers, and the world. It fundamentally requires that you serve without expecting anything in return—because it is the right thing to do. It means leading with passion and authenticity, and combining that with a purpose of doing good for others. For example, in his organization, rather than firing employees, Bryant worked even harder. As a leader, he gave more and got much more in return. As a leader, he also gave to the citizens they served. As a servant leader, you are a steward of the resources—human, financial, and otherwise—that your organization provides. Leaders serve those inside and outside the organization and at the same time focus on achieving results in line with the organization's mission and values. Robert Greenleaf first coined the concept of servant leadership in 1977 in terms of employees, but the concept has been expanded much more widely. He wrote, "The best test, and difficult to administer, is: do those served grow as persons? Do they grow while being served, become healthier, wiser, freer, more autonomous, more likely themselves to become servants?" (Greenleaf, 1998)

Former president Bill Clinton is one of the role models of servant leader demonstrating the way of giving to the society. For example, he regarded the act of giving as an example of good selfishness because it will almost always make you feel good, or in the case of businesses, it will result in positive things for your bottom line. His foundation is a wonderful example of this. They now have 1.4 million people accessing AIDS medicines under agreements that they've negotiated with dozens of pharmaceutical companies—but the companies that give them this medicine make money. They insist that they do. They just make money in a different way. Instead of making a higher margin on a lower volume, they make money selling a higher volume with a lower margin, and they keep more people alive. They try to show people and companies that doing good and doing well can be one and the same. The wise person comes to understand that selfishness and enlightened selfishness are one and the same.

Case in Point: YKK Philosophy: "Cycle of Goodness"

The YKK Group was founded in January 1934 by Yoshida Tadao. The YKK is currently engaged in business in hundreds of countries/regions around the world. Ever since YKK's founding, the spiritual pillar of all YKK Group business activities has been the "*Cycle of Goodness*" YKK Philosophy as indicated in Fig. 10.2, which embodies their belief that *no one prospers without rendering benefit to others.*

YKK understand well that an enterprise is an important member of society, and as such it must coexist with other elements of society. The value of its existence will be recognized by the benefits it shares with society. In pursuing their business, YKK has devoted great attention to the way in which they can realize such mutual prosperity—that this can be best achieved by the continual creation of new value through innovative ideas and inventions. This would result in business expansion for the YKK Group, which in turn would bring prosperity to consumers, community and business partners, and thus benefit society as a whole.

Every YKK company around the world shares the "*Cycle of Goodness*" philosophy and the management principle "YKK seeks corporate value of higher significance." "Fairness" is the standard on which we base our conduct. Tadao Yoshida,

Fig. 10.2 Business philosophy of YKK

YKK's founder, carefully considered this need for mutual prosperity as he planned his business endeavours. For example, if a more efficient machine can be developed, productivity will be enhanced; or, if the material loss rate can be reduced, lower cost in the final product will be attained while making the best use of limited resources. Also, Tadao Yoshida felt strongly that the fruits of these innovative ideas must not be retained by any individual. Instead, they should be distributed widely to society, thereby circulating the benefit. In this way, one can prosper while making a contribution to the enrichment of all humankind.

Courage Is the Key to Great Leadership

> The best leaders blend courage with compassion.
> – Sharma Robin, the author of The Monk Who Sold His Ferrari

According to Laozi's wisdom, *compassion leads to courage*. Compassion is more powerful than courage, because with courage we can conquer a world, but only with compassion can we heal and build it. However, Daisaku Ikeda, Japanese Buddhist philosopher and educator says that courage and compassion are two sides of the same coin. Compassion without courage is not genuine. You may have a compassionate thought or impulse, but if you don't do or say anything, it's not real compassion. Winston Churchill claims that courage is the first of human qualities because it is a quality which guarantees the others. Aristotle called courage the first virtue, because it makes all of the other virtues possible.

Courage is the most important human virtue, and also the most important business virtue. Without courage, other important business concepts like leadership, innovation and sales wither. Because leadership takes courage to make bold and often unpopular decisions. Innovation takes courage to involve creating groundbreaking but tradition-defying ideas. Sales takes courage to require being repeatedly rejected before closing a deal. Take away courage, sales, innovation and leadership lose their potency. Therefore, the great leaders need to blend courage with compassion.

As virtue courage implies a quality of strength; it enables us to hold our own against opposition, difficulty, or temptation often after repeated failed attempts. Every form of true courage and strength has its basis in love and serves justice. Courage fortifies us against the vice of cowardice (a vice of deficiency) and restrains us from recklessness (a vice of excess) (Hickey, 2011). It is the middle path between timidity and temerity. There are some things courage is not courage is not about the absence of fear, but about having fear and overcoming it. Bravery in the service of ignoble purposes is not courage; it is recklessness. And not all courage is physical, as physical strength is not always involved. Courage may be shown by mental or moral courage in facing public shaming, prejudice, exclusion or mockery for taking an unpopular stance.

Courage and Creativity

Courage can also be demonstrated by a person's open and honest response to one's own wrongdoing which has resulted in a reprimand or scandal. Without risk, there can be no personal growth in courage. We often grow through challenge, adventure, or adversity because what doesn't destroy us always makes us stronger. Therefore, those who are compassionate to others are courageous and can overcome the fears and take challenges. Those who face the challenges, risk and crisis must be knowledgeable and creative in figuring out new ideas and ways to solve the problems, and create new opportunities.

Henri Matisse says, "*Creativity takes courage*". *Compassion is also defined as creativity put to the service of justice,* and can be achieved for both humanity and the environment as the interconnectedness of all things are recognized. This implies that creativity (knowledge) and compassion must be interconnected and not be separated. There will be no compassion without creativity and no creativity without imagination. Victor Weisskopf, an Austrian-born American theoretical physicist says "*Human existence is based upon two pillars: Compassion and knowledge. Knowledge without compassion is inhuman. Compassion without knowledge is ineffective.*" Creativity without compassion may lead to megalomania or selective blindness about the destructive effects of our behaviour (Zsolnai, 2015).

Courage and Four Styles of Leadership

Courage is about making tough choices, but those choices more often than not involve the little things we do. Courage is the virtue that's needed if we are truly going to transform our lives. Courage is the virtue that's needed if we are going to enact anything that is significantly important to us. Courage is the virtue that's needed if we are going to change the status quo. Leadership is about taking people to places they've never been before, and we can't go to those places without courage. Leadership is courage in action. Courage gives us the energy to move forward. Courage gives us the confidence to believe we can make it. Courage gives us the strength to sustain ourselves in the darkest hours. Courage enables us to leave a legacy that declares, "I was here and I made a difference" (Kouzes & Posner, 2006). Throughout the ages, people have searched for the precise alchemy of ingredients that constitute great leadership. In measured proportions, great leaders are said to demonstrate bold but reasoned judgment, spirited but calculated risk-taking and an assertive but reflective disposition. Complicating the matter are the expectations and needs of those being led. Followers want leaders who make decisions decisively but inclusively, interpret situations with rational and emotional intelligence and exude confidence and humility.

The research of McGarvie and Kraft (2009) shows that a leader with high courage quotient (CQ) has the additional ability, such as a sense of curiosity, emphatic sense,

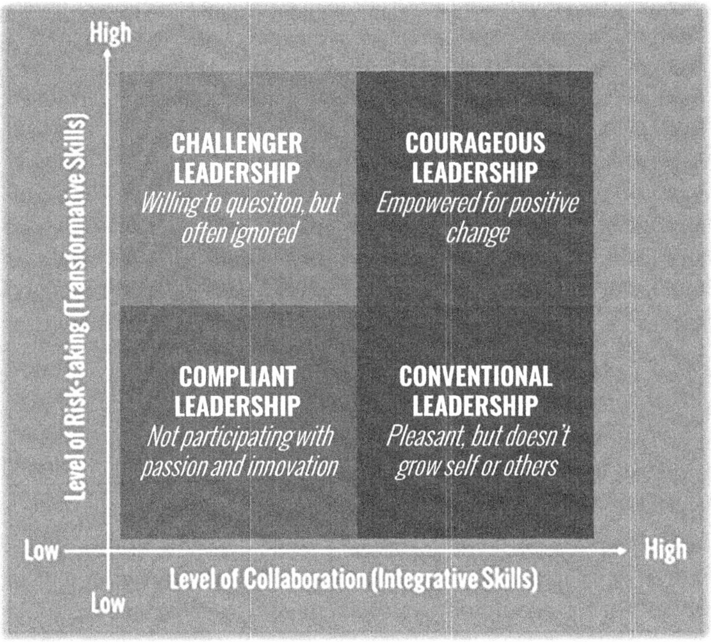

Fig. 10.3 Courage and leadership. Source: Adapted from Blythe J. McGarvie (2009): Shaking the globe: courageous decision-making in a changing world

competence and perseverance to stand out at the opportune moment. While individuals who have a sense of curiosity turn emotions and ideas into action and those who have an emphatic sense spur collaboration and the cultivation of relationships around them, courageous leaders inspire those around them to tackle bold, new opportunities. Two other factors that drive a leader's CQ are competence and perseverance: the abilities to drive accomplishment through hard work and innovation combined with a desire for continual self-improvement.

Leaders with high CQ scores are effective at standing out by moving their organization toward new opportunities that create long-term value for all stakeholders. In addition, they understand how to work with others within their organization—navigating the political and operating systems—to get things done in the face of obstacles, criticism, or even in the wake of their own mistakes. Figure 10.3 shows the different kinds of leaders based on level of courage which is decided by the level of cooperation that individual is comfortable with and level of risk that the individual is willing to take.

The level of collaboration is measured by the integrative skills which include financial acuity, integrity and linkages, and the level of risk-taking by transformative skills which include learning, perspective and global citizenship. Financial acuity refers to understanding how the company makes money, and measures its financial success, builds confidence. Integrity means doing the right things in the right way in order to preserve the reputation of the company, creates stakeholder trust. Linkages work to build and leverage a wide and effective network of stakeholders in order to provide access to new people and new ways of thinking, open the door to opportunity. Learning is continuously open to new disciplines and ideas, fosters creativity and innovation. Perspective is to develop and share insight that raises the performance bar personally and professionally for an individual and collectively for the organization, is critical to bringing balanced judgement into decision-making. Global citizenship is the ability to think broadly and operate in a world that is increasingly interconnected and interdependent, creates the skill of flexibility and adaptability to uncertain environments. Figure 10.3 shows the four styles of leadership.

Conventional Leadership A leader is capable of collaborating with stakeholders to get things done but lacks the risk orientation that drives higher level of performance. The conventional leader can be helpful in implementing current strategies but will not demonstrate the risk orientation needed to raise the performance bar and develop innovative strategies and plans.

Compliant Leadership A compliant leader wants to show up for work, collect a paycheck and focus more on what has been, rather than what is or will be. The individual neither has an appropriate focus on collaborating nor will take prudent risks in order to support the strategies and goals of the organization. The individual may agree to follow the rules and plans, and then proceed to do something quite different.

Challenger Leadership The individual has the perspective and risk orientation to make innovative and perhaps even breakthrough contributions. However, the individual seeks to impose his or her point of view on others without understanding the full situation and others' point of view.

Courageous Leadership The individual takes personal risk or sacrifice to make a difference. Their passions and energy are devoted to a cause. They process a real desire to improve the future of their companies throughout their chosen parts of the globe. The individual is capable of collaborating and willing to take risks in order to get short-term results and create a long-term value.

The courageous leader is a valued member of the organization and often serves as a pace setter for stimulating learning and change. Courageous leaders serve as both thought catalyst for change and as effective change agents. They are willing and able to take the risk required in change and willing and able to build the collaborative relationships that make performance sustainable. The courageous leader is a role model and exemplifies the values and actions appreciated by the organization. Everyone has the potential to be a courageous leader.

Courage: Action to Respond in Times of Crisis

> Those who act with compassion win in the offense,
> Those who act with compassion stand their ground in the defense.
> Heaven rescues and insures them with compassion.
> – Laozi, Tao Te Ching, Ch. 67

> Those who act bravely will perish.
> Those who act courageously will live.
> Of those two, one is beneficial and one is harmful.
> What Heaven detests, who knows why?
> Even the sage considers it difficult.
> – Laozi, Tao Te Ching, Ch. 73

Compassion is the core virtue of Tao, and is a trait of Tao. The compassionate is treated the same by Tao. Compassion breeds compassion. Therefore, whether you are in the defensive or in the offensive position, you must remain compassionate; you will succeed in achieving your goal, because as Laozi says that compassion empowers you with courage and strength. Even Heaven agrees on this. So, fate seems to work in favor of those who remain compassionate. However, Laozi also claims that courage without compassion leads to calamity. He illustrates this point in the verse 73: Those who are brave to dare will perish, and those who are courageous to dare will live. Those who act bravely without compassion will perish—bravery sometimes leads to stupidity. Those who act courageously with compassion will live, because courage embraces judgement.

Courage entails a cause, most commonly love, passion, compassion, concern, etc. Bravery maintains its essence even without a cause. Courage is a result of mindfulness; it is one's decision to fight despite one's fears. Bravery is an inherent characteristic; it does not involve much thinking and manifests itself as second nature in those who are brave. Another unique element that sets the two virtues apart is the presence or absence of mindfulness. Acts of bravery do not necessarily require critical judgment. Most of the time, the quality becomes inherent due to family and societal values, and therefore effortlessly manifests itself as second nature.

A brave person can eat a worm when told to, without putting much thought into reasons and consequences of their action. In contrast, courage is a result of a deep understanding of the matter; Courage implies firmness of mind and will in the face of danger or extreme difficulty. A courageous person truly understands what they're getting themselves into and who or what they're doing it for. For instance, a courageous man knows he might die if he enters a burning building to save his son. He shivers at the thought of burning to death, but proceeds anyway—because of the love he has for his child. A leader with courage possesses a mindset that allows himself or herself to respond to crises that he or she may not have sought, but which were nonetheless presented.

When he discussed with his disciples the importance of courage for leadership, Confucius says, "*Those who are faced with what is righteous leave it undone, they show a lack of courage. Those who are righteous are definitely courageous, but those who are courageous are not necessarily righteous*". In other words, those who are courageous do the right thing right, not only do the thing right. A courageous leader is the individual who are always righteous and do the right thing right in times of crisis.

Laozi describes two different strategies that corporations usually adopt to respond to the crisis in the business world: offensive and defensive. Companies can *pursue an effective CSR policy of either offense ("corporate social opportunity") or defence (CSR as "brand insurance")* (Chandler, 2016).

CSR Offense Policy The innovative, proactive CEO who is convinced of the intrinsic value of CSR sees it as an opportunity to utilize core competencies and identify new competitive advantages. Firms implementing a CSR perspective innovate in ways that make them more competitive. Companies with a progressive and innovative mind-set see benefits that range from being an attractive employer (helping retention and recruitment), to greater acceptance among government agencies (facilitating needed zoning and tax relief), to better relations with social activists (such as greenpeace). Timberland, for example, believes that its Path of Service program, which grants "full-time staff an annual benefit of (up to) 40 paid hours and part-time staff an annual benefit of (up to) 20 paid hours for community service," raises morale and increases retention, thereby lowering training costs while inducing new skills and stoking corporate pride.

CSR Defence Policy In terms of defence, CSR still has value by protecting the firm's reputation—avoiding criticism and implementing effective crisis management. In this instance, CSR is a rational choice that acts like a brand insurance policy, minimizing stakeholder disillusionment in response to perceived CSR transgressions. A good example of this approach is USCAP (United States Climate Action Partnership), formed by a group of energy and manufacturing firms, which "supports the introduction of carbon limits and trading" as a means of mitigating federal legislation designed to control carbon emissions: executives find it difficult to apply cost-benefit analysis to avoid future problems of uncertain likelihood. But these are the ideal conditions for insurance—not an insurance that pays off after a crisis, but more like traditional boiler insurance, one that focuses on preventative protection. The reason why firms need CSR is not because they necessarily have a pressing problem at the moment, but so that they can avoid (or, at least, lessen) problems that under- mine their brand going forward.

Either approach (offense or defence) assumes an up-front investment of some kind. When to introduce CSR into the strategic process, however, depends on the driving force behind its implementation. For those managers convinced of CSR's strategic potential, there is no time like the present. Innovative ideas and policies that create market opportunities, minimize costs, and increase productivity can produce immediate benefits. For managers yet to be persuaded by the argument for CSR, however, the temptation exists to delay as long as possible. Worse, cynical managers might see CSR as a public relations exercise, assuming they can postpone hard CSR choices and avoid the expense altogether. Perhaps this is analogous to someone who imagines that, as long as they remain healthy, they will be able to avoid outlays for health insurance.

Nevertheless, a crisis point can arise. Once stakeholder backlash becomes sufficient to warrant a genuine reaction, however, it may be too late. In 2011, for example, Walmart announced it would create "new programs aimed at helping women-owned businesses and women workers." Though commendable, this announcement was made within 3 months of the US Supreme Court's decision on the decade-long class-action lawsuit filed against Walmart claiming sex discrimination in its employment practices. As such, the announcement, which amounted to commitments totalling only "a small percentage of Wal-Mart's overall budget," served primarily to remind stakeholders of the alleged discrimination and failed to persuade anyone who was already sceptical that the firm had introduced a meaningful new approach to supporting female business owners.

In short, firms introduce CSR for different reasons. Implementing CSR proactively throughout the firm can generate efficiencies and new opportunities, as well as potential legitimacy benefits associated with first-mover status. Further, the genuine implementation of CSR, whether for offensive or defensive reasons, generates insurance-like benefits that can reduce the impact of subsequent transgressions. Whatever the motivation, there is a CSR threshold that varies for each firm (depending on whether it is the market leader or a smaller player), industry (some industries are more susceptible to stakeholder backlash than others), and culture (different societies place different expectations on corporations). The variable nature of this threshold (which can also ebb and flow with changes in public perception and the media news cycle) suggests why some companies perceive CSR to be of greater importance at different points in time. Still, why do different thresholds exist? An important part of the answer lies in the firm's business-level strategy.

Empathy and Courage: Two Hallmarks of Responsible Learners

Those leaders who have empathy and courage can weave environmental and social concerns into very strategic decision, revise policies and procedures to support sustainability efforts, and measure their progress toward sustainability goals. They must have the vision of Martin Luther King, Jr. "As soon as there is poverty in the world, I can never be rich.... As soon as diseases are rampant, I can never be healthy.... I can never be what I ought to be until you are what you ought to be."

Before analysing how business leaders take the courage to respond to social and environmental challenges, I want to start to explain what factors of courage can transform business by employing the findings of Merom Klein. Klein in the book of The Courage to Act has highlighted various domains in which courage is critical to performance (Merom Klein, 2003).

Courage to Face the Truth and to Express It Lucidity is one of the first signs of courage. Many people prefer not to admit there is a problem, rather than recognize it and be forced to respond. The lack of courage is therefore often insidious, because it is easier for people to think of themselves as ignorant as cowardly! Furthermore, being aware of a problem is not sufficient if one does not dare to express it. At every company, there are impassioned hallway discussions where people vigorously express what they would have liked to say in a meeting "if they could have." However, repeated acts of "minor cowardice" can ultimately undermine the performance of a team or a company.

Courage to Rely on Others A second form of courage indispensable to companies is daring to rely on others. Everyone knows that efficient delegation is critical to performance. However, the degree of courage to delegate is generally underestimated: you must be ready to relinquish control over results, you control over results, be ready to call into question, share information, etc.. Likewise, collaborate with others inevitably carries an element of risk. Work effectively in teams therefore requires this form of courage.

Courage to Make Decisions in Risky or Uncertain Situations Making decisions without being able to weigh the consequences in detail, or to collect all desired information is difficult but essential. Companies need employees able to show initiative, which may sometimes mean daring to take action without receiving prior approval from superiors. Conversely, someone can be courageous in deliberately choosing not to take action despite pressure from shareholders, superiors or employees.

Courage to Work Outside Our Comfort Zone Top-performing teams are those that dare to move outside the comfort of what they know, and push the limits. Setting ambitious objectives and having the persistence to pursue them in the face of adversity is a particularly critical form of courage in the business world. When confronted with a situation that is relatively satisfying, how many are willing to upset things to continue to improve?

Courage to Impose Rigorous Standards Finally, a dimension that is often underestimated consists in imposing discipline and rigor on ourselves and others. Clarifying the rules and ensure they are followed is an essential part of the job of team manager or leader. This idea appears to clash with the vision of the glorious leader ready to take risks with its own perils. And yet, imposing discipline does take real courage: it takes a lot of motivation to define obligations whose benefits may not be visible in the short term. And work relentlessly to ensure that these rules are applied, especially since those thus constrained are unlikely to give thanks in return!

A leader with courage possesses a mind-set that allows himself or herself to respond to crises that he or she may not have sought, but which were nonetheless presented. There are various general approaches to social responsibilities and can be divided into four basic stances: Obstructionist, Defensive, Accommodative, and Proactive (Dollak, 2008) . Based on Laozi's wisdom in the verse 73 and the principles of corporate social responsibility, I developed the four basic strategies

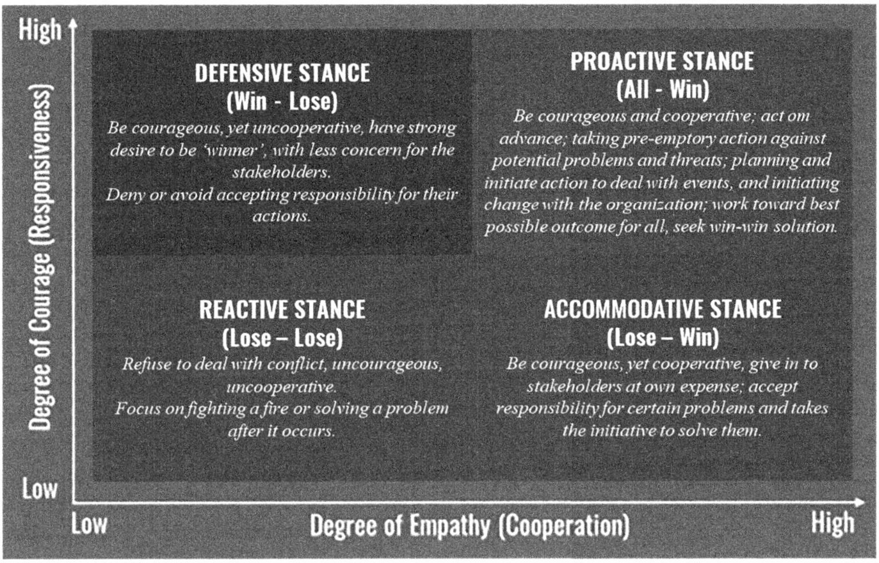

Fig. 10.4 Corporate social responsive strategy: courage and empathy

of corporate responsiveness to social and environmental crises as indicated in Fig. 10.4.

Reactive Stance with Low Cooperation and Negative Responsiveness An organization which holds a reactive stance tries to block and stop what is going on and avoid corporate social responsibility. When an obstructive company cross the ethical or legal line that separates acceptable from unacceptable practices, their typical response is to deny or avoid accepting responsibility for their actions by blocking any attempts to point out the company's lack of social responsibility to defend its economic priorities. An obstructive company does not make social responsibility an effort, instead making profits the most important aspect of its business. Some people view obstructive businesses as immoral since they may exploit their employees, pollute natural lands or deceive customers (Kanobi, 2018).

Defensive Stance with High Responsiveness and Low Cooperation In most cases, companies that take a defensive stance towards social responsibility are not particularly responsible, and deny or avoid accepting responsibility for their irresponsible actions. Companies respond with strong desire to be winner, but less concern for the stakeholders. Whatever they do only is required by law and nothing more. These companies may consider themselves neutral, and they make profits a more important motive than performing actions in a socially responsible way. They make a point of following the law to ensure that others cannot take legal action against them.

A company may create more waste than necessary, but it will remove of the waste in a legal method rather than dumping it illegally. For examples, there are companies like Camel, R. J. Reynolds, and Phillip Morris that are all tobacco companies that take a defensive stance to social responsibility. They do things such as placing warnings on the packs. These companies wouldn't put the warnings on the packages if it weren't for the law. In countries where that is not the law, they go above and beyond to sell their products, even if that means discarding their warnings. They will not purposely advertise the risks involved with the products in fear consumers will not buy them.

Accommodative Stance with High Cooperation and Low Responsiveness Accommodative stance means "approach to social responsibility by which a company exceeds legal minimums in its commitments to groups and individuals in its social environment". A business that employs an accommodative stance to social responsibility provides information and facts and doesn't try to hide things. Social responsibility is a term referring to the accountability businesses have to balance out their commitments to people, including customers, other businesses, investors and employees. Accommodative social responsibility is a strategy used when a company chooses to accept responsibility for certain problems and takes the initiative to solve them.

An accommodative stance signifies that a company believes social responsibility is important—and perhaps as important as making a profit. These companies satisfy all legal requirements and attempt to meet ethical standards, but will also go beyond these obligations in selected cases (Kanobi, 2018). Such firms voluntarily agree to participate in social programs, but solicitors have to convince the organisation that the programs are worthy of it support, or else the organisations do not proactively seek such avenues for contributing (Griffin, 2013). Besides, an accommodating company does not attempt to hide its actions and remains open about why it takes specific actions. For example, it may decrease its creation of waste, source products that are not tested on animals and pay its employees a fair wage. The company would keep its records open to the public. Though these companies are often socially responsible, they may change their policies in response to criticism (Kanobi, 2018). Walmart, Disney, and Google are great examples of companies going above and beyond. The three companies have been known to give great benefits to their employees, and even match contributions made by their employees to selected charitable causes.

Proactive Stance with High Responsiveness and High Cooperation The highest degree of social responsibility that a firm can exhibit is the proactive stance. A proactive stance, as opposed to a reactive one, involves acting in advance of a future situation rather than simply responding to a situation that has already happened. Ultimately, a proactive organization actively provides and tries to figure out how to help instead of being reactive. Logically, customers are much more trusting of such companies. Firms that adopt this approach take to heart the arguments in favour of social responsibility. They view themselves as citizens in a society and proactively seek opportunities to contribute.

Proactive behaviour aims at identification and exploitation of opportunities and in taking pre-emptory action against potential problems and threats, whereas reactive behaviour focuses on fighting a fire or solving a problem after it occurs. Companies can be either proactive or reactive in responding to events that impact them. Companies that take a proactive stance plan in advance and initiate action to deal with events, instead of merely responding to events. Besides, proactivity is about initiating change within the organization. In the area of customer service, for instance, a company may take proactive action to recall a product if it finds that there is a problem with it, rather than waiting for consumers to complain and then reacting to the issue (Kinsey, 2019).

An excellent example of proactive stance is the Ronald McDonald House program undertaken by McDonald's. These houses, located close to major medical centres, can be used by families for minimal cost while their sick children are receiving medical treatment nearby. This program has been widely applauded. Another example for proactive stance is The Toro Company, Exmark Manufacturing and Dixon Industries Inc. They collectively recalled 62,000 faulty commercial riding mowers. These companies worked directly with their dealers, distributors and customers during the recall campaign to proactively fix or replace the affected units already on the market (Bass, 2013). Nike is another example of a company that took a proactive stance, responding to criticisms about the labour conditions in the company's supply chain. Nike has taken a proactive stance to labour issues as part of the company's corporate social responsibility goals. The company has decided to take the offensive in terms of responding to criticism about labour conditions in the company's supply chain, according to a Nike corporate responsibility report. Nike sees this as a better option, recognizing that "waiting means we risk facing a forced requirement to shift on someone else's timeline." Kingfisher, a company that owns the British chain B&Q, has successfully implemented a proactive stance on waste reduction, chemicals and green issues in 2007. The company had goals for waste reduction and use of certified timber, sourcing the majority of its timber from sources that the Forest Stewardship Council has certified. Kingfisher's policies on chemicals in 2007 required its operating companies to have an action plan available by 2008 to identify products containing certain chemicals and to work with vendors on plans to remove or substitute them (Kinsey, 2019).

References

Armenteros, S. M. (2018). *Compassion counts! The power of compassion at work: Empirical findings from several multi-sample studies*. Universitat Jaume I.

Bass, B. (2013). *Examples of organizations that use proactive stances*. Retrieved October 20, 2020, from http://smallbusiness.chron.com/examples-organizations-use-proactive-stances-19368.html

Bryant, J. H. (2009). *Love leadership: The new way to lead in a fear-based world*. Jossey-Bass.

Chandler, D. (2016). *Strategic corporate social responsibility: Sustainable value creation*. Sage Publications.

Choi, J. (2006). A motivational theory of charismatic leadership: Envisioning, empathy, and empowerment. *Journal of Leadership & Organizational Studies, 13*(1), 24–43. https://doi.org/10.1177/107179190701300105 01

Cousineau, T. (2018). *The kindness cure: How the science of compassion can heal your heart and your world*. New Harbinger Publications.
Dollak, A. R. (2008). *How should American businesses approach social responsibility?* Retrieved October 20, 2020, from http://voices.yahoo.com/how-american-businesses-approach-social-responsibility-2131442.html?cat=3
Dutton, J. E., Workman, K. M., & Hardin, A. E. (2014). Compassion at work. *Annual Review of Organizational Psychology and Organizational Behavior, 1*(1), 277–304. https://doi.org/10.1146/annurev-orgpsych-031413-091221
Ferrucci, P. (2006). *The power of kindness: The unexpected benefits of leading a compassionate life*. Tarcher and Perigee.
Fox, M. (1999). *A spirituality named compassion: Uniting mystical awareness with social justice*. Inner Traditions.
Grassdoor. (2018, November 6). *20 Companies where employees are the happiest*. Glassdoor. Retrieved November 18, 2019, from https://www.glassdoor.com/blog/companies-employees-happiest/
Greenleaf, R. K. (1998). *The power of servant-leadership*. Berrett-Koehler Publishers.
Griffin, R.W. (2013). *Management* (11th ed.). South-Western, Cengage Learning.
Hickey, M. (2011). *Get goodness: Virtue is the power to do good*. University Press of America.
Kanobi, B. (2018, June 27). *What are the four basic approaches to social responsibility?* Retrieved 20 October 2020 from https://classroom.synonym.com/what-are-the-four-basic-approaches-to-social-responsibility-12083190.html
Keltner, D., Marsh, J., & Smith, J. A. (2010). *The compassionate instinct: The science of human goodness*. W. W. Norton.
Kinsey, A. (2019, June 17). *Companies that used proactive stance*. Retrieved October 20, 2020, from https://bizfluent.com/list-7300790-companies-used-proactive-stance.html
Kirschenbaum, H., & Henderson, V. L. (1989). *The Carl Rogers reader*. Houghton Mifflin.
Klein, S., & Dollenmayer, D. (2014). *Survival of the nicest: How altruism made us human and why it pays to get along*. The Experiment.
Kouzes, J. M., & Posner, B. Z. (2006). *A leader's legacy*. Jossey-Bass.
Kukk, C. L. (2017). *The compassionate achiever: How helping others fuels success*. HarperOne.
Lakoff, G. (2011, May 25). Empathy, sotomayor, and democracy: The conservative stealth strategy. *Huffington Post*. https://www.huffpost.com/entry/empathy-sotomayor-and-dem_b_209406
McGarvie, B. J., & Kraft, R. (2009). *Shaking the globe: Courageous decision-making in a changing world*. Wiley.
Merom Klein, R. N. (2003). *The courage to act: 5 factors of courage to transform business*.
Poorkavoos, M. (2016). *Compassionate leadership: What is it and why do organizations need more of it?*.
Rifkin, J. (2009). *The empathic civilization: The race to global consciousness in a world in crisis*. Tarcher.
Tagore, R. (2014). *Gitanjali*. General Press.
Ventura, M. P. (2018). *Applied empathy: The new language of leadership*. Touchstone.
Worline, M., & Dutton, J. E. (2017). *Awakening compassion at work: The quiet power that elevates people and organizations*. Berrett-Koehler.
Zsolnai, L. (2015). *The spiritual dimension of business ethics and sustainability management*. Springer.

Chapter 11
Doing Business with Conservation: Ecological Responsibility

> *Our planet is broken; humanity is waging war on nature. This is suicidal. Nature always strikes back—and it is already doing so with growing force and fury. Biodiversity is collapsing. One million species are at risk of extinction. Ecosystems are disappearing before our eyes. Deserts are spreading. Wetlands are being lost. Every year, we lose 10 million hectares of forests. Oceans are overfished—and choking with plastic waste. The carbon dioxide they absorb is acidifying the seas. Coral reefs are bleached and dying. Air and water pollution are killing 9 million people annually—more than six times the current toll of the pandemic. And with people and livestock encroaching further into animal habitats and disrupting wild spaces, we could see more viruses and other disease-causing agents jump from animals to humans. Today, we are at 1.2 degrees of warming and already witnessing unprecedented climate extremes and volatility in every region and on every continent. We are headed for a thundering temperature rise of 3 to 5 degrees Celsius this century.*

These are the challenges that Mr. Guterres, UN Secretary General voiced in his speech entitled State of the Planet at Columbia University on 2 December 2020. He also warned the world that:

> *The fallout of the assault on our planet is impeding our efforts to eliminate poverty and imperilling food security. And it is making our work for peace even more difficult, as the disruptions drive instability, displacement and conflict. It is no coincidence that seventy per cent of the most climate vulnerable countries are also among the most politically and economically fragile. As always, the impacts fall most heavily on the world's most vulnerable people. Those who have done the least to cause the problem are suffering the most. Even in the developed world, the marginalized are the first victims of disasters and the last to recover.*

Therefore, Mr. Guterres encourages every country, city, financial institution and company to adopt plans for a transition to net zero emissions by 2050, and to take decisive action now to put themselves on the path towards achieving this vision. He stressed that making peace with nature is the defining task of the twenty-first century. It must be the top, top priority for everyone, everywhere.

As I discussed in Chap. 8, one of Laozi's "three treasures" is conversation. Conservation is more meaningful and important to tackle today's ecological crisis. Conservation is emerging on the global stage with a new vision that emphasizes the

L. Zu, *Responsible and Sustainable Business*,
https://doi.org/10.1007/978-3-030-91117-1_11

importance of connecting nature and people. Interconnectedness of people and the natural world must guide conservation efforts (Kareiva and Marvier 2007). This is because just as Mr. Guterres described in his speech, today's global society is much further removed from nature than in the past. More than half of humanity now lives in cities, cut off from the daily realities of nature. This is especially true of the world's rich and powerful elites. Even more dangerous, the human impacts on nature are for the first time in human history so great that they threaten the planet's core biophysical functioning. We have reached, or will soon reach, dangerous thresholds of human activity that fundamentally threaten life (Sachs 2011).

Conservation efforts to preserve biological diversity must therefore find ways to draw upon novel ecosystems to meet the conservation goals of the future. Given that efforts to return these systems to their historical reference point are increasingly problematic in a rapidly changing world, we explore how ecosystem stewardship can contribute to conservation efforts and how accepting and exploiting the reality of novel ecosystems may facilitate these activities.

Therefore, ecosystem stewardship must be developed as a strategy to respond to and shape social—ecological systems under conditions of uncertainty and change to sustain the supply and opportunities for use of ecosystem services to support human well-being. These services include resources such as food, fuel and water, the capacity of ecosystems to regulate interactions among ecosystems (e.g., movement of water, fire or pollinators among ecosystems), the cultural connections between people and ecosystems and the underlying ecological processes that support these services. Stewardship is seen as a framework for managing these services under the environmental change scenarios predicted for the twenty-first century (Clark and Dickson 2003). The goals of this framework are to sustain required ecosystem services and support human well-being as societies attempt to improve the well-being of disadvantaged segments of an ever-growing human population. This program requires a global perspective to be successful and therefore must address changes that occur at scales ranging from local to global (Hobbs et al. 2013).

We must also integrate our gratitude and reverence into the principle of conservation. Such attitudes can help us enter into a direct relationship with life—a relationship of respect in which we are not higher or lower, but equal. And they help us relate to life with conscious recognition of how we are provided for by this planet and by the many people who have worked to feed us. Such attitudes keep us from felling distant from the many ways that life sustains us and bring closer to the real nourishment of life.

Taoism and Deep Ecology

Taoism's wisdom regards sustainability as the whole ecosystem, an interconnected web of life with its vast and rich diversity of species. It is in line with the principles of deep ecology, which considers the ecosystem as a living whole of which humanity is only one part. In this complex web of interrelationships all species are dependent upon each other, and it is this dynamic pattern of inter-relationship that needs to be sustained. No one part can be considered as separate from the whole, and the idea that the environment is just here to support our human civilization is a travesty of real environmental consciousness.

From the perspective of Taoism's wisdom, we know that the concept of sustainability moves beyond the Newtonian idea of humanity being separate from the world in which we live—the image of humanity and its environment. It does not see humanity as a "superior" species, which the rest of the ecosystem should support in a subservient manner, or that nature is for humanity to master and control. Rather than embracing a Darwinian concept of the survival of the fittest.

Laozi sees life from the perspective of cooperation and interdependence. It brings into question whether our present civilization, with its model of continued economic and material growth, is ethically or environmentally sustainable, whether it is right that our human needs and desires take precedence over the whole of creation, to the point of unprecedented species depletion, pollution, and destruction of natural habitat—as well as constellating a climate change that is bringing our whole ecosystem into a dangerous state of imbalance, And whether creation is an interdependent whole, how long we can all endure this present ecocide.

An interdependent ecosystem is closer to the dynamics of particle physics, which we begin to understand as underlying our physical world. Here not only is no one part separate from another, but everything is interacting, both locally and at a distance. And consciousness itself is not separate from physical reality. We are interdependent in ways we are only just beginning to understand. And yet we still live in a civilization dominated by an outdated Newtonian image of separation. Once we step into the reality of a holistic consciousness that is truly in "interrelationship" with the whole, we will find our self in a very different world in which everything is interacting with us in a continually dynamic state. Even our consciousness is affecting the physical world.

Prudence and Judgement for Visionary Leadership

Prudence and forethought are the proper qualities of a leader.
Reason and calm judgment:
The qualities especially belonging to a leader.
—Publius Cornelius Tacitus,
Roman historian and politician, AD 56-120

Those who lead people and serve the planet,
Shall hold firm to virtue of prudence.
To be prudent is to be forethought,
Those who are forethought have an abundance of virtue (of prudence),
Those who have virtue can rise to any challenges.
Those who can rise to challenges discover new sources of strength,
Those who can discover new sources of strength have power to lead.
Those who hold to virtue of prudence can thrive.

Fig. 11.1 Tree as a Metaphor of Laozi's wisdom of prudence

> *This is just like "planting tree roots deeply and firmly".*
> *This is the Tao of sustainability*
> —Laozi, Tao Te Ching, Ch. 59

Laozi claims that those who would lead people and serve the planet or in our modern word, the common good, need to develop virtue of prudence. Prudence enables leaders to perceive situations in all their complexity and uncertainty, and make wise decisions in accordance with this perception. Those who cultivate virtue of prudence are able to develop a good strategy to respond and mitigate challenges and risk, and navigate perfect storm in an uncertain world. The key logic Laozi made in this passage is that sustainable development is rooted in prudence in terms of conservation and preservation of human and natural resources. Prudence is declared to be the chief among all virtues. I want to use a tree as a metaphor to illustrate Laozi's wisdom of prudence.

Figure 11.1 shows that trees are symbols of the interconnectedness of life and represent the interwoven web of everything magical. Trees are not just pretty backdrops or landscape additions, they are wise, conscious beings, and they have been here on earth for an unthinkably longer time than we have. Leading an organization like planting a tree. Whether the tree is sustainable or not completely depends on the roots which uphold the tree. If the roots are planted deeply and firmly in the ground. The roots are able to spread out so that the tree can stand strong in the ground and grow strong and big, and produce fruits. Planting a tree requires us to identify right place and right time (prudence-foresight), well select the tree (forethought), and cultivate it with soil and water (virtues).

All the factors decide whether the roots can go deep into the ground and spread out. The deep and firm roots uphold the tree, particularly the truck to rise to any challenges in hard time, or in times of crisis. There's something visionary about them. They give a direction to where you're going, to the choices you're making. The depth of awareness or the depth of consciousness is what we see as part of the trunk of the tree. It's what brings the tree together, the roots and the branches. The trunk is a platform or a value base that one builds one's life on. The branches, which spread out into different areas. We sit in different branches as we explore the consequences of our deep experiences. The branches represent a planning stage regarding what we are doing in different aspects of our life. We explore the different branches, perhaps as a family person or perhaps as a student or a consumer or politician and so on. We have to integrate the values and visions from the roots and trunk into these different branches. The final level concerns the fruits of the tree. These are concrete actions, decisions made in concrete situations in your daily lived experience. Now we are living our values and our visions.

Prudence in Chinese means *"sè"*, it is about foresight, forethought, and providence in the use of resources. Prudence is the application of universal principles to particular situations. To be prudent means that one spends more time preparing and preventing than repairing and repenting. As the Chinese proverb goes, "*The more you sweat in peace, the less you bleed in war.*" This means that an anticipated outcome that is intended or that guides your planned actions. Prudence is one of the four classic western cardinal virtues. Aristotle recognized prudence is what makes it possible to decide correctly what is good and what is bad for man.

For Aristotle, prudence—*phronēsis*, sometimes rendered as "practical wisdom"—referred to the true prudence, as distinguished from what Aristotle calls "mere cunning," is oriented toward right ends. Taoism's wisdom is practical wisdom, and prudence of one of the most important virtues of Taoism's wisdom. Prudence—practical wisdom- requires good judgement to take each wise step. According to Aristotle, good judgment is about 'knowing how' more than 'knowing that,' is not at all reducible to logical rules or factual knowledge, and countless observers ever since have repeatedly verified that it is integrative, whole brain judgment drawing from well-digested experience, not abstract or specialist knowledge. Leslie Paul Thiele claims that practical wisdom, prudence, practical judgment, moral judgment, and political judgment are synonymous terms (Thiele 2006).

Prudence, however, is not merely an intellectual virtue; it is also a moral virtue. A moral virtue is a habit that makes its possessor good. One may be brilliant and learned without being morally good, but it is not possible to be prudent and not morally good. The prudent man is one who does the good, as opposed to one who merely knows the good. But since prudence deals in particulars, in the here and now of real situations, a number of other intellectual qualities are also necessary if one is to choose rightly, qualities that one does not necessarily acquire in a classroom setting. St. Thomas refers to these as integral parts of prudence, without which there is no prudence, just as there is no house without a roof, walls, and a foundation. If prudence is the proper application of universal principles to particular situations, then prudence demands that one continue to ponder the implications of the first principle of morality and the secondary precepts of natural law.

The common view of prudence is one of good deliberation: thinking things through, looking at options, considering the circumstances, and discerning an appropriate course of action. Laozi provided us with this principle of deliberation and forethought in Tao Te Ching. We can also learn the specific stages of how to think deliberately from St Thomas's theory of practical reason and prudence: The activity of reason goes through three stages. The first is deliberating the possibilities, in order to discover the means to the end; the second is making a judgement about the results of deliberation (so far this is like theoretic reason); but practical reason, which is connected to action, goes further: its third stage consists in executing the results of deliberation and decision. Since the last stage of action is the one closest to the whole point of practical reason, it is the principal act of practical reason and of prudence.

Examples of prudent people are helpful in clarifying the nature of right practical reason. For Aristotle it was Pericles, model statesman. When St. Thomas discussed different kinds of prudence, he added military leadership and household management, because both are practically oriented. The general (not his theoreticians or advisers) is the example of prudence, because he combines strategy with execution. He must think well, react quickly, and be good at organizing, communicating, and supervising the execution of the plan. The woman who somehow manages a home, family, and career is not usually in need of more theory or advice. Prudence in this demanding situation is more the ability to manage things, keep the schedule of events, juggle several things at once, respond to emergencies without panic, and maintain a level head in spite of fatigue or irritation.

Developing a Sustainable Future in a VUCA World

In this passage, Laozi mapped out a pathway to a sustainable future in a VUCA world. The Chinese classical philosophy emphasizes processes of change: the rhythm of the seasons, the rise and fall of empires and emperors, the alternation of poverty and affluence in society, the phases in human life from birth to death. Everything is in constant flux. A good example of Yin and Yang can illustrate the constant change. Yin and yang are opposites, but each concept implies its opposite. Yang stands for light, initiative, force and clarity. Yin represents darkness, passivity, flexibility and hidden qualities. The heavens are pure yang, the earth is pure yin. Change is the result of yin–yang interaction. This idea was elaborated in the Book of Changes, the Yi Jing, which offers a method of understanding situations and thinking about the future. This dialectical way of thinking—thinking in pairs of mutually opposing concepts—differs from Western logic. It accepts that something is the case and that the opposite is also the case. This acceptance of contradiction is related to the pragmatic emphasis in Chinese thinking: understanding that there are different opposing tendencies is more practical than deciding on a unique truth. Nobody can predict when and how change will happen. Laozi says,

> *"Good fortune leans on misfortune,*
> *Misfortune lurks behind good fortune.*
> *Who knows when one shall change to another?*
> *No paradigm can be followed.*
> *Normal can change to abnormal,*
> *Good can change to evil.*
> *People have been deluded for a long time."*
> —Laozi, Tao Te Ching, Ch. 58,

Laozi teaches us that "uncertainty is the only certainty there is, and knowing how to live with insecurity is the only security." We live in a new world, which is *interconnected, interdependent, nonlinear and volatile*. Over the past few decades, an acronym has emerged within the business community to identify the fundamental internal and external conditions that affect organizations within this more complex environment. This acronym is called VUCA, and it stands for volatility, uncertainty, complexity, and ambiguity. The Taoism's wisdom in this passage provides us with the principles of how to develop strategies for operating within this VUCA environment.

Figure 11.2 shows that achieving a sustainable future in an era of VUCA requires leaders to embrace virtue of prudence which combines memory to remember the past, intelligence to draw lessons in the present and foresight to use these lessons to anticipate wise action in the future. Prudence means "*seeing ahead, foresight, sagacity*", and is the ability to govern and discipline oneself by the use of reason. It is often associated with wisdom, insight, and knowledge. In this case, the virtue is the ability to judge between virtuous and vicious actions, not only in a general sense, but with regard to appropriate actions at a given time and place. Although prudence itself does not perform any actions, and is concerned solely with knowledge, all virtues have to be regulated by it. Distinguishing when acts are courageous, as opposed to reckless or cowardly, is an act of prudence, and for this reason it is classified as a cardinal (pivotal) virtue.

The function of prudence is to point out which course of action is to be taken in any concrete circumstances. It has nothing to do with directly willing the good it discerns. Prudence has a directive capacity with regard to the other virtues. It lights the way and measures the arena for their exercise. Without prudence, bravery becomes foolhardiness; mercy sinks into weakness, free self-expression and kindness into censure, humility into degradation and arrogance, selflessness into corruption, and temperance into fanaticism.

Building a sustainable future needs a prudent leader. Figure 11.1 illustrates, prudent leaders must have a foresight which can foresee and make provision for what may happen and advance consideration of future eventualities. Then, leaders must have an insight, which enables them to gain clear or deep perception of a complex situation or problem and grasp the inner nature of things intuitively. Insight might cause leaders to revise their forecast. After they move ahead with an action, their experience might cause them to revise their insight or their foresight. Foresight,

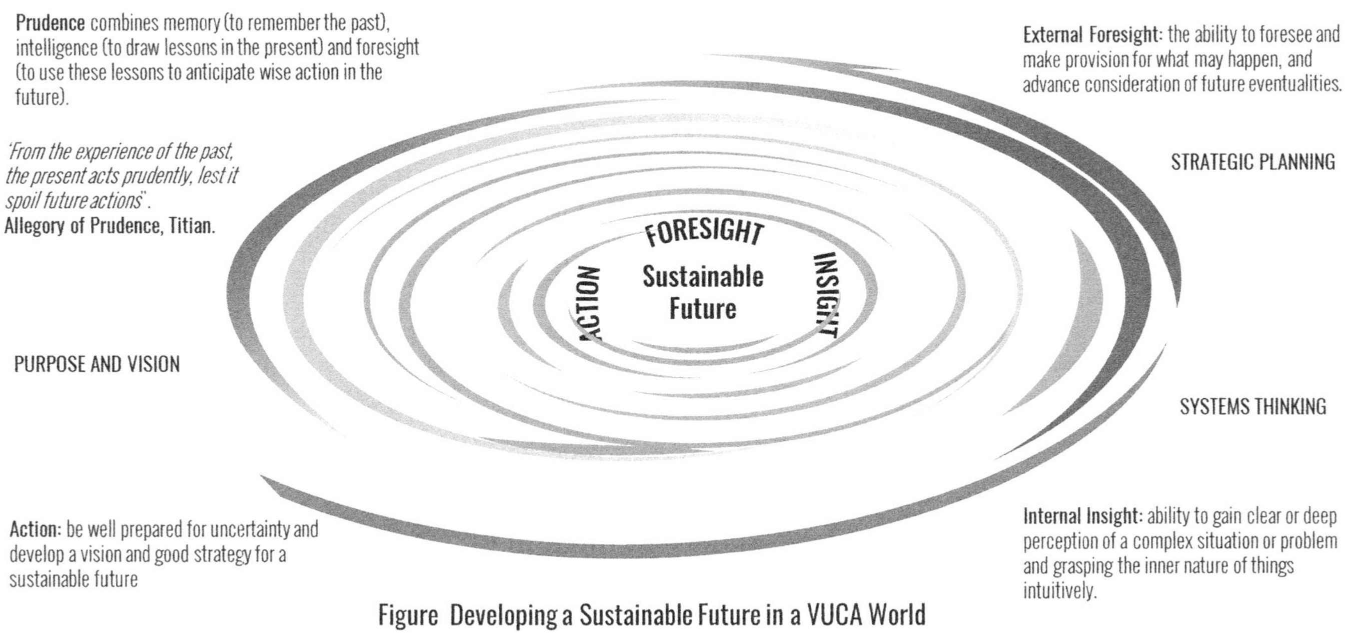

Fig. 11.2 Developing a sustainable future in a VUCA world. Source: the author adapted from Bob Johansen (2009), "Leaders Make the Future: Ten New Leadership Skills for an Uncertain World", and based on Tao Te Ching, Ch. 58

inevitably, links in some way to prudence. Prudence combines memory to remember the past, intelligence to draw lessons in the present and foresight to use these lessons to anticipate wise action in the future. 'From the experience of the past, the present acts prudently, lest it spoil future actions" (Allegory of Prudence, Titian). The goal of futures thinking is to use foresight to induce the kind of head-jerking turn that happens as you read a great story or play a great game: an abrupt shift in leader's thinking. Once leaders have had an insight, they can't go back to their old way of thinking. Insight changes them. Ultimately, foresight is about sense making in a future world where sense is in short supply. Our foresight was that the fun would become increasingly important for everyone because of all the uncertainty in the world around us. The VUCA world, our forecast suggested, will make the shared experience of fun and fear even more important. Everyone wants to have immersive fun experiences, but parents will be very concerned about safety.

Prudence is not only insight and foresight. It is also imperium or command. It directs the implementation of decisions expeditiously and with authority. Prudence is not timorous; leaders run great risks in making decisions. "Nobody," says Drucker, "learns except by making mistakes. The better a man is the more mistakes he will make—for the newer things he will try. I would never promote a man into a top-level job who has not made mistakes, and big ones at that. Otherwise, he is sure to be mediocre. Worse still, not having made mistakes he will not have learned how to spot them early and how to correct them." If arrived at prudently, a mistaken decision is not necessarily a wrong decision, just as a decision that turns out well is not right if it was imprudently made. A prudent decision may turn out to have been a mistake and an imprudent one a success because new factors came into play during implementation that could not be foreseen during the deliberation phase. It is advisable, therefore, not to judge a leader's capacity for prudential judgment on the basis of the results of just some of his decisions. Rather, it should be judged on the totality of the results achieved under his stewardship.

I found that the foundation principles of prudence naturally blend with VUCA Prime. The VUCA Prime was developed by Bob Johansen, distinguished fellow at the Institute for the Future and the author of Leaders Make the Future. The true leaders do not wait for the future passively. Instead of being negative about the VUCA term, they take proactive steps to shape it. Figure 11.2 shows that leading in a VUCA world is about transmuting Volatility to clarity of Vision; Uncertainty to Understanding; Complexity to Clarity and Ambiguity to Agility.

Leaders must learn how to make the future in an era of VUCA. The discipline of foresight can help leaders make better decisions today. We need not passively accept the future. It is hard to even think about the future if you are overwhelmed by the present, yet that is exactly the time when foresight can be most practical. A global futures perspective can help leaders make sense out of the chaotic patterns of change in the external world. Looking to distant possibilities can provide new insight for the present. Leaders are already experiencing volatility, uncertainty, complexity, and ambiguity, but many of their responses are not constructive and the prospects for leadership in the future are not secure. Some leaders will judge too soon and draw simplistic conclusions while others will decide too late and pay a price for their lack

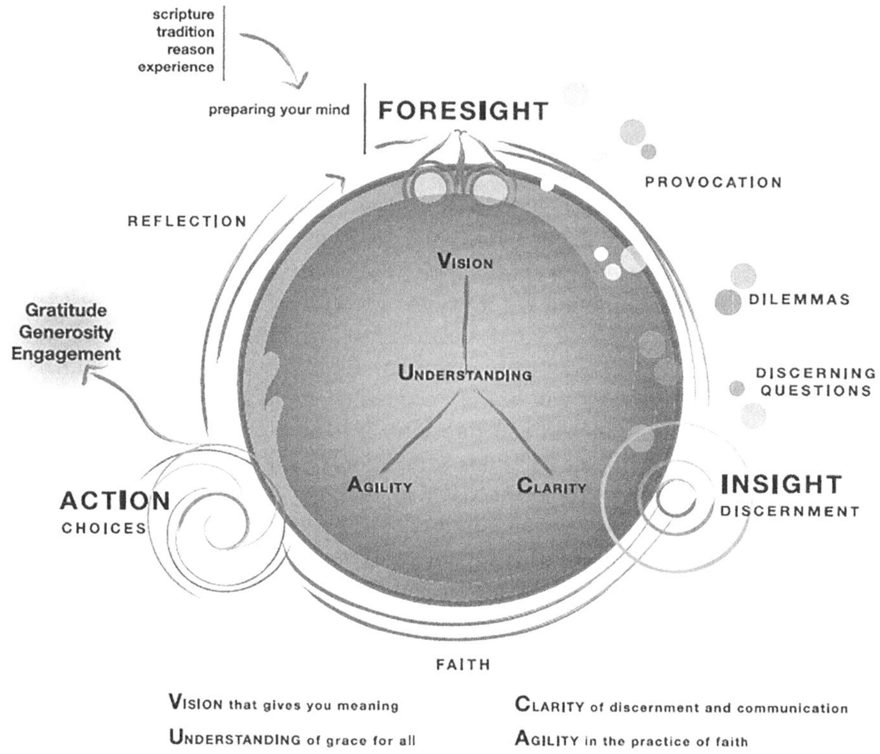

Fig. 11.3 Foresight to insight to action cycle. Source: Bob Johansen (2009), "Leaders Make the Future: Ten New Leadership Skills for an Uncertain World"

of courage or inaction. Some will be overwhelmed by a sense of helplessness while others will become cynical and question everything around them. Some will react with anger. Some will pick a side and start to fight. And some leaders will deny the crisis or truly believe that the chaos will just go away. Such leadership responses are both understandable and dysfunctional.

Leaders need not be overwhelmed and pummelled by the world of VUCA. The future will also be loaded with opportunities. Leaders must have the skills to take advantage of those opportunities, as well as the agility to sidestep the dangers (Fig. 11.3).

The case of COVID-19 pandemic reminds us that the future will be more volatile, more uncertain, more complex, and more ambiguous. To understand the future leadership skills, we must learn these emerging principles that form a profile for future leadership. The VUCA world of the future will be formidable and loaded with opportunities. The biggest danger is not being prepared—and we can control that by preparing ourselves and our organization. The best way to be prepared is to look many years ahead. Johansen claims that to survive and thrive in a VUCA world, leaders in the future will need to have Vision, Understanding, Clarity, and Agility.

These four skills will be able to turn the negative VUCA around with effective leadership that follows the principles.

Volatility Yields to Vision

Leaders need a compelling sense of the future they want to create. In a world of dilemmas, future intent is needed to provide a sense of focus and grounding. Bio-empathy helps to shape leadership vision, since natural principles provide important clues about where to go and what to avoid. Leadership vision must include a quest for new commons—new shared assets that a wider community can use in constructive ways. Leadership vision, however, should be carried out with your own personal style of quiet transparency and strength.

Uncertainty Yields to Understanding

Leaders need to immerse themselves in the cross-cultural worlds they will be serving, and they will need to listen and learn in order to figure out how to turn around the dilemmas they will face. Immersive learning ability will be critical to understand worlds that are unfamiliar and possibly threatening. Some situations will need to be depolarized before any progress can be made. Bio-empathy can help, since natural principles often yield new insights about what's really going on. Finally, the maker instinct provides curiosity to spur leaders on to a better understanding of what's going on and how things can be improved.

Complexity Yields to Clarity

Since clarity will be rewarded even if it is wrong, leaders need to be not only clear, but trustworthy, accurate, and transparent. The urge for clarity will seduce people toward polarities and extremes because absolute statements are comforting and are usually stated with great confidence. Clarity must be both compelling and simple—but not simplistic. Bio-empathy can help leaders make sense out of complexity and find a deeper clarity in the principles of nature. The best leaders will express clarity calmly and quietly yet powerfully in ways that people find meaningful. They will need to be very clear about the commitments they are making and the commitments they seek. There is a big difference between leadership clarity, which asks for commitment, and blind faith, which demands obedience. Shouting commands will not be enough.

Ambiguity Yields to Agility

Leaders need great flexibility within the frame of their vision. The best ones will have great agility making the future. Indeed, all the future leadership skills require agility in order to bring them to life:

- *The maker instinct encourages an ongoing cycle of new projects, which needs an agile mind to orchestrate them all.*
- *Clarity is like the martial arts principle of being cantered in the pit of your stomach, so you can respond with agility to attack.*
- *Dilemma flipping depends upon the agility of absorbing and reacting with creativity—without stumbling.*
- *Immersive learning ability often leads to disorientation, and you will need agility to recover your balance in the new setting where you are learning.*
- *Bio-empathy teaches agility in the form of resilience, a basic principle of successful natural systems.*
- *Constructive depolarization, which often necessitates delicate footwork, will be mandatory to cope with the extreme polarities of the future.*
- *Quiet transparency, a nimble balance of strength and humility, is the best leadership style for the future.*
- *Rapid prototyping is all about agility and learning on the fly. The best leaders will be perpetual prototypes.*
- *Smart mobs require dexterity to grow organically in the midst of fluid times, using various media.*
- *Commons creating demands a certain deftness to stretch into complex new territory where there can be multiple winners and shared assets.*

Leaders need to understand all of these future leadership skills, but don't need to do them all at once or all by themselves. These skills are challenging to master, but each of them can be learned and there are many resources. Moving from the negative VUCA (volatility, uncertainty, complexity, and ambiguity) to the positive VUCA (vision, understanding, clarity, and agility) will be the ultimate challenge for leaders in the future. As leaders of the future, they will need to have the future leadership skills in a mix that is all their own.

Case in Point: Prudent Leadership for a Better Future

Fan Li: Five Strategies for Successful Business in the Uncertainty

I'd like to start with the most famous and successful business leader in the ancient times, his name was Fan Li. He was also known as Lord Taozhu. Fan Li was a great politician and businessman in the Chinese history. He lived in the State of Yue in the

Spring and Autumn Period. Sima Qian, a Chinese historian highly praised Fan Li as "*a man who was very loyal to serve his country, courageous to triumph over the enemy, protected himself from calamity with his wisdom, and did great business for his wealth.*"

The ideas of Fan Li in politics and business had been shaped by Taoist thought. Thus, Fan Li was undoubtedly one of perfect representatives of Laozi's thought. Fan Li practiced Laozi's thought throughout his life. For example, after his successful political life in the government, Fan Li resigned and renamed himself Zhugong and began his career in business, farming and husbandry. Fan Li showed extraordinary talent in doing business. He had cashed in on business three times over 19 years. Fan Li was also a responsible business leader because when his business was flourished, he made a great contribution to the public welfare projects, therefore, he was well known for his social responsibility and regarded as a model of responsible business in Chinese history.

Fan Li's success in business was attributed to five strategies he developed built on his study of time and virtue of prudence in the uncertainty. The Tao of his success in doing business was "*to compete with the times, but not to blame others*". In other words, successful business is done by competing with the times, leveraging circumstances, grasping a good opportunity, rather than competing with specific people. Because the world is rapidly changing, those who want to be successful must understand the change. Those who know when the change will take place, must catch up with the change, and will become successful. We can discover the virtue of prudence and business philosophy he embraced from his five strategies of doing good business.

Strategy One: "seeking good business opportunity at the right time in uncertainty". Fan Li found out that the year in water was a bad year, the year in wood was a good year, the year in gold was a good year, the year in fire was a dry year, the year in earth was a neither-good-nor bad year. There was one good year, and one neither-good-nor bad year in every six years. There was a great famine in every twelve years. In an agricultural society, grain was the first commodity, and the fluctuation of grain price inevitably caused a series of fluctuations of other kinds of commodities. Therefore, if people wanted to do a good business in ancient times, they must understand the knowledge and phenomenon of astronomy, and particularly, be prudent.

Strategy Two: "when there was a flood, buying in carriages; when there was a drought, buying in boats". The best way to seize a good opportunity is to go against the trend. Fan Li advocated doing business with carriages in times of floods, and boats in times of droughts. Once the flood was over, the carriages would be scarce and the price would rise.

Strategy Three: "keeping coins flow". It referred to keep money awake, let it circulate to obtain the benefits with time. To increase the accumulation of wealth, cash should do the maximum turnover in the shortest possible time, so that goods and money flow around like flowing water. Since we want to speed up the circulation, we should not just pursue high prices and sell at small margins as fast as possible.

Strategy Four: "being prudent of expensive and cheap prices". The prices of good commodities are never stable, they are in the fluctuations, sometimes high, sometimes low, always in the process of transformation to the opposite side. In other words, when the price goes to the most expensive, it changes to the opposite of cheap; when the price becomes the cheapest, it goes to its opposite of expensive. Because when the price of goods is very expensive, it is bound to attract more people to engage in the production of this product, which leads to the low price; conversely, the price of a commodity is cheap, few people are willing to produce, then, the supply exceeds demand, the price rises.

Strategy Five: "When price of goods keeps rising, selling out just like throwing the garbage; when price of goods keeps declining, buying in just like gold and jade." According to the law of price fluctuations, when the price of a commodity is high, it should be sold out like dirt and garbage without hesitation, because the price will soon fall; when the price of a commodity is extremely low, it should be immediately brought in like gold and jade, because the price will soon rise. You must be courageous and decisive like a great entrepreneur.

Oil and Gas Industry

The oil and gas industry has experienced a turbulent few year. A combination of economic uncertainty, geopolitical risk and supply disruptions have fuelled volatility in oil and gas prices.

The recent 2021 Oil and Gas Industry Outlook issued by Deloitte in 2020 shows that global oil demand fell by 25% in April and it has rebounded sharply since then, cutting its losses to just 8%. Looking ahead, 2021 oil demand is expected to recover strongly but remain lower than pre-COVID-19 levels, about 4% lower in the base case and about 7% lower in Rystad Energy's second-wave scenario.4 Similarly, oil prices and energy stocks have underperformed base metals and the broader S&P 500 index by about 10–25% and 6–10%, respectively, between July to November 2020. Mass layoffs and heightened cyclicality in employment continue to challenge the industry's reputation as a reliable employer. US O&G companies laid off about 14% of permanent employees in 2020, and our research shows that 70% of jobs lost during the pandemic may not come back by the end of 2021 (Deloitte 2020).

The oil and gas industry are used to the highs and lows of economic cycles. The downturn caused by COVID-19, however, is unlike any other. With the survival of many companies at risk, coupled with a longer-term decline in petroleum demand, the next decade could look very different for the oil and gas market.

In our VUCA world, the Oil and Gas Sector's stuttering performance is having a considerable effect on the global economy. Many organisations are seeking to have dramatic cost savings in its supply chain. It may be ambitious, but ultimately, non-sustainable as suppliers find that they are unable to deliver sought savings over the long term and remain in business. The situation offers an opportunity to embrace innovation-driven change. Within the Oil and Gas context, prudent leaders must develop the new leadership literacies:

Vision: Leadership mindfulness that 'nudges' the organization in an empowering strategic direction. Technical innovation is embraced wholeheartedly capturing 'hearts and minds' in a compelling manner. Delivering common shared goals e.g., "Digital Dream: broadband in every home, e-governance". See, hear and feeling the impact of our Leadership 'shadow'. In Scandinavia the organizational question "Why did you feel it was necessary to shut down?" has changed to "Why did you feel it is safe to start up?"—nudging the organization in safe delivery.

Understanding: Clear communications gives focus, deeper knowledge and understanding. This facilitates multi organization collaboration where empowered people are supported in developing and maintaining operational excellence.

Clarity: An open culture where clarity of purpose is embedded into the organization with shared ownership of delivery. Advanced technology risks and rewards are balanced in a pragmatic cost-efficient manner. Leverage points are understood and optimized wherever possible.

Agility: Organisational agility is a 'watchword' for all. Opportunities to develop change capacity are grasped with vigour—this is the 'life blood' of the health and wellbeing of twenty-first century organization. An integrated supply chain brings value added to many facets of the business. This develops alliances that have shared ownership—installing pride in world -class delivery.

The oil and gas industry has always changed, and has caused changes in the societies in which it operates. The schismatic changes of the 1970s opened a new era. The combination of changes that the industry now faces requires epic rather than incremental responses, for the industry to evolve and prosper. Those responsible both inside and outside the industry need to try to understand what is happening now and how it may affect the future, to explain their strategies clearly and to adapt to new situations as they develop. In a world where technology and environmental threats are changing industries and society so rapidly, the slowly turning super tanker is not an image that excuses inertia in oil and gas companies and those who deal with them. All who are in the industry or who are involved with it need to share clear thinking about the future.

Navigate Perfect Storm in a Disrupted World

2020 has seen the whole world suffering the disruption in all areas, particularly massive societal change and demographic shifts. The lessons we all learned from the pandemic is how we can navigate perfect storm and thrive in tomorrow's disruptive environment. Deloitte issued an insight report by the end of 2020 which answer the question. It is also every timely case study for me to illustrate the virtue of prudence in Taoism's wisdom. Deloitte's report offers the government with three skills which can enhance capacities of navigating a disrupted world in the future: *foresight,*

Fig. 11.4 Navigating disruption in today's world. Source: Deloitte report, "How governments can navigate a disrupted world: Foresight, Agility, and Resilience" https://www2.deloitte.com/us/en/insights/economy/covid-19/governments-navigating-disruption.html

agility, and resilience (Fig. 11.4). I am sure that these skills are important not only for the government, but also for all leaders in other organizations.

While future events may not take the same shape as the pandemic, they will require leaders to navigate profound disruptions nimbly and effectively. Prudent leaders will need enhanced capabilities in three areas to help navigate both current uncertainties and tomorrow's more uncertain world (Eggers et al. 2020):

- *Foresight. Identifying forces and events that could place unprecedented demands on governments and their mission but could also create new opportunities for governments.*
- *Agility. Adjusting quickly to changes affecting customers, operations, and the broader ecosystem.*
- *Resilience. Withstanding and recovering from disruptions.*

Consider this metaphor: If your organization is a ship navigating dangerous waters, then foresight is your ability to anticipate changes in sea and weather, scanning the horizon for immediate threats and anticipating more distant hazards to be able to act in uncertainty. Agility is how quickly and effectively you can steer your ship to respond and adapt to unexpected conditions. Resilience is the ability of your ship and crew to withstand distress and disruption.

Sometimes, elements of all three abilities are lumped together as "strategic foresight," "future proofing," or increasingly during the pandemic, "resilience." This can be a useful conversational shorthand, but it's worth the effort to examine

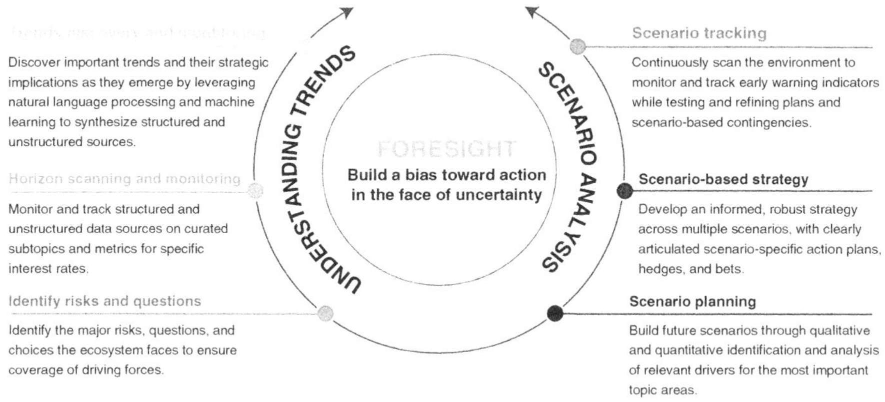

Fig. 11.5 Foresight approach to uncertainty, trends and risks. Source: Deloitte report, "How governments can navigate a disrupted world: Foresight, Agility, and Resilience" https://www2.deloitte.com/us/en/insights/economy/covid-19/governments-navigating-disruption.html

each ability separately to understand their distinctive qualities and how they fit together.

Foresight The current pandemic events have brought attention to the downside of disruptive change; effective foresight can be used to identify and embrace opportunities. Government looking ahead to the potential benefits of a disruptive technology such as AI is an example of foresight, focused on opportunity rather than risk.

Foresight abilities generally focus on two themes—understanding trends and uncertainties and analysing scenarios. Figure 11.5 lays out an approach to foresight planning, and how an organization could build a bias toward action in the face of uncertainty. While most government agencies should have some foresight capabilities, it doesn't necessarily require a separate foresight unit. Organizations can build these abilities through numerous avenues, engaging with academia, business, and others to understand risks and their implications.

Understanding Trends: Horizon Scanning, Monitoring, and Trends Discovery

Not all unpleasant surprises result from sudden events. Social behaviour, technology, and businesses are constantly evolving and can catch governments by surprise. Without the ability to sense emerging trends, government leaders and regulators risk finding themselves perpetually trying to catch up with changing citizen expectations, new business models, and innovative technologies. Sensing and horizon-scanning capabilities can help them stay ahead of the game.

Scenario Analysis: Strategy, Tracking, and Planning

Even if one attempts to understand ongoing trends, high impact "black swan" events such as the pandemic can always occur. Scenarios address such uncertainty not by predicting the future but by considering a range of possible futures. They help in perceiving risks and opportunities more broadly and developing strategies that could be used across multiple scenarios. Traditionally, scenarios are associated with longer-term futures and truly disruptive black swan events. But near-term scenarios also can be useful in times of great uncertainty. This can be seen in how scenarios are aiding governments as they move toward a post-COVID-19 world. Scenario planning, strategy, and tracking can help governments address uncertainty and disruption in the near and long terms (Fig. 11.6).

The specific form of scenario work will vary depending on factors such as levels of formality, openness, and time horizon. Classic scenario planning and strategy often focuses on the longer term—five to ten years in the future and beyond—crafting multiple futures against which various actions can be developed and tested. One can imagine several different paths the world may take as a result of COVID-19 and use these possible near-term futures or broader longer-term futures as a backdrop to consider the implications for any government agency.

Agility will be more important than ever in a post-COVID-19 world. Governments should institutionalize their ability to identify, act, and learn as circumstances change—capabilities that can be deployed not only in a crisis, but at all times. Agility requires organizational characteristics that allow resources, data, and staffing to flow and adapt as needed. This means, becoming an adaptable organization, driven by fast, flexible decision-making that learns and adapts constantly. It also requires a break from past orthodoxies. The agile organization should embrace

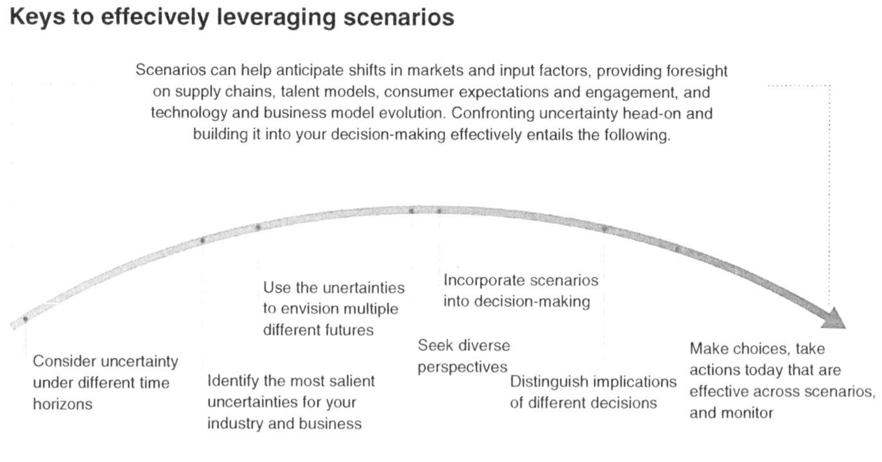

Fig. 11.6 Keys to effectively leverage scenarios. Source: Deloitte report, "How governments can navigate a disrupted world: Foresight, Agility, and Resilience" https://www2.deloitte.com/us/en/insights/economy/covid-19/governments-navigating-disruption.html

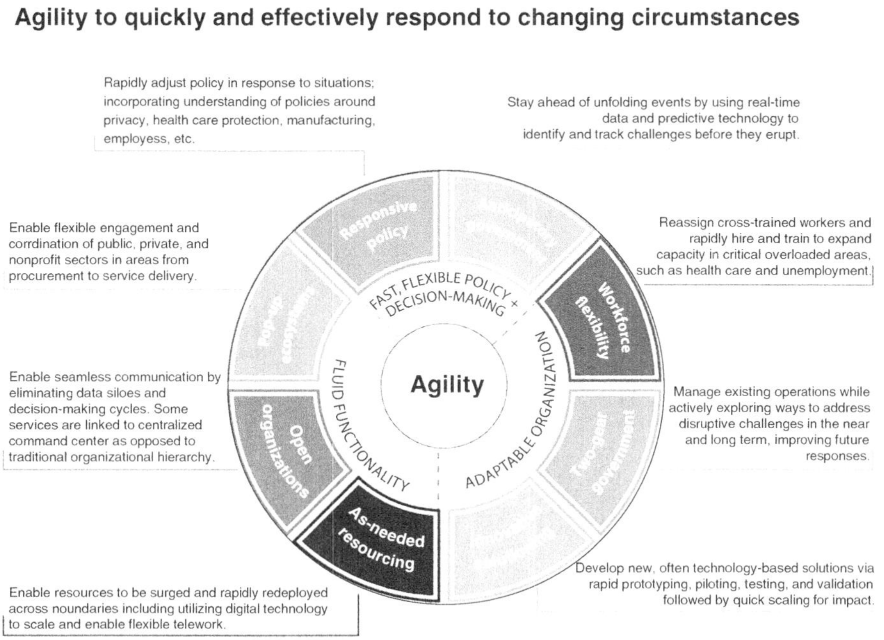

Fig. 11.7 Agility to quickly and effectively respond to changing circumstances. Source: Deloitte report, "How governments can navigate a disrupted world: Foresight, Agility, and Resilience" https://www2.deloitte.com/us/en/insights/economy/covid-19/governments-navigating-disruption.html

models that integrate not only across traditional boundaries between functions and units, but across the larger ecosystem, since disruptive change often alters the roles, relationships, and activities of interrelated parties (Fig. 11.7).

Policymaking traditionally moves in a "waterfall" fashion where design is done in a vacuum, and the failure points are only discovered when the finished item meets the real world—when it is too late to change. Changes after implementation often prove cost-prohibitive or politically impossible, so everything should be accounted for in advance. All too often, the result is slow, inflexible, and characterized by implementation failures caused by poor policy designs never tested in the real world. Responsive policy development is a core component of an agile government. This calls for rapid iteration and scaling to meet shifting needs and demands. Lessons learned from small prototypes, pilots, sandbox exercises, and staged rollouts can be used to avoid larger failures down the road.

Resilience Investing in resiliency can help organizations structure their processes, resources, and systems to better withstand future disruptions, so that performance will remain relatively unaffected or "bounce back" quickly (Fig. 11.8). The pandemic has prompted considerable discussion on making processes more robust for future pandemics. But government agencies also must be able to withstand as well as bounce back from shifting customer needs, technological innovation, economic and

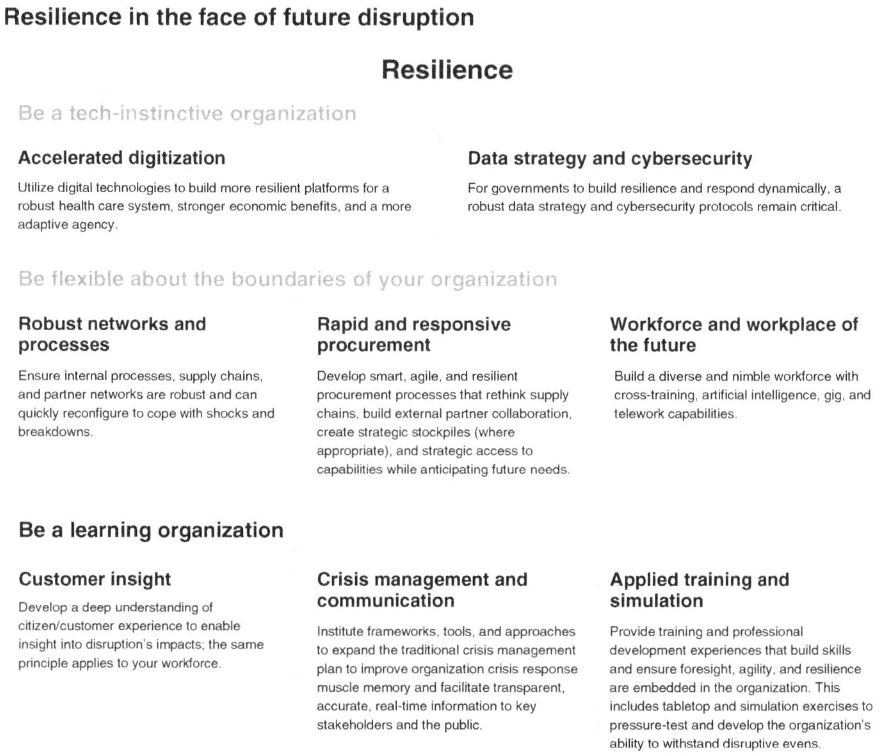

Fig. 11.8 Resilience in the face of future disruption. Source: Deloitte report, "How governments can navigate a disrupted world: Foresight, Agility, and Resilience" https://www2.deloitte.com/us/en/insights/economy/covid-19/governments-navigating-disruption.html

social upheaval, natural disasters, the actions of foreign powers, and more. If a crisis moves the organization to embrace telework, it shouldn't then become more vulnerable to a cyberattack; resiliency must remain robust in the face of all kinds of challenges, as well as in the face of growth in the scale and scope of the challenges faced.

To thrive in a world in which new challenges continue to evolve, building resilience isn't—and can't be—a "one-and-done" activity. The challenges are dynamic, so the approach to resilience should be as well. This means the organization should be a learning organization, investing in building and practicing the skills it needs to respond to disruption. A learning organization recognizes the importance of insight into the citizens it serves. The critical importance of customer experience has been reinforced by the pandemic, which has required segmenting the population into "at-risk," "essential workers," and so forth. To assess and improve resilience, agencies must understand the implications of disruption through the eyes of their customers, however they define them.

Deloitte's report has examined a series of abilities—*foresight, agility, and resilience, they are related, and best managed as an integrated portfolio*. Foresight can never be perfect, but greater agility can make up for imperfect foresight, just as better foresight improves agility by increasing lead times and easing demand on the organization. Resilience includes the investments in technology, people, and systems needed to support these key abilities. Contingency plans for agility, as well as the skills, practices, data, and IT infrastructure that goes with them, result from a focus on resilience. The resilient organization's embrace of uncertainty and change can lead to the institutionalization of foresight as a pervasive activity. While these interactions may seem obvious, they're often undercut in practice. Foresight may be only a quadrennial strategy exercise, with no real funding for monitoring and tracking. Agility can be promoted in IT investments, but the same organization may run some critical units "lean and mean," leaving no slack for an agile response. Resilience may be practiced with regard to natural disasters, but in investment decisions for IT infrastructure, managers may pursue labour savings rather than enhanced resilience. This piecemeal approach can undermine each ability and make the positive dynamics fostered by interaction impossible.

What's required is a cultural shift, one that recognizes that mission success requires the ability to anticipate, adapt to, and withstand disruptive events. Leaders should embrace these capabilities for the organization while developing their own skills in foresight, agility, and resilience. The pandemic has brought home the costs of acting without readiness for change. The ship of state is always sailing into unpredictable and potentially dangerous waters.

Case in Point: Joseph Is Prudent Leader

I want to close this section with the story of Joseph in Bible which could vividly to illustrate virtue of prudence.

In 2018 when I watched an Iranian TV series on Prophet Joseph, I found Joseph was really prudent and visionary leader. The series are replete with themes on filial love, personal journey through life (within family and on one's own), personal character, submission, prayer, prophethood, idolatry, monotheism, loyalty, betrayal, carnal desires, nature of various kinds of love, separation, abandonment, slavery, social organizations at various levels, nature of political authority, governance, strategy, various ideologies (and their implications), anticipation, and finally, forgiveness and salvation.

I remember well one of the stories in Bible about how Joseph accurately interpreted the Pharaoh's dreams, and that became a powerful leader for about decade's years in Egypt (Genesis 41: 40–41). Because of his prudent leadership, he was able to lead Egypt through seven years of plenty and the following seven years of famine.

The story goes like this. One day, Pharaoh, the king of Egypt sees himself standing over the Nile River, and, behold, there came up out of the River seven cows, handsome and fat of flesh, and they fed in the reed grass. And, behold, seven other cows came up after them out of the River, ugly and lean of flesh, and stood by the other cows upon the bank of the River. And the ugly and lean cows ate up the seven handsome and fat cows (Genesis 41:1–4). In the second dream, Pharaoh sees seven thin, shrivelled ears of grain swallow seven fat ears of grain. None of the wise men of Egypt can offer Pharaoh a satisfactory interpretation of his dreams. Then, the "young Hebrew slave," Joseph, is summoned from the dungeon to the palace. Joseph interprets the dreams to mean that seven years of plenty, symbolized by the fat cows and fat grain, will be followed by seven years of hunger, reflected by the lean cows and the shrivelled ears. The seven years of famine will be so powerful that they will "swallow up" and obliterate (destroy completely) any trace of the years of plenty.

After successfully interpreted the Pharaoh's dreams, Joseph then advises Pharaoh to deal with the situation: "Now Pharaoh must seek out a man with insight and wisdom and place him in charge of Egypt. A rationing system will have to be set up over Egypt during the seven years of surplus", Joseph explains, "in which grain will be stored for the upcoming years of famine." Pharaoh is blown away by Joseph's vision. "Can there be another person who has God's spirit in him as this man does?" Pharaoh asks his advisors. "There is none as understanding and wise as you," he says to Joseph. "You shall be over my house, and according to your word shall all my people be ruled; only by the throne will I outrank you." Joseph was thus appointed viceroy of Egypt.

The wisdom of Joseph's presentation to Pharaoh prove that he was a visionary and prudent leader who had insight, foresight and knew what and how to take action. Here is the essence of Joseph's wisdom: You must develop the virtue of prudence, never detach the years of plenty from the years of famine. When you experience plenty, do not let it blind your vision and desensitize you from what is truly important in life. The priorities you cultivate during your "good times" should be of the kind that will sustain you during your "bad times" as well.

Effectiveness vs. Efficiency: Doing the Right Things Right

To me success means effectiveness in the world,
That I am able to carry my ideas,
And values into the world—
That I am able to change it in positive ways.
—Maxine Hong Kingston

A good traveller leaves no traces.
A good speaker makes no slips.
A good reckoner uses no devices.
A well-shut door needs no bolts, and yet cannot be opened.
A well-tied knot needs no cord, and yet cannot be untied.
Therefore, great leaders always
Make the best of anyone, and no one is left behind.
Make the most of anything, and nothing is left to waste.

> *This is the paradigm of invisible wisdom.*
> —Laozi, Tao Te Ching, Ch. 27

Laozi's wisdom in this verse is really too mysterious and abstract to be understood. This is one of the verses in Tao Te Ching that is interpreted in different meanings and sometimes, very much confuse people. In fact, Laozi talks about the ecological wisdom here or the relationship between effectiveness and efficiency, or the two different concepts of leadership and management.

Laozi began with the metaphor of different actions that lead to different outcomes to illustrate the relationship between effectiveness and efficiency. For example, being a good traveller or passenger, no tracks are left whenever he travels; a good speaker make no slips whenever he speaks; a good accountant makes no miscalculation even he does not use calculator; a good locker keeps doors unlocked even he does not use bolts; and a good knotter keeps knots untied even he does not use cord. You might wonder how it is possible, and how it happens. That is why Laozi call it invisible wisdom, just like the light is covered in the earth, it is not easy for us to discover it. Thus, when you really discover it and learn it, you will be empowered with the wisdom and live a better life; when leaders discover and learn, you will become wise leaders.

This is one of the most important principles that Laozi expects leaders to learn and apply it in their life and work. Laozi describes the two important concepts, tactics and the impact in this passage. Furthermore, Laozi maps out the strategy for great leaders to build a sustainable organization and to best serve their organizations and the society as a whole. The Tao and tactics can be interpreted as effectiveness and efficiency from the perspective of modern management. Being a great leader, he or she must have a noble purpose, and be effective in what he or she does (doing the right things), and then executes efficiently what he or she wants to achieve (doing the things right).

From perspective of Taoism, effectiveness refers to efficacy of the Tao, and efficiency is concerned with tactics. The Tao has its particular efficacy. This efficacy is named in the title that Laozi was later given "Tao Te Ching". It is also translated as "*The Classical Scripture of the Way and its Efficacy*." Te is the efficacy or "power" (as it can be translated as well) of the Tao. Te is defined as morality (to do what is right) from a social perspective, and as inner power, efficacy and integrity from an individual perspective. Efficacy is the power or capacity to produce a desired effect. The word efficacy has to do with the ability or capacity to do something, but not about how something is done. Efficacy equals effectiveness, but different from efficiency. Effectiveness refers to successfully producing the expected or desired result; it's the degree to which you achieve your objectives, solve problems, and realize profits. In business, effectiveness is summed up by "doing the right things." Efficiency is the accomplishment of a job with the minimum expenditure of time, effort, and cost—the shortest distance between a goal and a checkmark. In business, efficiency is summed up by "doing the things right."

The difference between efficiency and efficacy is that efficiency means acting or producing with a minimum or waste, expense, or unnecessary effort, while efficacy has to do with whether or not something is able to be done at all, efficiency has to do with how something is done and whether or not it is done without must waste, effort, or time. Therefore, being effective means being adequate to accomplish a purpose; producing the intended or expected result. Being efficient means performing or functioning in the best possible manner with the least waste of time and effort.

Laozi uses the metaphor of people who achieve intended results in various areas to illustrate how important is for a great leader to combine effectiveness and efficiency to do the right things right to yield the most profitable and quickest route a leader can take to execute purpose. Laozi argues that great leaders must have the purpose, i.e., "to be good". They must have the purpose of doing the right things. Secondly, they must have the efficient instruments and tools to realize their purposes. The efficient way for good people in this passage are traveling without feet and vehicle, speaking without words, calculating without device, locking without bolts, and knotting without cord. Finally, the expected goals are no footprint and tracks, no spoken slips, no calculating mistakes, unlocked doors, and untied knots.

Why is it so important for leaders and organizations to adopt both principles of effectiveness and efficiency? It is easier to understand if we take a look at the metaphor of river and boat. Effectiveness is like river, efficiency like boat. Effectiveness is like rudder, and efficiency like paddle. Boat is useless without river, there is no way to cross a river without boat, there is no way to navigate without rudder, and there is no way to start voyage without paddle (to generate power). Kenichi Ohmae, the Japanese organizational theorist and management consultant has the same view, "Rowing harder doesn't help if the boat is headed in the wrong direction." Peter Drucker also said, "*There is nothing more wasteful than becoming highly efficient at doing the wrong thing*." Therefore, those who are effective but inefficient, are the victim of a frame-up, their strengths cannot be made full advantage of. Those who are efficient, but ineffective, cannot grow and thrive. Only are those who both effective and efficient are wise leaders and can achieve intended goals.

Another way to illustrate efficiency vs. effectiveness is with the 2 × 2 grid in Fig. 11.9. By referring to this chart, leaders can find an optimal balance between effectiveness and efficiency.

Quadrant I: Sustainable Business (Business Succeeds and Thrives): Highly Effective & Highly Efficient

Businesses that pursue the right purpose, integrate CSR and sustainability principles into their business strategy efficiently thrive and are sustainable. They can meet strategic targets earlier than anticipated, and can go on to meet more challenging strategic targets, so as to sustain their ability to thrive.

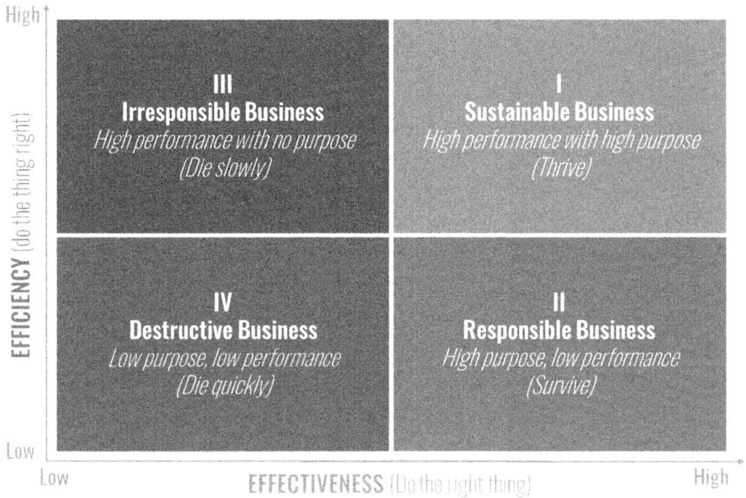

Fig. 11.9 Effectiveness vs. efficiency and four styles of business. Source: the author developed based on Laozi, Tao Te Ching, Chap. 27

Quadrant II: Responsible Business (Business Survives): Highly Effective & Inefficient

The business leaders articulate the right purpose for their organizations, but don't have the right strategy for using their limited resources. They show potential but never attain the growth that they should be capable of. This can be due poor management or inefficient practices.

Quadrant III: Irresponsible Business (Die Slowly): Ineffective & Inefficient

The business lacks a clear vision and right purpose of what it is trying to achieve, and so lacks the right strategies or has weak strategies on which to execute. The lack of clear strategies means that the short-term plans and tactics are lacking. As such the business delivers poor results for several years and are in a state of steady decline before the business eventually 'dies'.

Quadrant IV: Destructive Business (Die Quickly): Ineffective & Highly Efficient

Here the business is executing very well, but on the wrong strategies which drive it into a state of rapid decline. The business leaders are not learning from their mistakes, or are not aligned with the market's realities, and by doing so negatively compound the effects of their wrong strategies.

Organizations usually seek to increase and improve the efficiency of their operations and processes. After all, when working with limited resources, they would prefer to maximize the use of each of these resources, from natural resources, human resources, technology and time. However, by pursuing efficiency at all costs, some of these organizations are missing a valuable chance to take a step back and look at their overall effectiveness from a big picture perspective.

To be responsible and sustainable is to always pursue the top right box—pursuing the right goals and being efficient, by making use of resources and technological advances, not wasting time, and having better alignment and collaboration of between employees. Many organizations have their hearts in the right place—they know what goals they want to achieve, but are inefficient in achieving those goals. Other organizations are tightly run ships, with all employees working together, humming along and all singularly focused on the task at hand...but what if the task at hand is the wrong goal? For businesses to be sustainable they need to get both their efficiencies (right strategies) and effectiveness (right purpose) aligned—have the right direction and the right actions to help you bridge the gap between where you are now and where you want to be.

The purpose of the metaphor Laozi uses at the beginning is to let us have a better understanding of wisdom paradigm:

Great leaders always
Make the best of anyone, and nobody is left behind,
Make the most of anything, and nothing is left to waste.

As we discussed, the effectiveness focuses on value and purpose and is adequate to accomplish a purpose; producing the intended or expected result. When leaders know effectiveness first, they can care for all creatures whether they are good or bad. When the effective leaders care for all creatures, they need efficient methods and tools to fulfil their missions. Efficiency is about the ability to avoid wasting materials, energy, efforts, money, and time in doing something or in producing a desired result. In a more general sense, it is the ability to do things well, successfully, and without waste. It is also a great virtue. The goals of efficiency and fairness (equity) go hand in hand. Promoting fairness also promotes efficiency.

Figure 11.10 illustrates Laozi's wisdom paradigm. Laozi requires leaders to serve as the inclusive leader to build and maintain an effective, productive human and natural resources and in the meantime, to avoid the *pareto efficiency* which is a state of allocation of resources in which it is impossible to make any one individual better off without making at least one individual worse off.

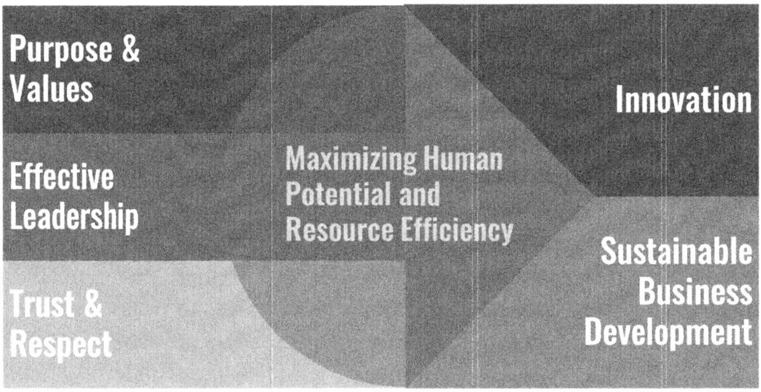

Fig. 11.10 Maximizing human potential and resource efficiency for sustainability. Source: author developed based on Tao Te Ching, Ch.59 and Michael C Bush (2018)

Purpose and values are important in new ways when it comes to maximizing human potential and succeeding. Purpose and values also are what leaders use to make decisions that cannot be made using spreadsheets and data analysis alone. They are the bedrock principles that guide executives' choices in complex, difficult matters—like hiring, firing, geographic expansions, doing more for customers, and mergers. When companies live out strong values, employees buy in figuratively while customers buy in literally. Given shifts in the business landscape toward a more purpose-conscious public, heightened transparency into companies, and increased expectations that business leaders will lead on social issues, meaningful values are only growing more valuable.

Effective leadership means connecting with your teams on a strategic and personal level, unlocking the full potential of your people and your organization. In practice, this means:

- *Forging meaningful, respectful, caring relationships with employees in a fundamentally fair way*
- *Establishing high levels of interpersonal trust and successful collaboration within the executive team itself*
- *Creating and communicating a coherent strategy that cascades to every level of the organization*
- *An executive team that reflects the demographics of the organization and the wider community*

Trust and respect are the cornerstone of effective leadership. Trust and respect are one of the cornerstones of integrity and character. It is a genuine will to lead and behave "at cause" and to become known to "do the right things". Trusted and respected leaders have a proven track record that they consistently do what they said they would, and don't break promises no matter how large or small. That is also what is considered to be an important tenet of integrity. Trust—specifically, a relationship of trust between employees and leadership—remains as important today as it was then. That's because while business conditions have changed dramatically, people are still people. Trust is a universal requirement for positive interactions. How do you build a high-trust culture? We believe the key elements of trust are credibility, respect, and fairness. Employees trust leaders when they see them as credible, as respectful, and as fair. Leaders must behave in a scrupulously fair way and demonstrate respect to everyone in the organization. They also must show themselves to be competent in running the business and consistent in living up to their word.

Maximizing human potential is pivotal to business success as a leader and a business. It requires leaders to bring out the best in their people—all of them. Enabling them to reach their potential as human beings; to be as creative, knowledgeable, and productive as possible. This means leaders are reaching heights they may not have thought possible in terms of projects they undertake, skills they develop, inspiration they feel.

Innovation When organizations maximize human potential through effective leadership, meaningful values, and a foundation of trust, good things happen. One of them is innovation. At a time when new competitors can spring up suddenly across the globe, organizations today must innovate constantly—in terms of new products, new business lines, and internal systems to optimize efficiency and profitability. In recent years, it has become clear that listening to the "wisdom of the crowd" and seeking good ideas from everywhere leads to better results. What's needed today is what might be called Innovation by All. That is, tapping the insights and ideas of employees from every level of the organization.

Sustainability is now the key driver of innovation. The findings of Nidumolu, Prahalad and Rangaswami's research show that sustainability is a mother lode of organizational and technological innovations that yield both bottom-line and top-line returns. Becoming environment-friendly lowers costs because companies end up reducing the inputs they use. In addition, the process generates additional revenues from better products or enables companies to create new businesses (Nidumolu et al. 2015). Because those are the goals of corporate innovation, they find that smart companies now treat sustainability as innovation's new frontier. The quest for sustainability is already starting to transform the competitive landscape, which will force companies to change the way they think about products, technologies, processes, and business models. The key to progress, particularly in times of economic crisis, is innovation. By treating sustainability as a goal today, early movers will develop competencies that rivals will be hard-pressed to match. That competitive advantage will stand them in good stead, because sustainability will always be an integral part of development.

The practical wisdom of Taoism in this section has applied in the business world. For example, built on the relationship between effectiveness and efficiency, Stack (2006) creates 3 T leadership: *Strategic Thinking, Teamwork, and Tactics*. She argues that twenty-first-century leaders and managers can obtain profitable, productive results by managing the intersection of two critical values: effectiveness and efficiency. Effectiveness, Stack says, is identifying and achieving the best objectives for your organization—doing the right things. Efficiency is accomplishing them with the least amount of time, effort, and cost—doing things right. If you're not clear on both, you're wasting your time. As Drucker put it, "There is nothing so useless as doing efficiently that which should not be done at all (Stack 2006)." Stack's 3 T Leadership offers the practices that will enable executives to be effective and efficient.

Eco-Effectiveness vs. Eco-Efficiency: From Cradle to Cradle

Laozi's ecological wisdom, "*make the most of anything, and nothing is left to waste*" has been validated by modern science and has more significance for today's environmental sustainability. When we apply Laozi's ecological wisdom in our modern world, we must start from transformation of our traditional thinking as indicated in Figs. 11.11 and 11.12, e.g., from "*cradle to grave*" *to* "*cradle to cradle*", from "*reductionist thinking*" *to* "*systems thinking*". Michael Braungart and William McDonough, scientists and authors of "Cradle to Cradle: Remaking the way we make things (2002*)*" and "The Upcycle: Beyond Sustainability—Designing for Abundance (2013)" have made a great contribution to building a sustainable world in recent years.

Cradle to Cradle design (also referred to as Cradle to Cradle, C2C, cradle 2 cradle, or regenerative design) embraces the ecological wisdom of Taoism. C2C has been promoted as a biomimetic approach to the design of products and systems. It models human industry on nature's processes viewing materials as nutrients circulating in healthy, safe metabolisms. It suggests that industry must protect and enrich ecosystems and nature's biological metabolism while also maintaining a safe, productive

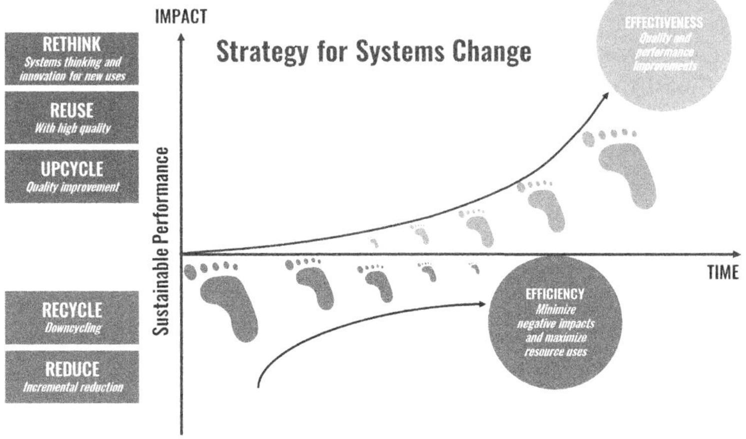

Fig. 11.11 Eco-effectiveness and eco-efficiency for sustainability. Source: Adapted from Cradle to Cradle. https://epea.com/nl/en/about-us/cradle-to-cradle. Retrieved on 28 October 2020

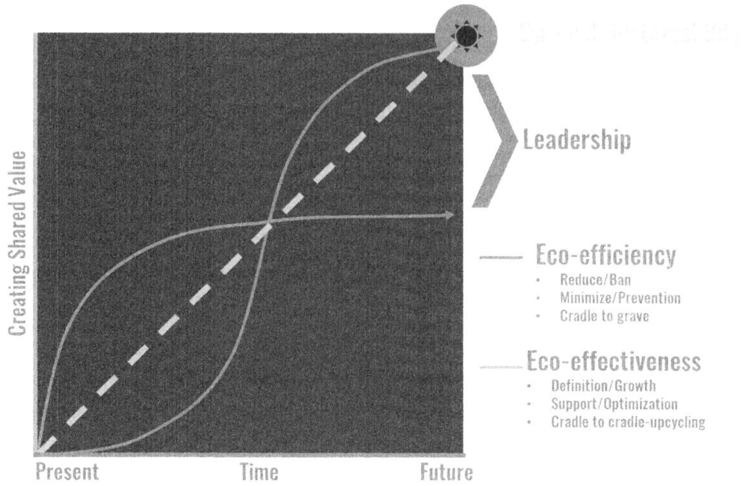

Fig. 11.12 Eco-effectiveness, shared value and sustainable development. Source: adapted from Ignasi (Cubina 2009), "From Efficiency to Eco-effectiveness"

technical metabolism for the high-quality use and circulation of organic and technical nutrients. Put simply, it is a holistic economic, industrial and social framework that seeks to create systems that are not only efficient but also essentially waste free. The model in its broadest sense is not limited to industrial design and manufacturing; it can be applied to many aspects of human civilization such as urban environments, buildings, economics and social systems. Transformation from "cradle to grave" to "cradle to cradle", implies that the C2C model is sustainable and considerate of life and future generations.

Eco-efficiency has been proposed as one of the main tools to promote a transformation from unsustainable development to one of sustainable development. It is based on the concept of creating more goods and services while using fewer resources and creating less waste and pollution. The term was coined by the World Business Council for Sustainable Development (WBCSD) in its 1992 publication "Changing Course," and at the 1992 Earth Summit, eco-efficiency was endorsed as a new business concept and means for companies to implement Agenda 21 in the private sector. As defined by WBCSD, "eco-efficiency is achieved by the delivery of competitively priced goods and services that satisfy human needs and bring quality of life, while progressively reducing ecological impacts and resource intensity throughout the life-cycle to a level at least in line with the Earth's estimated carrying capacity." "Eco-efficiency combines the goals of business excellence and environmental excellence, and creating the link through which corporate behaviour can support sustainable development."

Figure 11.11 shows that eco-efficiency begins with the assumption of a one-way, linear flow of materials through industrial systems: raw materials are extracted from the environment, transformed into products, and eventually disposed of. In this system, eco- efficient techniques seek only to minimise the volume, velocity, and toxicity of the material flow system, but are incapable of altering its linear progression. Some materials are recycled, but often as an end-of-pipe solution, since these materials are not designed to be recycled. Instead of true recycling, this process is actually down-cycling, a downgrade in material quality, which limits usability and maintains the linear, cradle-to-grave dynamic of the material flow system. In contrast to this approach of minimisation and dematerialisation, the concept of eco-effectiveness proposes the transformation of products and their associated material flows such that they form a supportive relationship with ecological systems and future economic growth. The goal is not to minimise the cradle-to-grave flow of materials, but to generate cyclical, cradle-to-cradle "metabolisms" that enable materials to maintain their status as resources and accumulate intelligence over time (upcycling). This inherently generates a synergistic relationship between ecological and economic systems, a positive recoupling of the relationship between economy and ecology.

Figure 11.11 also indicates that the perspective on sustainability is different in a circular economy (systems thinking, effectiveness, reuse and upcycling, etc.) than in a linear economy (efficiency, recycle, reduce, and down-cycling, etc.). When working on sustainability within a linear economy, the focus is on eco-efficiency. This is to minimise the ecological impact for the same output. This will extend the period in which the system becomes overloaded (Di Maio et al. 2017).

Within a circular economy, sustainability is sought in increasing the eco-effectiveness of the system. This means that not only the ecological impact is minimized, but that the ecological, economic and social impact is even positive (Kjaer et al. 2019). This difference can be illustrated with the production of beef. Raising cows for beef results in emissions of methane gas, a strong greenhouse gas. In a linear economy, the production of beef is made more sustainable by changing the way cows are fed, so that they emit less methane gas for the same amount of meat. This makes production more eco-efficient. In a circular economy, production is made more sustainable by not making beef from cows, but by imitating it as a meat substitute. For the beef substitute, plants are then grown that contribute to biodiversity, employment and landscape management. In this way, the ecological, economic and social impact of the same production of beef is increased.

Figure 11.12 illustrates another example of how eco-effectiveness system can create shared value to the society as a whole. Creating shared value (CSV) is a business concept first introduced in Harvard Business Review article "*Strategy & Society: The Link between Competitive Advantage and Corporate Social Responsibility*" (Porter and Kramer 2007). The central premise behind creating shared value is that the competitiveness of a company and the health of the communities around it are mutually dependent. Recognizing and capitalizing on these connections between societal and economic progress has the power to unleash the next wave of global growth and to redefine capitalism. Companies can create shared value opportunities in three ways:

- *Reconceiving products and markets—Companies can meet social needs while better serving existing markets, accessing new ones, or lowering costs through innovation*
- *Redefining productivity in the value chain—Companies can improve the quality, quantity, cost, and reliability of inputs and distribution while they simultaneously act as a steward for essential natural resources and drive economic and social development*
- *Enabling local cluster development—Companies do not operate in isolation from their surroundings. To compete and thrive, for example, they need reliable local suppliers, a functioning infrastructure of roads and telecommunications, access to talent, and an effective and predictable legal system*

Many approaches to CSR put businesses against society, emphasizing the costs and limitations of compliance with externally imposed social and environmental standards. CSV acknowledges trade-offs between short-term profitability and social or environmental goals, but focuses more on the opportunities for competitive advantage from building a social value proposition into corporate strategy.

Ecological accounting challenges: a significant challenge of CSV resides in accounting for ecological values and costs that are generated within the realm of agricultural production. Up to 90% of the ecological footprint in food processing can be attributed to land management activities outside the control of corporations. An eco-commerce model that accounts for ecosystem services at the production unit (farm) level allows "shared value" to emanate from the production unit outward. Centering the shared value at the farm level allows for utilities, biomass processors, food processors, environmental liability insurers, landlords, and governments to participate in the shared value process (Gieseke 2011). This eco-commerce shared value process accounts for and includes positive (environmental) externalities within the economic system.

Most systems designed for eco-efficiency are based on getting more output from less input. Some of these systems may be based on dematerialization, extended life of the product, multiple recycling, reducing pollution or toxicity, or obtaining more output from the resources. These strategies are all based on a linear flow of materials from their source to the landfill, or from cradle to grave. (Braumgart 2002) proposed a five-step system that leads to eco-effectiveness, or cradle to cradle.

Get Free of Known Undesirable Substances There are many substances that are known to be harmful and thus undesirable in products utilized by businesses or consumers. Most companies are not aware of the toxicological impact of substances in products through their supply chain. However, they should have a general knowledge of the most dangerous substances in their products. These are referred to as X-substances when referred to eco-effectiveness. For companies like this, a first step in moving toward eco-effectiveness is to find replacements for the X-substances in their products. This includes substances like mercury, cadmium, and lead that are known or suspected carcinogens, polyvinylchloride (PVC), mutagens, or endocrine disruptors. Removal of X-substances is almost always a step in the right direction, but such an approach has to be applied carefully to ensure that replacement substances are indeed better than those that are replaced.

Follow Informed Personal Preferences Once the most undesirable substances have been removed from a product, the next step is to begin to make educated choices about those substances that should be included in the product. The best way to do this may be to have a detailed knowledge about the impacts of a particular substance on ecological and human systems throughout its life cycle. But this is often impractical or even impossible. Furthermore, different substances may have different types of impacts in different end products. Some products may require an additive that could be one of several different materials. Each of these may have a different impact such as persistency in the environment, contribute to climate change, or harm plant life. Without a detailed scientific knowledge of a substance's toxicological profile and its fate throughout the life cycle of a product, these decisions can be difficult to make. Sometimes it may be necessary to bring a product to the market without really knowing the eventual impact. Without complete knowledge of these substances, the best way to make decisions about which chemicals and materials to include in a product comes down to personal preferences based upon the best available information. Though decisions guided by personal preferences may not always result in the most eco-effective design choices, they generally will result in a product that is at least less bad than its predecessors. Although it is "less bad," it is on its way to become eco-effective.

Creating a "Passive-Positive" List This step includes a systematic assessment of each ingredient in a product to classify it according to its toxicological and eco-toxicological characteristics, especially its capability to flow within biological and technical metabolisms. For products of consumption, the criteria to examine should include impacts like toxicity to humans (acute, delayed, developmental, reproductive), aquatic toxicity, persistence and bioaccumulation in nature, sensitization potential, mutagenicity, carcinogenicity, and endocrine disruption potential. Based upon the assessment of a material or chemical according to these criteria, a passive positive list can be generated, which classifies each substance according to its suitability for the biological metabolism. This list can be used to determine the degree of additional optimization necessary for a particular product to be a true product of consumption. One can also use this process for service-type products although the impacts may be different. Cadmium, for instance, is a highly toxic heavy metal and is often applied in photovoltaics in the form of cadmium telluride which may not necessarily be bad. Although cadmium telluride is not an ideal substance from an ecological perspective, its application in photovoltaics as a product of service may be considered acceptable until something better is found and employed.

Activate the Positive List In this step, the objective is to determine which component materials provide a positive technical or biological nutrient. In the step three, the objective is to optimize the amount of the material to minimize its impact, whereas in the step four, the objective is to optimize the component to its fullest extent. An example is an upholstery fabric whose constituent materials are positively defined as biological nutrients. This was designed by McDonough and Braumgart and others for a German company and is a completely biodegradable and compostable fabric. Each component was selected according to the manufacturer's positive listing methodology for its positive environmental and human health characteristics and its suitability as a biological nutrient.

Reinvention The concept of reinvention addresses the interconnected nature of ecological, social, and economic systems by considering the biological and technical impacts of existing product and service forms. Strategies for reinvention view products from the perspective of the services they provide and the needs they fulfil for customers. They also consider the broader context of social and ecological systems. While most companies try to design a product with minimal negative impacts, reinvention considers the design of a product with maximum positive impacts. An example may be to design a car whose emissions can be considered nutritious for nature or industries. Perhaps it could burn a fuel that emits water vapour that can be turned back to water and used for some end purpose. Or perhaps the carbon dioxide released from the exhaust can be captured and converted to carbon, which can be used in the manufacture of rubber tires. As more cars are manufactured and driven in the world, more nutrition will become available. This five-step process to develop an eco-effective product, system, or service will take a trial-and-error process along with time, effort, money, and creativity.

Eco-efficiency is not limited simply to making incremental efficiency improvements in existing practices and habits. It should stimulate creativity and innovation in the search for new ways of doing things. Nor is eco-efficiency limited to areas within a company's boundaries, such as in manufacturing and plant management. It is also valid for activities upstream and downstream of a manufacturer's plant and involves the supply and product value chains. Consequently, it can be a great challenge to development engineers, purchasers, product portfolio managers, marketing specialists and even finance and control. Companies can use eco-efficiency as an integral cultural element in their policy or mission statements. They can also set eco-efficiency objectives for their environmental or integrated management systems. And it is a useful tool for monitoring and reporting performance, and for helping the firm's communication and dialogue with its stakeholders.

However, developing an optimal sustainability for the future requires effective leaders to transform mindsets from efficiency to effectiveness by creating shared value to the society. The bridging the gap between sustainable and unsustainable development lies in leadership, and therefore, development of effective leadership is essential.

The Case in Point: Diderot Effect and Sustainable Consumption

Those who seal opening and shut doors of desires
Prevent calamity from life;
Those who widen opening and indulge in desires
Bring no hope to life.
Those who can discern subtleties,
Underlying trends and events are wise.
—Tao Te Ching, Ch. 52

When we apply the wisdom of prudence in our life, Laozi requires us to shut all senses of our organs, in other words, to cleanse and purify our minds and hearts, get rid of our own greed, self-indulgence, self-interest, short-sightedness and competition, and to avoid securing more than we need or limit where resources would naturally flow. Then we are able to prevent all dangers and troubles from happening in our life.

The wisdom of "*discerning the subtleties underlying trends and events are wise*" teaches us to be prudent, we must have foresight and insight to anticipate development trend of things, identify keenly opportunities and avoid risks and calamity. They should find the truth from everything that others ignore, and observe carefully the subtle from all things, care about it and analyse it insightfully.

However, if we cannot hold to the principle to restrain us from indulging ourselves in possessions, we are not only threatening our own health, prosperity and well-being, but our very future. Mahatma Gandhi says "*Earth provides enough to satisfy every man's needs, but not every man's greed.*" We have observed the phenomena: the global temperature is rising, the ice caps are melting, and levels of pollution across the world have reached unprecedented heights. We have seen *"the vanishing face of Gaia"* (Lovelock 2009). According to eminent scientist James Lovelock, in order to survive an assault from her dependents, the Earth is lurching ever closer to a permanent "hot state." Within the next century, we will almost certainly be forced to give up many of the comforts of western living as supplies are threatened. Only the fittest—and the wisest—will survive.

The wisdom of Laozi offers an essential wake-up call for the human race. Let me start with two different stories from China and France to illustrate the Diderot effect.

The effect was first described in Diderot's essay "*Regrets on Parting with My Old Dressing Gown*". In the paper, he tells how the gift of a beautiful scarlet dressing gown leads to unexpected results, eventually plunging him into debt. Initially pleased with the gift, Diderot came to rue his new garment. Compared to his elegant new dressing gown, the rest of his possessions began to seem tawdry and he became dissatisfied that they did not live up to the elegance and style of his new possession. He replaced his old straw chair, for example, with an armchair covered in Moroccan leather; his old desk was replaced with an expensive new writing table; his formerly beloved prints were replaced with more costly prints, and so on. "I was absolute master of my old dressing gown," Diderot writes, "but I have become a slave to my new one . . . Beware of the contamination of sudden wealth. The poor man may take his ease without thinking of appearances, but the rich man is always under a strain."

The Diderot Effect is also called "*the Matching Effect*", which means "*the more one get, the more he needs.*" One usually feels balanced when he hasn't got a certain thing, so he could live a stable life. However, once he gets a certain thing, he starts to feel dissatisfaction instead and thinks that he should get more. The Diderot Effect states that obtaining a new possession often creates a spiral of consumption which leads you to acquire more new things. As a result, we end up buying things that our previous selves never needed to feel happy or fulfilled.

Another story about the ivory chopsticks which happened in Zhou of Shang Dynasty. About 4000 years ago, King Zhou of Shang had a pair of chopsticks made of ivory. His wise minister, Jizi felt very worried. Jizi knew that the ivory chopsticks couldn't be matched with ordinary pottery, one must want to have the precious cups made of rhinoceros horn or jade to match with it. And then the vegetarian soup made of beans wouldn't match with the jade cup and ivory chopsticks, and must be used for rare delicious such as yaks, elephant or leopard foetus, and that when one ate yaks, elephants or leopard foetus, he wouldn't be wearing short clothes made out of coarse cloth and wouldn't be living in a thatched hut; instead, he would be wearing multi-layered clothes made out of brocade and living in spacious horse and towers. If he continued to pursue things like these, all the wealth in the world wouldn't be enough for him to enjoy or squander.

Jizi was quite afraid that his would bring about unintended consequence, so he felt great fear for such a beginning. After five years, King Zhou of Shang entertained himself with the "tree of meat", started the "hot bronze pillar" torture, and mounted the hill piled up with distillers' grains to look down at ponds filled up with wine. King Zhou also started to kill his officials and subjects cruelly. Finally, the people rebelled and put an end to the Shang Dynasty and King Zhou's life.

That was why when he observed the ivory chopsticks, Jizi was afraid of "Diderot Effect" which would brought the disasters to his country. The Diderot effect states that purchasing one item can lead to a shopping spree of more things. The Diderot effect is a social phenomenon related to consumer goods that comprises two ideas. The first posits that goods purchased by consumers will be cohesive to their sense of identity, and as a result, will be complementary to one another. The second states that the introduction of a new possession that is deviant from the consumer's current complementary goods can result in a process of spiralling consumption.

Sociologist and economist Juliet (Schor 1999) use the term in her bestselling book, *"The Overspent American: Why We Want What We Don't Need" to* describe processes of competitive, status-conscious consumption driven by dissatisfaction. Schor's 2005 essay "Learning Diderot's Lesson: Stopping the Upward Creep of Desire" explains the effect in contemporary consumer culture in the context of its negative environmental consequences. The term has become common in discussions of sustainable consumption and green consumerism, in regard to the process whereby a purchase or gift creates dissatisfaction with existing possessions and environment, provoking a potentially spiralling pattern of consumption with negative environmental, psychological and social impacts.

The Diderot Effect has been espoused by the green movement as well. They use the same language, replacing existing wasteful goods with more durable, cleaner, more responsibly-made goods. Eventually, when we learn how such things are made, and how many "products" there are in the "ecological line," we stop being the people who buy a few green things and become people whose life is based on making sustainable choices.

References

Braumgart, W. M. M. (2002). *Cradle to cradle: Remaking the way we make things*. North Point Press.

Bush, M. C. (2018). *A great place to work for all*. Berret-Koehler Publisher.

Clark, W., & Dickson, N. (2003). Sustainability science: The emerging research program. *Proceedings of the National Academy of Sciences of the United States of America, 100*, 8059–8061. https://doi.org/10.1073/pnas.1231333100

Cubina, I. (2009, November, 2009). *From efficiency to eco-effectiveness*. European Conference on Waste Reduction Barcelona.

Deloitte. (2020). *2021 Oil and gas industry outlook*.https://www2.deloitte.com/us/en/pages/energy-and-resources/articles/oil-and-gas-industry-outlook.html

Di Maio, F., Rem, P. C., Baldé, K., & Polder, M. (2017). Measuring resource efficiency and circular economy: A market value approach. *Resources, Conservation and Recycling, 122*, 163–171. https://doi.org/10.1016/j.resconrec.2017.02.009

Eggers, W. D., Chew, B., Datar, A., & Sng, D. (2020). *How governments can navigate a disrupted world: Foresight, agility, and resilience*. Deloitte. How governments can navigate a disrupted world:Foresight, Agility, and Resilience.

Gieseke, T. (2011). *EcoCommerce 101: Adding an ecological dimension to the economy*.

Hobbs, R. J., Higgs, E. S., & Hall, C. (2013). Novel ecosystems: Intervening in the new ecological world order. , .

Kareiva, P., & Marvier, M. (2007). Conservation for the people. *Scientific American, 297*, 50–57. https://doi.org/10.1038/scientificamerican1007-50

Kjaer, L. L., Pigosso, D. C. A., Niero, M., Bech, N. M., & McAloone, T. C. (2019). Product/service-systems for a circular economy: The route to decoupling economic growth from resource consumption? *Journal of Industrial Ecology, 23*(1), 22–35. https://doi.org/10.1111/jiec.12747

Lovelock, J. (2009). *The vanishing face of Gaia: A final warning*. Basic Books.

Nidumolu, R., Prahalad, C. K., & Rangaswami, M. R. (2015). Why sustainability is now the key driver of innovation. *IEEE Engineering Management Review, 43*(2), 85–91. https://doi.org/10.1109/EMR.2015.7123233

Porter, M., & Kramer, M. (2007). Strategy and society: The link between competitive advantage and corporate social responsibility. *Harvard Business Review, 84*(78–92), 163.

Sachs, J. (2011). *The price of civilization: Reawakening American virtue and prosperity*. Random House.

Schor, J. (1999). *The overspent American: Why we want what we don't need*. William Morrow & Co.

Stack, L. (2006). *Doing the right things right: How the effective executive spends time*.

Thiele, L. P. (2006). *The heart of judgment: Practical wisdom, neuroscience, and narrative*. Cambridge University Press.

Chapter 12
Doing Business with Compliance: Business Ethics

In the Taoism's wisdom, compliance is about the awareness that seeing oneself as being above or ahead of other people can only lead to failure, and knowing when to act and when not to act, being able to anticipate potential problems. Simply put it, compliance refers to a personal expression of changed attitude or behaviour in complying with the requests of others.

As we analysed in the preceding chapters, from the perspective of Taoism, compliance is concerned with humility, integrity, accountability, etc. When the practical wisdom of Tao is applied in business ethics, compliance means adherence to, or conformance with, rules, laws, standards, and policies. It also implies a sense of accountability and an obligation to uphold pertinent codes of conduct. Compliance forms the foundation for a company's program and the code of ethics/conduct. While the code of conduct helps set the overall corporate tone toward compliance expectations, a company's program should be a series of integrated mechanisms designed to address all aspects of compliance breaches. A company's program can only emerge when basic operational components of a program are in place.

Many people engaged in business activity, including accountants and lawyers, are professionals. As such, they are bound by codes of conduct promulgated by professional societies. Many firms also have detailed codes of conduct, developed and enforced by teams of ethics and compliance personnel. Business ethics can thus be understood as the study of professional practices, i.e., as the study of the content, development, management, and effectiveness of the codes of conduct designed to guide the actions of people engaged in business activity.

Nidumolu's research views compliance as opportunity. They claim that companies must take on the long march to sustainability usually arise from the law. Compliance is complicated: environmental regulations vary by country, by state or region, and even by city. In addition to legal standards, enterprises feel pressured to abide by voluntary codes. These standards are more stringent than most countries' laws, particularly when they apply to cross-border trade (Nidumolu et al. 2015).

A key element of responsible leadership is having the ability to make informed ethical judgments about existing norms and rules. Especially when overseeing global

L. Zu, *Responsible and Sustainable Business*,
https://doi.org/10.1007/978-3-030-91117-1_12

business operations, where leaders face a diversity of rules and regulations, have to engage with various cultural norms and operate in contexts where there might be insufficient legal guidance. Responsible leaders should be able to critically question norms of business conduct they deem wrong.

Humility: Defined from Perspective of Taoism' Wisdom

Humility opens the door to progress.
—John Marks Templeton.

Always be humble, but not by bowing your head
Which is external humility.
Real humility is internal and has its origin in wisdom.
—Rabbi Nahman of Bratslav

Humility as a virtue essential to wisdom has deep roots. When humility combines with the virtues of truthfulness and obedience it produces proper self-realization, self-esteem, and self-image. Laozi stresses the virtues of simplicity and humility; he placed much emphasis on "*who one is*" as compared to "*what one does* (being vs. doing). Laozi always advocates living a simple and humble life, because humility is in harmony with nature and the wisdom of the universe, and simplicity and humility were the basis of greatness. In Tao Te Ching, a favourite natural symbol Laozi used to depict humility is water, a simple substance seeking the lowest places:

Supreme goodness is like water.
It benefits all creatures without contention.
It stays in low position where others dislike,
Thus, water comes nearest to the Tao.
—Laozi, Tao Te Ching, Ch. 8

Laozi loves to use water as a metaphor to describe the qualities of great leaders. Water is always humble to serve, stays in the low place whether water can flow in. This is the quality of a humble person. The arrogant person is quite the opposite in always seeking the highest most visible spot. Thus, we can say that water embodies the Tao of humility. It is the natural kind of humility that never needs to be faked or forced, and exactly the kind that we need to cultivate in ourselves.

Although water is soft and gentle, it is persistent and powerful. If drops of water keep pounding at a rock for years, even the hardest rock will yield to water. Over time, water can cut through the hardest rock, forming valleys and canyons. The style of leaders should be similarly gentle and soft, but also persistent and powerful. Here is an example of what we could learn from water:

Nothing in the world
Is as yielding and receptive as water;
Yet in attacking the firm and inflexible,
Nothing triumphs over it.
—Laozi, Tao Te Ching, Ch. 78

Since there is nothing softer than water, yet nothing better for attacking hard and strong things, there is no substitute for it. Its softness enables it to tolerate all kinds of environments, gathering strength without wearing it off at an earlier stage. And the resolute and perseverance of water help it to cut its path through hard rocks and wear away mountains. It is very important for a leader to know the dialectical relationship as such and to acquire the resolute and persevering characteristics of water.

Humility is also viewed as the science of the self-examined through a trustful understanding of one's strengths and weaknesses, involving not only honest self-appraisal but also an ability to forget the self and appreciate the value of all things. Humility demonstrates not only a willingness to see the self accurately, but also a strong desire to serve others. Selflessness and altruism lead to humility. The Taoist leaders, like water, also place themselves lower and maintain a low profile and are humble and modest. Being humble and modest is necessary for good leaders to appreciate and understand the Tao of things, and to always be ready to learn and be alert to overconfidence in the self, and to avoid a sense of authority, assertiveness, aggressiveness, and competitiveness. The virtue of modesty and humility, willingness to help and serve others are qualities which are essential to a leader who wants to influence others. They are the leaders who embrace Taoism's wisdom:

Why seas and rivers become leaders of hundreds of valleys
Is because they stay in low position.
Thus, great leaders who
Want to stand above people, must speak to them from below;
Want to stand ahead of people, must place themselves behind.
Therefore, when great leaders
Lead from above, people do not feel burdened;
Lead from behind, people do not feel obstructed.
Thus, people are never tired of exalting and supporting them.
—Laozi, Tao Te Ching, Ch. 66

Those who are humble and modest not only exist in good harmony with others, but are effective leaders, just like the river and sea. The sea, for instance, can govern a hundred streams of valleys because it has mastered being lower. Being humble is important for leaders because it enables them to accept people's goals as their own and to attract and unite people around themselves. Just as the sea accepts and embraces all streams coming its way—muddy or clear, large or small—leaders who humble themselves before people draw people towards them and gain their trust. This does not belittle leaders, but strengthens them instead. When leaders do not discriminate against those coming their way, they will have people of all abilities around them. When they place themselves below people and praise them for their abilities, leaders will boost the self-esteem and confidence of the people, who will in return be more eager to carry out tasks to their full potentials.

Humility is regarded as a positive characteristic possessed by leaders who are more likely to trust others. Humility is defined as a desirable personal quality reflecting the willingness to understand the self (identities, strengths, limitations), combined with perspective in the self's relationships with others. Mishra and Mishra posited that leader humility encourages leaders to be vulnerable to their followers and motivates followers to trust one another by acknowledging their collective vulnerability (Mishra and Mishra 2012). Without humility, the practice of every other virtue could be reduced to selfish-pride. With humility, we are empowered to relinquish self-will, self-love, and self-interest; it is the proof of the presence and practice of every other virtue. As Gregory The Great said, "He who gathers the other virtues without humility is as one who carries straw against the wind."

Compliance, Authority, and Humility

Great leaders are barely known by their people
Good leaders are loved and praised by their people
Mediocre leaders are feared by their people, and
Bad leaders are despised by their people
Those leaders who distrust people are not trusted by people.
Those leaders who empower people are trusted by people.
Therefore, when accomplishing their work,
People all say, "we did it ourselves!"
—Laozi, TTC, Ch. 17

Laozi describes the four styles of leaders and art of leadership. The difference among the styles of leadership lies in the core qualities of leaders: humility, trustworthiness, authority (power) and compliance. The four styles of leadership can be categorized as two main leadership models: those who lead with high trustworthiness, high humility, and utilitarian power (benevolence) lead to high compliance and high performance (great and good leaders); those who lead with low trustworthiness, low humility, but with coercive power (manipulation) lead to low compliance and low performance (mediocre and bad leaders).

The findings of Chiu and Hung (2020) research claims that leader humility is a vital component of effective leadership, corresponding with subordinate deep involvement (compliance), or effective leadership needing to be more trustworthy. Great leaders are humble and dependent on their followers, and the followers are on leaders. Therefore, leader humility fosters the shared sense of trustworthiness between leaders and subordinates, thus increasing compliance and performance.

Authority is defined as a kind of legitimate power that can be assigned to specific persons or positions (Katz and Kahn 1966). A mover with power is able to influence others to execute his/her orders, or to achieve the scope that others have supported. (Etzioni 1975) categorized three kinds of power: utilitarian power used by leaders to reward subordinates based on performance, coercive power used to force followers to meet power holders' expectations, and normative power used to reach controls based on common beliefs among members. In contrast to Etzioni's (1975) congruent power-involvement relationships, French and Raven (1959) proposed that the powers are not only come from positions (harsh powers, such as rewards, coercive and legitimate powers), but also from persons (soft powers, such as giving expert and referent advices). Those who want to exercise control over others and to advance personal interest are concerned about maintaining their authority positions.

Compliance refers to a personal expression of changed attitude or behaviour in complying with the requests of others (Taylor et al. 2006). Bass (1990) regarded leadership as a respectful and cooperative process that leaders are willing to initiate and followers are willing to go along with. Compliance, therefore, is indicative of a significant relationship among subordinate attitudes and behaviour and effective leadership (Becker et al. 1996).

Chinese pundits posited that, "Leadership is a kind of influential process which takes time to gradually convince followers of complete compliance" (I-Ching, Tuan Zhuan); and that, "When one causes men to submit by virtue instead of by force, they submit to him sincerely and willingly" (Mencius, Gon Sun Chou I). It is suggested that Power and Virtue are essential elements for effective leadership, which is consistent with compliance theory. According to McClelland (1975), leaders with a preference for personalized power (i.e., those at the lower levels of power motivation) are more likely to use power for the betterment of the self and tend to manifest dominance-submission as well as win-lose relationships between the leader and others. Personal satisfaction for these leaders stems from winning, specifically by conquering others.

The findings of many researchers have validated Laozi's wisdom that humble leaders (great and good leaders) engage in more of a bottom-up approach to leadership, because they acknowledge themselves as the ones who can't figure all the answers out at the top (Senge 2006). Humble leaders are perceived to genuinely care about their subordinates and convey this authentic concern in relationships. Humble leaders better reflect the values and opinions of followers and further enhance follower commitment and motivation toward the mission (Conger and Kanungo 1998). Moreover, leader humility can enhance the creation of trust (Argandoña 2015). Alawati et al. (2018) maintain that humble leaders heighten followers' trust and commitment; hence, leader humility, characterized from a trustful understanding of the self and serving others, is argued to be trustworthy and to facilitate subordinate compliance.

The study that Chiu and Hung (2020) conducted on examining how leader humility affects the relationship between authority and trustworthiness, and its effect on subordinate compliance shows that the most effective form of leadership to facilitate subordinate compliance is comprised of high humility with high authority and high trustworthiness; whereas, high leader humility with low trustworthiness illustrates the lowest compliance when authority is low. These conclusions may clarify the idea that, in order to effectively increase compliance, leader humility can be viewed as a strength when combining high trustworthiness under high authority, but may be regarded as weakness when both authority and trustworthiness are low. They also found that both trustworthiness and authority positively impact compliance, which is consistent with previous research that showed power sources and the ways power may be used can influence subordinates' compliance.

Humble Leadership vs. Narcissistic leadership

Those who are not self-absorbed are outstanding.
Those who are not self-righteous are distinguished.
Those who are not self-aggrandized are given credit
Those who are not self-concerted become a leader
—Tao Te Ching, Ch. 22

Those who stand on tiptoes cannot stand firm,
Those who stride forward cannot walk far.
Those who are self-absorbed cannot be outstanding,
Those who are self-righteous cannot be distinguished,
Those who are self-aggrandized cannot be given credit,
Those who are self-conceited cannot become a leader.
—Tao Te Ching, Ch. 24

Laozi describes two styles of leadership in the passage 22 and 24: humble leadership and narcissistic leadership. We discussed in the preceding chapters the humble leaders who are water-like leaders. Let's look at the traits of narcissistic leaders. Narcissistic leadership is a leadership style in which the leader is only interested in him/herself. Their priority is themselves—at the expense of their people/group members. This leader exhibits the characteristics of a narcissist: arrogance, dominance and hostility (Neider 2010). It is a sufficiently common leadership style that it has acquired its own name.

A considerable amount of psychological research over the last thirty years has produced a picture of the narcissist as a person with inflated self-regard, feelings of superiority and entitlement, and a ravenous, almost insatiable hunger for attention and praise-values clearly antithetical to almost anyone's notion of wisdom.

"We know that narcissism correlates with lower ethics in business and with white-collar crime," said Campbell (2009), a psychologist at the University of Georgia who studies narcissism. "What it really does predict is the emergence of leadership, in groups and among strangers. But over time, it's humility, coupled with drive, that correlates with performance." He added that narcissism has a pervasive effect on decision making "that's generally bad." As Chatterjee and Hambrick put it, "Narcissists rate themselves highly (and more highly than is objectively warranted) on an array of agentic dimensions, including intelligence, creativity, competence, and leadership abilities."

The findings of Weinzimmer and McConoughey (2012) have validated Laozi's wisdom in terms of what constitutes a narcissistic leader. Their research reveals three primary styles or modes of self-absorbed leadership became evident. Some self-absorbed leaders are narcissists, in love with themselves; some are arrogant, either believing or acting as if they know best or simply are best; some suffer from hubris, or a blind faith in their own infallibility. Some spectacularly self-absorbed leaders exhibit all of these characteristics—and do massive and often permanent damage to their organizations and their own careers. These three modes seem similar, but each may characterize a different facet of self-absorbed leadership.

Narcissism The concept of narcissism took its name from Greek mythology: the beautiful Narcissus was so infatuated with his own reflection in a pool of water that he could not tear himself away and eventually died. According to Sigmund Freud, we are all narcissistic to some extent. It is healthy to love yourself. But a true narcissist has a personality disorder. If you are a narcissist, you don't merely love yourself; you're infatuated with yourself. Everything you do is right, because according to yourself, you are perfect. Moreover, for narcissists, everything is about them, and others exist to support the narcissist's self-image. Narcissists always want to be the center of attention.

Arrogance Arrogance is similar to narcissism in that it involves an inflated sense of self, and in some cases, arrogance is actually a result of narcissism. In other cases, however, arrogance may be a result of insecurity and low self-esteem. If challenged, you will aggressively attack others to protect your ego. Unlike the narcissist, arrogant leaders don't always have to be the center of attention, but they always have to be right.

Hubris In a leadership context, self-absorption is ultimately manifested in poor decision making. When a leader makes critical decisions while blind to his own faults and weaknesses, we say he shows hubris. The word hubris also has Greek roots—it originally referred to individuals who saw themselves as equal to the gods; Aristotle pointed out that one of the biggest reasons that humans fail is because of this blinding pride. Hubris often is a result of too much success; a leader may begin to feel he is "on a roll" or has the "Midas touch." He feels omnipotent, and that's when very bad things start to happen.

Taking all three of these attributes together creates the perfect storm: a self-absorbed leader who is destined to fail, and in the worst case scenario, take down his company with him. It is virtually impossible for a self-absorbed leader to be effective in the long term. Not only is it annoying for employees to work under them, but the entire work environment suffers. A self-absorbed leader can cut off healthy dialogue and kill motivation. Often a self-absorbed leader surrounds himself with co-dependents (aka "yes people") to support his ego. This often leads to poor performance as outside perspectives and ideas that challenge the leader are not tolerated. It is not uncommon for the self-absorbed to profess they are committed to supporting company values and goals. But when push comes to shove, it is all about them. Rather than using company resources to achieve organizational goals, self-absorbed leaders often use organizational resources to support their own personal goals.

Many self-absorbed leaders are trying to compensate for self-doubt and low self-esteem. These self-absorbed leaders become isolated to a degree that they cannot be trusted to act in the best interests of the company. The only people who interact with them are the politically inclined who feel the need to "play the game." For those subjected to a self-doubting and self-absorbed leader, either by choice or by their place in the organizational hierarchy, the environment can become toxic. "Here's what happens," Silverman contends. "I'm worried that other people are going to realize that I'm not very competent at my job, so I'm going to put other people down, criticize others, and belittle my employees because somehow I think I'm going to look better that way."

Healthy vs. Destructive Narcissistic Managers

Narcissism is most often described as unhealthy and destructive. Narcissistic leadership (preferably destructive) is driven by unyielding arrogance, self-absorption, and a personal egotistic need for power and admiration. However, not all narcissistic behaviours or managers are helpful. Therefore, we need distinguish healthy narcissism and destructive narcissism. Lubit (2002) compared healthily narcissistic managers versus destructively narcissistic managers for their long-term impact on organizations.

Table 12.1 shows that healthy narcissism has some differences in the areas of self-confidence, desire for power, wealth and administration, relationships, ability to follow a consistent path and foundation. For example, in terms of desire, healthy narcissism doesn't pursue power at all costs, but just enjoys power they might have. I will discuss two examples in business world to illustrate the healthy and destructive narcissism and impact on the organizational performance.

In 2007, two economists at Pennsylvania State University's Smeal College of Business published a study that, indirectly, says a lot about humility in the executive suite. They had set out to explore the relationship between the performance of companies in the computer business and the narcissism of their respective CEO. In order to wrap their arms around this admittedly elusive quality, Chatterjee and

Table 12.1 Healthy vs. destructive narcissistic managers

Characteristic	Healthy Narcissism	Destructive Narcissism
Self-confidence	High outward self-confidence in line with reality	Grandiose
Desire for Power, Wealth and Administration	May enjoy power	Pursue power at all costs, lacks normal inhibitions in its pursuit
Relationships	Real concern for others and their ideas; does not exploit or devalue others.	Concerns limited to expressing socially appropriate response when convenient; devalues and exploits others without remorse.
Ability to follow a consistent path	Has values; follows through on plans	Lacks values; easily bored; often changes course
Foundation	Healthy childhood with support for self-esteem and appropriate limits on behaviour towards others	Traumatic childhood undercutting true sense of self-esteem and/or learning that he/she doesn't need to be considerate of others

Source: Lubit, R. (2002). The Long-Term Organizational Impact of Destructively Narcissistic Managers. Academy of Management Executive, 16(1), 127–138

Hambrick (2007) catalogued several indirect measures of corporate vanity in order to gauge the dimensions of any given CEO's ego:

- *the size of the leader's photograph in company documents,*
- *the length of entries in Who's Who,*
- *the frequency with which the CEO was mentioned in corporate press releases, and*
- *the number of times the CEO used the first-person singular (I, me, mine, my, myself) in interviews.*

This is obviously a squishy metric, but reading their analysis (entitled "It's All About Me") through the prism of the 2008 financial panic and the 2009 executive bonus boondoggle, we may find the results eerily informative. Narcissistic CEOs, they reported, were more acquisitive, tended to make more "extreme choices," and, in essence, were the corporate equivalent of drama queens, typically pursuing abrupt shifts in business strategy. Chatterjee and Hambrick (2007) wrote that "CEO narcissism is also related to extreme and volatile company performance. Narcissistic CEOs, who tend to pursue dynamic and grandiose strategies, also tend to generate more extreme performance—more big wins and big losses than their less narcissistic counterparts (as measured both by accounting and shareholder returns)." The bottom-line conclusion: Executive narcissists bring a lot of drama into the boardroom, but that drama does not produce systematically better corporate performance.

Narcissistic CEOs may, however, contribute to financial panics. In an interview, Hambrick dated the rise of boardroom narcissism to, of all things, a publishing event in the 198os. "It all got launched by Lee Iacocca and his autobiography," Hambrick said, referring to the iconic executive of the (now bankrupt) Chrysler Corporation. "Prior to that, ninety-five percent of the American public would not have been able to name the CEO of any company. So there has been a spiral of flamboyance, of more narcissistic types drawn to these jobs, to the kind of compensation that would attract that kind of person. Everything became more extreme, jazzier, more colourful. And this," he added, speaking about a month after the collapse of the U.S. financial industry, "is where it's left us."

Perhaps the best explicit treatment of humility in the executive suite (and in almost all the social sciences) has come from management researcher Jim Collins. In his 2001 book Good to Great, and in an article in the Harvard Business Review based on the same research, Collins's findings in a series ratified the same paradox apparent in Gandhi. Exceptional business leaders, according to the five-year study, blend "extreme personal humility with intense professional will." Business executives who "possess this paradoxical combination of traits is catalysts for the statistically rare event of transforming a good company into a great one" (Collins 2001).

Among the traits associated with these humble (but great) business leaders were a reluctance to seek public adulation; a style of leadership that emphasized organizational standards rather than personal charisma; a willingness to subsume personal ambition to the larger ambitions of the company; and an eagerness to apportion credit to others combined with a willingness to accept responsibility for failures. Collins anticipated the Penn State findings when he noted that "boards of directors frequently operate under the false belief that a larger-than-life, egocentric leader is required to make a company great." It's worth commenting on the methodology here, too: Collins's research project began by identifying eleven companies that significantly outperformed the general market and also competitors in their field; it was only in an attempt to explain why these companies had performed so exceptionally that the pattern of humble but strong-willed executive leadership emerged.

Integrity: Accountability and Trust

Great leaders are not egocentric, and selfless to serve other interests
They are good to those who are good,
They are also good to those who are not good,
Then, it leads to genuine goodness.
They trust those who are trustworthy,
They also trust those who are untrustworthy,
Then, it leads to genuine trust.
—Laozi, Tao Te Ching, Ch. 49

The great leaders that Laozi always admires are those who are selfless and place people's interests above their own. Great leaders embody their genuine integrity and goodness, and are held accountable for any wrongdoing and bad consequences. Trust ultimately is a function of people doing the right things. Being trustworthy is one of the keys to leadership success and an essential component of successful working relationships between leaders and followers. When a leader is considered trustworthy, he or she enables cooperation, encourages information sharing, and increases openness and mutual acceptance with the people he or she manages. Great leaders place trust in people that do the right things. Accountability determines what people will do. If leaders reward people for something, they'll do more of it. If leaders punish people for something, they'll do less of it. If leaders are accountable for determining what people are accountable for, then leaders ultimately control whether or not they will trust them.

Figure 12.1 shows that when trust is low, if leaders hold people accountable to the wrong things, they'll forever micromanage them. If trust is high and leaders hold people accountable to the wrong things, their trust is misplaced. In both situations, success will be a matter of luck. Leaders will get more of the wrong thing than the right thing. When trust is low, if leaders hold people accountable to the right things, trust will grow as people do more and more of the right things.

When trust is high and leaders hold people accountable to the right things, they demonstrate leadership. Leaders lead by holding people accountable to the right things and they don't get in their way, leaders don't control how they do things. In both of these situations, success will largely be a function of talent. In fact, the right thing had better be how we define success.

There is power in being trustworthy. In the economy of trust, what goes around comes around. The more leaders look out for others, the more they look out for

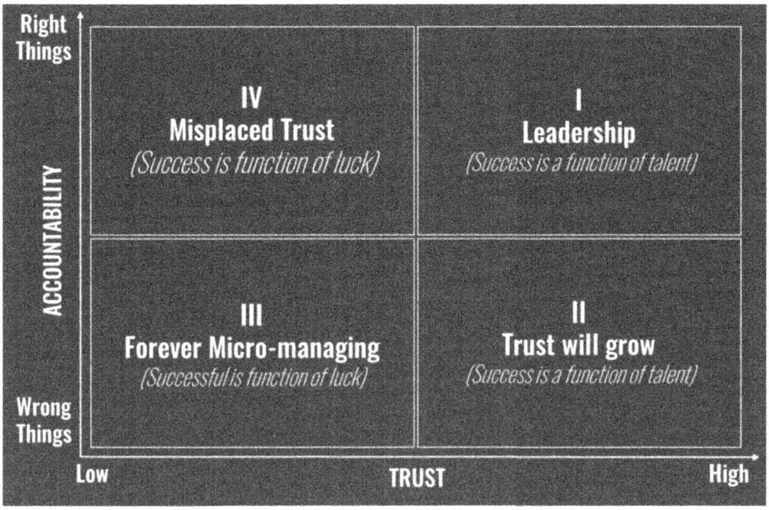

Fig. 12.1 Accountability and Trust Matrix. Source: Adapted from http://www.weshigbee.com/trust-and-accountability/. Retrieved on 16 October 2020

themselves. Distrust begets distrust, trust begets trust. The more leaders trust, the more leaders are trusted. When trust is the medium of exchange, people collaborate and altruism can grow, again to everyone's benefit.

Case in Point: Edelman Trust and Leadership

Edelman 2020 report defines the trust based on two distinct attributes: competence (delivering on promises) and ethical behavior (doing the right thing and working to improve society). The 2020 Edelman Trust Barometer reveals that none of the four institutions is seen as both competent and ethical. Figure shows that business ranks highest in competence, holding a massive 54-point edge over government as an institution that is good at what it does (64 percent vs. 10 percent). NGOs led on ethical behavior over government (a 31-point gap) and business (a 25-point gap). Government and media are perceived as both incompetent and unethical (Fig. 12.2).

Trust is undeniably linked to doing what is right. After tracking 40 global companies over the past year through our Edelman Trust Management framework, they found that ethical drivers such as integrity, dependability and purpose drive 76 percent of the trust capital of business, while competence accounts for only 24 percent.

Edelman Trust Barometer claims that the "mass-class" trust divide has become chronic, reaching record levels in more countries than ever, with a global 14-point gap between informed public and mass population trust in institutions. In developed markets, less than one in three people believe that they will be better off in five years.

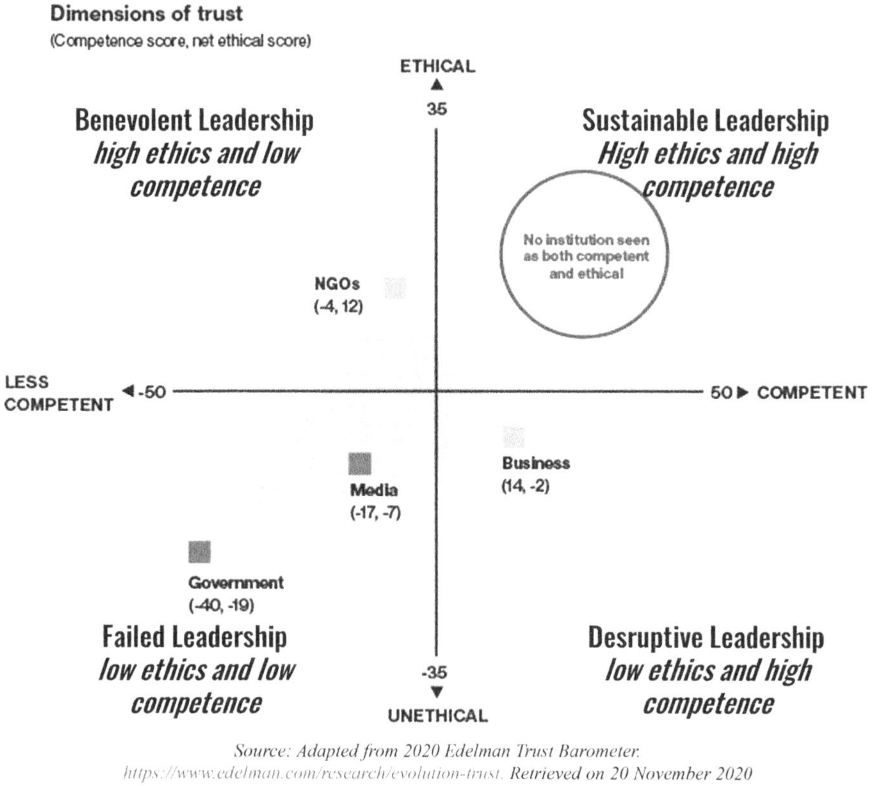

Fig. 12.2 Edelman Trust (competence and ethics) and Leadership. Source: Adapted from 2020 Edelman Trust Barometer. https://www.edelman.com/research/evolution-trust. Retrieved on 20 November 2020

Under 20 percent of the general population express confidence in the system, and 73 percent are looking for change. More than half of our respondents believe that capitalism causes more harm than good, and that democracy is losing its effectiveness.

Business has been prompted to action by the recognition that stakeholders now have new expectations of the corporate sector. A stunning 92 percent of employees surveyed in the 2020 Edelman Trust Barometer say that they expect their employer's CEO to speak up on one or more issues ranging from income inequality to diversity and training for jobs of the future. Seventy-three percent of employees expect a prospective employer to offer the opportunity to shape the future of society in a positive way. Consumers share this determination; our 2019 "In Brands We Trust?" study found that nearly two-thirds of consumers buy based on their beliefs, and 81 percent agree that "a brand I can trust" is one of their top reasons for purchase. Our Edelman 2020 Trust Barometer respondents told us that customers and employees are over five times more important to a company's long-term success than shareholders.

2020 Trust Barometer reveals startling imbalances among the institutions. Business ranks highest in competence, holding a gigantic 54-point gap over government as an institution that is good at what it does. NGOs are much more trusted on ethical behaviour than government (a 31-point gap). Government is trusted more than twice as much as business to protect the environment and close the income inequality gap. The four existential issues of the next decade—income inequality, sustainability, information quality and artificial intelligence—will require higher levels of cooperation among our institutions; no single entity can take on these complex challenges alone. But only about one-third of people believe that business does a good job of partnering with NGOs or government. Currently business and government are like children of different weights on an unbalanced playground seesaw; government, perceived as both incompetent and unethical, is unable to provide the necessary counterbalance to business, which is considered highly effective but too self-interested. Business must stop pushing government away.

The Edelman Trust Barometer requests business to take the lead on solving the trust paradox because it has the greatest freedom to act. Its immediate mandates are clear. An overwhelming number of respondents believe that it is the duty of business to pay decent wages (83 percent) and provide retraining for workers whose jobs are threatened by automation (79 percent). Yet less than a third of people trust that business will do these.

References

Alawati, H., Sayed, R., & Caldwell, C. (2018). *Transformative ethics and moving toward "greatness" – problems and realities.*

Argandoña, A. (2015). Humility in management. *Journal of Business Ethics, 132*, 63–71. https://doi.org/10.1007/s10551-014-2311-8

Bass, B. M. (1990). *Bass & Stogdill's handbook of leadership* (3rd ed.). The Free Press.

Becker, T., Billings, R., Eveleth, D., & Gilbert, N. (1996). Foci and bases of employee commitment: Implications for job performance. *Academy of Management Journal, 39*, 464–482. https://doi.org/10.5465/256788

Campbell, W. K. (2009). *The Narcissism Epidemic: Living in the age of entitlement.* Atria Books.

Chatterjee, A., & Hambrick, D. C. (2007). It's all about me: Narcissistic chief executive officers and their effects on company strategy and performance. *Administrative Science Quarterly, 52*(3), 351–386. https://doi.org/10.2189/asqu.52.3.351

Chiu, T.-C., & Hung, Y. (2020). Impacts of leader humility between authority and trustworthiness on compliance: Tests of three-way interaction. *Psychological Reports.*. https://doi.org/10.1177/0033294120973942.

Collins, J. (2001). *Good to great: Why some companies make the Leap and others don't.* HarperBusiness.

Conger, J., & Kanungo, R. (1998). *Charismatic leadership in organizations.* Sage.

Etzioni, A. (1975). *Comparative analysis of complex organizations: Revised and enlarged edition* (Revised and enlarged edition ed.). The Free Press.

French, J. R., & Raven, B. (1959). The bases of social power. In D. Cartwright & A. Zander (Eds.), *Group dynamics*. Harper & Row.
Katz, D., & Kahn, R. (1966). The social psychology of organizations. *American Sociological Review, 31*, 745. https://doi.org/10.2307/2091895
Lubit, R. (2002). The long-term organizational impact of destructively narcissistic managers. *Academy of Management Executive, 16*, 127–138. https://doi.org/10.5465/AME.2002.6640218
McClelland, D. (1975). *Power: The inner experience*. Irvington Publishers.
Mishra, A. K., & Mishra, K. E. (2012). *Becoming a trustworthy leader: Psychology and practice*. Routledge.
Neider, L. (2010). *The dark side of management*. Information Age Publishing.
Nidumolu, R., Prahalad, C. K., & Rangaswami, M. R. (2015). Why sustainability is now the key driver of innovation. *IEEE Engineering Management Review, 43*(2), 85–91. https://doi.org/10.1109/EMR.2015.7123233
Senge, P. (2006). *The fifth discipline: The art and practice of the learning organization*.
Taylor, S. E., Peplau, L. A., & Sears, D. O. (2006). *Social psychology* (12th ed.). Pearson.
Weinzimmer, L. G., & McConoughey, J. (2012). *The wisdom of failure: How to learn the tough leadership lessons without paying the price*. Jossey-Bass.

Part IV
Building Wise Strategy for Sustainable Business Development

Chapter 13
Purpose-Driven Leadership: A New Revolution

Why Heaven and Earth exist forever is.
Because they do not live for themselves.
Thus, they are sustainable.
—Laozi, Tao Te Ching, Ch. 7

The man without a purpose is like a ship
Without a rudder—a waif, a nothing, a no man.
—Thomas Carlyle

In recent years, the topic of "purpose" has been widely discussed by the academic scholars and business practitioners. The purpose revolution has significantly changed the way companies are doing businesses today. There is growing consensus among leaders today that business exists not to make money, but to make the world better to live. As early as 2500 years ago, Laozi discovered power of purpose in life and universe, and offered his wisdom in the bible of Tao Te Ching.

Laozi claims that the Tao is the source of all existence, and it is the purpose of everything. Wisdom of Taoism has inspired and guided people with precepts of compassion, harmony, cooperation, integrity, humility and prudence. Taoism's thought as the master virtue allows individuals, organization, and society to cultivate purpose for a sustainable life, and directs leaders to pursuit a basic blueprint of not only doing good, but also being good.

In this chapter, I will combine the Taoism's wisdom with management to discuss the concept of purpose and relationships from philosophical, business and Taoism's perspectives, but with the focus on purpose-driven leadership. I will walk you through the key text of Tao Te Ching and introduce five core principles for purpose-driven leadership: *self-awareness* for mindful leadership, *self-cultivation* for authentic leadership, *leading with humility* for Level 5 leadership, *transcending ego* for servant leadership, and *doing the right things right* for sustainable leadership. The principles are the guidelines and strategies for directing leaders to develop purpose-driven organization.

L. Zu, *Responsible and Sustainable Business*,
https://doi.org/10.1007/978-3-030-91117-1_13

From CSR Revolution to Purpose Revolution

Decades ago, when I began to turn my research interest to corporate social responsibility (CSR), I was struck by CSR revolution in academic and business world. The revolution is not only about cutting carbon, reducing energy use, monitoring factories, or donating to charities, but about reimagining companies from within: innovating new ways of working, instilling a new logic of competing, identifying new possibilities for leading, and redefining the very purpose of business (Hollender 2010). The revolution has caused expansive debate over business's role in society among academic scholars and business executives around two opposing arguments. Those who are against CSR state that social issues are peripheral to corporate agenda. The sole purpose of business is to generate shareholder value. Those who are for CSR take the stand that companies, which care for social and environmental issues and positively contribute to society will see the benefits to their reputation and subsequently their bottom line.

The long-term debate over CSR is actually concerned with whose interest should be attended to, shareholders or stakeholders. As a result, the debate leads to two competing theories, i.e., shareholder theory and stakeholder theory, which seek to examine the purpose of modern business firm. Each provides a framework for economic and social performance of business. Shareholder theory emanates from an economic perspective, focusing on the firm's purpose of creating wealth for its owners while minimizing both the importance of the firm's interaction with its other constituencies and its role in society; While stakeholder theory broadens the shareholder's perspective, recognizing the importance of wealth creation as well as the firm's relationships with its multiple constituent groups—shareholders, employees, customers, suppliers, local communities, and environment—and impact on society at large (Pfarrer 2010).

In recent years, we have seen CSR revolution morphed into purpose revolution, the fundamental shift from the "for-profit" model to "for-purpose". The explosion of the interest in purpose has taken place not only in business, but in all other areas. Psychologists describe it as the pathway to happiness. Scientists point to it as essential to brain health and well-being.

Business experts make the case that purpose is a key to exceptional productivity and organizational credibility, and medical professionals have found that people with purpose in their lives are less prone to disease and even live longer. Ernst & Young noted that "public discourse about 'corporate/organizational purpose' has increased fivefold since 1994, now trending at an exponential rate that surpasses the rate of public discourse about sustainability" (EY Beacon Institute 2016). 73 percent of business leaders say that corporate purpose is a key to success in navigating the uncertainties of the economy and today's volatile world (EY Beacon Institute 2017).

Today the company that declared it has a purpose beyond profit is eagerly trumpeted in response to growing demands from employees for work that is meaningful, from customers for brands that inspire, and from society for companies to be responsible. These might be also the drivers of the emergence of purpose. The forces and megatrends that drive the emergence of purpose have been identified. The study of EY reveals six forces that are challenging companies' old sense of identity and operating models—forcing them to rethink value and how it is created: the trust deficit; the sustainability imperative; rising social inequality; conflicting time horizons; diminishing brand control and the threats and opportunities of digitalization (EY Beacon Institute 2016). The forces mean that many employees, customers, investors, communities and other stakeholders are asking profound questions about the structure of society and the role of the corporation in that society. The global megatrends, such as population growth, urbanization and demographic change; resource scarcity and role of renewables; digitalization; climate change, and responsibility and compliance, represent many long-term opportunities and challenges for companies in the future. They are also driving demand for sustainable solutions, new technologies and responsible business practices (UPM 2017). The forces and megatrends demand business leaders to concern more with social and environmental issues and integrate them into business purpose.

Purpose, CSR and Stakeholder Theory: Discovering Their Links

By examining the recent studies on purpose, CSR and stakeholder theory, I have found that they are closely linked. I believe that purpose revolution is the uninterrupted wave of CSR revolution and debate of shareholder and stakeholder theories. The terms of purpose, CSR, sustainability, stakeholders, and the like are now common sentiments expressed in many business circles. CSR is a branch of stakeholder-related theory, and it befits a stakeholder view of the role of business in society. CSR means promoting environmental integrity, economic development and social justice as part of the firm's overall strategy to gain competitive advantage. Therefore, I believe that business purpose has a lot of things to do CSR and sustainable development.

However, some researchers have treated the emerging concept of purpose differently from CSR and sustainability. Dan Pontefract argues that CSR is not purpose of business, and business purpose is not its CSR strategy. Using CSR as a substitute for purpose is corporate social irresponsibility. It's the dark side of CSR. Because he argues that an organization's purpose centres around five "Good DEEDS" he identified (Pontefract 2017):

- *Delight your customers. Working with and for the customer always remembering why an organization exists in the first place.*
- *Engage your team members. Team members need purpose in their role to flourish, and they need to know they are able to create value while simultaneously feeling valued.*
- *Ethical within society. Decisions need to be made—be it financially, environmentally, socially—that are always ethical in nature.*

- *Deliver fair practices. Consistent and positive people practice inside the organization to unleash the creativity and productivity of team members.*
- *Serve all stakeholders. The organization has a responsibility in society to positively affect customers, team members, the community, environment and owners alike.*

It doesn't matter what Pontefract calls it, the essence of Good DEEDS in fact embraces dimensions of CSR: the internal dimension is engagement of employees, team members and quality of products and services, and external dimension is customers, community and environment. It is obvious that Pontefract incorporated the principles of CSR in DEEDs, which is concerned with contribution to or positive impact on society and environmental sustainability by delivering benefits for all stakeholders. From this perspective, CSR ought to be a critical component to be an organization's operating purpose and values. The recent EY survey shows that purpose is part of a shift toward business becoming a partner in global problem solving, mirroring a shift from value creation for its own sake, through value creation without harm (a CSR approach), to value creation for and with a broader set of stakeholders (a stakeholder approach) (EY Beacon Institute 2016; Mourkogiannis 2014) claims that Purpose is preparation for doing what is right and what is worthwhile. As such it creates a sense of obligation. But this obligation is not a weight or a drag in any way—it's a way of knowing what you can and cannot do. "Do the right thing and do well (purpose)" is a new way of saying "Do well by doing good (CSR)".

Nevertheless, there is a slight difference among purpose, CSR and stakeholder theory. Purpose is built on the perspectives of CSR, shareholder and stakeholder theories. A purpose-driven company or organization is inspired by a clear role in the world that offers it a reason for being. Let's put it simply, purpose is concerned with WHY: why does a company exist? CSR is more with WHAT and HOW: what responsibilities should a company take while doing business in society: economic, social or environmental? How should a company do business: in a socially responsible manner or irresponsible? And stakeholder theory is more with WHO: who are constituents that a company should be responsible for: shareholder, community, employees, or customers?

Purpose is crucial and the primary source of business success because purpose is about a set of values and beliefs that defines an organization and inspires and motivates its employees. Rather than organization and structure, ideas are what cause companies to go from good to great. It determines its goals and strategy. Purposeful companies contribute meaningfully to human betterment and create long-term value for all their stakeholders (Mourkogiannis 2014). Therefore, when organizations activate their clear purpose, they will be able to define their version by incorporating CSR and sustainability concerns into business strategy and server all stakeholders' interests.

The Tao Is Purpose of Everything

Purpose is the reason for which something is done or created or for which something exists. It reveals the underlying dynamics of any human activity. Everything in nature has its purpose, and no single purpose is more important than another. But not all purposes are effective and successful. A purpose's effectiveness depends both on its relevance to the problems that leaders face today, and on its connection to the shared value and culture of humanity. It needs to draw on philosophical ideas that have stood the test of time. Not all ideas are born equal. A successful purpose both drives an organization forward and helps build sustainable competitive advantage (Mourkogiannis 2014). In this sense, we need the philosophical ideas of the Taoism, which have stood the test of over 2000 years. The Tao is a central concept of Taoism, and is purpose of everything. The Tao embeds in everything and pervades everywhere. Laozi, an ancient Chinese philosopher, the founder of philosophical Taoism, discovered the power of the Tao or purpose in meaningful life and universe. Laozi describes the power and role of the Tao in Tao Te Ching:

> *The great Tao flows everywhere like water,*
> *All things depend on it to exist, and yet*
> *It does not demand for obedience.*
> *All things depend on it to fulfil their purpose, and yet*
> *It does not claim credit.*
> *All things depend on it to nurture and grow, and yet*
> *It does not possess them.*
> —Laozi, Tao Te Ching, Ch. 34

The Tao is used symbolically in its sense of '*way*' as the '*right*' or '*proper' way* of existence and it is the source and ideal of all existence, in our modern language, the Tao is the ultimate reason why everything has happened or the purpose behind what has happened in the universe. Taoism's thought as the master virtue allows individuals, organization, and society to live in a successful life, and as well directs leaders to pursue a basic blueprint of not only doing good, but also being good.

What is Purpose? The Philosophical, Taoism and Business Perspectives

Purpose: The Philosophical Perspective

Like any other emerging concepts, there is no universal working definition of purpose. I will try to examine the concept and definitions of purpose from the perspectives of philosophical, Taoism and business.

From the philosophical standpoint, the concept of purpose is generally defined as the reason for which something is done or created or for which something exists. Aristotle, the ancient Greek father of western philosophy called that purpose, *telos*.

The word can mean 'purpose,' 'intent,' 'end,' or 'goal,' but as usual, Aristotle used it in a more specific and subtle sense—*the inherent purpose of each thing, the ultimate reason for each thing being the way it is, whether created that way by human beings or nature*. The root sense of telos is wholeness or completion, and Aristotle's "teleology" is his teaching that all natural events aim at producing or maintaining the wholeness of natural beings, understood not only in a bodily and biological sense but also as the wholeness of being-at-work that constitutes their lives. In human beings, the achievement of this wholeness of life requires choices carried out in action; hence the end appears as a purpose, the accomplishment of which completes the action. The purpose behind all other purposes would be the human end that is complete simply (Sachs 2002). Aristotle observed that every person is drawn by a telos or purpose in their lives. Aristotle argues that living happily requires living a life of virtue. Someone who is not living a life that is virtuous, or morally good, is also not living a happy life, no matter what they might think. Someone who does live according to virtue, who chooses to do the right thing because it is the right thing to do, is living a life that flourishes. Human beings discover these things rather than creating them. We do not get to decide what is right and wrong, but we do get to decide whether we will do what is right or what is wrong, and this is the most important decision we make in life (Aristotle 1995). For Aristotle, teleological concepts help us capture what sorts of things living things are—namely, purposively organized entities that strive to achieve various aims—and what properties they possess.

In the wisdom of Heraclitus, a Greek philosopher of the late sixth century BCE, and one of the great philosophers before Socrates and Plato, purpose is interpreted as the word "*logos*" which stands for "the reason for why", the purpose behind what took place and the force that shapes their lives. He believed in the necessity of scientific enquiry, probing the natural world, asking how and why things were the way they were. He looked for patterns or laws to see if he could deduce some logic behind the operation of the natural world. For example, when he looked at life (bios) he looked for the logos; when he studied the weather (meteor) he sought the logos. This concept now appears in our words for the study of different areas in science: biology, meteorology, geology, psychology, sociology, etc. Thus, Heraclitus said that the logos is 'the reason why'. Every branch of science is looking for the logos, the reason why things are as they are. The literal Greek "logos" is translated as "word", and sometimes rendered as "account". It is unseen force, not that different from the biblical "Word" or the "Tao" in Taoism, which regulates and runs the universe. Humans can only act in a right way if their actions are in attunement with the Logos (Butler-Bowdon 2017).

William Damon (2008) defined purpose as a stable and generalized intention to accomplish something that is at the same time meaningful to the self and consequential for the world beyond the self. This purpose consists of three main components: *long-term intention, actual action plan and commitment, and beyond-the-self motivation* (Damon 2008). In this sense, purpose can be interpreted as moral virtue from the perspective of virtue ethics. Purpose can be regarded as a virtue in virtually all eras and cultures, including Western, Taoism, Confucianism, and Buddhism cultures, although there might be minor differences in the concepts of purpose in each cultural background. For instance, Christianity regards purpose of life associated with a calling from God as one of the most fundamental elements for a meaningful and valuable life (Warren 2002). In Eastern cultures, achieving the ultimate purpose of life, such as the completion of self-cultivation in Taoism and Confucianism or true enlightenment and Nirvana in Buddhism, has been morally admired (Rahula 1974; Ho 1995).

Han (2015) argues that purpose is naturally a moral virtue that enhances flourishing. But it is a second-order virtue that plays a corrective role and moderates the performance of other first-order virtues and the strength of motivational force of behaviour. Purpose provides other virtues with the proper direction where they should aim, and when and where they should be put into practice. For instance, courage without purpose would be meaningless. Without purpose, although a person might possess and exercise individual moral virtues at a certain moment, all of those individual virtues, or virtue-like things, cannot appropriately facilitate the achievement of his/her flourishing at the end. Purpose is a second-order virtue that enables a person who possesses it to decide which actions to take and which virtues to exercise at a specific moment for the achievement of his/her noble long-term goal, and ultimately for flourishing. Purpose plays a corrective role to maintain the level of behavioural motivation at an appropriate level. A person with this virtue, a purposeful person, can maintain an appropriate level of behavioural motivation to achieve his/her ultimate goal at the end. This person knows when to act and when to stop, and where to spend and concentrate energy and where not to pay attention (Bronk 2012). Thus, purpose can correct the two non-productive motivational statuses and guide a person to the ultimate happiness. Therefore, purpose can play a corrective role to decide a proper thrust and focus of endeavours, and to control the degree of behavioural motivation between two extreme ends: insufficient and excessive behavioural motivation.

Leider (2015) claims that our purpose is the essence of who we are and what makes us unique. Our purpose is an active expression of the deepest dimension within us—where we have a profound sense of who we are and why we're here. Purpose is the aim around which we structure our lives, a source of direction and energy. Through the lens of purpose, we are able to see ourselves—and our future—more clearly. You have a purpose no matter what age you are, how healthy you are, or what your economic or social situation is. Purpose is actively living your values, leaning toward compassion for others, and getting up in the morning to contribute value to the world. Purpose is what gives life a meaning.

Izzo and Vanderwielen (2018) claim that purpose is transcendent. It ties you to what matters most, to something bigger than yourself, something enduring that offers a deeper sense of meaning. Purpose connects your place as a leader to the larger world of relationships and events. Purpose is altruistic. It is not about you but about the well-being of people and environment outside your-self—how you enrich society or the planet. Purpose is forward thinking. It points you and others forward toward a compelling vision, focusing attention and energy on the creation of a better future reality. Throughout history, humans have sought to make sense of their lives, searching for meaning through prayer, retreat, art, music, nature, community, gratitude, forgiveness, and multiple other ways. Traditionally, purpose was connected with the spiritual aspect of people's lives, and healers, priests, and shamans were the ministers who helped people connect with the sacred to restore bodies and souls to health and wholeness (Leider 2015). Cashman (2017) also agrees that purpose is the natural flow of our gifts as they serve those we touch. Sometimes we may inhibit or ignore this flow, but it is always there, seeking expression. How it manifests depends on our ability to open up to it and the particular circumstances we may be facing at the time. Purpose is constant, the manifestation of purpose is always changing to serve the situation.

Purpose: The Taoism's Perspective

The descriptions and definitions of purpose I discussed in the preceding section touch on the core principles of Taoism: the reason of being, source of direction and energy, compassion for others, transcendent, altruistic, forward thinking, spiritual aspect of people's lives, wholeness, constant, natural flow, etc. I will elaborate the principles in the following sections.

We know that the Tao is origin and source of all things in the universe, the law of nature and ultimate reality. But the Tao is also seen as the spiritual law. The simplest interpretation of the Tao, or spiritual law, is: "This is how things work." One way to comprehend this law is to realize that it expresses the relationship between a person's mind and the thoughts and ideas of the mind, a person's emotions and how they are expressed, and the physical activities that give expression to those thoughts, feelings, and ideas. A definite relationship exists between the invisible thoughts and feelings of our mind and heart and the visible actions we take because of them. Spiritual law is a timeless law or principle and being of spirit, and is not visible. It is not shaped or determined by any person's current opinion or whim. Spiritual laws are impartial in that they apply equally to everyone, everywhere throughout our world. They work without prejudices or bias at all times and in all places. These laws are self-enforcing and are not dependent on human authority or commandants. Laozi makes it clear that if people can embrace the spiritual law or Tao (the power of mind) and cultivate the virtues (the law of mind action), they won't fail and are able to thrive (Templeton 2002).

By recognizing and aligning ourselves with these laws, humans can attain a state of being which combines the experience of total freedom with one of complete connectedness to life's processes—being at one with the Tao. To help gain this level of existence, Taoist writings offer us various principles to be followed in the course of everyday living. Understanding and adopting these values presents the opportunity to become whole and complete, to consciously become an inseparable part of life's flow.

In modern language, we can interpret the Tao (power of mind) as the Why, purpose or cause. Some of the elements of the power of the mind may be familiar to us: vision, imagination, intent, belief, positive or negative thinking, etc.. Everyone uses these elements of mind frequently throughout the day. But many people may not realize the important contribution these aspects of the mind make toward defining the character and personality of an individual. So, understanding the quote, "When you rule your mind, you rule your world," can provide powerful insight into some of the ways we function as an individual.

The virtues (the law of mind action) can be translated as the HOW, strategy, effect, or principle. It plays its role in every person's life. How does the law of mind action affect a person and his world? One answer offers the premise that thinking is the connecting link between the universal mind of Tao and man. Awareness of this law and its application can help you shepherd your thoughts and ascertain that they are positive and of art of everything. Within the mind of every individual abides the starting point of a person's thoughts, spoken words, actions, and even one's feelings. What you think about the Creator of all, ourselves, our family, our neighbours, our acquaintances, our work associates, or others, make a great deal of difference in our daily life. In fact, every aspect of our life can be affected by the way we think! As Joseph Addison once said, "One of the most difficult things for a powerful mind is to be its own master!" It is important to be aware of the situations and circumstances around you. It is also important and helpful to possess certain qualities in life: sincerity of purpose, dedication to ideals, commitment to integrity, and a continual thirst for knowledge.

Now let's discuss the Taoism and purpose. The first question we may ask what the purpose of Taoism is. The purpose of Taoism is to create the World of *Da-Tong*, which refers to a harmonious and peaceful World or Great Unity for Common Good. Laozi never drew the blueprint in his teaching of TTC, but he did depict an ideal world where there is ideal people—simple and honest—in Tao Te Ching, verse 65, ideal leaders—humble to serve people—in verse 66, and ideal nation—small with little population—in verse 60. Confucius mapped out the vision and blueprint of ideal world that Laozi depicted in the Book of Rites (*Li Ji*), a collection of texts describing the social forms, administration, and ceremonial rites of ancient time. This is what the World of *Da-Tong* looks like as Confucius described:

When the Great Tao (perfect order) prevails,
the world is like a Commonwealth State shared by all, not a dictatorship.
Virtuous, worthy, wise, and capable people are chosen as leaders.
Honesty and trust are promoted, and good neighborliness cultivated.
All people respect and love their own parents and children, as well as the parents and children of others.
The aged are cared for until death; adults are employed in jobs that make full use of their abilities; and
children are nourished, educated, and fostered.
Widows and widowers, orphans and the old without children,
the disabled and the diseased are all well taken care of.
Every man and woman has an appropriate role to play in society and in the family.
They hate to see resource lying idle or cast away, yet they do not necessarily keep them for themselves.
They hate not to make use of their abilities, yet they do not necessarily work for their own self-interest.

> *Thus intrigues and conspiracies do not arise, and thievery and robbery do not occur; therefore, doors need never be locked.*
> *This is the ideal world—a perfect world of equality, fraternity, harmony, welfare, and justice.*
> *This is the world called "Da-Tong."* (Hwang 2010)

The World of *Da-Tong* is the state "of the people, by the people, and for the people", and characterized by ideal leaders—virtuous, worthy, wise, and capable, and ideal people—honest, trustworthy, caring and respectful. And most importantly, every people have purpose—social responsibility and environmental sustainability, for example, every man and woman have an appropriate role to play in society and in the family, they do not necessarily work for their own self-interest, and they hate to see resource lying idle or cast away, yet they do not necessarily keep them for themselves. In Chinese history, we do have a few dynasties that achieved the World of Da-Tong, for instance, the Tang Dynasty. Emperor of Taizong Tang, Li Simin was the second emperor of the Tang Dynasty. He is typically considered to be one of the greatest emperors in China's history and henceforth. He is typical Taoist and purpose-driven leader. His reign became regarded as the exemplary model against which all future emperors were measured. His era, the "*Reign of Zhenguan*" is considered a golden age in Chinese history and was the World of Da-Tong.

To realize the World of Da-Tong, leaders must embrace and cultivate three core virtues or principles of Taoism, Laozi calls them three treasures or I call it 3C as we discussed in the preceding chapters:

> *I have three treasures to hold and enshrine,*
> *The first is compassion,*
> *The second is conservation,*
> *The third is compliance.*
> —Laozi, Tao Te Ching, Ch. 67

Compassion—a caring, kindness or charity toward all things in the world—is the most important and primary virtue of Tao Te Ching, and is the foundation of other two virtues: conservation and compliance. The whole idea of compassion is based on a keen awareness of the interdependence of all these living beings, which are all part of one another and all involved in one another. Compassion is an important, even critical skill for leaders worldwide. This has been proved by the scientific evidence. The Study of the compassion and leadership has demonstrated the compassion leads to strong leadership. Conservation—moderation, prudence and effectiveness—traditionally, refers to the act of preserving, guarding or protecting natural resources, environment or cultural heritage, etc. But from the perspective of Taoism, it focuses on frugality, thrift and prudence in not only natural resources, but also in the human's spirits, energy, and managing and leading people knowing when and how to avoid wasting one's resources in terms of time and energy, and direct them in a meaningful way, in accordance with one's purpose in life. Compliance—humility, integrity and accountability—means confirming to a rule, code of conduct, standards or to comply with relevant law and regulations. But in wisdom of Taoism, it is concerned more with "not daring to put oneself ahead of others", in other words, with the qualities of humility, un-contentedness, integrity, and accountability. It refers to the act or action of yielding in relationship with others and environment. It stresses cooperation over competition. Compliance requires human beings to live in harmony with each other to avoid the crisis, conflicts and disasters in the process of economic development and growth.

Purpose: The Business Perspective

Inge Thulin, president, CEO, and chairman of 3M once said, "An enterprise not focused on sustainability for their own products and those of their customers will not exist in 50 years." EY Beacon Institute research reveals that businesses need to embrace and integrate a humanistic, multi-stakeholder-oriented purpose to navigate today's volatile, uncertain economy. Businesses need to be driven by a purpose higher than maximizing profit, and they must ensure optimal benefits to all stakeholders. Only if that happens can capitalism deliver to all humanity the full societal benefits it is capable of.

Over the past decades, CEOs and executives, and management scholars have over focused on vision, mission, and strategy. Is there any difference from business purpose? Of course, it is (Kenny 2014) claims that your company's purpose is not its vision, mission, or values. Business leaders have to clarify it and place in meaningful relationship for their company to thrive. I pull together the terms and distinguishes these terms from one another: vision is about what is possible for us to become; mission is about what business the organization is in (and what it isn't) both now and projecting into the future; strategy is about how we will get there; and purpose is about why it is so important that we exist in the world or what is the reason for being (Cashman 2017). The explanation of purpose of Johnson Controls tells us how it defines the relationships among the concepts of vision, strategy and purpose. Johnson Controls, a 130-year-old company has treated purpose as a key driver behind its success. Kim Metcalf-Kupres, Chief Marketing Officer explained his company's purpose to EY Beacon Institute, "The heart of our motivation and inspiration is really to find and stick to what Johnson Controls is good at. The purpose behind our company has really been captured in a vision that we've used for many years about creating a more comfortable, safe and sustainable world. Our strategies have evolved with that vision in mind. And as we look for the next century and the megatrends that are driving the world, we think the things that we bring to the world are very relevant. As we look at the makeup of the company and the implications for us as an organization, that's challenged us in this age of activism to really understand what fits in our core and what does not." We should not be confused with specific goals or business strategies. We might achieve a goal or complete a strategy, but we cannot fulfill a purpose; it's like a guiding star on the horizon—forever pursued but never reached.

However, we have found that most companies already have a purpose, be implicit or explicit, which dates from their creation. For example, I was surprised when I found as early as 1947, Forrest E. Mars, Sr. started to be aware of power of purpose,

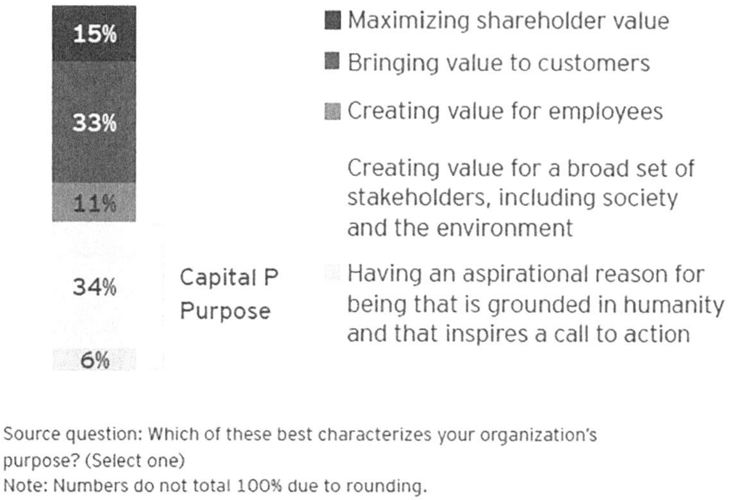

Fig. 13.1 The definitions of purpose. Source: EY Beacon Institute, "How Can Purpose Reveal a Path through Disruption? Mapping the Journey from Rhetoric to Reality", report 2017

and defined the purpose of the Mars, the candy company as "*the manufacture and distribution of food products in such manner as to promote a mutuality of services and benefits among consumers, distributors, competitors, suppliers, governmental bodies, employees and shareholders*." Obviously, the purpose of Mars is multi-stakeholders-centricity. The International Institute for Management Development (IMD) echoes these ideas, defining purpose as "a company's core 'reason for being.' The organization's single underlying objective unifies all stakeholders and embodies its ultimate role in the broader economic, societal and environmental context."

IMD defines purpose by blending a CSR approach (the value creation without doing harm to society and environment) and a stakeholder approach (the value creation for and with multi-stakeholders). EY Beacon Institute (2016) describes a corporate purpose as an aspirational reason for being that is grounded in humanity and inspires a call to action.

In 2017, EY came up with the brand-new concept of capital P Purpose based on the result of their survey. Having analysing the extent and impact of different characterizations of purpose, they define it as the purpose that focuses on creating value for a broad set of stakeholders. The study they conducted focused on five definitions of purpose: maximizing shareholder value; primarily creating value for customers; primarily benefiting employees; serving all stakeholders and improving society; and having an aspirational, human-centric mission designed to inspire a call to action. Combining the last two, which both speak to a broad, socially engaged Purpose, produced the top-ranking answer, given by 40% of the business leaders they asked (Fig. 13.1).

The definitions I introduced above are all concerned with who and whose interests business should serve, creating value for a single stakeholder, like shareholder, employee, customer or for multiple stakeholders.

Izzo and Vanderwielen (2018) define purpose from the perspectives of individual and organization. For the individual employee or worker, purpose is the belief that work serves to make a difference in a way that is meaningful to that person. It is the part of work that is not simply about earning a salary or having status but a sense that the work itself has meaning, with an underlying feeling that the job serves society or their personal values in a positive way. For organizations they define purpose as an aspirational reason for being that is about making life better now and in the future for all stakeholders, especially customers, society, and the planet. A purposeful organization is one that has built its entire enterprise around this core reason for existence. Though the organization may manufacture products, provide services, and generate profits, its entire system revolves around this desire to make life better for customers, employees, society, and the environment now and in the future.

We can see from the definitions given by practitioners and academic scholars that purpose often means slightly different things to different companies, in the same way that people define their individual purposes in slightly different ways. Nonetheless, the common theme is that business should create value for its full set of stakeholders. The consensus among scholars and practitioners is that purpose is not about making money, but about making the world better to live. Whenever making money becomes a company's primary purpose, losing sight of what's best for customers and the world at large, it is often the beginning of a downward spiral that can be halted only when purpose once again becomes paramount. Volkswagen emissions scandal is a typical case to illustrate the point. The decision to deceive regulators on emissions from diesel cars was clearly good for business in the short term, as it allowed the company to promote and sell its vehicles as "clean alternatives." But what allowed that decision to be made? The best guess is that VW was not staffed by evil people who could care less about the environment. Instead, there is a very good chance that the focus on clean vehicles at VW was being driven mostly as a strategy rather than as a belief in doing what's right and making the world a better place. The distinction between "doing what's right" and the business case may feel like mere semantics, and there is no doubt that the difference can be subtle. There are the occasional companies like Enron, run by people whose basic ethics turn out to be purely self-oriented, but most of the biggest purpose problems likely come from this focus on purpose as a means rather than an end.

Purpose: The Pathway to High Performance

According to Korn Ferry's latest study, consumer companies that focused their employees on the organization's purpose boasted annual growth rates that were nearly triple the annual rate for the whole sector. And the benefits go beyond financial. The study also found that having an authentic purpose can help recruit and retain talent, win over customers, and have positive impacts on broader society (Korn Ferry Institute 2016).

The study, called "People on a mission," examined a broad set of purpose-driven organizations, including interviews with 30 founders, CEOs, and senior executives at consumer companies with visible and authentic purposes, engaged employees, customer-oriented cultures, and strong financial results. "We have found that organizations that take the challenging steps to define their core purpose and values, and integrate these throughout their operations—beyond slogans or advertising gimmicks—see not only strong bottom-line results, they also find this approach transforms all aspects of their business," said Elaine Dinos, principal of Korn Ferry's Global Consumer Market practice. "When an organization has a clear purpose, it unleashes the power and drive of the entire workforce, harnessing and focusing that combined effort in one aligned direction." Indeed, the study found that companies with the proper focus posted compounded annual growth rates of 9.85% compared to a 2.4% for the whole S&P 500 Consumer Sector.

EY Beacon Institute research has consistently shown that purpose enables organizations to perform well in times of volatility. The research joins a growing body of evidence demonstrating that a strong and active purpose raises employee engagement and acts as a unifier, makes customers more loyal and committed to working with you, and helps to frame effective decision making in an environment of uncertainty. Global Leadership Forecast 2018 finds that getting purpose right builds organizational resilience and, crucially, improves long-term financial performance as seen in the figure below.

They found that the real benefits come when leaders walk the walk by behaving in a manner that exemplifies their organization's purpose (DDI 2018). Tony Hsieh, the visionary CEO at online retailer Zappos is one of the exemplary leaders. He shows in his book of In Delivering Happiness: A Path to Profits, Passion, and Purpose how connecting employees with values and meaning serves as one path to happiness. Today, he's also building a consultancy, Delivering Happiness at Work, around the importance of a values-based culture in achieving both happiness and business success. Zappos' renowned culture, remarkable growth, and robust financial performance stand testament to this philosophy and approach.

The DDI's survey also shows that of 1500 global C-Suite executives surveyed, 84 percent say their business operates in an increasingly disrupted environment. In this world, purpose is a North Star—fixed point to help navigate through change and uncertainty. To understand the impact of purpose, they identified three types of organizations: those without a purpose; those with a purpose statement and purposeful organizations where leaders bring the stated purpose to life through behaviours.

They found clear evidence that companies in this third category are earning a significant performance premium (see Fig. 13.2) (DDI 2018).

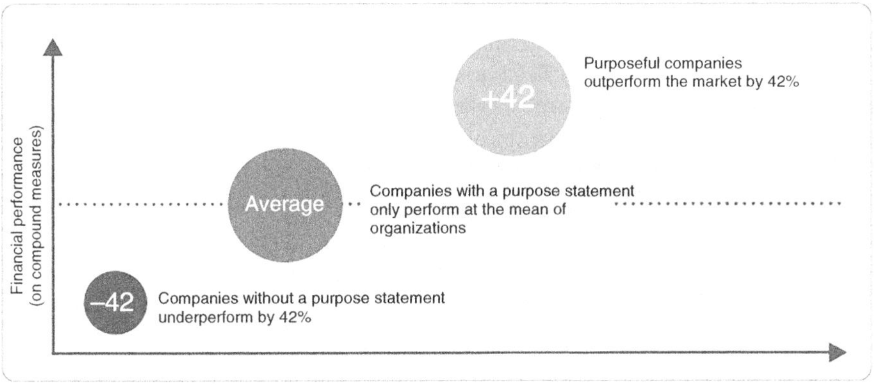

Fig. 13.2 Impact of purpose on financial performance. Source: DDI (2018), Global Leadership Forecast 2018: 25 Research Insights to Fuel Your People Strategy

What Does Purpose Matter to Leadership?

There is growing consensus among leaders today that business exists, not to make money, but to make the world better, and most agree that both employees and customers want to associate with enterprises that provide a sense of purpose. 90% of executives have said that their company understands the importance of purpose, but "only 46 percent said it informs their strategic and operational decision-making." (Izzo and Vanderwielen 2018). Every leader must have a purpose, and they have a responsibility to address this significant question: why do we exist? Why is it so important that we exist? what is the contribution we want to make? Why is the world better because we are here? A successful purpose both drives a company forward and helps build sustainable competitive advantage. In the hands of an effective leader, purpose becomes the engine of a company, the source of its energy (Mourkogiannis 2014).

Imbuing an organization with a core purpose can be hard work, requiring a deep and abiding commitment from the top. The commitment needs to be backed up by key best practices, including hiring people who connect with the organization's purpose, transparency in leadership's actions, and incentive plans based on an employee's holistic contributions to the organization. Leading in the purpose revolution must begin with each of us as a leader discovering our own purpose—the reason we are leading that is greater than the massing of profits. You need to find your personal purpose to contribute to something that is greater than yourself or even your company. Your actions must be imbued with meaning because what you say and do matters, maybe even more than you realize. It's not just a question of your values but of your future and legacy, and it all starts with finding and living your purpose.

Korn Ferry's study shows that CEOs loom large in purpose-driven organizations. They are the chief advocates of their organizations' core purposes. Typically, they are inspired to be part of something larger than themselves, and they work hard to affect others' lives in positive ways. They strive to maintain a laser-like focus on serving all stakeholders (not just shareholders), and the greater world. Through their communications, actions, and behaviours, these leaders set clear examples of how their organizations pursue purpose while adhering to shared values. "If we stay exceptionally true to the foundation of this company, we will continue to do really well," said Jim Alling, CEO of TOMS. "We do well when people want to read past the superficial layer. The minute we become a sell-out brand is the minute we die" (Korn Ferry Institute 2016).

An organization that benefits society as well as shareholders requires leaders at all levels who never stop reflecting on who they are and who they want to be, who can blend their own personal purpose with those who see the world differently, who tell the truth about obstacles and recognize their own personal responsibility in creating them, and who know there are no final answers or formulas.

A great example of a leader who found his personal purpose—transforming the company he worked for in the process—is Paul Polman, CEO of the consumer goods company Unilever. He calls on leaders to use their position to take a stand and be courageous about what they believe in. When Polman joined Unilever, he helped refocus the business around social and environmental values. Under his leadership Unilever created the Sustainable Living Plan, which includes plans to "reduce our absolute environmental impact. . .and increase our positive social impact." He realized that addressing these issues required a fearless long-term strategy, not short-term thinking. He told Forbes: The big changes we need to make to transform this world, if you want to, are changes that will be made against the odds—lots of naysayers and sceptics. So, to fundamentally make these changes, you need to have a certain level of courage, especially at the CEO level...[so] we certainly need more courageous leaders. Defining courage as "the ability to put the interests of others ahead of your own and be able to absorb personal risks," he encourages us "to fight your way through that." Having met scores of Unilever team members at all levels, we can personally attest to the way Polman's personal purpose, and his willingness to speak openly about it, has inspired deep loyalty and commitment throughout the company.

The Power of Purpose and Values: From the perspective of Taoism

What Drives Your Life?

Purpose is not everything, but it trumps everything else. Every organization must also have strong leadership, management, succession planning, execution, strategy and tactics, innovation, and more, but Spence (2011) believes that it all has to start with a purpose. That is the hinge that everything else hangs upon. Everyone's life is driven by something. There are hundreds of circumstances, values, and emotions that can drive your life. Rick Warren identified five of the most common ones: Those who are driven by guilt are manipulated by memories. They allow their past to control their future. They often unconsciously punish themselves by sabotaging their own success. Those who are driven by resentment and anger often miss great opportunities because they're afraid to venture out. They play it safe, avoiding risks and trying to maintain the status quo. Those who are driven by materialism desire to acquire becomes the whole goal of their lives, and always want more based on the misconceptions that having more will make them more happy, more important, and more secure. Those who are driven by the need for approval allow the expectations of parents or spouses or children or teachers or friends to control their lives. There are other forces that can drive your life but all lead to the same dead end: unused potential, unnecessary stress, and an unfulfilled life (Warren 2002).

The wisdom of Taoism shows us how to live a purpose-driven life—a life guided, controlled, and directed by the great Tao or spiritual law. Without a purpose or the Tao, life is motion without meaning, activity without direction, and events without reason. Without a purpose, life is trivial, petty, and pointless. For example, one of the benefits that purpose-driven life is that those who know their purpose can simplify their life. It defines what you do and what you don't do. From the Taoism's viewpoint, this is one of key principles of Taoism—*no-doing or non-action, wu-wei. Wu-wei* refers to behavior that arise from a sense of oneself as connected to others and to one's environment. *Wu-wei* must be your purpose that sets the standard that you use to evaluate which activities are essential and which aren't. Without a clear purpose you have no foundation on which you base decisions, allocate your time, and use your resources. You will tend to make choices based on circumstances, pressures, and your mood at that moment. People who don't know their purpose try to do too much-and that causes stress, fatigue, and conflict.

Laozi explains why purpose is powerful and what impact purpose-driven leaders have on others.

> *Those who hold true to the great Tao are*
> *Followed by people in the world*
> *People not only follow them, but do no harm to them.*
> *Music and delicious-looking food tempt people's senses,*
> *But they are like busy travellers' stopover.*
> *Tao is odorless and tasteless when it is expressed in word*
> *Invisible when it is looked at,*
> *Inaudible when it is listened to,*
> *But inexhaustible when it is used.*
> —Laozi, Tao Te Ching, Ch. 35

Laozi here begins with the influence and power of leaders who align themselves with purpose. Laozi says that those who hold true to the great Tao are followed by people in the world, because they cultivate themselves with virtue. They are like the North Star around which is revolved by other stars. Confucius also says, "*Those who lead people with virtue are like the North Star, which stays in its place, and all the other stars turn towards it.*" The virtuous or purpose-driven leaders are role model of their followers and show respect and concerns for others so that the followers are inspired and empowered to act spontaneously. Therefore, Laozi says, "*Great leaders who do not speak gets a good response; great leaders who do not summon is obeyed and followed*". Great leaders who follow the Tao are able to inspire people to act. Those who are able to inspire give people a sense of purpose or belonging that has little to do with any external incentive or benefit to be gained. Those who truly lead are able to create a following of people who act not because they were swayed, but because they were inspired. For those who are inspired, the motivation to act is deeply personal. They are less likely to be swayed by incentives. Those who are inspired are willing to pay a premium or endure inconvenience, even personal suffering. Those who are able to inspire will create a following of people—supporters, customers, workers—who act for the good of the whole not because they have to, but because they want to.

Then, Laozi reminds us of another style of leadership which is opposite to the purpose- driven leadership. They are profit-driven leaders. Laozi uses the metaphor of music and food as the temptation and desires that people run after in their life. It is normal that what we perceive is what we see and hear, so we need to go in the direction pointed out by our senses—yet, constantly reminding ourselves that there is more to it and that the Tao reaches farther than we are able to detect. If we hold on to it and go where it leads, we will find that the whole world complies and benefits as well. Although Tao is hard to see or hear, and words to describe it become far from spectacular, it's inexhaustible. That's because it's not a thing or a creature, but a principle, a natural law that governs the universe. Tao is the way the universe works. The whole universe may dissolve without the law of its fate doing so. Like a formula it can be used over and over and over, without suddenly ceasing to function.

Values and Purpose

Many practitioners and scholars have concluded that purpose can have a real impact only if executives' and employees' understanding and commitment to this core belief are strongly aligned. Core values constitute the guiding principles the business uses to realize its purpose. Core purpose operates at the high-performing intersection where our core talents and core values come together. It is the value-creating, catalytic moment when our gifts make a meaningful, enduring difference. Leadership purpose is rooted in your values and your authentic self. You must be true to who you really are and to the ethics, principles, and causes that are most meaningful to you. Developing personal purpose involves getting in touch with our values and our unique contribution to the world. As you think about your own purpose as a leader, you need to clarify your deepest values and concentrate on what sincerely matters to you (Izzo and Vanderwielen 2018).

Laozi discovered purpose and core values in pattern of one's behaviour. The pattern of one's behaviour is shaped by its identity of values and purpose. Laozi claims that different values and purpose lead to different patterns of behaviour. Laozi says,

Those who follow Tao are at one with Tao
Those who cultivate virtue are at one with virtue (Te),
Those who forgo Tao and virtue (Te) are at one with deprivation
Those who are at one with the Tao are embraced by the Tao,
Those who are at one with virtue (Te) are embraced by virtue (Te),
Those who are at one with loss of Tao and virtue are embraced by deprivation.
—Laozi, Tao Te Ching, Ch. 23

Put it simply, the verse means that I am what I think, I think Tao, the Tao is released in me, and I am wise with the wisdom; I think the Virtue, the Virtue is released in me, and I am virtuous. I think the loss (forgo Tao and Virtue), the Loss is released in me, and I am a failure. Your purpose is why you exist. Your values define who you are, what you stand for, and how you behave. Your mind is your world. Your thoughts are the tools with which you carve your life story on the substance of the universe. When you rule your mind, you rule your world. When you choose your thoughts, you choose your results (Shanklin 2005). This is the Tao of cause and effect in action. If people's thought is good, their actions and deeds are good, so they will surely receive blessings. If people's thought is bad, their actions and deeds are also bad, so they will surely bring on misfortune. Good and bad thought are the cause of events, receiving blessings and bringing on misfortune are the effect of events. When there is a cause, it will surely have an effect. It cannot be that the fruit of good seed is not good, nor can it be that the fruit of bad seed is not bad. The consequences of good and bad are like shadows following forms, certain and invariable. It is all a matter of choosing between planting good and planting evil, distinguishing what is good and what is bad. Therefore, great leaders consider the beginning when they do things; being careful about things in the beginning, they are able to complete them in the end (Liu 1988).

Laozi also showcased the comparison of himself (Taoist or a purposeful leader) with other people to illustrate different values and purpose lead to different behaviours.

Other people are busy pursuing after enjoyment
As if they were ascending the terrace in spring and celebrate a sacrificial feast.
I alone remain stoic, quiet and indifferent,
Like a newborn baby who is pure and innocent,
And I alone appeared to be lost like one who has nowhere to go.
Other people possess more than they need,
While I alone seem wanting.
I have the mind of a fool—so ignorant!
Other people are bright and shrewd, but I am alone stupid.
Other people are narrow-minded, but I am alone open-minded:
My heart is as boundless as the sea that embraces everything;
My soul is as free as the wind that blows everywhere.
Other people are talented, but I alone appeared unlearned.
Why I am different from others is that I hold on to the Tao or purpose.
—Laozi, Tao Te Ching, Ch. 20

Laozi's wisdom offers us with the principles and standards for purpose-driven leaders. We must understand what our values and how to do with alignment with our purpose. Different values result in different purpose, and different purpose leads to the different performance. Jim Collins's recent study has validated the principles of Taoism. In Good to Great, (Collins 2001) wrote about the preservation of what he calls "core legacy," the combination of core values and core purpose, as a feature of enduring companies that went from "*good to great, to build to last.*" Collins explains that there are not necessarily any "right" or "wrong" values, but there is the necessity to have them and live them, because they provide a reason for being beyond making money. Enduring great companies preserve their core values and purpose while their business strategies and operating practices endlessly adapt to a changing world.

Drawing upon what he saw in the visionary companies, Collins has created a practical two-part definition of core ideology: Core Ideology = Core Values + Purpose. Core Values = The organization's essential and enduring tenets—a small set of general guiding principles; not to be confused with specific cultural or operating practices; not to be compromised for financial gain or short-term expediency. Purpose = The organization's fundamental reasons for existence beyond just making money—a perpetual guiding star on the horizon; not to be confused with specific goals or business strategies.

Thomas J. Watson, Jr., former IBM chief executive, commented on the role of core values (what he calls beliefs) in his 1963 booklet A Business and Its Beliefs:

I believe the real difference between success and failure in a corporation can very often be traced to the question of how well the organization brings out the great energies and talents of its people. What does it do to help these people find common cause with each other? ... And how can it sustain this common cause and sense of direction through the many changes which take place from one generation to another? ... [I think the answer lies] in the power of what we call beliefs and the appeal these beliefs have for its people.... I firmly believe that any organization, in order to survive and achieve success, must have a sound set of beliefs on which it premises all its policies and actions. Next, I believe that the most important single factor in corporate success is faithful adherence to those beliefs.... Beliefs must always come before policies, practices, and goals. The latter must always be altered if they are seen to violate fundamental beliefs.

Whole Foods Market is the case in point. Whole Foods Market's core values succinctly express the purposes of the business—purposes that include making profits but also creating value for all of the major constituencies. Their core values are these: selling the highest-quality natural and organic products available, satisfying and delighting their customers, supporting team member happiness and excellence, creating wealth through profits and growth, caring about their communities and the environment, creating ongoing win-win partnerships with their suppliers, and promoting the health of their stakeholders through healthy eating education. John Mackey, co-founder and co-CEO of Whole Foods Market, contended that companies with a "conscious culture" and "higher purpose" inspire employees to reach their greatest potential, as well as help support the fight against the current "purpose crisis" in America. "Businesses in the twenty-first century need to shift focus from profit maximization to purpose maximization," argued Mackay. "In fully aligning your organization's strategies, systems, and structures around a higher purpose", he said, "You will almost certainly realize business results—making more money than you thought possible." Whole Foods' purpose-driven business model focuses on "whole foods, whole people, whole planet," and the model empowers the company's 62,000 employees and plays a huge role in the organization's success. For example, Whole Foods' Total Health Immersion Program, an internal initiative whereby at-risk employees receive intensive health and wellness education geared toward sustaining positive lifestyle changes. With great passion, Mackey underscored the power of purpose and values and a conscious culture: it energizes and engages employees, promotes creativity and innovation, and helps businesses achieve a sustainable competitive advantage (Armstrong 2012).

References

Aristotle. (1995). *Nicomachean ethics*.http://www.iep.utm.edu/aris-pol/#H5.

Armstrong, B. T. (2012, 26 April 2012). The power of purpose and values: Leadership lessons from the great place to work conference. *Forbes*. Retrieved April 18, 2018, from https://www.forbes.com/sites/barbaraarmstrong/2012/04/26/the-power-of-purpose-and-values-leadership-lessons-from-the-great-place-to-work-conference/#50a3f6d82dca

Bronk, K. C. (2012). A grounded theory of the development of noble youth purpose. *Journal of Adolescent Research, 27*(1), 78–109.

Butler-Bowdon, T. (2017). *50 Philosophy Classics: Your shortcut to the most important ideas on being, truth, and meaning*.

Cashman, K. (2017). *Leadership from the inside out: Becoming a leader for life*. Berrett-Koehler Publishers.

Collins, J. (2001). *Good to great: Why some companies make the Leap and others don't*. HarperBusiness.

Damon, W. (2008). *The path to purpose: How young people find their calling in life*. Free Press.

DDI. (2018). *Gloabal leadership forecast 2018 report: 25 research insights to fuel your people strategy*. https://www.ddiworld.com/glf2018/purposeful-leadership

EY Beacon Institute. (2016). The state of the debate on purpose in business.

EY Beacon Institute. (2017). How can purpose reveal a path through disruption? *Mapping the Journey from Rhetoric to Reality*.

Han, H. (2015). Purpose as a moral virtue for flourishing. *Journal of Moral Education, 44*(3), 291–309.

Ho, D. Y. F. (1995). Selfhood and identity in confucianism, Taoism, Buddhism, and Hinduism: Contrasts with the west. *Journal for the Theory of Social Behaviour, 25*(2), 115–139.

Hollender, J. B. B. (2010). *The responsibility revolution: How the next generation of businesses will win*. Jossey-Bass.

Hwang, M. S.-M. (2010, 1 July 2010). *The purpose of Taoism*. Translation Compiled Retrieved April 18, 2018, from http://www.with.org/classics_datong.html

Izzo, J., & Vanderwielen, J. (2018). *The purpose revolution: How leaders create engagement and competitive advantage in an age of social good*. Berrett-Koehler Publishers.

Kenny, G. (2014, 3 September 2014). *Your company's purpose is not its vision, mission, or values*. Harvard Business Review. Retrieved April 26, 2018, from https://hbr.org/2014/09/your-companys-purpose-is-not-its-vision-mission-or-values

Korn Ferry Institute. (2016). *Korn Ferry report 2016 on people on mission: How purpose drives performance*. K. F. Institute. https://www.kornferry.com/institute/purpose-powered-success.

Leider, R. J. (2015). *The power of purpose: Find meaning, live longer, better* (3rd ed.). Berrett-Koehler Publishers.

Liu, I.-m. (1988). *Awakening to the Tao: Translated from the Chinese by Thomas Cleary*. Shambhala.

Mourkogiannis, N. (2014). *Purpose: The starting point of great companies*. St. Martin's Press.

Pfarrer, M. D. (2010). What is the purpose of the firm? Shareholder and stakeholder theories. In J. D. M. O'Toole (Ed.), *Good business: Exercising effective and ethical leadership*. Routledge.

Pontefract, D. (2017, 25 April, 2018). *Stop confusing CSR with purpose*. Forbes. Retrieved November, 18, 2019, from https://www.forbes.com/sites/danpontefract/2017/11/18/stop-confusing-csr-with-purpose/#67949cf23190

Rahula, W. (1974). *What the Buddha taught*. Grove Press.

Sachs, J. (2002). *Aristotle Nicomachean ethics: Translation, glossary, and introduction essay*. Focus Publishing/R. Pullins Company.

Shanklin, I. O. (2005). *What are you?* Unity.

Spence, R. M. (2011). *It's not what you sell, it's what you stand for: Why every extraordinary business is driven by purpose*. Portfolio Trade.

Templeton, J. (2002). *Wisdom from world religions: Pathways toward heaven on earth*. Templeton Foundation Pr.

UPM. (2017). *Annual report 2017 on aiming higher with biofore*. http://www.upm.com/Investors/Reports-Presentations/2017/Pages/default.aspx

Warren, R. (2002). *The purpose driven life: What on earth am i here for?* Zondervan.

Chapter 14
Five Principles of Taoism for Purpose-Driven Leadership

We discussed in Chap. 13 the concepts and definitions of purpose and its power and impact on organizational performance. This chapter will offer five principles for leaders who want to cultivate and activate their purpose from perspective of Taoism's wisdom. I am assumed if purpose and values provide the compass, and principles give leaders a set of directions.

We know that to be purposeful leader or purposeful company is not easy, even companies and leaders who recognize power of purpose have a hard time getting on board with purpose. They may not have the right mindset or the necessary resources at their disposable. There are many reasons why companies fail to truly close the purpose gap or activate purpose. For example, many leaders make the mistake of treating purpose just like any other plan to win talent and customers, or like making money or marketing program, etc. Izzo and Vanderwielen (2018) have come up with the best practices for avoiding purpose pitfalls and point out what traits constitute the purpose:

- *Purpose must be authentic and cannot be viewed as another short-term business strategy or way to garner customer attention;*
- *Shift the dialogue from profit to purpose;*
- *Align your brand's core competencies with your social platform by making a clear, authentic purpose statement;*
- *Be willing to update your purpose and vision with the changing times, keeping in mind the expectations of tomorrow's generation as well as today's.*

Now the most difficult part might be the application of the best practices in reality if leaders do not change their ideology and mentality, transform fixed mind-set to growth mindset. Laozi ascribed failure in cultivating the Tao or purpose to different mindsets.

> Those who have high wisdom hear of the Tao diligently practice it;
> Those who have low wisdom hear of the Tao doubt it and
> Those who have no wisdom hear of the Tao laugh loudly at it.
> – Laozi, Tao Te Ching, Ch. 41

L. Zu, *Responsible and Sustainable Business*,
https://doi.org/10.1007/978-3-030-91117-1_14

If we interpret the passage in our modern business language, it might be easy to understand Laozi's ideas. Laozi described three types of people who embrace three different mindsets: growth mindset, mixed mindset and fixed mindset. Those who have growth mindset believe that abilities can be developed. They have high wisdom and perseverance, and never give up even in the face of struggle. They take negative feedback and apply it to their own work the next time they do a task. Therefore, they are positive to activate and practice purpose in organization; those who have mixed mindset have low wisdom and low perseverance, and try hard until they face a struggle. They need a strategy before they can overcome the obstacle on perseverance. They are inspired to do better by feedback, but they need to consider the source in order to take it seriously. Therefore, they are in hesitation and unable to bring purpose statement to life. Those who have fixed mindset are smart, but have no wisdom, and believe that abilities are fixed. They do not persevere and gives up after the littlest inconvenience and they feel intimidated by negative feedback and do not apply the corrections. Therefore, they are negative and unwilling to develop purpose in organization.

Developing a purposeful organization and purpose-driven leadership requires transformation in mindset from fixed, mixed to growth mindset. Wisdom of Laozi offers us principles, which can guide and transform leaders' mindset. In this chapter, I will walk you through that the text of Tao Te Ching to identify the five principles of Taoism for effective leadership. The principles of Taoism have been tested in the fires of real life, with real people. These essential leadership principles encourage true growth and real change.

The purpose of the five principles of Taoism is to offer guide and direction for development of holistic (whole) leadership. From the discussions I did in the preceding chapters, you may understand that one of the fundamental principles of Taoism which is clearly stated in Tao Te Ching is "Oneness" meaning that every being in the universe is a manifestation of the Tao. The Tao births every being, sustains them, defends them, cares for them, eases them, and in end takes all beings back to itself. Following oneness is the dynamic balance. Dynamic balance is the equality of the two distinctions in nature represented by yin and yang. This pair of yin and yang symbolizes opposite forces such as the sun and the moon, heaven and earth, light and dark, and chaos and order; one of the purposes of Taoism is to find harmony between these polar opposites. Weakness was produced from strength, and strength created weakness. The fundamental principles of Taoism govern the ways to live and view life.

Dhiman (2017) claims in his book, "Holistic Leadership: A New Paradigm for Today's Leaders" that the solution to the current leadership crisis lies in leaders' self-cultivation process, emanating from their deepest values and culminating in their contribution to the common good. Traditional approaches to leadership rarely provide any permeating or systematic framework to garner a sense of higher purpose or nurture deeper moral and spiritual dimensions of leaders. Learning to be an effective leader requires a level of personal transformation on the continuum of self, spirit, and service.

Synthesizing the best of contemporary approaches to leadership in a holistic manner, this chapter will present a unique model of leadership that is built on the sound principles of self-awareness for mindful leadership; self-cultivation for authentic leadership, transcending ego for servant leadership, humble to serve for Level-5 leadership and doing the right thing right for sustainable leadership.

The five principles are logically integrated and interacted with each other. Self-awareness is at the centre of a purpose-driven leader's compass, and the foundation of authenticity. To develop your self-awareness, you must cultivate yourself with virtue, the power of Tao. Self-cultivation is a path to be authentic and achieve the ultimate purpose of life. Humility is the heart of a leader, and is a quality of certain types of leaders. A sense of humility is essential because it authenticates a person's humanity. John Buchan, a Scottish novelist, historian says, "Without humility there can be no humanity". Mahatma Gandhi says that attempting to sustain truth without humility is doomed to become an "arrogant caricature" of truth. Humility is a trait that can enhance leadership effectiveness. Humility is one of core virtues of Taoism for a wise leader to cultivate. When you cultivate your humility and transcend your ego, you have the power to serve others. However, to be an effective and sustainable leader requires the principle of "doing the right things right". This is the pathway for purpose-driven leaders to achieve a sustainable business.

Self-Awareness: Mindful Leadership

The history reveals that nearly all individuals who achieve high levels of personal and professional success have a keen sense of self-awareness. A purpose-driven leader must start with self-awareness. Leading others begins by first leading yourself, and measure yourself before you measure others. Peter Drucker claims that we can't manage others unless we learn to manage ourselves (Drucker & Wartzman, 2010). Once you discover the purpose of your leadership, you'll find the true leader inside you.

Self-awareness is the foundation of authenticity, and thus it is at the centre of a purpose-driven leader's compass. You develop it by exploring your life story and then understanding the meaning of your crucibles. As you do this, you need to understand who you are at a deeper level. This is hard work, but an essential step in your development as a leader. A foundation of self-awareness leads to self-acceptance and ultimately self-actualization so that you can fulfill your greatest potential (George, 2015).

Since the ancient times, much more attention has been devoted to promoting self-awareness: "finding ourselves," "knowing who we truly are." Many traditions, including certain schools of Western psychology, regard this discovery and acceptance of self as central to personal well-being, an important step on the path of individual transformation. It is also the belief of certain social thinkers and activists that, without a high degree of individual self-awareness and responsibility, it will remain impossible to resolve the many social and environmental problems currently facing mankind.

What guidelines does Taoism offer in this area? How can we manifest our virtue, know our true selves in a manner that connects us with the rest of our world? Laozi demands Taoist leaders to not only know themselves, but also transcend themselves. Because Laozi claims that:

> Those who know others are smart,
> Those who know themselves are wise.
> Those who transcend others have strength.
> Those who transcend themselves have inner power.
> – Laozi, Tao Te Ching, Ch. 33

Laozi encourages a wise leader to take the time to get to know yourself and find your passion. Look inside, to find your power, your purpose. If you find and go with this flow, you will make a difference in our world and you will find joy in the journey. Laozi's wisdom on self-awareness reflects the ancient Greek aphorism "Know Thyself": *understanding your inner world, bright and dark sides, personal strengths and weaknesses.* Sayings based on great wisdom, such as this one, all have one thing in common, regardless of the time and place in which they occur: they are encouragements to engage in conduct that is demanding and out of the ordinary, but nevertheless offers prospects of great reward.

Laozi's teaching is a classic illustration of this point. Why did the ancient sages attach a great importance to "Know thyself"? "Know thyself" is always an immensely difficult task. There are the four impediments to knowing thyself, which include everyday distractions that encourage a superficial and non-analytical existence; psychological obstructions that shade our eyes from the glare of troublesome truths; hedonism, the lack of courage to face and address painful and inconvenient realities; and the distorted imagery of mass media presentation (Soupios & Mourdoukoutas, 2014). Those who are courageous to know thyself must be able to:

- *Explore the dark side of their inner being, the frauds and deceits that nurture a counterfeit reality;*
- *Reveal psychological deficiencies and troublesome truths;*
- *Cast a harsh and unforgiving light at self-exonerating falsehoods, and*
- *Commit to an agenda of spirited self-indictment —an honest self-discovery process designed to dispel self-induced frauds.*

Burnison (2016) claim that anyone can have the right hands-on skills, but true leadership finesse lies in the much tougher realm of developing self-awareness to lead yourself first; navigating by a fixed point of personal and organizational purpose; journeying with others who want to follow you; and plotting a course that's beyond the line of sight of what everyone sees.

To lead others, you must continually measure yourself—not overestimating your strengths, and not underestimating your weaknesses. To do so, you must be able to look humbly in the mirror. After all, self-awareness and honesty go hand in hand. Let others illuminate your blind spots as you improve yourself and, by extension, the organization.

According to Laozi, a great leader not only know himself, understand inner mind, but also should know others, understand outer world. Because self-awareness and awareness of others are the keys to happiness, to personal satisfaction, and to successful relationships. If we want to be successful and happy, we must take responsibility for our feelings, thoughts and behaviours. We must not blame others for our choices.

Paradoxically, as we become more self-aware, we become less self-conscious—less worried about how we look to others and about what others think of us. This allows us to be more self-less and better able to work with, support and give to others. Self-awareness also provides us with a richer inner life and the ability to identify and focus on what really matters to us—the people we love. Only do those who know their inner mind and outer world have power and strength to transcend themselves and fulfil themselves, and become a mindful leader.

Hougaard et al. (2016) argues that mindfulness is a foundational skill for effective leadership. Mindfulness is about developing high levels of self-management by switching off the autopilot and getting in the driver's seat of your life. Mindfulness also cultivates the ability to be more aware of others, which is a cornerstone for leading people and leading an organization.

A mindful leader is simply a leader who uses mindfulness to gain deeper knowledge of himself and makes a conscious effort to use this knowledge to manage himself better, taking personal responsibility for his actions and striving to be the best leader he can be. Mindful leaders provide calm, clarity and a clear sense of direction, carefully balancing the needs of the organization with the needs and aspirations of the workforce. Mindful leaders monitor themselves to maintain a focus on present- moment reality, their impact on other people, and their reactions to stressful situations. Mindful leaders experience the reality and vividness of what's going on in any given moment, without knee- jerk reactions based on negative mind states (such as anxiety, fear or anger) responding with a calm awareness and care for themselves and others (Adams, 2016).

Hougaard et al. (2016) have created a framework for mindful leadership which can help to explain the challenges many leaders face and how they can be overcome. The framework looks at what the cultivation of mindfulness—that is, high focus and awareness—enables for self and others and, subsequently, what that enables in terms of leadership. Impactful leadership begins with mindfulness as defined in quadrant 2 of Fig. 14.1. This is where they have strong focus and open awareness directed toward their own self. It enables them as individuals to be calm and clear-minded in how they think and behave. In this state, they mindfully monitor our thoughts and emotions and use our values and goals to guide our actions. This mind state is a prerequisite for everything else.

As they are developing greater self-awareness, they are simultaneously cultivating the ability to have greater empathy for others. Once they can see and understand their own struggles and challenges, we have a greater ability to recognize those in people around us. Therefore, moving from a high degree of mindfulness of self

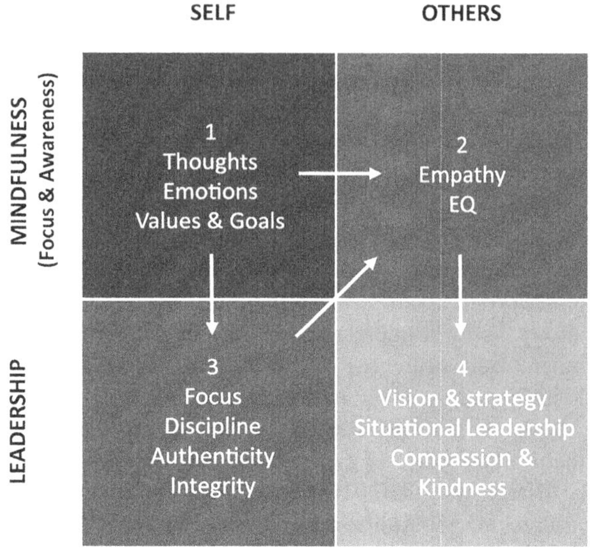

Fig. 14.1 Mindful leadership framework. Source: Rasmus Hougaard et al. (2016), Mindful leadership: achieving results by managing the mind

toward mindfulness of others is a natural transition. Once we have developed a high level of self-awareness, it is also very easy to move down in the framework toward effective self-leadership. This is where we have the discipline to focus on the right things and take the time to know what those right things are. Specifically, the "right things" come from tuning in with your authentic self and having a high degree of integrity in everything you do.

Once we have the foundations of mindfulness of self and others as well as leadership of self, leadership of others becomes much easier. In particular, if you take these skills as the foundation and introduce strategic and tactical management tools and techniques such as defining vision and strategy and applying situational leadership you have a pretty robust framework for success. And the more you cultivate these skills in your leadership of others the greater your capacity for compassion and wisdom. All these together, in a dynamic, ongoing, ever-changing development road map, define mindful leadership.

Self-Cultivation: Authentic Leadership

Bill George, the former Chairman and CEO of Medtronic, the author of Authentic Leadership has done many studies on authenticity and impact on leadership over the past years. His study shows that those leaders who gained self-awareness was central to becoming authentic leaders. When you know yourself, you can find the passion that motivates you and the purpose of your leadership (George, 2015). Bill George's approach to leadership, based on self-awareness and authenticity, is widely considered the gold standard in the field. Thus, self-awareness and authenticity are two important traits of every proven leader. That is why most of the business leaders have seen the importance of authenticity as one of core ingredients of purpose-driven leaders. Just as John Replogle, CEO of Seventh Generation claims that authenticity is everything you cannot fake purpose.

As I discussed in the preceding section, leadership purpose is rooted in your values and your authentic self. You must be true to who you really are and to the ethics, principles, and causes that are most meaningful to you. When purpose becomes personal, it becomes real and powerful. From this place, you will be able to establish a clear mission in life, focus attention on what is most important, find courage to do what is right, and, as a leader, activate purpose in others. In considering your personal purpose, you need to be honest about your deepest values and know how to leverage your unique, distinctive qualities, skills, and position to make a difference, to your people, your customers, and the world.

Most academic scholars agree that the CEO must define, and almost personify, a company's purpose. In particular, the literature often characterizes purpose as being inextricably linked to the perceived authenticity of the CEO. Success is ascribed partly to this authenticity, along with clarity and consistency of the CEO's communication. Many articles also flag the potential vulnerability of leaders if they are perceived as not living up to their avowed purpose (EY Beacon Institute, 2016).

Our Chinese sage, Laozi always emphasizes the role of authenticity and integrity in life and leadership. He encourages wise leaders to *embody integrity, and keep away from hypocrisy; embrace authenticity, and keep away from vanity* (Tao Te Ching, Ch. 18).

Purpose-driven leaders are authentic leaders, who are the people with the highest integrity, and committed to building sustainable organizations. They are the leaders who have a deep sense of purpose and are true to their core values. They are also the leaders who have the courage to build their companies to meet the needs of all their stakeholders, and who recognize the importance of their service to society. Authentic leaders genuinely desire to serve others through their leadership. They are more interested in empowering the people they lead to make a difference than they are in power, money, or prestige for themselves. Authentic leaders are dedicated to developing themselves because they know that becoming a leader takes a lifetime of personal growth.

Self-cultivation is a path to develop authenticity and achieve the ultimate purpose of life, and thus occupies a central position in the philosophical Taoism. Self-cultivation empowers leaders to emanate from their deepest values and culminate in their contribution to the common good. Laozi stresses the importance of self-cultivation and its influence on team, community, organization and beyond:

> Those who cultivate themselves with virtue become authentic.
> Those who influence their family with virtue harmonize family;
> Those who influence their community with virtue sustain community;
> Those who influence their country with virtue prosper country;
> Those who influence the world with virtue pacify the world.
> – Laozi, Tao Te Ching, Ch. 54

Those leaders who hold to the great Tao cultivate themselves are authentic. Those who are authentic have the power to influence others, and those who are influential have the capacity of leading others. Leadership is more about influence and enabling the right things to happen rather than lining up a shot and making it happen. Real power of leaders is derived from influence through authentic leadership, rather than the perception of authority.

The wisdom of Taoism tells us that we are all connected and interdependent on each other in the universe. These connections and interdependence stretch like an incredibly interwoven and complicated tapestry. Each of us exists within this tapestry. Our thoughts and actions are like a stone dropped in a pond and can create ripples that travel outward. Everything we do and think affects the people in our lives and their reactions in turn affect others. The choices we make have far-reaching consequences. Each of us carries within us the capacity to change the world in small ways for better or worse. We can use the principles of the ripple effect to magnify our actions and their effects.

Laozi's wisdom also implies that if you want to be a positive and influential leader in the world, first you must get your own life in order. Ground yourself in the universal principle so that your behaviour is wholesome and effective. If you do that, you will earn trust and respect, and be a powerful influence. Your behaviour influences others through a ripple effect. A ripple effect works because everyone influences everyone else. Powerful people are powerful influences. If your life works, you influence your organization. If your organization works, your organization influences the community. If your community works, your community influences the nation. If your nation works, your nation influences the world. If your world works, the ripple effect spreads through the cosmos. It is important to remember that your influence begins with you and ripples outward. So, be sure that your influence is both potent and wholesome.

Building on Laozi's wisdom in the passage 54, I developed the five waves of virtue or purpose to elaborate the ripple effect. Figure 14.2 shows that the five waves of virtue start with leaders. The leader's purpose is to cultivate authenticity with virtue. The authentic leaders have the charismatic power, because the virtue is radiance that others can detect. Virtue (efficacy) will spread wherever things are arranged according to ideal structure of the Tao. This begins with the individual (self), and it extends to the family (teams in organization), the community (organization), nation (society), until it reaches the whole cosmos. Leading with influence requires a clear purpose and the ability to develop authentic connection with others.

When you lead based on a genuine desire to serve, and your decisions are shaped by your core values and true respect for others, it is easy to develop authentic relationships. When relationships are grounded in mutual respect, they thrive. And when relationships thrive, so do the organizations that they serve. This mutual synergy fosters greater organizational cohesiveness and more prolific collaborations, and helps leaders to establish more robust platforms steeped in influence. Let me explain the waves of virtue and leadership influence.

The first wave of virtue and influence is to lead yourself, and to be authentic leader. As a leader, your actions, starting with your own state of being, affect other

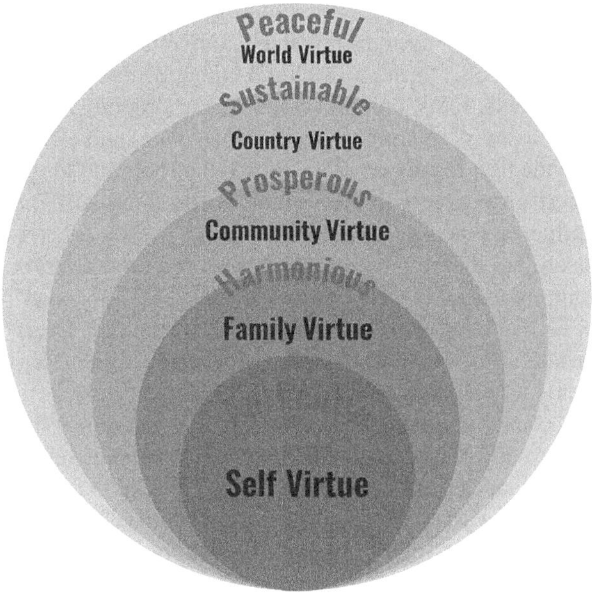

Fig. 14.2 The five waves of virtue or purpose of authentic leadership. Source: Author developed based on Laozi, Tao Te Ching, Ch. 54

people and your organization. When the leader shows up with his or her strengths, values, and actions all aligned, you can feel it. Leaders who understand how to master leading themselves are more powerful and influential than those who don't. As a leader, your state of being and doing influences many different layers of your organization: personal, interpersonal, and organizational. Proactive attention to how you as a leader are showing up and taking action can enable you to make bigger, more positive impacts with others.

Second, lead others—influence each person in a genuinely positive way. As a leader, your actions, starting with your own state of being, affect how other people work on an individual level and your organization. This isn't about you the leader versus a sea of followers. When the leader, already powerfully aligned with himself or herself, respects and builds an enabling relationship with each follower on an individual basis, the entire group of followers is enabled to build strong relationships with each other. As a leader, how you manage and present yourself dramatically impacts your followers, and the way you connect with each of them dramatically impacts every person in the organization. For example, imagine getting passionate about a new direction you believe your organization needs to pursue. To some, your passion will come across as exciting and empowering. To others, it may seem dictatorial and oppressive, or even distracting and needless. While you can't control how your passion is received, understanding how each person might react or respond to how you are showing up will enable you to build stronger relationships with each person in your business, thereby helping you achieve better results together. And this web of relationships is surrounded by resources, policies, and processes—the organization.

Third, lead the organization (in Fig. 14.2, it refers to family and community)—influence your systems positively. Organizations function not only through relationships but also through structural components like habits, practices, resources, measurements, rules, and processes. These structures are designed in harmony for both effectiveness (getting the right things done) and efficiency (get things done right) to get the best results possible in both the short and long term. While the influence you exert on people will cause them to do things differently within the structure, the influence you exert directly on the organizational layer changes the support structure itself and thereby affects everyone in the organization. Therefore, leaders' actions, starting with their own state of being, affect how other people work on an individual level, and the systems in which they operate. Everyone benefits from improved results as well as from a more able and resilient organization. Your initial action starts a chain reaction that causes positive impacts to others and the organization. The benefits of this chain reaction trigger ripples through the entire organization. They add energy and enthusiasm to the people and processes that make the organization successful. This is the ripple effect in action. And with enough momentum, people outside the organization benefit as well.

Ultimately—create ripples beyond your organization (including nation and the world). As a transformational leader, the ultimate outcome of your work is to create an organization that can have a lasting, positive impact on clients and customers. In turn, those people will work to make a lasting, positive impact on their clients and customers. And the stone keeps skipping. . .For example, imagine that you lead a non-profit like Heifer International. They raise and donate pregnant animals to people in need around the world. The recipient of a gift is then charged to pass the next offspring to another family in need. Or imagine you lead a for-profit company that refines material used by other companies to make cancer-fighting drugs. Your company's output is critical to saving people's lives. In these pay-it-forward examples, it's easy to see how each action you take as leader—your skipping stone—goes from you to others in your organization, to the organization itself, to others creating their own product or service, and to the people who benefit from that product or service. This ripple effect continues indefinitely so long as well-intentioned leaders continue to skip stones for positive impact. While you cannot predict the future, you can influence it. With the right stones and right leadership mindset, you can create amazing ripples that travel quite far indeed.

Transcending Ego: Servant Leadership

At the beginning of this chapter, I analysed Laozi's three types of leaders who embody three different mindsets. One of them is one with fixed-mindset. The fixed mindset leaders preen their egos and look for the next self-image boost. They start with the belief that some people are superior. They all have the need to prove and display their superiority. They use their subordinates to feed this need, rather than fostering the development of their people. They all end by sacrificing their organizations to its need. The fixed-mindset teaches us the lesson and let us understand where gargantuan egos come from, how they operate, and why they become self-defeating (Dweck, 2006).

We have many leaders with growth mindset who serve a larger purpose beyond their careers and themselves. However, serving others is a noble purpose which demands leaders to transcend their ego. To be selfless to serve people is one of most core virtues that Laozi requires leaders to cultivate in their leadership. Laozi describes the qualities of servant leaders who transcend ego to care for others.

> Great leaders place themselves behind; and
> Find themselves ahead.
> Great leaders lay down their lives, and
> Find themselves thrive.
> Give no thought to themselves, and
> Find themselves fulfilled.
> – Laozi, Tao Te Ching, Ch. 7

> Great leaders who want to stand above people,
> Shall speak to them from below;
> Great leaders who want to stand ahead of people,
> Shall place themselves behind.
> Therefore, when great leaders
> Lead from above, people do not feel burdened;
> Lead from behind, people do not feel obstructed.
> Thus, people are never tired of appreciating them.
> – Laozi, Tao Te Ching, Ch. 66

The verse 7 depicts profile of servant leadership, which is defined as guiding others with the ultimate purpose of improving their wellness. In Laozi's heart, the altruistic leaders who model themselves on Heaven and Earth do not exist for themselves, they make no conscious effort for their own sake, always place their people's interests above their own. They think of nothing but others, they are free themselves from being egocentric, and are always concerned over other people's rights and interests. As a result of their altruism, they are respected and followed by people, and end up fulfilling themselves and achieve their purpose.

Laozi in verse 66 reveals the quality that servant leadership shall develop. Laozi offers one of the core principles for those who want to be great leaders, which is great leaders should lead from behind, not from the front. However, it doesn't mean that Laozi is not against the way that leaders lead from the above or the front. It sounds paradox. But it is the art of leadership. In leading from the front, leaders must be humble to what they do and say; and in the meantime, they must place people's interests before their own.

Those who embrace the qualities of humility and selflessness never contend with others, and claim any credits from others, but they are willing to take any risks and accountability whenever something goes wrong or in crisis. Therefore, when they lead from the above and the front, people never feel oppressed and harmful. As a result, people exalt and follow them voluntarily and cheerfully. Nelson Mandela is a typical Taoist leader. He has aligned himself with the principles of Taoism. He said,

"It is better to lead from behind and to put others in front, especially when you celebrate victory when nice things occur. You take the front line when there is danger. Then people will appreciate your leadership". This is the exact wisdom of Laozi. In his autobiography, Mandela (1995) equated a great leader with a shepherd: *"He stays behind the flock, letting the most nimble go out ahead, whereupon the others follow, not realizing that all along they are being directed from behind*" (Mandela, 1995).

Leading from behind doesn't mean abrogating your leadership responsibilities. After all, the shepherd makes sure that the flock stays together. He uses his staff to nudge and prod if the flock strays too far-off course or into danger. For leaders, it's a matter of harnessing people's collective genius. Doing so entails two primary responsibilities—and they are not easy to get right. First, leaders must ensure their organizations are willing to innovate. This is fundamentally about building community. Some leaders refer to this function as "creating a world to which people want to belong." In these communities, people are valued for who they are and have the opportunity to contribute to something larger than themselves. These communities have a common purpose, values and rules of engagement about how people should interact and problem-solve together. A shared purpose brings the people together and makes them willing to do the hard work of innovation. Second, leaders must build the organizational capabilities necessary for engaging in the innovation process. The three essential organizational capabilities are: creative abrasion (the ability to generate ideas through intellectual discourse and debate); creative agility (the ability to test and refine ideas through quick pursuit); and creative resolution (the ability to make decisions in an integrative manner). Those who are exceptional at leading from behind are likely to be different than those who excelled at leading from the front (Hill, 2010).

Those who follow wisdom of leading from behind are servant-leaders. In the heart of Laozi, servant-leaders should like the ones he states in Tao Te Ching:

> Great leaders are not egocentric,
> But selfless to serve other interests.
> They are good to those who are good,
> They are also good to those who are not good,
> Then, it leads to genuine goodness.
> They trust those who are trustworthy,
> They also trust those who are untrustworthy,
> Then, it leads to genuine trust.
> Great leaders lead people
> By letting go of their egotism.
> – Laozi, Tao Te Ching, Ch. 49

Laozi stresses two qualities or virtues for servant-leaders: goodness and trust or integrity. Virtue is the power, and is the power to do good; trust is a principle of power. Servant-leaders shall have the power to activate goodness, build a high-trust organization, and transform the world through doing good.

Those who embrace the virtues of goodness and trust can forgo ego and self-interest, but place their mind and heart on what people think and need. They always cultivate these two important virtues in their lives. Servant-leaders are completely different from the average persons. They treat everyone equally, whoever is good or bad, trustworthy or untrustworthy. They are the magnanimous persons with the greatness of soul. When faced with choices in lives, servant-leaders tend to pursue what is most noble, and what form them in excellence and benefit others most. They strive for greatness at the heart. This is the virtue by which servant-leaders pursue what is great and honourable in their lives, even if it is difficult.

Humble to Serve: Level 5 Leadership

Purpose with humility is the best way we humans can pursue a noble cause passionately without risking the perils of seeing our efforts do more harm than good. This is also the most important quality for purpose-driven leadership. When passion for a noble purpose turns into self-righteousness, we lose our capacity to learn from our mistakes or even to notice when we are making mistakes. We must always be on guard to make sure that the justifiable satisfaction that we earn with a life of purpose does not become pridefulness, which has been long been recognized, for good reason, as a deadly sin. Pride harms us, harms those we are trying to help, and ultimately harms the purpose that we are trying to accomplish. The only way to avoid this constant danger is to keep a healthy perspective on ourselves (Damon, 2003).

Humility is the heart of a leader. Great leaders have the humility, courage, and insight to admit that they can benefit from the expertise of others who have less power than them. They actively seek the ideas and unique contributions of their followers that they serve. This is how great leaders create a culture of learning, and an atmosphere that encourages followers to become the very best they can.

Humility is always one of the core virtues that Taoist nurtures and cultivates in life, and most essential to holistic leadership. Humility, in Taoism, is defined as a refusal to assert authority or a refusal to be first in anything and that the act of daring, in itself, is a refusal of wisdom and a rush to enjoin circumstances before you are ready. Along with compassion and conservation, humility (one of virtues of compliance) is one of the three treasures (virtues) in the possession of those who follow the Tao. Laozi describes the qualities that a wise leader should embrace:

> The humble is the foundation of the noble,
> The lower is the foundation of the higher.
> Thus, ancient leaders treated themselves as
> the orphaned, the lonely and the unworthy.
> Are they really low and mean? No, they are not.
> Therefore, the ultimate honour is no honour.
> Do not seek to be shiny and glorious like jade,
> But to be plain and firm like stone.
> – Laozi, Tao Te Ching, Ch.39

Laozi offers advice to a wise leader who *does not to seek to be shiny like jade, but to be plain and firm like stone*. In other words, Living a simple and humble life, like a plain and firm stone. Laozi understood humility as being in harmony with nature and the wisdom of the universe. In wisdom of Taoism, simplicity and humility were the basis of greatness.

It is clear that the qualities of a stone are the traits that modern "Level 5 Leadership" needs to embrace. "Level 5 leadership" is the new concept that was coined by Collins and is seen as the highest level of management development and thinking. (Collins, 2005) believes that the key ingredient that allows a company to become great is having a Level 5 leader: an executive in whom genuine personal humility blends with intense professional will. Collins regards "Level 5 Leadership" as the starting point in the process to becoming great. Level 5 leaders channel their ego needs away from themselves and into the larger goal of building a great organization. It's not that Level 5 leaders who have no ego or self-interest. Indeed, they are incredibly ambitious—but their ambition is first and foremost for the institution, not themselves. Level 5 leaders are driven, infected with an incurable need to produce sustained results. They are resolved to do whatever it takes to make an organization great, no matter how big or hard the decisions.

To justify his arguments, Collins explains the traits of Level 5 leadership by drawing on the theory of Yin and Yang from perspective of Taoism. Personal humility represents Yin, which demonstrates the qualities of a compelling modesty, shunning public adulation; never boastful. It acts with quiet, calm determination; relies principally on inspired standard, not inspiring charisma, to motivate. It channels ambition into the company, not the self; sets up successors for even more greatness in the next generation. It looks in the mirror, not out the window, to apportion responsibility for poor results, never blaming other people, external factors, or bad luck. Professional will is concerned with Yang. It creates superb results, a clear catalyst in the transition from good to great. It demonstrates an unwavering resolve to do whatever must be done to produce the best long-term results, no matter how difficult. It sets the standard of building an enduring great company; will settle for nothing else. It looks out the window, not in the mirror, to apportion credit for the success of the company—to other people, external factors, and good luck.

In addition to metaphor of stone, Laozi also used another favourite natural symbol—water—as the good qualities of humility and willpower for great leaders. The qualities of water are also embedded in Level 5 Leadership.

> The supreme good is like water,
> Which benefits all creatures without contention.
> It stays in the low position where others dislike.
> Thus, it comes nearest to the Tao.
> – Laozi, Tao Te Ching, 8

Furthermore, Laozi illustrated the qualities of an unwavering resolve water:

> Nothing in the universe is much softer and weaker than water
> But nothing triumphs over water in overcoming the hard and strong

> Nothing substitutes for water in dissolving the hard and strong.
> – Laozi, Tao Te Ching, Ch.78

The metaphor of water reminds us that what really drives success is not "genius" but a unique combination of passion and long-term perseverance. Those who nurture and embrace the qualities of stone and water are courageous to take responsibility in a time of organizational crisis and are able to become a great leader. Those are the leaders that Laozi wish them to develop the qualities of water.

> Only those who are able to endure humiliation that
> A country suffers can lead a country;
> Only those who are successful to meet crisis that
> A country faces can lead the world.
> – Laozi, Tao Te Ching, Ch.78

Those who embrace qualities of water such as yielding but persistent, humble but courageous to serve people in times of crisis, become Level 5 leaders. When people and country are facing challenges and crisis, they can stand up to protect them, and are able to be entrusted to lead them. There is nothing quite like a crisis to test our leadership. It will make or break us as a leader. Crises have brought down many leaders and their organizations with them, while other leaders have risen to the challenges to prove their mettle. What makes leading our organization through difficult situations so hard? Like being in a war, crises test us to our limits because the outcome is rarely predictable. We not only have to use all our wisdom to guide our organization through it, we must dig deep inside ourselves to find the courage to keep going forward (George, 2009). Leaders aligned with wisdom of Taoism can be prepared to guide their organizations through severe situations because they know who they are. They have the self-awareness, self-confidence, and resilience to take responsibility for their failings and lead others through the rapidly unfolding—and often unpredictable—sequence of events. They rise to the occasion, find leadership abilities they never knew they had, and come through with shining colours. Lou Gerstner, IBM CEO, and Anne Mulcahy, CEO of Xerox are two great Taoist leaders who took up themselves in times of organizational crisis. Lou Gerstner saved IBM in the mid-1990s and Anne Mulcahy took the helm at Xerox. Inheriting companies facing bankruptcy, they showed great leadership, not just in saving their companies but restoring them to leadership in their respective fields.

Collins showcases Darwin E. Smith, CEO of Kimberly-Clark as the typical Level 5 Leader. Smith was named as CEO when the old paper company was in great trouble in 1971, and turned it into the leading consumer paper products company in the world. Smith's turnaround of Kimberly-Clark is one the best examples in the twentieth century of a leader taking a company from merely good to truly great. Smith is a classic example of a Level 5 leader-an individual who blends extreme personal humility with intense professional will.

Collins's research also found other unique qualities of Level 5 Leaders besides humility and professional will. He created the window and the mirror concept. It is a simple yet powerful concept exemplified by leaders of companies that made the Good to Great transition: Level 5 leaders, inherently humble, look out the window to apportion credit-even undue credit-to factors outside themselves. If they can't find a specific person or event to give credit to, they credit good luck. At the same time, they look in the mirror to assign responsibility, never citing bad luck or external factors when things go poorly. Conversely, the comparison executives frequently looked out the window for factors to blame but preened in the mirror to credit themselves when things went well. The funny thing about the window-and-mirror concept is that it does not reflect reality (Collins, 2001). The window and the mirror model, which focuses on look out the window and give credit to those responsible for positive outcomes, and look in the mirror and take ownership of negative outcome, exactly reflects the wisdom of Taoism.

> The Great Tao flows everywhere like water,
> All things depend on it to exist,
> Yet it does not demand for obedience.
> All things depend on it to fulfil their purpose,
> Yet it does not claim credit.
> All things depend on it to nurture and grow,
> Yet it does not possess them.
> – Laozi, Tao Te Ching, Ch. 34

The Taoist leader that Laozi describes are those who are willing to help and serve others, but never take credits, and don't dominate and control them, and therefore, they have the power of influencing others. A recent Catalyst study backs up Laozi's thought, showing that humility is one of critical leadership factors for creating an environment where employees from different demographic backgrounds feel included. In a survey of more than 1500 workers from Australia, China, Germany, India, Mexico, and the U.S., they found that when employees observed altruistic or selfless behaviour in their managers—a style characterized by

- *Acts of humility, such as learning from criticism and admitting mistakes;*
- *Empowering followers to learn and develop;*
- *Acts of courage, such as taking personal risks for the greater good; and*
- *Holding employees responsible for results.*

Employees who perceived altruistic behaviour from their managers also reported being more innovative, suggesting new product ideas and ways of doing work better. Moreover, they were more likely to report engaging in team citizenship behaviour, going beyond the call of duty, picking up the slack for an absent colleague—all indirect effects of feeling more included in their workgroups (Prime & Salib, 2014).

Doing the Right Things Right: Sustainable Leadership

The previous analysis makes us understand that purpose is a reason that something exists or why something is done or created. But if we want to understand whether something has a purpose, we need to develop awareness of the correlation between the resource exchange and the perceived or expected value to be gained.

Effectiveness results from the purposeful utilization of our resources. For example, one resource that we all have available to exchange is time. However, time is limited. We cannot get more of it. For this reason, time is our most valuable resource. From an external perspective, this may not appear to be the case. Many of us spend a great deal of our time thinking and doing things that don't have much purpose. Becoming aware of what we value and what matters in life is a great way to start thinking and acting with greater purpose. Having a clear understanding of the 'why' behind our existence—our purpose—as a business or organization is an important factor of effectiveness. Laozi was aware of the close relationship between effectiveness (purpose) and efficiency (tactics), and positive impact of purpose on organizational sustainability. I have identified three keys in the text of Tao Te Ching, particularly, verse 27 and 54 which are the qualities of sustainable business: *knowing your purpose (WHY), maximizing your human and material resource potential (WHAT), and investing in your strengths (HOW).*

> A good traveller leaves no traces.
> A good speaker makes no slips.
> A good reckoner uses no devices.
> A well-shut door needs no bolts, and yet cannot be opened.
> A well-tied knot needs no cord, and yet cannot be untied.
> – Laozi, Tao Te Ching, Ch.27

> A good founder builds what will last,
> A good entrepreneur sustains what is built,
> A good successor carries on what it has for generations.
> – Laozi, Tao Te Ching, Ch.54

The Laozi's idea is whatever we do must have a purpose in our job, your organization and your leadership. Purpose allows us to fulfil ourselves effectively and efficiently. I analysed the verse 27 in Chap. 11 from the perspective of ecological sustainability and pointed out that Laozi uses the metaphor of people who occupy different jobs to illustrate impact of purpose on their performance. A good traveller's purpose is to leave no tracks and footprint wherever he/she travels; a good speaker's purpose is to make no slips whenever he/she speaks; a good accountant's purpose is to make no miscalculation even he/she does not use calculator; a good locker's purpose is to keep doors unlocked even he/she does not use bolts; and a good knotter's purpose is to keep knots untied even he/she does not use ropes.

I start to analyse Laozi's wisdom with job purpose. In our modern business philosophy, job purpose is different from job function. Job function is the set of tasks a person performs in their role, whereas job purpose is the intended outcome of the job in terms of its impact on organization, community, customers, society or environment (Izzo & Vanderwielen, 2018). Those who have high purpose in their jobs and lives work effectively and efficiently, and are less prone to waste of resources. As a result, whatever they do have a positive impact on environment and society. The purpose-driven or effective leaders must understand the distinction between job function and job purpose, and instil a sense of purpose in their job and act on it.

The wisdom of Taoism also tells us that building a sustainable enterprise, leaders must identify a noble purpose in the enterprise they serve so that the enterprise can sustainable for at least three generations. We can interpret the verse 66 as "*A purpose-driven founder can build an enterprise to last; a purposeful entrepreneur can keep the enterprise that has been built, and transform it from good to great; a purpose-driven successor who succeed the enterprise and transform it from great to be sustainable*".

The studies, conducted by Collins, et al, have offered us some evidence to justify Laozi's ideas. Collins calls the built-to-last enterprise "visionary company", which is one that is a premier institution in its industry, is widely admired by knowledgeable businesspeople, made an imprint on the world, had multiple generations of CEOs, had multiple product/service life cycles. Collins claims that transition from good to great enterprise require Level 5 Leaders who are humble, but driven to do what's best for the enterprise, and right people on the bus. Every institution is vulnerable, no matter how great. No matter how much you have achieved, no matter how far you've gone, no matter how much power you've garnered, you are vulnerable to decline. There is no law of nature that the most powerful will inevitably remain at the top. Anyone can fall and most eventually do (Collins, 2009). Just as Laozi says that

> What hasten to grow in the heyday leads to decay,
> For it is against the Tao.
> What is against the Tao shall soon perish.
> – Laozi, Tao Te Ching, Ch. 55

It means that decline can be detected early and avoided. How far can a company fall before the path toward doom becomes inevitable and unshakable? How can companies reverse course? The research project that Collins has undertaken for many years of research of several thousand companies offers leaders the well-founded hope that they can learn how to stave off decline and, if they find themselves falling, reverse their course.

Laozi provides three keys for business leaders to stop enterprise from failing. The first key is that sustainable business should have a clear purpose—when properly conceived—has a profound effect upon an organization beyond what core values alone can do, and that organizations should put more effort into identifying their purpose. The visionary companies had a set of core values that were unchanging and a core purpose that fuelled everything the organization did. Collins put it: core purpose is the organization's fundamental reason for being. An effective purpose reflects the importance people attach to the company's work—it taps their idealistic motivations—and gets at the deeper reasons for an organization's existence beyond just marking money. The powerful purpose statements that had propelled some of the most visionary companies of our day to great success. For example, the purpose of Merck is to gain victory against disease; Hallmarking Disney is to use their imaginations to bring happiness to millions; Johnson & Johnson to alleviate pain and suffering; Packard and his peers did not begin as corporate giants, they began as entrepreneurs and small business people. From there, all of these companies built small, cash-strapped enterprises into some of the world's most enduring and successful corporations.

From perspective of Taoism's wisdom, purpose-leaders must first understand the relationship between effectiveness and efficiency. Because being effective means being adequate to accomplish a purpose; producing the intended or expected result. Being efficient means performing or functioning in the best possible manner with the least waste of time and effort. We discussed in Chap. 11 that effectiveness is about efficacy of the Tao, and efficiency is concerned with strategy. The word efficacy has to do with the ability or capacity to do something, but not about how something is done. Efficacy equals effectiveness, but different from efficiency. Effectiveness refers to successfully producing the expected or desired result; it's the degree to which you achieve your objectives, solve problems, and realize profits. In business, Effectiveness is doing the things that get you closer to your purpose. Efficiency is performing a given task (whether important or not) in the most economical manner possible.

Effectiveness is summed up by "doing the right things." Efficiency is the accomplishment of a job with the minimum expenditure of time, effort, and cost—the shortest distance between a goal and a checkmark. In business, efficiency is summed up by "doing things right." Laozi uses the metaphor of people who achieve intended results in various jobs to illustrate how important is for an effective leader to use effectiveness and efficiency to do the right things right, and to yield the most profitable and quickest route a leader can take to execute purpose. Laozi also claims that great leaders must have the purpose, i.e., to do good and be good. No matter whether you are a traveller, a speaker, an accountant, a blocker, and a knotter, you must have the purpose of doing the right things. You must have the strategy and efficient instruments to achieve their purposes.

What does it matter to leadership? Misguided efficiency—being efficient at the expense of being effective, or being efficient at doing the wrong thing—is a common mistake among leaders. With a focus on efficiency, leaders often disregard the outside environment, and the primary concern becomes the operation of the firm itself. Conversely, when leaders focus on effectiveness, they view their organization as a part of a greater whole, as a single piece of the puzzle. Recognizing the impact of effectiveness (purpose) and efficiency on leadership effectiveness requires leaders to embrace the second key principle of Taoism to maximize resource potential.

> Effective leaders
> Make the best of anyone, and no one is left,
> Make the most of anything, and nothing is left to waste.
> – Laozi, Tao Te Ching, Ch. 27

When the effective leaders care for all creatures, they must develop efficient strategy and tools to fulfil their purpose. Efficiency has to do with minimizing waste. Something that has a perfect of efficiency will have no waste. That's the way Laozi requires leader to serve as the conscientious leader who focuses on maximizing human potential and resources efficiency. Building and maintaining an effective, productive human and natural resources is the first step toward responsible and sustainable business. Human resources are the most important source for business success. Maximizing human potential is central to a purposeful organization and is pivotal to our success as a leader and a business. In modern business, "human potential" means bringing out the best in our people, and enabling them to reach their potential as human beings—to be as creative, knowledgeable, and productive as possible. This means they are reaching heights they may not have thought possible in terms of projects they undertake, skills they develop, inspiration they feel. Work is not a deadening place or one that is stressful to the point of being debilitating. It is a place where people come alive, where they get in "the flow." Where, in the framework of psychologist Abraham Maslow, they can "self-actualize." If you are not maximizing the human potential in your organization—getting the most from everyone—you cannot realize the full potential of your business. And that spells trouble over time, as competitors are working to realize the full potential of their businesses (Bush, 2018).

The new study undertaken by Korn Ferry Institute shows that by 2030, there will be a global human talent shortage of more than 85 million people. Talent shortage could result in about $8.5 trillion in unrealized annual revenues (Korn Ferry Institute, 2018). Acute global talent shortages are clearly a looming threat, and they're driven by a shortage of skills rather than a shortage of people. Mitigating the talent crunch requires a fundamental redefinition of the social contract between individuals, organizations, and governments. The future of work doesn't just require different skill sets, but entirely new ways of working, therefore, leaders at different levels must be mindful of their citizens' employability in the context of a global talent market. It's essential that governments and companies focus on building and maintaining skilled talent pipelines and provide continuous access to both formal and on-the-job learning opportunities. In the new networked economy, organizations will increasingly rely on an extended ecosystem of workers rather than a large permanent workforce, using people, technology, and partners to execute their strategies in different ways.

The second factor that is influential to business success is natural resources efficiency. Eco-effectiveness is one of the central principles of Taoism for environmental sustainability: "*making the most of anything, and nothing is left to waste.*" The essence of eco-effectiveness is "waste equals food", or "waste is something that is placed in the wrong place". The concept was developed in response to some of the perceived limitations of eco-efficiency which critics claim only slow down the rate of environmental depletion and do not reverse the production of unused or non-recycled waste. Waste should be seen as a resource instead of just waste.

We are all aware that environmental degradation is one of the largest threats that are being looked at in the world today. The United Nations International Strategy for Disaster Reduction characterizes environmental degradation as the lessening of the limit of the earth to meet social and environmental destinations and needs. Environmental degradation is the deterioration of the environment through depletion of resources such as air, water and soil; the destruction of ecosystems; habitat destruction; the extinction of wildlife; and pollution. Environmental degradation is of many types. When natural habitats are destroyed or natural resources are depleted, the environment is degraded. Therefore, waste and inefficiency has become the biggest threat to planet. Modern economies are now consuming resources at a rate to many more times the planet's actual capacity, this leads to the fact that waste overtakes pollution as the major environmental threat in the twenty-first century.

Laozi might not see the environmental crisis we are facing today, but we learnt from his wisdom that he had foreseen the nature and resource challenges in our modern time. In recent years, governments, businesses and scientists have realized that the waste of resources has become the biggest threat to our planet, and taken concerted efforts to counteract this problem including environmental protection and environmental resources management. Scottish governments have urged businesses, farmers and manufacturers in Scotland to adopt a "one planet prosperity" policy designed to cut their energy use, greenhouse gas emissions, waste and resource use. Scottish leaders have regarded sustainable growth as the core objective of its regulatory strategy, and defined their statutory purpose as delivering environmental protection and improvement in ways which also create health and wellbeing benefits and sustainable economic growth.

In the business world, IPM is one of the responsible companies which lead in sustainable solutions to the biggest threat to planet. UPM is a Finnish forest industry company. The production of UPM is based on renewable raw-materials which are biodegradable and recyclable. Recently, UPM has created the term "Biofore" to describe new forest industry. "Bio" stands for sustainable solutions and environmental performance. "Fore" stands for forest and the company's position at the forefront of the development. UPM provides sustainable and safe solutions to the growing global consumption demand, and offers alternatives to replace non-renewable fossil-based materials. They understand from its vision, purpose and strategy the efforts that UPM has made in creating a sustainable society. The vision of UPM is to lead the forest-based bioindustry into a sustainable, innovation-driven, and exciting future by holding on to the competence and integrity and drive of their people. The purpose of UPM is to create value by seizing the limitless potential of bioeconomy. The strategy of their Biofore strategy is to use renewable and recyclable raw materials in a sustainable way, which means consuming resources such as raw materials, water and energy, in a prudent and responsible way while achieving energy, production and cost efficiency. By recognizing its great achievement in sustainability, UPM is the only paper company which is listed in the Dow Jones Sustainability Indices and the only forest industry company invited to the United Nations Global Compact LEAD sustainability leadership platform.

Maximizing human and resource potential must start with effective leadership. Effective leaders not only understand their own strengths, but are able to invest in other strengths. This comes to the third key of Laozi for effective leaders: *understanding and investing people's strengths*. Laozi requires effective leaders to apply the principles of maximizing human potential in their organization. As we pointed out the effectiveness focuses on value and purpose. When focusing on effectiveness first, leaders can care for all creatures whether they are good or bad.

> The good is the mentor for the bad to follow,
> The bad is the lesson for the good to learn.
> Those who neither model themselves on the good
> Nor learn from the bad is bewildered, though they are knowledgeable.
> – Laozi, Tao Te Ching, Ch. 27

The rationale behind this idea is that systems intelligence and philosophy of oneness reminds us that in the interconnected world, all creatures are interdependent and interacted with each other. There is nothing so useless as doing efficiently that which should not be done at all (Drucker, 1963). Whether they are good or bad, they are all valuable resources for organizational growth, and each of them can play a different role in life. The Tao is oneness. As a consciousness of oneness sees and values the patterns and needs of an entire system, it also recognizes the intrinsic values of each individual part. Nothing is excluded. John Muir said: "*When we try to pick out anything by itself, we find it hitched to everything in the universe*". Juan Manuel Carrion, a biologist and ornithologist stressed this point with his study:

> There is a great lesson I've learned from nature, from the birds, the insects, from the ecosystems: The awareness that everything has its reason to exist in nature, nothing is redundant; nothing is insignificant. A spider is as important as a dragonfly, an insect, a bird, a mammal or a huge tree. Perhaps a tiny plant has a specific and important function that makes it as important as a giant tree. This is the awareness that everything has its purpose and nothing is insignificant because everything has its own nature. (Global Oneness Project, 2013).

Nothing is separate from us or from anything else. People and creatures are not the instruments or objects for our goals. They are just like us, real beings with their own hopes, joys and pains. No one's suffering is worse than another's, and no one's life is more valuable. By aligning ourselves with oneness (Tao), we find ourselves in a very different world—a world in which our contributions matter, where we are given what we need in order to make a difference, and where we see outer life as more flexible, more accessible, more part of us than we thought. In these ways, oneness is essentially empowering, helping us build communities that facilitate the flow of all resources—including the deepest resources of love and meaning—throughout the interconnected web of life. As we become more conscious of oneness, we see there is no hiding from our impacts on each other. There is no backyard that is not our backyard, there is even no such thing as "waste". Everything in life is re-usable.

Effective leaders have the power of connecting with employees and teams on a strategic and personal level, unlocking the full potential of people and organization. When organizations maximize human potential through effective leadership, meaningful values, and a foundation of trust, good things happen. The effective leaders are able to connect on a human, emotional level with employees, no matter who they are or what they do in the organization. They forge meaningful, respectful, caring relationships at work and do so in a fundamentally fair way. Fairness in relationships is particularly vital. It means being aware of implicit biases we all have as human beings (Bush, 2018).

The new way of thinking about effective leadership is embodied in three simple, but powerful, principles: *(a) Each is valuable; (b) No one is sufficient; and (c) All are required for the enduring success of the organization* (McCloskey, 2014). These three principles explicitly elaborate the principles of Taoism: "*The good is the mentor for the bad to follow, the bad is the lesson for the good to learn.*" First, effective leaders embrace, embody, and extend the conviction that "each is valuable." (McNamee, 2004) observes, "In the New Normal, enterprises will increasingly recognize the value of individuals at all levels of the organization". This makes good sense, as sustainable effectiveness depends on the efforts of many motivated and talented members-leaders who are ready and willing to contribute to the welfare and progress of the organization. Second, effective leaders embrace, embody, and extend the conviction that "no one is sufficient." Recognizing their assets and liabilities, New Normal Leaders know they cannot do it all. They appreciate the impossibility of staying abreast of a rapidly changing external environment. They know the limits of their interpretive capacity in processing the vast amount of data and experience each day brings their way. Third, effective leaders embrace, embody, and extend the conviction that "all are required for the enduring success of the organization." If each is valuable and no one is sufficient, it follows that no qualified member is excluded from the leadership work. Collaborative engagement calls for the wide distribution of leadership opportunity up, down, and across the organization, with the maximum participation of members a part of everyday organizational life.

The Case in Point: Johnson & Johnson, Lego and Microsoft

I am going to close this chapter with the cases Johnson & Johnson, Lego and Microsoft to illustrate the principles of Taoism I discussed in this chapter.

The Case of Johnson & Johnson

Johnson & Johnson is one of only a handful of companies that have flourished through more than a century of change. It is the company that aligns itself with the principle of Taoism:

> A good founder builds what is to last,
> A good entrepreneur keeps what is built,
> A good successor succeeds to what it has for generations.

When Robert W. Johnson founded Johnson & Johnson in 1886, he did so with the idealistic aim "to alleviate pain and disease." By 1908, he had expanded this into a business ideology that placed service to customers and concern for employees ahead of returns to shareholders. In 1935, Robert W. Johnson, Jr., echoed these sentiments in a philosophy that he called "*enlightened self-interest,*" *wherein* "*service to customers comes first ... service to employees and management second, and ... service to stockholders last.*"

Later (in 1943), Johnson, Jr. added service to community to the list (still ahead of service to shareholders) and codified the J&J ideology in "Our Credo," printed on old-style parchment and captioned in the same lettering used in the American Declaration of Independence. "*When these things have been done,*" *he wrote,* "*the stockholders should receive a fair return.*" Although J&J has periodically reviewed and slightly revised the wording of the credo since 1943, the essential ideology—the hierarchy of responsibilities descending from customers down to shareholders and the explicit emphasis on fair return rather than maximum return—has remained consistent throughout the history of the credo. The values that guide decision-making of Johnson & Johnson are spelled out in their Credo. Put simply, Their Credo challenges them to put the needs and well-being of the people they serve first.

Robert Wood Johnson, former chairman from 1932 to 1963 and a member of the Company's founding family, crafted their Credo himself in 1943, just before Johnson & Johnson became a publicly traded company. This was long before anyone ever heard the term "corporate social responsibility." The Credo is more than just a moral compass, it is the noble purpose for business success. The Credo also reflect the invisible wisdom of Taoism:

> Make the best of anyone, no one is left,
> Make the most of anything, nothing is left to waste.

In reality, the wisdom of "*make the best of anyone, no one is left*" specially refers to the responsibilities J&J takes for maximizing their doctors, nurses and other employees' potential to serve patients, and in the meantime, to save patients' lives whatever is possible. The wisdom of "*Make the most of anything, nothing is left to waste*" refers to the responsibilities J&J takes for utilizing natural resources to manufacture medicine and medical devices, and as well managing medical waste. We can discover how J&J align their purpose with the wisdom of Taoism in the credo and practices.

The Credo of J&J centres on multi-stakeholders, such as doctors, nurses, patients who are the primary stakeholders which directly influence J&J's economic and social performance in the pharmaceutical industry. Therefore, they determined that their first responsibility is to the doctors, nurses and patients, to mothers and fathers and all others who use their products and services. In meeting their needs everything J&J does must be of high quality. They must constantly strive to reduce their costs in order to maintain reasonable prices. Customers' orders must be serviced promptly and accurately. Their suppliers and distributors must have an opportunity to make a fair profit.

The responsibility they take for other stakeholders includes employees, communities and stockholders. They are also important because they directly and indirectly influence company's economic performance and reputation. Their responsibilities for employees are to respect their dignity and recognize their merit; to ensure them a sense of security in their jobs; to offer fair and adequate compensation, and clean, orderly and safe working conditions; to help employees fulfill their family responsibilities; to provide employees with freedom of making suggestions and complaints; to offer them an equal opportunity for employment, development and advancement for those qualified, and finally to provide competent management in an just and ethical way.

J&J is responsible to the communities in which they live and work and to the world community as well. They want to be good citizens—support good works and charities and bear their fair share of taxes. They want to encourage civic improvements and better health and education. They want to maintain in good order the property they are privileged to use, protecting the environment and natural resources. J&J's final responsibility is to their stockholders. They make a sound profit and fair return to their shareholders through innovative research and programs; purchasing new equipment; providing new facilities, and lunching new products.

We found that J&J didn't put environmental sustainability in the credo, but recently they developed the Climate Friendly Energy Policy built on their credo, which states they must be good citizens in the global community; they must protect the environment and natural resources; and they must strive to reduce costs in order to maintain reasonable prices. They are committed to excellence in fostering the efficient, cost-effective, and environmentally responsible purchasing and use of energy.

Finally, I want to analyse the 1982 Tylenol crisis to illustrate wisdom of Taoism:

> The good is the mentor for the bad to follow,
> The bad is the lesson for the good to learn.

We observed from the J&J's Credo the comprehensive responsibilities that J&J promise to take for all stakeholders including environment. However, it is usually hard for most of companies to translate them into action-in organization structure, internal planning processes, compensation systems, strategic business decisions, and as a tangible guide in times of crisis. J&J has done it very well. We can discover it from how J&J used the credo as the basis for its response to the 1982 Tylenol crisis.

In October of 1982, Tylenol, the leading pain-killer medicine in the United States at the time, faced a tremendous crisis when seven people in Chicago were reported dead after taking extra-strength Tylenol capsules. Johnson & Johnson was faced with the dilemma of the best way to deal with the problem without destroying the reputation of the company and its most profitable product. Although Johnson & Johnson knew they were not responsible for the tampering of the product, they assumed responsibility by ensuring public safety first and recalled all of their capsules from the market.

Johnson & Johnson's response to the Tylenol poisoning crisis in the 1980s proactively and quickly, and successfully managed the crisis, on one hand, stems from the company's credo, but on the other, is attributed to their purpose-driven leadership. James Burke, the company's chairman, was widely admired for his leadership in the decision to pull Tylenol capsules off the market, and for his forthrightness in dealing with the media. James Burke, reacted to the negative media coverage by forming a seven-member strategy team. The team's strategy guidance from Burke was first, "How do we protect the people?" and second "How do we save this product?"

The Johnson & Johnson Tylenol crisis is an example of how an organization should communicate with the various publics during a crisis. The organization's leadership set the example from the beginning by making public safety the organizations number one concern. This is particularity important given the fact that Johnson & Johnson's main purpose with Tylenol is to enhance the public's well-being or heath. Today Johnson & Johnson has completely regain its reputation and recovered its market share lost during the crisis. The organization was able to re-establish the Tylenol brand name as one to the trusted over-the-counter consumer products in American.

Johnson & Johnson's successful handing of the Tylenol crisis is clearly the example of how company can transform the bad or bad luck to the good or good luck if they are socially responsible for all stakeholders. And do the right things right, regardless of cost. That's why Laozi says:

> Good fortune leans on misfortune,
> Misfortune lurks behind good fortune.
> – Laozi, Tao Te Ching, Ch.58

The Case of Lego

2017 Global RepTrak survey reveals why the top companies have a strong CSR Index. These are the five fundamental reasons:

- *Leadership actively engaged in CSR*
- *CSR aligns with corporate brand purpose*
- *CSR agenda is about action, not just about rhetoric*
- *CSR drives internal and external engagement*
- *CSR focus on human and social interest*

Let's take Lego for example. The Lego Group topped the Reputation Institute's 2017 Global CSR RepTrak list. Among a number of CSR initiatives, Lego introduced their Sustainable Materials Centre, a site "dedicated to research, development and implementation of new, sustainable, raw materials to manufacture LEGO elements as well as packaging materials." This is CSR at its utmost finest. LEGO has made great strides in sustainability, aligning product with purpose. A new kind of leader emerges: a CEO who thinks beyond profit and aligns leadership with societal contributions and highly ethical behaviour.

Good leadership is linked with societal contribution and ethical and transparent governing. For example, the Lego Group remains in the second place for 2 years on the Global RepTrak 100 survey because it is a leader in transparency and societal contribution. It is the only company to have a strong score in 'governance' and 'citizenship.' Then, what's Lego's purpose? Niels B. Christiansen, CEO of Lego reveals his purpose, which is *to inspire and develop the builders of tomorrow. It is what drives Lego and keeps Lego on their toes.* The public recognition of Lego doesn't happen by accident; it is the result of their dedicated colleagues prioritizing children first and delivering play experiences that help them develop those essential skills needed for the future. The Lego Group's Planet Promise is focused on leaving a positive impact and earning a trusted position among stakeholders. In 2018, it starts to materialize its promise by replacing the source material to make plastic from. It is an example of a company whose products are in complete alignment with its values on societal contribution and business transparency.

Case of Microsoft

Microsoft has been working to apply the power of technology to ensure corporate responsibility, safeguard human rights and protect planet. Their policies and business practices reflect a commitment to making a positive impact in communities around the globe. Building on the purpose of Microsoft, they concentrate on the three core areas:

Empowering People Building trust with customers and partners is central to their business success. Earning that trust starts with a foundation of principles to guide their own operations and how they impact the rights of people around the globe. At Microsoft, they strive to create a respectful, rewarding, diverse, and inclusive work environment that enables their employees to create products and services that help others to achieve more. Their leadership is focused on bringing out the best in people, supporting their goals, and allowing them to find deep meaning in their work.

Strengthening Communities Microsoft works to drive greater economic opportunity, inclusion, and empowerment of people around the globe. They leverage a broad set of resources in their quest to empower communities and individuals. Microsoft uses technology as a powerful force for good in a rapidly changing world, and through Microsoft Philanthropies, they're working to ensure that everyone has access to the economic opportunities it provides. Every day they donate nearly two million dollars in products and services to non-profits and they've pledged to donate one billion dollars in cloud services to non-profits and academic researchers over 3 years. Through their YouthSpark grants, they're working with non-profits in 58 countries to increase access to computer science education.

Beyond philanthropy, the company advances community empowerment with commercial offerings and other programs. For example, Microsoft's Africa Initiative provides a set of programs to empower African youth, entrepreneurs, developers and business and civic leaders by with skill development, access to technology, and support for local innovation.

Protecting Our Planet-Environmental Sustainability Microsoft is committed to leveraging technology to solve some of the world's most urgent environmental issues, and focusing on key areas where we believe we can have the most positive impact. Empowering every person and organization on the planet to thrive in a resource-constrained world. They focus their environmental sustainability work in the five areas where they believe they can have the greatest positive impact—carbon, energy, water, ecosystems (including food, agriculture, and biodiversity), and circular economy (including waste reduction). Across these areas, they work to reduce their impact within their own operations, collaborate with their partners to take advantage of digital transformations that reduce their footprint, and support innovation, R&D, and policies that help create a more sustainable future.

At Microsoft, they believe in the sustainable management of the water resources they use across their operations. To support this, they focused on increasing their understanding of water-related risks and impacts to their business and to the communities they serve, setting meaningful goals, improving their water efficiency, and advancing innovative solutions to water challenges. Partnerships with companies like Ecolab, and technology innovations like the free, publicly-available Water Risk Monetizer tool, are not just helping Microsoft address its water-related risks—they're also enabling other organizations to understand the true value, risks, and impacts of water in their operations. They make their efforts transparent by disclosing their annual water use, their water-related risks and governance of water through CDP.

In July 2017, Microsoft announced a new program called AI for Earth, aimed at putting the power of artificial intelligence towards solving some of the biggest environmental challenges of our time. As a technology company with a deep commitment to sustainability, they understand that their responsibility extends beyond their own operations to innovating towards a healthier and better future more broadly. To make AI more accessible to these important groups, Microsoft has designed a program based on three pillars:

Access They will improve access by making a new pool of grants available to help researchers and organizations gain access to cloud and AI computing resources. This includes access to Azure compute time and our data science virtual machine offerings on Azure. These grant applications are available today.

Education They will provide new training and educational opportunities to make sure people and organizations know what AI tools are available, how to use these tools and how the tools can help meet their specific needs. Their approach will be both broad and deep, reaching many people through general session trainings as well as small group faculty summits on single issue areas and training for grantees.

Innovation They also want to encourage others to innovate based on the power and potential of AI. They partnered with others on lighthouse projects that demonstrate how AI can deliver results more rapidly, accurately and efficiently.

Microsoft's vision for the future, and its purpose as a company, is becoming clear. Microsoft CEO Satya Nadella laid out the mission of Microsoft: "*To empower every person and every organization on the planet to achieve more.*"

References

Adams, J. (2016). *Mindful leadership for dummies*. For Dummies.
Burnison, G. K. B. (2016). *The leadership journey: How to master the four critical areas of being a great leader*. Wiley.
Bush, M. C. (2018). *A great place to work for all*. Berret-Koehler Publisher.
Collins, J. (2001). *Good to great: Why some companies make the Leap and others don't*. HarperBusiness.
Collins, J. (2005). *Level 5 leadership: The Triumph of humility and fierce resolve*. Harvard Business Review. Retrieved May 20, 2019, from https://hbr.org/2005/07/level-5-leadership-the-triumph-of-humility-and-fierce-resolve
Collins, J. (2009). *How the mighty fall: And why some companies never give in*. JimCollins.
Damon, W. (2003). *Noble purpose: The joy of living a meaningful life*.
Dhiman, S. (2017). *Holistic leadership: A new paradigm for today's leaders*. Palgrave Macmillan.
Drucker, P. (1963). Managing for business effectiveness. *HBR*(May), 53–60. https://hbr.org/1963/05/managing-for-business-effectiveness
Drucker, P. F., & Wartzman, R. (2010). *Drucker lectures: Essential lessons on management, society and economy*. McGraw-Hill Education.
Dweck, C. S. (2006). *Mindset: The new psychology of success*. Random House.
EY Beacon Institute. (2016). The state of the debate on purpose in business.
George, B. (2009). *Seven lessons for leading in crisis*. Jossey-Bass.
George, B. (2015). *Discover your true north* (2nd ed.). Jossey-Bass.
Global Oneness Project. (2013). *Living oneness: Restoring wholeness in a fragmented world*. http://www.resilience.org/resources/living-oneness-study-guide-restoring-wholeness-in-a-fragmented-world/
Hill, L. A. (2010). *Leading from behind*. https://hbr.org/2010/05/leading-from-behind
Hougaard, R., Carter, J., & Coutts, G. (2016). *Mindful leadership: Achieving results by managing the mind*. Wiley.
Izzo, J., & Vanderwielen, J. (2018). *The purpose revolution: How leaders create engagement and competitive advantage in an age of social good*. Berrett-Koehler Publishers.
Korn Ferry Institute. (2018). *Korn Ferry report 2018 on future of work: The global talent crunch*. https://www.kornferry.com/institute/talent-crunch-future-of-work?reports-and-insights.
Mandela, N. (1995). *Long walk to freedom: The autobiography of Nelson Mandela*. Back Bay Books.
McCloskey, M. W. (2014). *Learning leadership in a changing world: Virtue and effective leadership in the 21st century*. Palgrave Macmillan.
McNamee, R. (2004). *The new normal: Great opportunities in a time of great risk*. Penguin Group.
Prime, J., & Salib, E. (2014). *The best leaders are humble leaders*. https://hbr.org/2014/05/the-best-leaders-are-humble-leaders
Soupios, M., & Mourdoukoutas, P. (2014). *The ten golden rules of leadership: Classical wisdom for modern leaders*. AMACOM.

Chapter 15
Strategies for Managing Sustainability Risk in a VUCA World

Neglecting uncertainty is problematic,
Because it allocates all risk-related costs
To future generations,
Which contradicts the main tenet of
Sustainable development.

– Frank C. Krysiak Professor University of Basel

This chapter examines and analyses sustainable risk and crisis in today's business world and provide an overview of different approaches to risk management from the Taoism's perspective. Combining academic rigour and management science in the West with the Eastern thought—the wisdom and philosophy of Taoism—offers an important resource and approach for organization and business leaders concerned with sustainability and risk management.

Doing Business in an Era of VUCA

As early as 2500 years ago, Laozi observed the phenomenon of the uncertainty, and its impact on individuals and society. The uncertainty breeds risk and opportunity for organizations and individuals. Laozi describes the uncertain world as the following:

Good fortune leans on misfortune,
Misfortune lurks behind good fortune.
Who knows when one shall change to another?
No paradigm can be followed.
Normal can change to abnormal,
Good can change to evil.
People have been deluded for a long time.
– Laozi, Tao Te Ching, Ch.58

Jia Yi (201–168 BC), a Taoist, Chinese writer, poet and politician of the Western Han dynasty, also illustrates the phenomenon of the uncertain world in his famous poet, "On the Owl":

L. Zu, *Responsible and Sustainable Business*,
https://doi.org/10.1007/978-3-030-91117-1_15

All creation changes, nothing is at rest;
Ceaseless the flux - progression and retrogression -
Matter becoming immaterial in endless transformations,
Their infinite subtlety defying description!
In misfortune lies good fortune,
And in good fortune lurks misfortune.
Grief and joy knocking together at the door,
Good luck and bad luck inhabiting the same realm.
Thus, good fortune and bad are interlaced;
Fate is unpredictable,
And none knows what the end will be.
Water forced will spurt out,
An arrow drawn taut will fly far.
Nature is a ceaseless cycle
With everything transmuted, interacting.
Clouds gather and rain falls;
Endless the universal evolution;
None can fathom Heaven or make plans for the future.
Who knows how soon or late he must meet his fate?
– Jia Yi (201–169 B.C.) "The Owl"

Laozi and Jia Yi share the same point of view on the world we live that's constantly changing, becoming more unstable every day, where changes big and small are becoming more unpredictable—and they're getting more and more dramatic and happening faster and faster. As events unfold in completely unexpected ways, it's becoming impossible to determine cause and effect. In today's term, we call it "VOLATILITY". From the passages of Laozi and Jia Yi, we are also aware that it's becoming more difficult for us to anticipate events or predict how they'll unfold; historical forecasts and past experiences are losing their relevance and are rarely applicable as a basis for predicting the shape of things to come. It's becoming nearly impossible to plan for investment, development, and growth as it becomes increasingly uncertain where the route is heading. Thus, today we can term the phenomenon as "UNCERTAINTY". Since ancient times when Laozi and Jia Yi lived, we found that our world is getting more complex than ever. For example, problems and their repercussions are more multi-layered, harder to understand. The different layers intermingle, making it impossible to get an overview of how things are related. Decisions are reduced to a tangled mesh of reaction and counter-reaction—and choosing the single correct path is almost impossible. We can give it a name of "COMPLEXITY". In a volatile, uncertain and complex world, the solution of "one size fits all" and "best practice" didn't work anymore. They have been relegated to yesterday—in today's world it's rare for things to be completely clear or precisely determinable. Not everything is black and white—grey is also an option. The demands on modern organisations and management are more contradictory and paradoxical than ever, challenging our personal value systems to the core. In a world where the "what" takes a back seat to the "why?" and the "how?", making decisions requires courage, awareness, and a willingness to make mistakes. Therefore, we see the phenomenon as "AMBIGUITY". When we bring the four phenomena together, we get the new term, "VUCA".

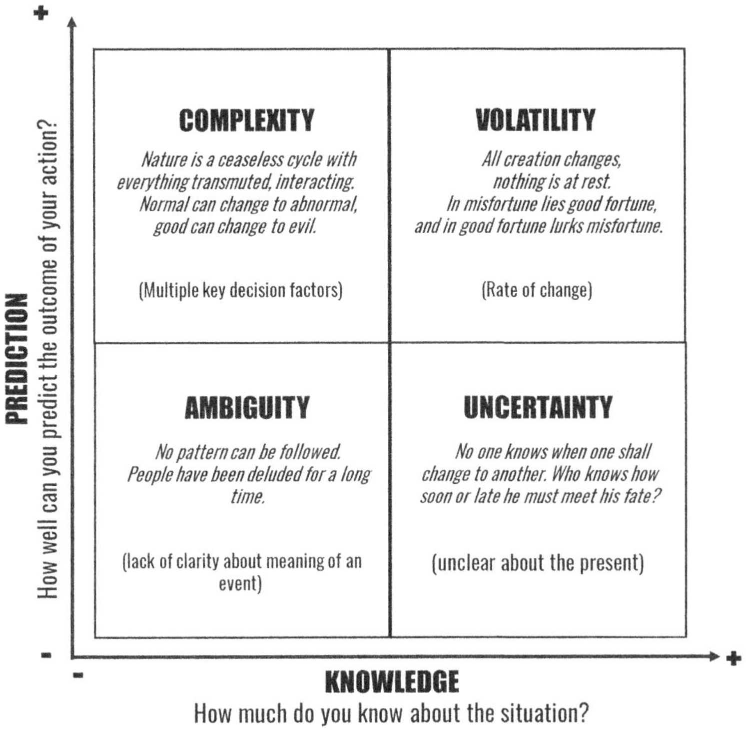

Fig. 15.1 Taoism's wisdom and VUCA. Source: Author developed based on Tao Te Ching and concept of VUCA

As I discussed in Part III, VUCA is a common acronym in today's managerial jargon that many have lost a full understanding of what VUCA means. Thus, in this chapter, I'll try to summarise the main aspects of this concept from the perspective of Taoism's wisdom, to understand how this affect individuals and organisations (see Fig. 15.1).

Volatility (Laozi and Jia Yi: all creation changes, nothing is at rest. In misfortune lies good fortune, and in good fortune lurks misfortune): refers to the speed of change in an industry, market or the world in general. It is associated with fluctuations in demand, turbulence and short time to markets, and it is well-documented in the literature on industry dynamism. The more volatile the world is, the more and faster things change.

Uncertainty (Laozi and Jia Yi: No one knows when one shall change to another. Who knows how soon or late he must meet his fate?): refers to the extent to which we cannot confidently predict the future. Part of the uncertainty is perceived and associated with people's inability to understand what is going on. Uncertainty, though, is also a more objective characteristic of an environment. Indeed, uncertain environments are those that don't allow any prediction, even not on a statistical basis. The more uncertain the world is, the harder it is to predict.

Complexity (Laozi and Jia Yi: Nature is a ceaseless cycle with everything transmuted, interacting): refers to the number of factors that we need to take into account, their variety and the relationships between them. The more elements, the higher their range and the more they are interconnected, the more complex an environment is. Under high complexity, it is impossible to analyse the situation and come to rational conclusions thoroughly. The more complex the world is, the harder it is to explain.

Ambiguity (Laozi and Jia Yi: No paradigm can be followed. People have been deluded for a long time): refers to a lack of clarity about how to interpret something. A situation is ambiguous, for example, when information is incomplete, contradicting or too inaccurate to draw definite conclusions. More generally it refers to fuzziness and vagueness in ideas and terminology. The more ambiguous the world is, the harder it is to interpret.

Each of these elements can be seen individually: i.e., we can have a situation that is volatile but not complex or ambiguous. The more of these four elements happen together, the more critical understanding of the scenario and reacting to it becomes.

Risk and Opportunity in the VUCA World

In Chaps. 10 and 11, I discussed how to lead with virtue of prudence in an uncertain world. I also pointed out that crisis and risk bring to business and industry not only threats and dangers, but also opportunities. That's the law of dialectics, or law of unity of opposites. Although risks need to be treated for their adverse effects, they can also be harnessed for their opportunities (Fig. 15.2).

This is also true of today's reality in a VUCA environment. Economic and financial globalization and the expansion of world trade have brought substantial benefits and opportunities to companies, but globalization also poses novel sources of uncertainty and risks. Multiple business indicators show that the level of uncertainty for corporate leaders has increased, due in large part to:

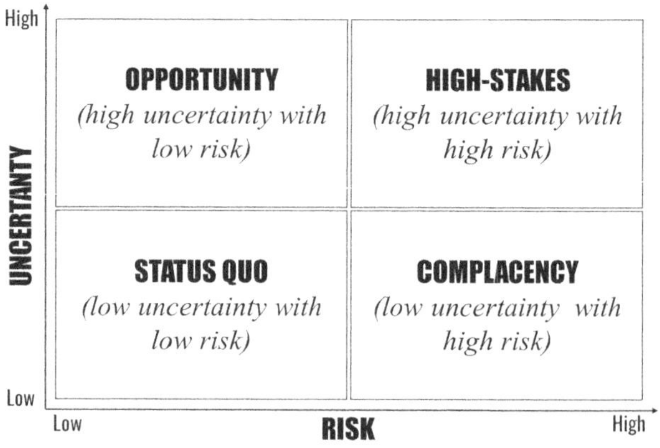

Fig. 15.2 VUCA and risk and opportunity. Source: adapted from Constance Dierickx (2018), Leading through Crisis with Courage, Judgment, and Fortitude

  - Large extended enterprises made up of independent organizations but with tremendous pressures to grow and perform as a unit;
  - Rapid rates of change in technology, connections and information flows as a result of globalization; and
  - Problems in managing scale using methods rooted in controlling all decisions across the entire extended enterprise (Kytle & Ruggie, 2005)

- The result of the greater interdependencies and hidden vulnerabilities that businesses now face is an increased number of uncertainties in corporate decision-making. Current network-based operating models highlight the growing importance of the extended enterprise by establishing greater connectivity among and between stakeholders across the globe. This connectivity has also created entirely new stakeholders and requires innovative forms of risk management.
- Most companies seem to do well when the future is reasonably predictable and uncertainty is low, but fail spectacularly in a discontinuity—a sudden change in the environment. Many companies seem to have difficulty adapting to a shock or a heightened level of uncertainty—something they are not used to. Many attempt to tackle uncertainty by trying to eliminate it through cleverly crafted hedges—mechanisms that allow them to remove uncertainty from one part of the business or the other. Attempting to eliminate uncertainty is costly and reducing uncertainty in one part of the business may increase the overall risk faced by the company and make it vulnerable to shocks. Increasing flexibility is a much better way to manage and to take advantage of uncertainty, reducing risk and increasing economic value. This is one of Taoism's principles: *reversal is the movement of the Tao* (Tao Te Ching, Ch.40). It means that the course of the Tao is one of reversal, situations turn around and change to their opposites. This can be said with respect to good and bad luck. In a VUCA world, business leaders must be able to equally accept the opposing segments or phases of the movement of the Tao without being one-sidedly attached to a singular element.

Figure 15.2 shows that in an era of VUCA, corporate continuity can be at stake because it faces the big changes of high uncertainty and high risk. The manifestation of VUCA can be seen in many forms—a massive collapse in climate change, oil and commodity prices, acts of terrorism, cyber security threats, natural disasters, technological glitches, and many more. While risk management principles will continue to be relevant, companies need to proactively adopt a VUCA lens when implementing risk management, including each phase of the risk management process. In other words, a risk-savvy company is one that proactively embraces VUCA—it is a risk survivor and also a risk overcomer. At the epicentre of its governance DNA is a smart, risk-based, decision-making process embedded across different levels of the organisation. In the corporate governance arena, the principle of establishing of a sound system of risk management is a generally accepted global norm in the code of corporate governance. Risk governance is gaining traction as a core competence along with other technical, business and personal skill sets. It is an integral part of a company's strategic initiative. Fundamentally, it facilitates the creation as well as the preservation of corporate values.

However, setting up a system of risk management is not a panacea. The framework and process must be continuously strengthened to be fit for purpose in the constantly-changing face of VUCA (Liang et al., 2016). In other words, the goal is how to navigate the company effectively at the speed of change in the VUCA environment.

The forces of VUCA can have a severe impact. As responsible stewards, the board and management must exercise due diligence to ensure that the company is resilient to the adverse impact of VUCA. Risk taking without boundaries is recklessness. The significance of having a risk appetite is to set an enterprise perimeter for risk taking and risk management. In recent years, there has been a growing awareness and adoption of risk appetite statements by companies. Such a statement serves to align the boundaries for risk taking in addition to expounding the exploitation of opportunity for the companies. For instance, it is common for some companies to disclose risk appetite statements in their annual reports. In its 2015 Annual Report, SingTel states that "the Group shall not compromise our integrity, values and reputation by risking brand damage, service delivery standards, severe network disruption or regulatory non-compliance". As a mechanism for opportunity seeking, it is "prepared to take measured risks to seek new growth in the digital space by providing global platforms and enablers, targeted at a global footprint, while leveraging our current scale and core strengths".

How to respond to VUCA risks and crisis? In Chap. 10, I discussed four types of crisis responses include reaction (avoidance), defence (reduction), accommodation (transfer) and pro-action (retention). In relation to the externalities and disruptive nature of VUCA, these risk responses call for greater contingency planning and collaboration with external stakeholders. Standard Operating Procedures (SOPs) can help but their effectiveness may be limited since the responses and the outcomes are dependent on external parties and other factors. In most cases, companies would have to adopt a "trial-and-error" approach when faced with VUCA risks. Without the certainty of outcomes, companies are increasingly considering secondary risks that may arise from the initial response. In a similar vein, VUCA risks manifest a business reality, that is, the companies' controls over them may be limited. There are no perfect solutions. Hence, the issue calls for systems thinking that we have already discussed in the preceding chapters. More precisely, it calls for thinking out of the box in a collaborative manner—harnessing a diversity of views to address VUCA.

Navigating the VUCA landscape is challenging. It is ever changing. Indeed, change is the only certainty. An important question to ask, therefore, is whether the risk management is appropriate for the VUCA context faced by the company. Put differently, is it fit for purpose? Sound stewardship requires the stewards to establish robust management practices, and having a sound system of risk management is no exception. Nevertheless, the question remains as to whether or not there are weaknesses and blind spots in existing practices. In this respect, a pillar of robust corporate governance is assurance, that is, having an independent eye that reviews whether risk management is VUCA-ready, design-effective, and operationally-effective. In today's environment, those charged with governance face a higher

		DIVERS	EFFECTS	DEMANDS
V	VOLATILITY	• Change nature • Change dynamics • Chang rate & speed	• Risks • Instability • Flux	Vision • Wider understanding • Different perspectives
U	UNCERTAINTY	• Unpredictability • Potential surprises • Unknown outcomes	• Direction • Paralysis to data overload	Understanding • Take actions • Probe changes
C	COMPLEXITY	• Tasks correlation • Multifaceted effects • Influencers	• Unproductive • Dualities	Clarity • Key focus • Flexible • Creative
A	AMBIGUITY	• Ideal vs. Actual • Misinterpretation	• Induce doubt & distrust • Lapses in decision making • Hurt innovations	Agility/Adaptation • Decision making • Innovation

Fig. 15.3 VUCA 1.0 vs. VUCA 2.0. Source: author developed based on Bill George (2017)

degree of oversight for the system of risk management. An independent, objective assurance (example, internal audit) serves to inspire confidence in key stakeholders that the system is fit for purpose in the creation and preservation of corporate values. More importantly, the openness to having an independent review goes a long way in conveying that the board and management take the threat of VUCA seriously—both in word and in the spirit of corporate governance excellence.

In response to challenges and crisis of VUCA, some scholars have come up with VUCA 2.0 as an alternative way of thinking for both organizations and individuals. For example, Bill George, a senior fellow at Harvard Business School, used the same letters V.U.C.A, but referring to four foundational qualities for the response: *Vision, Understanding, Clarity and Agility/Adaptability* (George, 2017). Figure 15.3 shows that these four modes (VUCA 2.0) are able to apply to every layer of human life, from governments to organisation, to single individuals. And should ensure the psychological safety that is required to live through a state of unknown.

Vision: paint a picture of the future we want; vision serves as a compass and for orientation to confer meaning and spark motivation—and to forge internal and external identity and effectiveness. Today's business leaders need the ability to see through the chaos to have a clear vision for their organizations. They must define the True North of their organization: its mission, values, and strategy. They should create clarity around this True North and refuse to let external events pull them off course or cause them to neglect or abandon their mission, which must be their guiding light. CEO Paul Polman has done this especially well by focusing Unilever's True North on sustainability.

Understanding: understand interconnections; make them transparent. Reflect on the context. Think and plan meta-strategically. Start from the result and work backwards. Harmonise skills. Embrace and exploit behaviours and reactions. Convert anxiety and resistance into productive energy. With their vision in hand, leaders need in-depth understanding of their organization's capabilities and strategies to take advantage of rapidly changing circumstances by playing to their strengths while minimizing their weaknesses. Listening only to information sources and opinions that reinforce their own views carries great risk of missing alternate points of view. Instead, leaders need to tap into myriad sources covering the full spectrum of viewpoints by engaging directly with their customers and employees to ensure they are attuned to changes in their markets. Spending time in the marketplace, retail stores, factories, innovation centers, and research labs, or just wandering around offices talking to people is essential.

Clarity: simplicity. Focus on what counts and what it's really about. Trust, transparent connections and processes. Apply energy and force exactly where they will be most effective. Now more than ever, leaders need the courage to step up to these challenges and make audacious decisions that embody risks and often go against the grain. They cannot afford to keep their heads down, using traditional management techniques while avoiding criticism and risk-taking. In fact, their greatest risk lies in not having the courage to make bold moves. This era belongs to the bold, not the meek and timid.

Agility/Adaptability: Flexibility, Scrutinise hierarchical management techniques. Promote a consistent culture for making decisions and accounting for mistakes. Interact transparently with objections. Facilitate innovation and build up resilience. If ever there were a need for leaders to be flexible in adapting to this rapidly changing environment, this is it. Long-range plans are often obsolete by the time they are approved. Instead, flexible tactics are required for rapid adaptation to changing external circumstances, without altering strategic course. This is not a time for continuing the financial engineering so prevalent in the past decade. Rather, leaders need multiple contingency plans while preserving strong balance sheets to cope with unforeseen events.

Sustainability Risk Is Emerging and Defined

Traditionally, when people are talking about business risk, they are more concerned about financial risk, operational risk, security risk or technical risk. But the late twentieth century has shown that any human and business activity can have many consequences on society and natural environment—foreseen and unforeseen, intended and unintended, beneficial and catastrophic. The companies as they go global have increasingly encountered social and environmental risk.

The increasingly significant risks traditionally fall into non-financial areas of business activity, often referred to as environmental, social and governmental (ESG) issues. These risks have been amplified by the butterfly effect in movement of corporate social responsibility, the increasing globalization, new technologies and a rising tide of expectations among stakeholders about the social and environmental role of business. These changes in the operating model have led to a significant shift in market power—not just to customers and traditional investors, but also, more importantly, toward stakeholders.

As a result of this shift in market power, "sustainability risk" is a rising area of concern for global corporations. Sustainability risks are growing and getting more

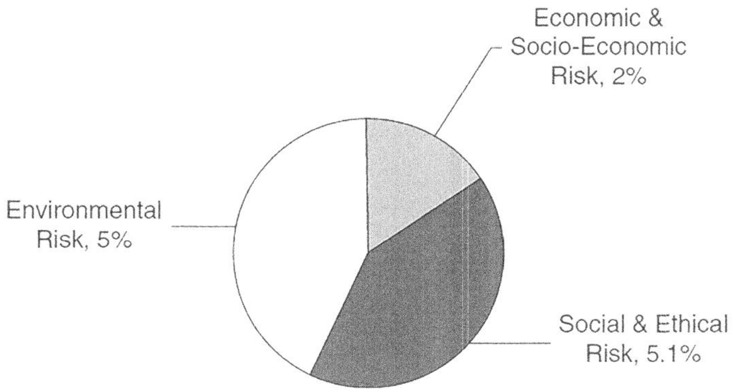

Fig. 15.4 Sustainability risks. Source: Spedding, Linda, Adam Rose. (2008). Business Risk Management Handbook: A Sustainable Approach. Burlington, USA: CIMA Publishing

attention from executives, investors, lenders and regulators. Because business executives realized that social responsibility risks threaten the license to do business. From a company perspective, sustainability risk, like any other risk, arises when its own behaviour or the action of others in its operating environment creates vulnerabilities. In the case of sustainability risk, stakeholders may identify those vulnerabilities and apply pressure on the corporation for behavioural changes. As the ability to listen to corporate stakeholders' perspectives on social and environmental issues becomes a competitive necessity, managing sustainability risks will need to become more fully embedded in corporate strategy. Sustainability risk management deals with emerging environmental and social justice risks. Risk managers will need to anticipate these risks and develop appropriate risk mitigation and strategies for them, but since many sustainability risks are new and emerging, the best strategies for dealing with corporate sustainability might not be apparent.

Experience and case studies demonstrate that the sustainability risks do have financial impacts upon organisations, both positively and negatively. Therefore, it highlighted the need for a review and reappraisal of corporate behaviour and accountability. In turn this had major implications for sustainable risk management. Business leaders must examine new areas of emerging risk and develop sustainable systems of risk analysis and management.

The confluence of risks and opportunities associated with environmental, social and economic performance has made sustainability a strategic priority for companies as part of their overall business strategy. Measuring an organization's environmental, social and economic performance is often referred to as the "triple bottom line."

Over the past years, we have seen the rising sustainability risks that affect thriving businesses, the environment sustainability, people and the society as a whole. Therefore, sustainability risk management issues have become a critical importance for businesses to be sustainable and competitive in the market. If we look at the pie chart in Fig. 15.4, we notice that the majority of operational risk from sustainability issues is derived from environmental risks, social and ethical issues. As Table 15.1

Table 15.1 Risk to value from sustainability issues

Risk to value from sustainability issues	Gross (inherent) risk (%)	Risk management factor (RMF)			Net (residual) risk (%)
Economic and socio-economic risk	2.9	/	1.4	=	2.0
Social and ethical risk	9.0	/	1.8	=	5.1
Environmental risk	8.2	/	1.55	=	5.4
Combined risk issues	20.1	/	1.6	=	12.5

Source: Spedding, Linda, Adam Rose. (2008). Business Risk Management Handbook: A Sustainable Approach. Burlington, USA: CIMA Publishing

reveals that the primary sustainability risk within the organisations reviewed is still as a result of environmental issues, representing a 5.4% risk to market value; followed by social and ethical issues at 5.1% (including health and safety issues) and economic 'sustainability' factors at 2.0% (Spedding & Rose, 2008).

Table 15.1 also shows that among the companies analysed by the sustainability enterprise management risk rating system (UK, EU and US markets), non-financial issues alone put at risk an amount equivalent to 20.1% of the total market capital if left untreated. This represents the "gross" or "inherent" risk borne by those companies by virtue of the nature of their current operations. The risk management measures actually adopted by those companies are taken into account to mitigate this risk, the sustainability of their risk management systems, and the value threatened falls to 12.5%—a measurement of the 'net' risk to market value of the organisations (Spedding & Rose, 2008).

Every year, the economists who meet in Davos at the World Economic Forum present an updated estimate of the major risks facing the business world and the global economy. They do this using a grid that shows the two dimensions of risk:

- *The likelihood or probability of the risk occurring (expressed as a percentage) and*
- *The severity or consequences if the risk does occur (expressed in monetary units)*

Figure 15.5 reveals that the risks that are most closely connected to environmental sustainability (climate change, extreme weather events and water scarcity, etc.) are marked in green, and socio-economic issues (income disparity, unemployment and fiscal crises) in red. Sustainability risks (environmental and social risks) have become more prominent over the past years. Many of these risks are interconnected, and a major crisis of one type could trigger a series of related crises, a domino effect (WEF, 2014) .

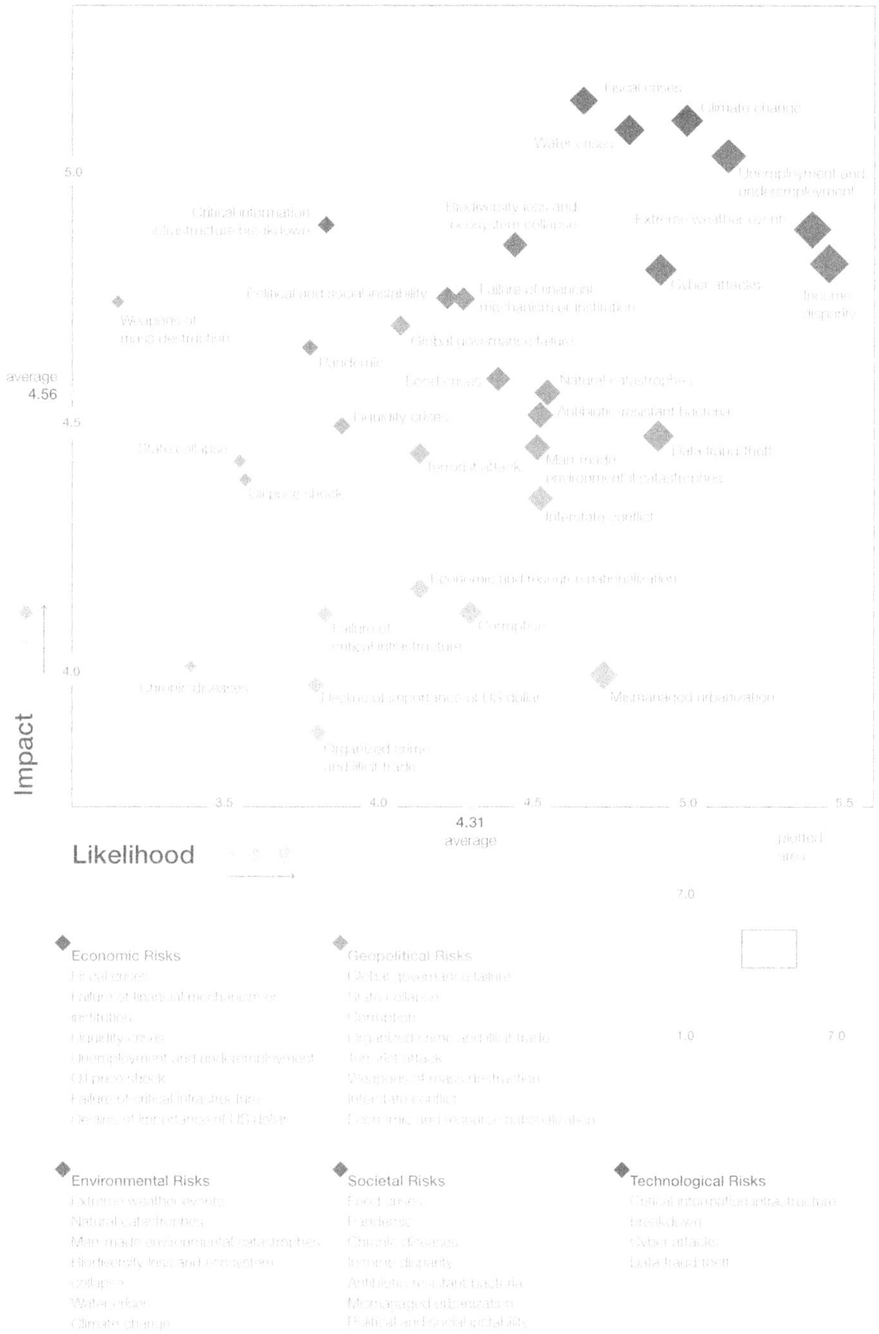

Fig. 15.5 Concern over sustainability risks is growing. Source: World Economic Forum Global Risk Report (2014)

COVID-19: An Emerging Sustainability Risk

COVID-19 is seen as an emerging sustainability risk because the immediate human and economic cost of COVID-19 is severe. It threatens to scale back years of progress on reducing poverty and inequality and to further weaken social cohesion and global cooperation. Job losses, a widening digital divide, disrupted social interactions, and abrupt shifts in markets could lead to dire consequences and lost opportunities for large parts of the global population. The ramifications—in the form of social unrest, political fragmentation and geopolitical tensions—will shape the effectiveness of our responses to the other key threats of the next decade: cyberattacks, weapons of mass destruction and, most notably, climate change.

We can find more evidence from the Global Risks Report 2021. The key findings of the latest Global Risks Perception Survey (GRPS) reveals that global risks perceptions among the highest likelihood risks of the next 10 years are extreme weather, climate action failure and human-led environmental damage; as well as digital power concentration, digital inequality and cybersecurity failure. Among the highest impact risks of the next decade, infectious diseases are in the top spot, followed by climate action failure and other environmental risks; as well as weapons of mass destruction, livelihood crises, debt crises and IT infrastructure breakdown (see Fig. 15.6).

When it comes to the time-horizon within which these risks will become a critical threat to the world, the most imminent threats—those that are most likely in the next 2 years—include employment and livelihood crises, widespread youth disillusionment, digital inequality, economic stagnation, human-made environmental damage, erosion of societal cohesion, and terrorist attacks. Economic risks feature prominently in the 3–5-year timeframe, including asset bubbles, price instability, commodity shocks and debt crises; followed by geopolitical risks, including interstate relations and conflict, and resource geo-politization. In the 5–10-year horizon, environmental risks such as biodiversity loss, natural resource crises and climate action failure dominate; alongside weapons of mass destruction, adverse effects of technology and collapse of states or multilateral institutions.

The Pandemic has caused economic fragility and societal divisions to increase. Underlying disparities in healthcare, education, financial stability and technology have led the crisis to disproportionately impact certain groups and countries. Not only has COVID-19 caused more than two million deaths at the time of writing, but the economic and long-term health impacts will continue to have devastating consequences. GRPS shows that the pandemic's economic shockwave—working hours equivalent to 495 million jobs were lost in the second quarter of 2020 alone—will immediately increase inequality, but so can an uneven recovery. Only 28 economies are expected to have grown in 2020. Nearly 60% of respondents to the GRPS identified "infectious diseases" and "livelihood crises" as the top short-term threats to the world. Loss of lives and livelihoods will increase the risk of "social cohesion erosion", also a critical short-term threat identified in the GRPS.

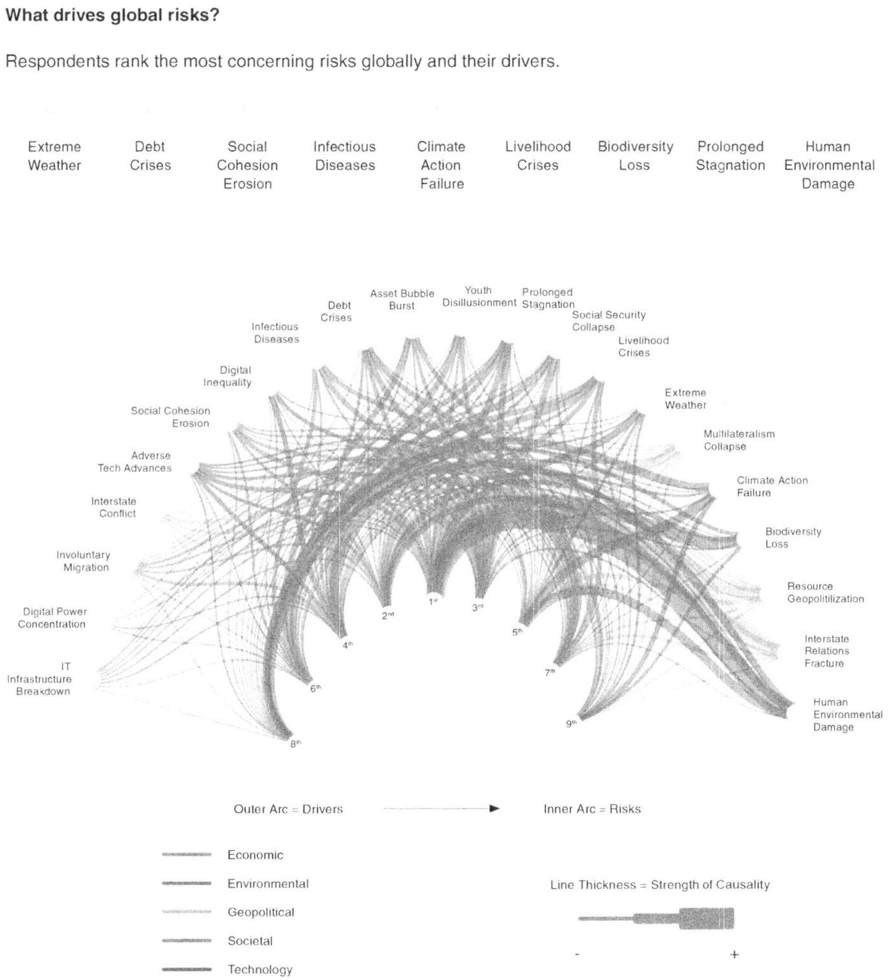

Fig. 15.6 Global risk network. Source: World Economic Forum (2021)

Growing digital divides and technology adoption pose concerns COVID-19 has accelerated the Fourth Industrial Revolution, expanding the digitalization of human interaction, e-commerce, online education and remote work. These shifts will transform society long after the pandemic and promise huge benefits—the ability to telework and rapid vaccine development are two examples—but they also risk exacerbating and creating inequalities. Respondents to the GRPS rated "digital inequality" as a critical short-term threat. A widening digital gap can worsen societal fractures and undermine prospects for an inclusive recovery. Progress towards digital inclusivity is threatened by growing digital dependency, rapidly accelerating automation, information suppression and manipulation, gaps in technology regulation and gaps in technology skills and capabilities.

A doubly disrupted generation of youth is emerging in an age of lost opportunity. While the digital leap forward unlocked opportunities for some youth, many are now entering the workforce in an employment ice age. Young adults worldwide are experiencing their second major global crisis in a decade. Already exposed to environmental degradation, the consequences of the financial crisis, rising inequality, and disruption from industrial transformation, this generation faces serious challenges to their education, economic prospects and mental health.

According to the GRPS, the risk of "youth disillusionment" is being largely neglected by the global community, but it will become a critical threat to the world in the short term. Hard-fought societal wins could be obliterated if the current generation lacks adequate pathways to future opportunities—and loses faith in today's economic and political institutions.

Climate continues to be a looming risk as global cooperation weakens. Climate change—to which no one is immune—continues to be a catastrophic risk. Although lockdowns worldwide caused global emissions to fall in the first half of 2020, evidence from the 2008–2009 Financial Crisis warns that emissions could bounce back. A shift towards greener economies cannot be delayed until the shocks of the pandemic subside. "Climate action failure" is the most impactful and second most likely long-term risk identified in the GRPS.

Responses to the pandemic have caused new domestic and geopolitical tensions that threaten stability. Digital division and a future "lost generation" are likely to test social cohesion from within borders—exacerbating geopolitical fragmentation and global economic fragility. With stalemates and flashpoints increasing in frequency, GRPS respondents rated "state collapse" and "multilateralism collapse" as critical long-term threats.

Climate Change Is One of the Top Sustainability Risks

Sustainability risk refers to the uncertainty in being able to sustain the growth of a given system (a corporation, household, community or economy) because certain practices may have negative externalities which result in the dilapidation of value chain of the system over a period of time or impact other related systems.

The starkest example that illustrates this scenario is rising sustainability risk across sectors of an economy to varying degrees because of climate change. Whether or not climate change is leading to significant disorders is not even a point of debate. Innumerable agencies, including the plus important Intergovernmental Panel on Climate Change (IPCC) have well established the adverse impacts that range from rising temperature to increase occurrences of extremes condition of flood and drought.

These climatic disturbances have already been directly impacting the profitability of corporations. For example, floods in the most important coal basins of the world, Queensland, Australia, led to an estimated loss of $6 billion, according to Forbes. Up to 40% of the global coke supply was impacted and supply disruptions caused coke contract prices to rise up to 30%. This led to delays in the production of steel and within 3 weeks after the flood, the steel prices had risen more than 10%. According to JP Morgan's senior economist Helen Kevans, the flood impact on production and demand could have shaved around 0.4% points off the Australian GDP. Such can be the economic impact of a flood. As the frequency of such events rise, we can very well imagine what the quantum of loss could be.

On 23 February 2021, António Guterres, UN Secretary-General addressed the Security Council on climate-related security risks to international peace and security. He pointed out that the climate emergency is the defining issue of our time. Because climate disruption is a crisis amplifier and multiplier. The impacts of the crisis are greatest where fragility and conflicts have weakened coping mechanisms; where people depend on natural capital like forests and fish stocks for their livelihoods; and where women—who bear the greatest burden of the climate emergency—do not enjoy equal rights.

Guterres also stressed that vulnerability to climate risks is also correlated with income inequality. In other words, the poorest suffer most. Unless we protect those most exposed and susceptible to climate-related impacts, we can expect them to become even more marginalized, and their grievances to be reinforced. High levels of inequality that climate change enhances, can weaken social cohesion and lead to discrimination, scapegoating, rising tensions and unrest, increasing the risk of conflict. Those who are already being left behind will be left even farther behind.

Therefore, Guterres called for more needs to be done to address the specific risks—the climate crisis—that poses to peace and security. He also came up with four priority areas.

First, a greater focus on prevention through strong, ambitious climate action. Guterres emphasized that we must get the world on track to achieve the goals of the Paris Agreement and avoid climate catastrophe. We must create a truly global coalition to commit to net-zero emissions by the middle of the century. And we must mobilize a decade of transformation through a successful COP26 in Glasgow. All companies, cities and financial institutions are requested to prepare concrete and credible decarbonization plans. It is the only way we will keep the 1.5-degree goal within reach.

Second, immediate actions to protect countries, communities and people from increasingly frequent and severe climate impacts. Guterres proposed a breakthrough on adaptation and resilience to dramatically raise the level of investments. All donors and multilateral and national Development Banks must increase the share of adaptation and resilience finance to at least 50% of their climate finance support. And we must make these funds accessible to those on the frontlines of the climate crisis. Developed countries must keep their pledge of channelling $100 billion annually to the Global South. Guterres also suggested to scale up early warning systems and early action on climate-related crises, from droughts and storms to the emergence of zoonotic diseases. We also need stronger social protection to support those impacted. These actions must start now, with transformative policies as we emerge from the pandemic. Economic and financial systems must incorporate climate risk into financial analysis, so that it is captured in business models and investment decisions.

We must invest in renewable energy and green infrastructure. In short, we must close the finance gap by increasing support to the countries and communities that are suffering the worst impacts of the climate crisis. That support must reach women and girls, who bear the brunt of the climate crisis; and constitute eighty percent of those displaced by climate change.

Third, embracing a concept of security that puts people at its centre. The COVID-19 pandemic has shown the devastation that so-called non-traditional security threats can cause, on a global scale. Preventing and addressing the poverty, food insecurity and displacement caused by climate disruption contributes to sustaining peace and reducing the risk of conflict. The Nobel Committee recognized this when it awarded the Nobel Peace Prize to the World Food Programme last year. Respect for human rights, particularly women's rights, the rule of law, inclusion and diversity, are fundamental to solving the climate crisis and creating more peaceful and stable societies. The 2030 Agenda and the Sustainable Development Goals are the global blueprint for action.

Fourth, deepening partnerships across and beyond the United Nations system. Guterres stressed the importance of leveraging and building on the strengths of different stakeholders, including UN Security Council, the Peacebuilding Commission, international financial institutions, regional organizations, civil society, the private sector, academia and others. The Climate Security Mechanism, which brings together the Department of Political and Peacebuilding Affairs, the United Nations Development Programme and the United Nations Environment Programme, is a blueprint for such collaboration within the United Nations System. Working to deliver these goals, the United Nations is striving to lead by example by making sure our own operations take full account of the climate crisis. We are working to ensure that our mediation strategies, analysis and reporting consistently reflect climate risks.

The climate crisis is the multilateral challenge of our age. It is already impacting every area of human activity. Solving it requires coordination and cooperation on a scale we have never seen before. The engagement of all multilateral bodies can play an important role in facing this challenge.

Assessments of Sustainability Risk

Sustainability risks by their nature are perceived to have a long lead-time and are difficult to anticipate. Thus, current risk assessment methods may not be suitable to assess the estimated value at risk. Effective risk identification and appropriate risk responses are vital to the sustainability of any organization. However, the identification and management of sustainability risks remains a major challenge for many businesses. The research of Business Council for Sustainable Development (WBCSD) shows that it is relatively easy to identify sustainability risks (e.g., economic, environmental or social) that might have a financial impact on the business. However, risk managers as well as sustainability experts are struggling to quantify such risks in a meaningful way that allows for business leaders to allocate resources. The absence of standardized approaches hampers this further (WBCSD, 2013).

In the absence of a universal standard, some companies have developed their own approach to quantifying sustainability risks by developing methodologies and models that assign a monetary value to human capital, or modelling the stock market price impacts linked to sustainability events that have attracted a negative reaction. By embedding sustainability into environment risk management (ERM) systems, companies increase the effectiveness of their overall risk management, as risks are looked at with a broader view.

Traditional concepts to risk management hardly cover all risks, especially social and environmental ones, and consequently do not meet the expectations of respective stakeholders. A risk management approach that also includes sustainability indicators provides management with a better and more complete view of the company's exposures. Conventional risk methods focus on risks that can be financially quantified such as rebuilding of a facility, or legal costs due to improper business behaviour. However, they rarely focus on risks concerning brand valuation or human rights and if they do so, it is from a qualitative perspective. These risks are more difficult to financially quantify and many companies are struggling to find ways to overcome this challenge. In addition, most risk models exclude the potential for extreme events as they are deemed improbable. By embedding sustainability into ERM systems, companies can increase the effectiveness of their overall risk management processes by capturing and prioritizing risks through a wider lens.

One theory put forward in the book "Surviving & Thriving in Uncertainty", by Rick Funston and Stephen Wagner, is that companies need to use unconventional methods to assess risks including sustainability risks. They argue that resilient companies are those that understand and appreciate the worst scenario that their business faces on the basis that the improbable can and does happen, sometimes with little warning. Tools have been developed to assist companies to perform scenario planning so they can be ready to react should an extreme event occur (Funston & Wagner, 2010).

Sustainability risks should not be treated differently than other risks. Once identified, sustainability risks have to be measured and mitigated. In addition, ERM processes should be updated periodically to consider new trends, emerging issues and stakeholder concerns. The most advanced risk management processes are those that proactively assess the following sustainability risks prior, during and after a project is completed: financial, legal, social, reputational, environmental and safety and health. Some companies routinely evaluate geo-political, economic and technological risks, and others also assess potential and strategic impacts and assign weights to each component to calculate an overall risk rating. Another best practice trend observed is when the management of sustainability risks is tied to financial compensation for employees. Additionally, some companies are incorporating sustainability metrics in supplier qualifications and in business development practices

The Future Leader Team (FLT) of WBCSD 2013 working group compared company-specific approaches to sustainability risk management and identified that some approaches could be classified as "best practices" and could be adopted by other companies to help create a standard in this area. Traditional risk assessment methods have a bias for monetizing risk since this is the accepted language of corporate reporting and investment analysis. However, embedding sustainability into business models and strategies has also been recognized as means to differentiate companies and create value. The traditional calculation for defining risk has been to multiply the financial impact of an event by the probability of its occurrence.

One key recommendation from the FLT 2013 working group is for risk managers and corporate sustainability experts to develop adequate methods that capture the respective needs of the individual company and its sustainability exposures. At the same time, a merger with conventional valuation methods, such as a discounted cash flow model to monetize sustainability risks, should be explored. It is recommended that companies develop analyses and tools to support their risk management approach. This can be done alone or in collaboration with other companies. Furthermore, companies need to change their thinking with regards to risk assessment. Companies need to review the whole value chain since there are major sustainability risks at the beginning or at the end of the value chain which may have an indirect but material impact on the company.

Therefore, risk assessment should try to cover all possible areas of events to identify the most critical elements for the survival and performance of the company. It is also critical that companies do not become blasé about excluding material impacts on the basis of their unlikelihood. It is prudent to estimate the vulnerability and resilience a business has to all scenarios including remote worst-case scenarios and how quickly they can occur. For all identified risks, including those that cannot be measured by probability, as they are classified as uncertain, risk managers have to assess scenarios on how bad can it get and how fast can it get bad.

Incorporating sustainability risks into risk management processes is becoming a strategic topic for management and boards of directors. By understanding and developing an appropriate response to sustainability risks, companies are able to gain a holistic and transparent view of their exposures and opportunities. These are also likely to be the companies that are able to cope with related challenges in a structured, cost-effective and efficient manner. Last but not least, such companies will most probably be in a better position to create business opportunities and gain competitive advantage.

Managing Sustainability Risk: The Core Stages

This section will discuss some stages and approaches from perspective of Taoism's wisdom, and present some cases in the business world to illustrate Taoism's philosophy.

Anticipating and Avoiding the Risk: Responding to Early Warning Signals

In an ancient time, Laozi observed one phenomenon:

> People usually fail
> When they are about to succeed in doing businesses
> – Tao Te Ching, Ch. 64

Today, an American business consultant, Collins (2011) observed the same one:

> Why do some companies thrive in uncertainty, even chaos, and others do not? When buffeted by tumultuous events, when hit by big, fast-moving forces that we can neither predict nor control, what distinguishes those who perform exceptionally well from those who underperform or worse?

As we discussed the alternation of good luck and back luck in the preceding section, we understand that there are some dangers or bad luck lurking; namely, past success can lead to both inertia and recklessness. Business success to date can lead to reluctance to change or even risk-aversion behaviour. Contrarily, the same success can breed a sense of invincibility and promote reckless action. Kwak (2002) refer to the latter as the "Icarus Paradox." Icarus is the mythical figure who was overconfident of his own powers and eventually fell back to earth after flying too close to the sun. Early success can promote both inertia and recklessness. Organizations that experience strong performance early in their history tend to become imprinted with change-inhibiting routines, and lead to the hubris. The hubris can take several different forms, ranging from refusing to take competitors seriously to overreacting to moves that might be interpreted as personal attacks.

In the book of "How the Mighty Fall", Collins examines how and why once great companies have since declined and identifies five stages of organizational decline: hubris born of success; undisciplined pursuit of more; denial of risk and peril; grasping for salvation, and capitalization to irrelevance or death. In the first stage of "hubris born of success", faith and confidence become pride and arrogance. Leaders become careless and workers become complacent. From his analysis, we see hubris in undisciplined leaps into areas where a company cannot become the best, hubris in a company's pursuit of growth beyond what it can deliver with excellence. We see hubris in bold, risky decisions that fly in the face of conflicting or negative evidence. We see hubris in denying even the possibility that the enterprise could be at risk, imperilled by external threats or internal erosion.

To avoid the decline and failure, Laozi advises

> Be prudent at the end just as at the beginning, and
> There will be no failure.
> – Tao Te Ching, Ch. 64

I want to explain Laozi's idea with Book of Change (I Ching). The ancient Chinese watched the cycles of the seasons, and comprehended that there also was a cycle of good times and bad times. When favourable situations came to their conclusion, unfavourable situations follow. In the Great Treatise of I Ching, Confucius says (Huang, 2010),

> What is danger?
> It arises when one is satisfied with his security and neglects danger.
> What is to perish?
> It arises when one is satisfied with his survival and neglects death.
> What is disorder?
> It arises when one is satisfied with things in order and neglects disorder.
> Therefore, the superior person does not forget danger
> When he is in security, nor does he forget death
> When he is well, nor does he forget disorder
> When his affairs are in order.
> In this way he gains personal safety and
> Is able to protect the empire.

It implies that in managing risk and crisis in a VUCA world, business leaders must be prudent and forethought, when the situation is favourable and peaceful, they should never forget about hard times or potential risk. On the other hand, when the situation is unfavourable, they should always look forward to the good. This is also the least costly and simplest way to control a potential risk and crisis.

> What is stable and peaceful is easy to hold,
> What is with no signs is easy to plan,
> What is fragile is easy to break,
> What is minute is easy to scatter, therefore,
> Being well-prepared to risk before it arises,
> Being precautious of chaos before it happens.
> – Tao Te Ching, Ch. 64

Laozi teaches us that acting before anything has happened and setting things in order before confusion arises. Do not think a mere sprout is not an omen. To act consciously and clutch at things is to court failure. Laozi also uses metaphorically the tree that grows from a slip to remind us of how importance of anticipating and preventing crisis and risk from happening at the beginning.

> A huge tree grows from the tiny shoot,
> A nine-story high terrace starts from a mound of earth,
> A journey of a thousand miles begins under one's feet.
> – Tao Te Ching, Ch. 64

When things are in a quiescent or incipient condition or are undergoing the initial changes, they are easy to deal with. Before the risk or crisis happens, it is easy to control and prevent, so organizations must develop the risk management system to prevent risk and crisis from happening or leading to the disasters. The frog can't feel the crisis which is going to happen, however, when the water is too hot to stand, it is too late to jump out of water. Thus, business leaders must anticipate and put the risk management system in place.

In order to be competitive, organisations must constantly review their methods and models to check they are operating correctly. In addition, they must examine new areas of emerging risk and develop sustainable systems of risk analysis and management. Business leaders must maintain hypervigilance and be prudent about any small changes, because it is relatively easy to maintain the situation when everything is peaceful and quiet. When the possibility for chaos is small or nearly non-existent, it is a simple task to keep it in check.

Preparing to Manage Risk: Maintaining Constant Vigilance

Most business leaders, preoccupied with the market pressures of the present quarter, are not inclined to pay much attention to planning for future risks and crises. However, it is important for business leaders to prepare for that circumstance when prevention doesn't work, that is, making a plan to deal with a variety of undesirable outcomes if disaster does strike. In preparing for the risks and crises, it pays to search for subtleties. It is instructive to recall the principle of Tao.

> Deal with what is difficult while it is easy,
> Do what is great while it is small.
> What is difficult in the world must be dealt with while it is easy,
> What is great in the world must be done while it is small.
> – Tao Te Ching, Ch. 63

The passage advises that being successful in planning to handle the risks and crises, business leaders shall make plans against eventual difficulties when things are still easy to resolve, because the difficulties inevitably grow out of easily resolvable troubles. They shall act on what is eventually big while it is still minute, because the big affairs necessarily grow out of minute ones. Only can business leaders who do not act upon things are in the end able to prevent risks and crises and complete their greatness.

Fink (2000), a prominent management consultant has the same opinion, he emphasizes that everyone in a position of authority "should view and plan for the inevitability of a crisis in much the same way [one] views and plans for the inevitability of death and taxes: not out of weakness or fear, but out of the strength that comes from knowing you are prepared to . . . play the hand that fate deals you." His survey of the Fortune 500's CEOs found that senior managers may suffer from a severe lack of crisis preparedness but certainly not from a lack of confidence that they can handle a crisis. 89% of those who responded said that crises in business are as inevitable as death and taxes, yet 50% said they did not have a plan for dealing with crises. Nevertheless, fully 97% felt confident that they would respond well if a crisis occurred (Fink, 2000).

Once leaders know the events, or black swans, they're looking for, they should set up signal detection mechanisms, enable open lines of communication and develop responses. These detection notifications can provide faster emergency response and give first mover advantage to changes in the marketplace. Laozi suggests,

> Prudent as if crossing a river in winter;
> Vigilant as if fearing danger from all around;

Respectful like a visiting guest;
Yielding as if ice is about to melt;
Humble like plain wood;
Magnanimous like a valley;
Inclusive like murky water.
– Tao Te Ching, Ch. 15

In their activities, business leaders shall be always "*prudent like crossing a frozen river in winter*". Whatever activity and strategy they undertake should be very careful to prevent possible risk and crisis from happening. The leaders shall be "*Vigilant as if fearing danger from all around*", because whatever business you do, they always have many competitors, of which, some are good competitors, and others hostile, thus, they must be alert all the time, follow this principle of the Tao. In their behaviour, business leaders must be "*respectful like a visiting guest*", this requires them to work with its partners and other stakeholders in responsible and ethical manner. Business leaders must be also "*yielding as if ice is about to melt*", they shall be patient and clam down, and follow it in a natural way when they face the risk and crisis. The character of business leaders should be "*humble like plain wood*", they shall concentrate on internal risk management, and remain so honest and calm that problems can be solved. When risk and crises happen, the outlook of business leaders should be expansive and their attitudes be open and receptive, as if a "deep valley", they have a big heart just like the valley, so broad and deep that you can defend any disturbance and seductions. The outward expression of business leaders can make them appear "*inclusive like murky water*", they must keep their head open and clear when facing the risk and crisis so that the reputation and image of company won't be damaged by the problems. Only "those who embrace this Tao to take precautions can get rid of risk and crisis, their businesses can be successful and sustainable".

Collins and Hansen (2011) studied companies that rose to greatness—beating their industry indexes by a minimum of ten times over 15 years (called 10Xers)—in environments characterized by big forces and rapid shifts that leaders could not predict or control. The research team then contrasted these "10X companies" to a carefully selected set of comparison companies that failed to achieve greatness in similarly extreme environments. They found that 10Xers differ from their less successful comparisons in how they maintain hypervigilance in good times as well as bad. Even in calm, clear, positive conditions, 10Xers constantly consider the possibility that events could turn against them at any moment. They believe that conditions will—with 100% certainty—turn against them without warning, at some unpredictable point in time, at some highly inconvenient moment. And they'd better be prepared. 10Xers maintain hypervigilance, staying highly attuned to threats and changes in their environment, even when—especially when—all's going well. They assume conditions will turn against them, at perhaps the worst possible moment. They channel their fear and worry into action, preparing, developing contingency plans, building buffers, and maintaining large margins of safety. 10Xers remain productively paranoid in good times, recognizing that it's what they do before the storm comes that matters most. Since it's impossible to consistently predict specific disruptive events, they systematically build buffers and shock absorbers for dealing with unexpected events. They put in place their extra oxygen canisters long before they're hit with a storm.

Recognizing and Containing the Risk

There is a Chinese proverb, saying that "a dike ten thousand feet long begins its crumbling with holes made by ants; and a room one hundred feet square begins its burning with sparks of fire leaping through cracks of chimneys." Why did the disasters happen? They didn't act in accordance with the principle of the Tao: "*Being well prepared for risk before it rises, being prudent about chaos before it happens* (Tao Te Ching, Ch.64)." In other words, it is always easier to act on something effectively when it is small. Take care of an issue as early as possible, before it really becomes an issue. Nip a potential problem in the bud so it doesn't get the chance to grow into something serious. "A lot of crises seem to happen overnight, but they have really long roots, like 10–15 years in terms of the source of the real problems." This is what Xerox CEO Anne Mulcahy said when she visited Harvard Business School class (George 2009).

We have also seen that there is a risk, business leaders refuse to face reality, and thus they often fail to see the crisis coming. Rather than acknowledging they should have recognized the signals in time, they blame external events and things outside their control. Companies sometimes misclassify a problem, focusing on the technical aspects and ignoring issues of perception. But it is often the public perception that causes the risks and crises.

Collins (2009) illustrates the story of his wife who suffered breast cancer in his book: *How the Mighty Fall: And Why Some Companies Never Give In*. He described that his wife looked like the picture of health, but she had already been carrying the carcinoma. The image of his wife, looking healthy yet already sick, stuck in his mind and gave him a metaphor. He's come to see institutional decline like a staged disease: *harder to detect but easier to cure in the early stages, easier to detect but harder to cure in the later stages*. An institution can look strong on the outside but already be sick on the inside, dangerously on the cusp of a precipitous fall. Machiavelli (2003) also has the same point of view in his book "*The Prince*": "If they be foreseen while yet remote, admit of easy remedy, but if their approach be awaited, are already past cure, the disorder having become hopeless; realizing what the physicians tell us of hectic fever, that in its beginning it is easy to cure, but hard to recognize; whereas, after a time, not having been detected and treated at the first, it becomes easy to recognize but impossible to cure."

China has the same thought-provoking story in the ancient time which can illustrate the problem. Bian Que was a well-known herbalist doctor in the Spring-Autumn & Warring States periods in ancient China. Once he went to visit Lord Huan of Cai. He observed him for a while and said, "Now your disease is at the surface of your skin. It will get serious if you do not cure it." But Lord Huan of Cai said, "I have no disease." After Bian Que went out, the Lord said to the people beside him, "It is a common fault for a doctor to cure those who are not ill. And finally, he would claim the credit for himself!" 10 days later, Bian Que came to visit Lord Huan again. After careful observation, he said, "Your disease has reached your muscle. If you do not cure it now, it will get worse!" Lord Huan still did not pay any attention to his words and was very unhappy. Another 10 days later, Bian Que said to Lord Huan, "Your disease is now in the digestive system. It would be even worse without curing!" Lord Huan again refused to take his advice and was unhappier. Another 10 days later, as soon as Bian Que saw Lord Huan, he left without saying anything. Lord Huan was curious and sent someone to ask Bian Que why. Bian Que said to the messenger, "When the disease was at the skin, in the muscle or in the digestive system, I am able to cure it. But now it is deep in the marrow and no one can cure it." Five days later, Lord Huan felt pain in his body and sent messengers to look for Bian Que, but Bian Que had escaped to the State of Qin. Soon after that, Lord Huan died of illness.

All the three stories have the same implication for a business leader when they manage risk. A business leader should be like a good physician, when treating diseases, attacks them when they are still in the capillary tubes. This means that they manage risk when it is small. Hence, the saintly man begins to attend to things when it is early enough. In our daily life and as well as business world, we should not overlook small defects because small problems may bring about disasters in the future. If you want to achieve success, you have to start out small. It also holds true for solving difficulties and risks. If you only focus on the disappointing trouble as a whole, you will lose heart.

Sanlu's melamine scandal in China is the case for illustrating the above problems. On 12 September 2008, the Chinese government ordered the nation's biggest manufacturer of milk powder, Sanlu Group, to halt production because its powdered infant formula was found to contain melamine, a nitrogen-rich chemical, ingestion of which could cause kidney stones. The national inspection agency further discovered that milk products manufactured by 21 other diary companies tested positive for melamine. Sanlu was reported to have received its first complaint of illness as early as December 2007. However, news of the problem only surfaced nationwide after Sanlu's New Zealand partner, Fonterra Cooperative Group, alerted the New Zealand government in September 2008.

Sanlu received the first complaint about its melamine-laced milk power as far back as December 2007. The first documented exposure of Sanlu's problematic powder was posted on a popular internet community by a consumer. Most of the other Sanlu milk contamination cases were found in Hebei, Jiangsu and Gansu provinces. About three months before the milk scandal leaked in September 2008, a local newspaper in Jiangsu had reported a rising number of babies diagnosed with kidney disease over the previous two months. Around the same period of time, the health department in Gansu also received a report from a local hospital in mid-July indicating a surge in cases of kidney ailments among babies, stating that most of the affected had been drinking Sanlu's infant formula. However, soon after the scandal broke, Sanlu apologised publicly for the incident, but denied about the urgency and severity of the challenges they were facing, and blamed external suppliers for their problems, for example, Sanlu said that its milk suppliers had added melamine to the milk before selling it to them. The company failed to explain the delay in alerting the public to the contamination. The local government of Shijiazhuang, where Sanlu was headquartered, was also blamed for holding back the news from the central government. By the end of September 2008, about 53,000 young children were found to have been sickened due to consumption of melamine-laced dairy products, and at least four babies had died from kidney failure. The melamine scare resulted in many countries recalling and banning goods using milk products from China. The milk crisis was soon regarded by the World Health Organisation as one of the largest food-safety events in recent decades.

Strategy for Responding to Sustainability Risk

In today's socially conscious environment, companies are exposed to scrutiny of stakeholders in social and environmental issues. Risks tied to perceptions of over-consumption of water and reputational risks linked to investments in projects with potentially damaging environmental consequences. Additional trends in sustainability risk include risks to financial performance from volatile energy prices, compliance risks triggered by new carbon regulations, risks from product substitution as customers switch to more sustainable alternatives, and risks associated with the way in which a company and its staff conduct themselves including matters such as culture, tone from the top, governance, how customers are treated, remuneration of staff and how companies deal with conflicts of interest. Therefore, companies are increasingly confronting the risks and crises emerging from corporate social responsibility and sustainability issues.

A business finds itself being criticized for some action it has taken or failed to take. The stakeholders and civil society have the power in exerting enormous pressure on businesses, and wielding significant influence on public opinion, causing firms to take or not take particular courses of action. Stakeholders need a quick response with information about how the company plans to resolve the risk and crises, as well as what they can do to mitigate negative effects to themselves. It is necessary to communicate specific issues to stakeholder groups, including remorse for the event, guidelines as to how the organization is going to address the crisis, and criteria regarding how stakeholder groups will be compensated for negative effects.

What strategies does a company take to respond to them leads to different consequences when the social and sustainable risks and crises emerge? The strategies that business response to risks and crises can be categorized as the reactive (or obstructionist), defensive-accommodative and proactive (Carroll & Buchholtz, 2008). The reactive strategy involves denying responsibility and doing less than is required. The defensive strategy acknowledges only reluctantly and partially the responsibility issues that may be raised by the firm's stakeholders. The accommodative strategy attempts to satisfy stakeholder demands and the proactive accepts and anticipates stakeholder interests.

Few leaders are willing to accept responsibility for their mistakes. Instead, many ignore problems and hope they go away. Most of business leaders take reactive (obstructionist), defensive strategies instead of accommodative and proactive. They often go into denial about the urgency and severity of the challenges they are facing. Or they tend to blame external events, people, or organizations for their problems. Without accepting that the problem is theirs to fix, they cannot understand what they are dealing with. Often the hardest part is to acknowledge their role in the origins of the crisis. Even when leaders acknowledge their responsibility, they may face significant resistance from their organizations in solving it because people have great difficulty in admitting their mistakes (George, 2009).

One of most important principles of Tao is softness and pliancy like water and feminine, and therefore, Laozi suggests a softer stance so as to reduce or avoid risks and crises that is accommodative and proactive stances. Laozi says,

> Nothing in the universe is softer and weaker than water,
> However, nothing triumphs over water in
> Overcoming the hard and strong
> Nothing substitutes for water:
> The weak overcomes the strong,
> The soft overcomes the hard.
> – Tao Te Ching, Ch. 78

Water appears to be the weakest and softest thing in the world, and is the ultimate symbol of the yielding and flexible aspect of the Tao. At the same time, there is also nothing better than water at dissolving the hardest and most unyielding rocks. This observation of water teaches us that despite a yielding, humble appearance, the weak overcomes the strong and the soft overcomes the hard. This is a principle that we can all understand, but somehow cannot put into practice in real life. We still have a tendency to meet force with force. Business leaders can learn from this wisdom that those who have the strength to accept problems and crises, they can possess the power embodied in water—seemingly soft and weak, and yet able to overcome the hard and strong. If they apply this power to business, they would achieve competitive advantage in the business world. Therefore, by embracing the seemingly weak and soft, a business leader can gain personal power to overcome risks and crises and achieve sustainable development.

However, if business leaders take the opposite stance, like obstructionist and defensive stances, they will bring about failure and calamity. Laozi always opposes these actions. He warns that:

> The living is soft and yielding;
> The dead is rigid and stiff.
> Living plants are flexible and tender;
> The dead is brittle and dry.
> Those who are stiff and rigid are the disciples of death.
> Those who are soft and yielding are the disciples of life.
> – Tao Te Ching, Ch. 76

Life is characterized by softness and pliancy, while death is characterized by stiffness and rigidity, just like our body and plants. We can generalize from this observation and link death to that which is hard and unyielding. Life would be linked that which is pliable and thus capable of growth and adaptation. This applies not only to flora and fauna but also to all aspects of human existence. For instance, an army that cannot adapt to the ever-changing conditions on the battle field will soon find itself outmaneuverred and defeated by an enemy that is more nimble and flexible. This implies for business leaders who are forceful and aggressive may seem to have the upper hand, but in fact occupies a lower position of disadvantage. Conversely, being yielding and flexible may be perceived as a weakness, but is in fact a great strength that occupies a higher position leading to victory and success.

The risk and crisis are not going to fix itself, so denying its existence can only make things worse. That reality must start with you and your acknowledgment of your role in the crisis itself. Then you have to guide your organization to face reality as well. John Hope Bryant (2009), who lived as a homeless person early in his life, is the founder of Operation HOPE. He has raised $500 million to focus on financial literacy for the poor and serves as vice chair of the President's Council on Financial Literacy. In *Love Leadership*, Bryant writes, "Vulnerability is power", he says:

> Admitting weaknesses and owning up to mistakes have counterintuitive benefits. When you are honest, people are more likely to forgive you any weaknesses and mistakes. You are also able to make a stronger connection with others. That ultimately gives you an ability to persuade and influence people, which in turn strengthen your ability to lead.

Laozi has the same view:

> Those who are courageous to dare will perish,
> Those who are courageous not to dare will live.
> ...
> Therefore, great leaders,
> Do not contend, yet, they win easily,
> Do not speak, yet they get a good response,
> Do not demand, yet, all their needs are met.
> – Tao Te Ching, Ch. 73

This passage reveals the wisdom which is those who possess courageous resolve but advance with caution are congruent with the Tao, and that is why they seem to be favoured by the heavenly powers. The lesson for business leaders is that they should know the distinction between courage and daring. Courage means being resolute, dauntless and firm; daring means throwing caution to the winds, full speed ahead and damn the torpedoes. One is an inner quality born of conviction; the other is an external display of bravado. Therefore, business leaders who possess this inner quality are similar to the Tao in the following ways:

- *Because they are unadventurous, they do not struggle against others, just as the Tao contends against no one. But despite this seemingly yielding nature, they consistently achieve their objectives in the long run.*
- *They are quiet and unassuming, just as the Tao does not speak. However, they remain ever responsive to changing conditions out of their sense of caution. When circumstances change, they are ready to alter their approach to better aim for a moving target.*

- *They are also fully present in all of their activities, just as the Tao is present in all things. They bring mindfulness to their work. By being totally aware in each moment of life, they enhance and deepen everything they do.*
- *They are composed and prepared, just as the Tao plans and coordinates its myriad movements in a relaxed and unhurried way. They see how flowers bloom when the season is right and not a moment sooner, so they also take their time in thoughtful planning. By being well-prepared, they are able to act with composure and maximize their chances of success... when the time is right, and not a moment sooner.*

Thus, it is exactly that only because he does not contend, no one is able to struggle with him. Compliance means fortune, and opposition means misfortune. That's why he excels in making people respond without speaking. He takes a low position; the people gravitate to him naturally. Heaven reveals good fortune and misfortune by hanging down the images in the sky, and the plan he sets are verified before things actually happen. While security, he does not forget the threat of danger, and makes plans while things are still in the pre-manifest stage.

Case in Point: Merk and Amgen

I want to examine the two business cases to illustrate the different responsiveness strategies and consequences. The first example is about the organizational denial which can be found in the difficult pharmaceutical maker Merck.

Merck had with its $2.5 billion pain-relief drug, Vioxx. After an intense battle with Merck over indications of cardiovascular effects from the drug, the FDA approved Vioxx for general marketing in 1999. As large numbers of patients began using the drug and additional studies were completed, concerns continued to arise about Vioxx's safety for cardiovascular patients. Sceptical because the concerns were based on nonrandomized data, Merck executives decided to conduct a 3-year randomized trial of high-risk cardiovascular patients while continuing to market the drug.

In September 2004, Merck halted the study at the midway point because results showed Vioxx patients were twice as likely to suffer a heart attack or stroke as those on placebo. Merck CEO Ray Gilmartin courageously pulled the drug from the worldwide market for all users, not just those at high risk of cardiovascular disease. By then Vioxx was linked to more than twenty-seven thousand heart attacks and sudden cardiac deaths and a rising flood of lawsuits from plaintiff's attorneys. Merck wisely chose to defend Vioxx on a case-by-case basis, which may have saved the company from insolvency. After 3 years of fighting the attorneys to a draw, Merck announced a $5 billion settlement with the plaintiffs in 2007. The company had finally put its agony behind it. Why did Merck, a company known for its scientific prowess, not take the more conservative course of restricting access to Vioxx? From the outside, it appears that Merck was so committed to using Vioxx to compete in the pain-relief market with Celebrex and other painkillers that it waited until proof was in from its own scientific study. When the study confirmed the problem, management immediately took action. By then, the damage was done.

Denying reality has destroyed more careers and organizations than incompetence ever did. The first reason is that people always prefer good news or a quick fix. Rarely are they willing to acknowledge that their organization is facing a crisis. Crises often start out in relatively benign ways, and then seemingly minor events escalate into major ones. Unless leaders face reality early, they can easily miss the signals of the deeper crisis that is waiting ahead. Until its leaders acknowledge the crisis, their organizations cannot address the difficulties (George, 2009). Many people find reality is just too horrible to face or they are too ashamed, so denial becomes a convenient defense mechanism. If you feel yourself getting defensive, ask yourself, "What am I defending against? How might denying reality make the situation worse?"

The second case is about the proactive responsiveness of Amgen. In 2007 Amgen, the world's largest biotechnology company faced growing safety concerns over Aranesp, its highly successful anaemia drug with $4 billion in annual sales. After 6 years on the market, a series of studies conducted by Amgen, Johnson & Johnson, and others revealed problems with off-label use of Aranesp. To deal with the growing crisis, CEO Kevin Sharer tasked his key executives with developing a plan to address the problems. But he found they wouldn't move until he acknowledged his own role in the crisis. "For a deeply reflective hour, I asked myself what I owned of this problem. I came up with a long list," said Sharer.

When he met with the executives to go over his list, they were stunned that their CEO would admit his errors. This freed them up to address their roles in the crisis and take necessary actions to get out of it. Well aware of the Merck experience with Vioxx, Amgen voluntarily agreed to more restrictive language on Aranesp package inserts. As a result, sales dropped by 26%, or more than $1 billion, but the company recovered. Aranesp is still on the market, albeit with a reduced patient population, and Amgen's relationship with the FDA is healthy once again.

Reflecting on what he learned from this crisis, Sharer noted, "The toughest thing was to embrace the reality that we had to take action because so many stakeholders had questions about the safety of Aranesp."

Our first reaction was to blame these problems on the FDA. We had to get above the fray and recognize that public health officials had legitimate questions about what was happening. First, I had to acknowledge my role in the crisis. Then we could face reality together by owning the problem and looking realistically at the decisions we had made.

Sharer stresses the importance of being adaptive to new realities in a crisis. He notes that many CEOs fail to adapt because they get stuck in a comfortable mind-set with their version of reality. He cites his favourite analogy from biology: "*What species survives? The biggest? The strongest? The fastest? No, it's the most adaptive.*" (George, 2009).

Risk Management, Competitiveness and Sustainability

A responsible and sustainable business in an uncertain world must be prudent to any threats of risks and crises, particularly be concerned about the social and environmental issues and emerging national and global regulations. Laozi offers us the roadmap for business to achieve a competitive and sustainable goal. He emphasizes in Tao Te Ching.

> Those who lead people and serve the planet,
> Shall hold firm to virtue of prudence.
> To be prudent is to be forethought,
> Those who are forethought have an abundance of virtue,
> Those who have virtue can rise to any challenges.
> Those who can rise to challenges discover new sources of strength,
> Those who can discover new sources of strength have power to lead.
> Those who hold to principle of prudence can thrive.
> This is just like "planting tree roots deeply and firmly"
> This is the Tao of sustainability
> – Laozi, Tao Te Ching, Ch. 59

We cited this verse in Chap. 11 of this book to discuss the virtue of prudence and visionary leadership. The wisdom of this verse is inexhaustible. In this section, this passage present business leaders with the sustainability roadmap: to be a sustainable company, Laozi stresses that people shall be prudent in conservation, valuing and using efficiently natural resources, and caring for environment. In doing so, business leaders must be well prepared at the early stage and be precautious of what they are doing so that when risk and crisis arises, they are well prepared to avoid and solve it. One of the important measures to avoid and solve risk and crisis is to cultivate virtues, i.e. doing business in socially responsible way, this can win in the competitive market, and therefore, thus, business leaders have the capacity of leading the people and governing organization. To thrive and sustain their organizations, business leaders must hold on to the principle of the Tao (the Way and Virtue). When it comes to serving the society and protecting natural resources and environment, there is nothing like the principle of conservation—the principle of valuing and using efficiently natural resources and caring for environment. The best way to conserve the resources is to be prudent and well prepared for risk and crisis in an uncertain environment. It is in business leader's responsibility to give up any business activities which can consume too many resources and deteriorate environment as soon as possible. Over-consuming resources and damaging environment can bring risk and crisis to the organization and society as a whole. The sooner business leaders stop wasting resources and energy in environment, the sooner they can start accumulating virtues—social and environmental values—in their organization.

When they accumulate virtues by take social and environmental responsibility, business leaders can become powerful and competitive, and there are no obstacles they cannot overcome. Once they move beyond the limits that hamper most people, business leaders can gain power over themselves, as well as a natural authority that people respond to. They are able to influence them effortlessly because their respect for them flows naturally. This is the mother principle of true authority. Unlike the transient power achieved through force or domination, it is a positive force that lasts. With this lasting power, business leaders will have a firm foundation upon which to build harmonious and enduring society. This positive force takes root deeply in the hearts of people and also in business leaders. It is the Tao of sustainability—a vision of everlasting harmony and leadership.

References

Bryant, J. H. (2009). *Love leadership: The new way to lead in a fear-based world*. Jossey-Bass.

Carroll, A., & Buchholtz, A. K. (2008). *Business and society: Ethics and stakeholder management* (7th ed.). Cengage Learning.

Collins, J. (2009). *How the mighty fall: And why some companies never give in*. JimCollins.

Collins, J., & Hansen, M. T. (2011). *Great by choice: Uncertainty, chaos and luck – why some thrive despite them all*. Random House Business.

Fink, S. (2000). *Crisis management: Planning for the inevitable*. http://www.backinprint.com/.

Funston, F., & Wagner, S. (2010). *Surviving and thriving in uncertainty: Creating the risk intelligent enterprise*. Wiley.

George, B. (2009). *Seven lessons for leading in crisis*. Jossey-Bass.

George, B. (2017, February 17). *VUCA 2.0: A strategy for steady leadership in an unsteady world*. Retrieved November 12, 2020, from https://www.forbes.com/sites/hbsworkingknowledge/2017/02/17/vuca-2-0-a-strategy-for-steady-leadership-in-an-unsteady-world/?sh=24046d0513d8

Huang, A. (2010). *The complete I Ching: The definitive translation, 10th anniversary edition*. Inner Traditions International.

Kytle, B., & Ruggie, J. G. (2005, March). *Corporate social responsibility as risk management: A model for multinationals*. John F. Kennedy School of Government, Harvard University.

Kwak, M. (2002). The perils of power. *Sloan Management Review, 43*(3), 13.

Liang, F. S., Lee, L., & Sang, C. N. (2016). *Risk management in a VUCA environment*. Deloitte. https://www2.deloitte.com/kh/en/pages/risk/articles/risk-management-in-vuca-environment.html.

Machiavelli, N. (2003). *The Prince*. Penguin Classics; Reissue edition.

Spedding, L., & Rose, A. (2008). *Business risk management handbook: A sustainable approach*. CIMA.

WBCSD. (2013). *Getting sustainability risks onto management's agenda: Moving from theory to opportunity*.

WEF. (2014). *Global risks 2014*. W. E. Forum.

World Economic Forum. (2021). *Global risks report 2021, insight report* (16th ed.).

Part V
Taoism's Wisdom and Sustainable Development Goals

Making peace with nature is
the defining task of the 21st century.
It must be the top, top priority
for everyone, everywhere."
—António Guterres
Un Secretary-General's speech
on the State of Planet
on 2 December 2020

Chapter 16
Responsible Leadership at United Nations

In the preceding chapters, I discussed the role of responsible leadership from the perspective of Taoism at business level in sustainable business development. This chapter will discuss the power of responsible leadership at societal level in transforming the world for a better future. I will, first of all, articulate the concept of responsible leadership for further discussion. The concept of responsible leadership can be interpreted at three levels:

- *On an individual level, it requires questioning the contemporary moral and social order, as well as moving beyond the skills and attributes dimensions, towards investing in the ethical and values dimensions of leadership;*
- *On a business level, it requires reframing the rules (the social contract with stakeholders) that guide business practices, which implies also critically engaging with approaches and paradigms of business education, and finally*
- *On a societal level, facilitating global citizenship and collaboration—moving from the 'me' to the 'we' to the 'us'.*

In terms of leadership at the societal level, the United Nations has been the leader in promoting and fostering peace, security, and social justice, sustainable and inclusive development since 1945. The UN responsible leadership reflects in its purpose stated in the UN Charter:

> To achieve international cooperation in solving international problems of an economic, social, cultural, or humanitarian character, and in promoting and encouraging respect for human rights and for fundamental freedoms for all without distinction as to race, sex, language, or religion; and to be a centre for harmonizing the actions of nations in the attainment of these common ends.

Embracing the UN purpose, the United Nations initiated the 2030 Agenda for Sustainable Development in September 2015 with inputs from business, academia and non-profit organizations globally, and it was adopted by all UN Member States. The Agenda for Sustainable Development Goals (SDGs) provide a roadmap for the future we all want, and it also provides a blueprint for peace and prosperity for

L. Zu, *Responsible and Sustainable Business*,
https://doi.org/10.1007/978-3-030-91117-1_16

people and the planet, now and into the future. The SDGs cover broad challenges such as economic inclusion, diminishing natural resources, geopolitical instability, environmental degradation and the multifaceted impacts of climate change.

Achieving Sustainable Development Goals is an urgent call for action by all countries—developed and developing—in a global partnership at macro-level, are also call for action by academia, politics and business at meso- and micro-level. Achieving SDGs requires academia, business and politics to create shared value for a world that is comprehensively sustainable: socially fair; environmentally secure; economically prosperous. Therefore, more responsible leadership is needed to inform, inspire and catalyze collective action across the SDGs. Being responsible leader, United Nations endeavours to create shared value by embedding sustainability into its core business, and investing in the stable development of societies across the globe.

In October 2019, the United Nations announced that 30 influential leaders from the corporate world will work together over the next 2 years in a bid to free up trillions of dollars from the private sector to finance SDGs. These responsible leaders have seized the sense of urgency, and are committing to cooperate across borders, across financial sectors and even with their competitors, because it is both ethical and good business sense to invest in sustainable development for all people on a healthy planet. To align business practices with the 2030 Agenda for Sustainable Development, academia, business and politics must transform their business paradigm and mind-set: transforming from doing well by doing good to doing good by doing good, and focusing on creating shared value in meeting the challenges of society whilst at the same time bringing strong economic returns.

Many companies have also been working to address environmental, social and economic issues. Leading companies have begun to recognize that they can only address the complex sustainability challenges by scaling up their efforts through collaboration with peers, industry and sector organizations, customers, governments, non-profit organizations, and society. SDGs provide a universal and visionary framework for this global cooperation and action, bringing all stakeholders together to proactively address and solve these challenges. However, according to the latest GlobeScan/SustainAbility Survey in 2019 shows that only nine percent of experts say the private sector has made a positive contribution to progress on SDGs so far. The UN's research suggests that there is no shortage of money from the private sector which could be invested in sustainable development. However, a combination of factors, including the policy environment, incentive structures and institutional conditions, tend to discourage the kind of long-term commitment that is needed.

Chapter 17
Sustainable Development: Harmony with Nature

Before the UN 2030 Agenda for Sustainable Development was adopted in 2015, given that environmental degradation, biodiversity loss, poverty, hunger, malnutrition, diseases and economic instability persist despite the analytical capability and technological capacity deployed by current civilization towards eradicating them, the United Nations adopted the resolution on Sustainable Development: Harmony with Nature in December 2009. The resolution supports the call to make use of the International Mother Earth Day to "promote activities and exchange opinions and views, experiences and principles for a life in harmony with nature" (United Nations, 2010). This resolution recognizes that "human beings are an inseparable part of nature, and that they cannot damage it without severely damaging themselves."

In the same year, the United Nations General Assembly proclaimed 22 April as International Mother Earth Day. In so doing, Member States acknowledged that the Earth and its ecosystems are our common home, and expressed their conviction that it is necessary to promote Harmony with Nature in order to achieve a just balance among the economic, social and environmental needs of present and future generations. The same year, the General Assembly adopted its first resolution on Harmony with Nature.

The General Assembly has widely acknowledged that the world's depletion of natural resources and rapid environmental degradation are the result of unsustainable consumption and production patterns which have led to adverse consequences for both the Earth and the health and overall well-being of humanity. The scientific community has well documented evidence that our present way of life, in particular our consumption and production patterns, has severely affected the Earth's carrying capacity.

Loss of biodiversity, desertification, climate change and the disruption of a number of natural cycles are among the costs of our disregard for nature and the integrity of its ecosystems and life-supporting processes. As recent scientific work suggests, a number of planetary boundaries are being transgressed and others are at risk being so in a business-as-usual world. Since the industrial revolution, Nature has been treated as a commodity that exists largely for the benefit of people, and

L. Zu, *Responsible and Sustainable Business*,
https://doi.org/10.1007/978-3-030-91117-1_17

environmental problems have been considered as solvable through the use of technology. In order to meet the basic needs of a growing population within the limits of the Earth's finite resources, there is a need to devise a more sustainable model for production, consumption and the economy as a whole.

Devising a new world will require a new relationship with the Earth and with humankind's own existence. Since 2009, the aim of the General Assembly, in adopting its five resolutions on 'Harmony with Nature', has been to define this newly found relationship based on a non-anthropocentric relationship with Nature. The resolutions contain different perspectives regarding the construction of a new, non-anthropocentric paradigm in which the fundamental basis for right and wrong action concerning the environment is grounded not solely in human concerns. A step in this direction was further reaffirmed in the outcome document of the United Nations Conference on Sustainable Development (2012), entitled "The future we want":

> We recognize that planet Earth and its ecosystems are our home and that "Mother Earth" is a common expression in a number of countries and regions, and we note that some countries recognize the rights of nature in the context of the promotion of sustainable development.

Harmony with Nature: International Actions

Figures 17.1, 17.2 and 17.3 show that since 1970, the United Nations has endeavoured to work with its member states to take actions to protect our planet, and build harmony with nature. For example, in 1972, the United Nations Conference on the Human Environment held in Stockholm brought the industrialized and developing nations together to delineate the "rights" of the human family to a healthy and productive environment. A series of such meetings followed, for example on the rights of people to adequate food, to sound housing, to safe water, to access to means of family planning. The recognition of the need to revitalize humanity's connection with nature led to the creation of global institutions within the United Nations system.

In 1980, the International Union for the Conservation of Natural Resources (IUCN) published the World Conservation Strategy, a precursor to the concept of

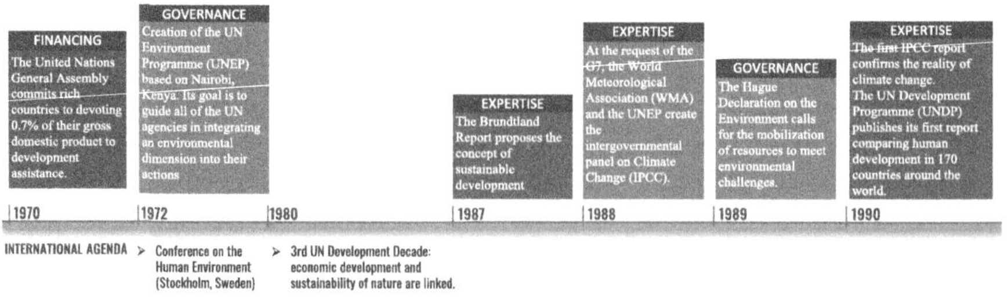

Fig. 17.1 United Nations—30 years of sustainable development: 1970–1990. Source: Adapted from Biagiotti and Martimort-Asso (2016)

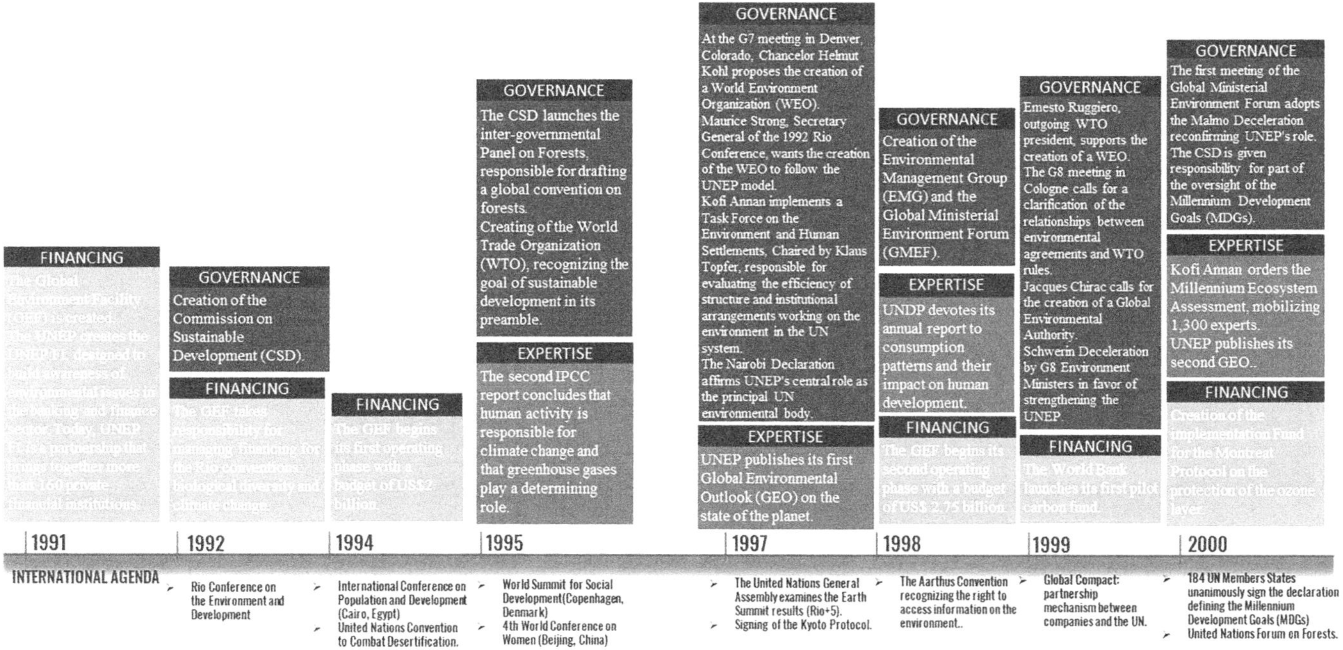

Fig. 17.2 United Nations—30 years of sustainable development: 1991–2000. Source: Adapted from Biagiotti and Martimort-Asso (2016)

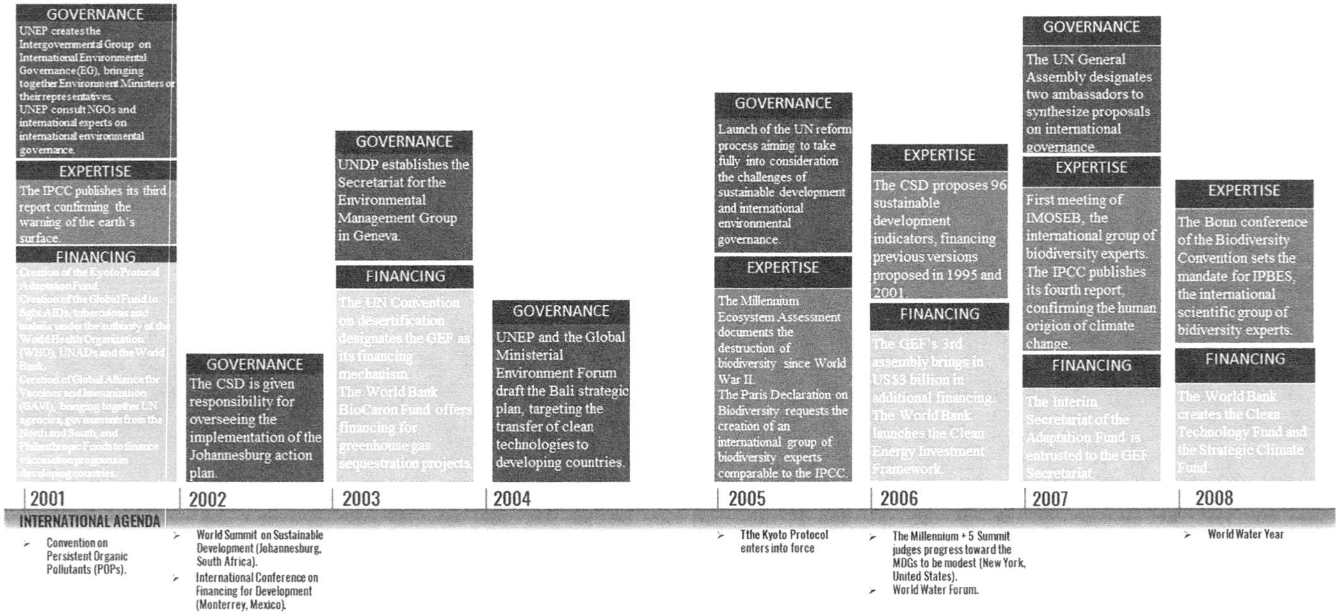

Fig. 17.3 United Nations—30 years of sustainable development: 2001–2008. Source: Adapted from Biagiotti and Martimort-Asso (2016)

sustainable development. The Strategy asserted that conservation of nature cannot be achieved without development to alleviate the poverty and misery of hundreds of millions of people, and stressed the interdependence of conservation and development in which development depends on caring for the Earth. Unless the fertility and productivity of the planet are safeguarded, the human future is at risk.

In 1982, 10 years after the Stockholm Conference, the World Conservation Strategy initiative culminated with the adoption of the World Charter for Nature. The Charter stated that mankind is a part of nature and life depends on the uninterrupted functioning of natural systems. In 1983, the World Commission on Environment and Development was created; by 1984, it was constituted as an independent body by the General Assembly, and asked to formulate a "global agenda for change". In 1987, in its report, "Our Common Future", the Commission advanced the understanding of global interdependence and the relationship between economics and the environment previously introduced by the World Conservation Strategy. The report wove together social, economic, cultural and environmental issues and global solutions. It reaffirmed that the environment does not exist as a sphere separate from human actions, ambitions, and needs, and therefore it should not be considered in isolation from human concerns. The environment is where we all live; and development is what we all do in attempting to improve our lot within that abode.

In June 1992, the first United Nations Conference on Environment and Development was held in Rio de Janeiro and adopted an agenda for environment and development in the twenty-first century, comprising the Rio Declaration on Environment and Development, which recognizes each country's right to pursue social and economic progress and assigned to States the responsibility of adopting a model of sustainable development; Agenda 21, a programme of action for sustainable development; and the Statement of Principles concerning forests. Agreements were also reached on the Convention on Biological Diversity and the Framework Convention on Climate Change. That Conference for the first time mobilized the major groups and legitimized their participation in the sustainable development process, which has remained a constant until today. For the first time also, the lifestyle of the current civilization was addressed in principle 8 of the Rio Declaration, in which the urgency of a deep change in consumption and production patterns was expressly and broadly acknowledged by State leaders (United Nations, 1992). Agenda 21 further reaffirmed that sustainable development was delimited by the integration of the economic, social and environmental pillars.

The spirit of the Conference was captured by the expression "Harmony with Nature", brought to the fore with the first principle of the Rio Declaration: "Human beings are at the centre of concerns for sustainable development. They are entitled to a healthy and productive life in harmony with nature" (United Nations, 1992).

In 1993, the Economic and Social Council set up the Commission on Sustainable Development to follow up on the implementation of Agenda 21. In June 1997, the General Assembly dedicated its nineteenth special session to designing a Programme for the Further Implementation of Agenda 21. In 2002, 10 years after the Rio Declaration, a follow-up conference, the World Summit on Sustainable

Development, was convened in Johannesburg to renew the global commitment to sustainable development. The Conference agreed on the Johannesburg Plan of Implementation and further mandated the Commission on Sustainable Development to follow up on the implementation of sustainable development.

Since the Rio Conference, sustainable development has become part of the international lexicon. The concept has been incorporated in many United Nations declarations and its implementation, while complex, has been at the forefront of world institutions and organizations working in the economic, social and environmental sectors. However, they all recognize how difficult it has been to grant the environmental pillar the recognition enjoyed by the other two pillars despite the many calls by scientists and civil society signalling the vulnerability and precariousness of the Earth since the 1960s.

Harmony with Nature: Taoism's Wisdom

Around the world, ancient civilizations have a rich history of understanding the symbiotic connection between human beings and nature. Ancient sites, many of which the United Nations Educational, Scientific and Cultural Organization (UNESCO) has recognized as part of the world heritage, have a part to play in the spiritual and material life of the twenty-first century. Chinese civilization recognized the vital links between humans, nature and the divine. Taoism, based on the Tao Te Ching, began teaching people to follow the patterns of nature. Tao in fact means "the way of nature", and Taoism judges affluence by the number of species. Taoism believes that nature itself is divine and that we should live in harmony with nature's cycles and systems.

The philosophy of Taoism with a focus on wholeness and holism, embodied in the concept of sustainable development, rests on an understanding that all things are interconnected and that nothing occurs in isolation. Wholeness and holism call for broader perspectives. As the spirit of holism begins to infuse the practice of health care, we come closer to that healing that is needed at all levels. As the wheel of medicine now turns towards a commitment to those principles that further the health of individuals, of society, and of the planet as a whole, so turns the wheel of sustainable development.

From perspectives of systems and wholeness/holism, Laozi claims that there are four greats: Tao, Heaven, Earth and Human beings. They are interconnected and interdependent in the universe.

> Tao is Great,
> Heaven is Great,
> Earth is Great,
> Human beings are also Great.
> There are four Greats in the universe,
> And human beings are one of them.
> Man models himself on Earth.

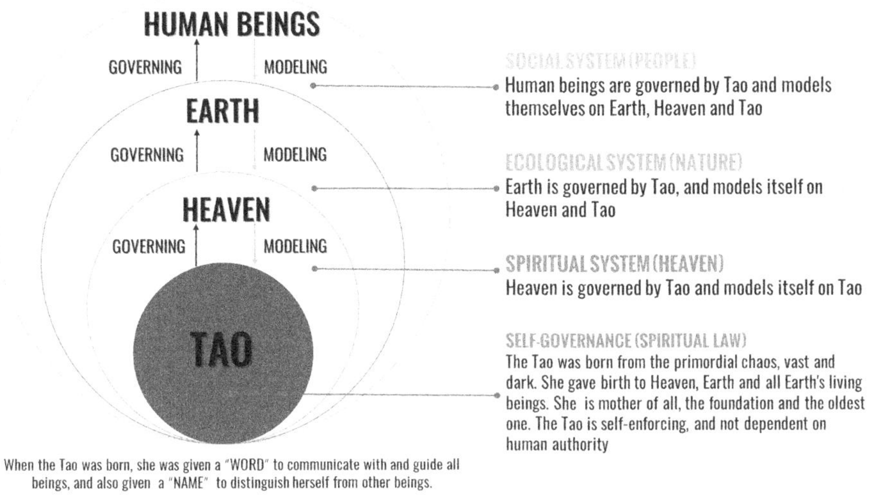

Fig. 17.4 Harmony with nature: Taoism's wisdom. Source: author developed based on Laozi, Tao Te Ching, Ch. 25

> Earth models itself on Heaven.
> Heaven models itself on the Tao.
> Tao functions on its own spontaneously.
> – Laozi, Tao Te Ching, Ch.25

To have a better understanding of this passage, I created Fig. 17.4 to demonstrate the relationships among the four greats of Tao, heaven, earth and human beings. Figure 17.4 shows that the four greats model themselves on another or learn from each other by observation. The circle poetically symbolizes integrity, interconnection and interdependence. A circle is integral, whole, complete, and entire; it has a firm, fixed centre, and is the sum of everything inside its perimeter. Expanding on this idea, the poetic symbol for the universe is four interlocking circles—ideally, the joining of an integrated the Tao, human, earth and heaven. Our well-being and quality of life depend on finding greater wholeness in life.

The interaction between these systems then involves the exchange of energy, matter and information. Human society and economy are deeply dependent upon the natural environment and this flow of natural resources of all kind from the ecosphere to the economy is called ecosystems services. These include broad categories of services like provisioning, such as the production of food and water; regulating, such as the control of climate and disease; supporting, such as nutrient cycles and crop pollination; and cultural, such as spiritual and recreational benefits.

Human beings (or phenomena) that are wholly in harmony with the Tao behave in a completely natural, uncontrived way. The goal of spiritual practice for the human beings is, according to Laozi, the attainment of this purely natural way of behaving, as when the planets revolve around the sun. The planets effortlessly do this revolving without any sort of control, force, or attempt to revolve themselves, instead engaging in effortless and spontaneous movement. Taoist philosophy recognizes that the Universe already works harmoniously according to its own ways; as a person exerts their will against or upon the world that they disrupt the harmony that already exists.

Taoism's central principle is that all life, all manifestations, are part of an inseparable whole, an interconnected organic unity which arises from a deep, mysterious, and essentially unexplainable source which is the Tao itself. Everything conceivable is contained within this principle. Various Western translators have compared this concept to the idea of God, Universal Mind, or Absolute Reality, to name but a few examples. Taoism views the universe and all of its manifestations as operating according to a set of unchanging, natural laws. As an inseparable part of the Tao, human beings can gain knowledge of these laws and become attuned to them. It is these natural laws that constitute the core principles of Taoism. Aligning ourselves with these principles provides a universal perspective and understanding and allows life to be lived in harmony with the Tao. Indeed, our way of life becomes the Way, a full expression of the Tao.

Taoism states that all life forces tend to move toward harmony and balance because it is in their nature to do so. Gaining an awareness of life's essential unity and learning to cooperate with its natural flow and order enables people to attain a state of being that is both fully free and independent and at the same time fully connected to the life flow of the Universe—being at one with the Tao. From the Taoist viewpoint this represents the ultimate stage of human existence.

In an interdependent and interconnected system like that of Earth, we cannot recognize the rights of the human part of the system without affecting the rest of the system. To re-establish balance with nature, we must acknowledge its intrinsic value and clearly establish the obligations of humans toward nature, and also recognize that nature has rights that should be respected, promoted, and defended. Just as human beings have rights, the Mother Earth also has the right to exist, the right to maintain its vital cycles, the right to regeneration, the right to be free from structural alteration, and the right to relate to the other parts of the Earth system. Without respecting and guaranteeing the rights of nature, it is not possible to guarantee human rights and achieve sustainable development.

Taoism's Wisdom and SDGs: Harmony vs. Happiness

From the preceding section, we understand that since 1970s, the international community has started to take actions to protect our planet by learning and drawing on the traditional wisdom from diverse national cultures in the world. Thanks to the endeavours and uniting of diverse cultures and faiths, in September 2015, Sustainable Development Goals was adopted by the uniting of nations. It was a uniting of diverse sectors of governments, business, and civil society. It was a coming together moment of the human species in transcending our own generation's narrow self-interests to envisage our common futures.

Fig. 17.5 SDGs and Taoism's wisdom: happiness vs. harmony. Source: author developed based on SDG pyramid and Taoism

The 17 SDGs reflects the roots of cultures and spiritual philosophies that have guided the lives of many communities around the world for centuries. As indicated in Fig. 17.5, SDG Pyramid was initially created out of this intent of aligning the seventeen goals with local culture and core values. Figure 17.5 portrays the 17 SDGs as a pyramid of these three key realms of people, ecological and spiritual that are pivotal in determining fundamental individual happiness and true sustainability.

The first ten Sustainable Development Goals (SDG1–10) from poverty to gender and inequalities relate to social needs, humanitarian, economic development, inclusiveness or people issues. The next five goals (SDG 11–15) from sustainable cities to climate change to nature relate to sustainability and ecology whilst the final goals (SDG 16–17) on peace and partnerships relate to the spiritual and values aspects.

The Sustainable Development Goals are intended to do at least two things. First, the Sustainable Development Goals communicate a vision for the world—a beacon on the horizon that serves as a compass for the world so that we can meet our responsibilities to succeeding generations. Second, the 17 Global Goals combine to provide a tangible guide to our daily lives—a set of reference points to advise us what to do as peoples, as consumers, producers, business, and policy makers.

The observation that SDGs are an expression of long held cultural and religious traditions is thus significant. An awareness that these goals are an expression of our cultures means that they can become part of our daily lives if we return to these roots and core values. They combine to give us a narrative for our lives. The universal theme of this narrative is about securing happiness, or balance and harmony of human beings within three realms. These three realms are spiritual realm, the ecological realm and the social realm.

Figure 17.5 shows when we look at the three realms of SDGs from the perspectives of Taoism, we understand that human beings/people must model themselves on Earth/nature, in other words, people must follow and observe the law of nature; nature/earth must follow spiritual law of heaven. The is the only way for human beings to build a harmonious and happy, and sustainable society.

However, if our development policies support one realm or one pillar of sustainability at the costs of the others, it ends up being unsustainable. Let us explore the example of wildlife conservation in Kenya. The aim was to save endangered animals and make progress in achieving SDG-15—life on land (ecological realm). Over the past few decades, rich countries have made significant contribution towards wildlife conservation in Kenya. This meant wildlife reserves became bigger and the animals were no longer endangered. However, this expansion came at a cost. The growing wildlife population started to encroach neighbouring communities' lands. These wild animals would often invade and damage local farmlands to restore the lands. The poor farmers were often found paying from their own pockets. This gave rise to high levels of poverty in these areas. The big wildlife reserves did attract rich tourists, but the tourism money rarely trickled down to these communities. In other words, trying to achieve SDG 15 made it more difficult to eradicate poverty. Favouring the environmental pillar (ecological realm) meant overlooking the social pillar (people realm).

In another case of China, we found that one of China's primary focus has been to drive economic growth. Started with a reform in 1978 that opened China's market to the world. Since then, China has been enjoying an explosive GDP growth. This has helped lift 850 million people out of poverty with only 3% of China's population currently below the poverty line. During this period of economic prosperity, China's environmental and social pillars (ecological and people realms) took a hit. A 2017 report estimated that China will suffer a health cost of 1.4 trillion dollars because of its air pollution. On top of this, China's geological survey reported that nearly 90% of Chinese cities had polluted ground water. Simultaneously, China is also dealing with land pollution, deforestation and poor animal welfare. To reverse this damage, the Chinese government have recently passed stricter environmental laws and regulations. The pollution levels have started to decline. However, in the end, China's development policy sacrificed its social and environmental pillar for the economic pillar.

It is clear that trying to address any of the three pillars of sustainability in isolation will often result in a trade-off. Imagine the three pillars as actual physical pillars supporting sustainable development. Even if one of the pillars is weak, the whole thing can collapse. Therefore, this will require a balancing approach—one where we try to pay equal attention to all the three pillars of sustainability. This is called an integrated approach—where each pillar is evenly shouldering the weight of sustainable development.

In Chap. 2, we discussed the 3D symptoms that Scharmer & Kaufer, discovered in his research. The 3D symptoms plague the world: ecological divide concerning the natural environment (self and nature); the social divide concerning the socio-economic divides that characterize our local, national and global communities (self and others); and the spiritual-values divides that become artificial barriers to our potential (self to potential self). The 3D symptoms were caused by imbalanced development policies for economic growth. This insight provides a simpler visually more pleasing narrative of the 17 Goals grounded in our existing core values. To get rid of the 3D, we need 3C Model of Taoism which I developed based on Laozi's Tao

Te Ching. The purpose of 3C Model is to develop a harmonious society where all people live a harmonious and happy life. 3C Model of Taoism can be depicted as human beings (people), earth (ecological), and heaven (spiritual). This is the philosophy of the three ways to happiness or the unity of the three way to harmony. These three ways referred to in principle are: *(1) harmony of people with people, (2) harmony of people with nature and (3) harmony of people with the spiritual or creation*. The principle of Taoism guides many aspects of people life. The Taoism's wisdom teaches that there is no separation between philosophy as theoretical guidance and practice or the practical exercise.

This notion of happiness is the destination of countless searches. The achievement of balance in the ecological, peoples and spiritual is the path to happiness. The world has been searching for this from efforts to develop sustainable national accounts that recognize the value of natural wealth to Bhutan's measurement of Gross National Happiness. The UN in its 2012 resolution establishing "Happiness Day" reflected that it was "conscious that the pursuit of happiness is a fundamental human goal ... recognizing also the need for a more inclusive, equitable and balanced approach to economic growth that promotes sustainable development, poverty eradication, happiness and the well-being of all peoples."

The Sustainable Development Goals can be an integral part of daily life in three tiers. When we view the SDGs from this traditional perspective, we see a narrative of the goals grounded in existing core values. This contrasts dramatically with the more common view from "media" reports that the Sustainable Development Goals are a list of discrete and separate goals prescribed by an external body. The Sustainable Development Goals pyramid map out in elegance and simplicity aspirations to happiness through harmony of people, ecology, and spiritual values that guide daily life.

On a separate context, reflecting a holistic perspective, the UN Secretary General, António Guterres, when taking his oath of office in December 2016, said that "... *Humanitarian response, sustainable development and sustaining peace are three sides of the same triangle...*" We believe this framework links closely to the concept of Happiness that the United Nations has presented in recent years. Former UN Secretary-General Ban Ki-moon commissioned the Sustainable Development Solutions Network (SDSN) in 2012, with goals such as ending world hunger and poverty, ensuring healthy lives, and promoting well-being. This network of leaders from academia, governments and the private sector published their first happiness report in 2012.

The 2017 ranking, prepared by the SDSN, shows that Norway has jumped from fourth place in 2016 to first place, followed by Denmark, Iceland and Switzerland in a tightly packed bunch. While recognizing the subjectivity of the concept, the SDSN used three different aspects to try to come to a general measure of the feeling: residents' evaluations of their situations, positive feelings about their lives (like joy and pride), and their negative ones (like anger and worry). The top four countries rank highly on all the main factors found to support happiness: caring, freedom, generosity, honesty, health, income and good governance. Norway moves to the top of the ranking despite weaker oil prices. It is sometimes said that Norway achieves and maintains its high happiness not because of its oil wealth, but in spite of it. By choosing to produce its oil slowly, and investing the proceeds for the future rather than spending them in the present, Norway has insulated itself from the boom-and-bust cycle of many other resource-rich economies. To do this successfully requires high levels of mutual trust, shared purpose, generosity and good governance, all factors that help to keep Norway and other top countries where they are in the happiness rankings.

All of the other countries in the top ten also have high values in all six of the key variables used to explain happiness differences among countries and through time—income, healthy life expectancy, having someone to count on in times of trouble, generosity, freedom and trust, with the latter measured by the absence of corruption in business and government.

I have found in China in recent years, Taoist leaders have launched "One Village, One Paradise" project for a harmonious and happy community. The project was built on Taoism's wisdom, particularly refers to Tao Te Ching, Chapter 80:

> In a tiny country with small population,
> People never used them,
> Even if there were availability of instruments.
> People more cared about where they lived,
> And did not travel far away from home.
> People never took them,
> Even if there were availability of boats and carriages.
> People never resorted to them,
> Even if there were availability of armour and weapons.
> People worked in the natural way of knotted rope to record things.
> People were enjoying tasty food,
> Wearing beautiful clothes,
> Living in comfortable home, and
> Appreciating the customs.
> – Laozi, Tao Te Ching, Ch.80

The farmers who participated in the project was encouraged to cultivate the farmland and agriculture without using any chemical products by holding to the Law of Natural Agriculture:

> Revering and respecting Heaven and Earth,
> Cultivating with gratitude and love,
> Living in harmony symbiosis with all creatures, and
> Caring the earth for sustainable development.

For example, the Taoist leaders set up Natural Farming Training Course in Luoyang, China. While learning the wisdom of Tao Te Ching about the preciousness of natural farming methods, they cultivated agriculture without using chemical fertilizers, pesticides and herbicides. They ended up harvesting food, vegetables and fruits. When they tasted the organic products, they feel very happy because they seem to try the taste of heaven and earth! Luoyang Ecovillage was one of the successful examples of "One Village, One Paradise" practices. I believe this is also the good practice of SDG happiness pyramid in China.

References

Biagiotti, I., & Martimort-Asso, B. (2016, December 21). *United Nations – 30 years of sustainable development: 1970–2008*. Retrieved May 15, 2020, from http://regardssurlaterre.com/en/united-nations-30-years-sustainable-development

United Nations. (1992). Report of the United Nations conference on environment and development. *Environment and Development, Rio de Janeiro*.

United Nations. (2010). *Report of the secretary-general on sustainable development: Harmony with nature*. United Nations.

Chapter 18
Ensuring No One Is Left Behind: The Case of Youth

> *We cannot always build the future for our youth,*
> *but we can build our youth for the future.*
>
> *– Franklin D. Roosevelt (1882–1945)*

> *Making the best use of anyone, no one is left behind,*
> *Making the most use of anything, nothing is left to waste.*
>
> *– Laozi, Tao Te Ching, Chapter 27*

> *For the world civilization, for the mankind happiness,*
> *we, the youth, shall dedicate ourselves to building*
> *a family of youth,*
> *a country of youth,*
> *a nation of youth,*
> *the mankind of youth,*
> *the earth of youth, and the universe of youth.*
>
> *– Dazhao Li,*
>
> *Co-founder of the Communist Party of P. R. China*

The UN 2030 Agenda for Sustainable Development is the framework for making the greatest impact for people and planet, and in the end for advancing the well-being of humankind. One of the fundamental principles of the Agenda is to *ensure no one is left behind.* It is completely in alignment with the Chines traditional wisdom of Taoism. The target population for the pledge to leave no one behind is various, some may focus on disadvantaged groups of society, and others focus on reducing inequalities between countries, but in this chapter, "Ensuring no one is left behind" will focus on the youth. Because young people are especially vulnerable group, although they are the most vibrant, dynamic and energetic; and constitute the most valuable human resource that forms the foundation of future development of any nation, they are more exposed to risks.

Since 2020, we have seen the COVID-19 global health emergency and its economic and social impacts which have disrupted nearly all aspects of life for all

L. Zu, *Responsible and Sustainable Business*,
https://doi.org/10.1007/978-3-030-91117-1_18

groups in society. People of different ages, however, are experiencing its effects in different ways. But young people have suffered considerable risks that the COVID-19 poses in the fields of education, employment, mental health and disposable income. Moreover, while youth and future generations will shoulder much of the long-term economic and social consequences of the crisis, their well-being may be superseded by short-term economic and equity considerations.

According to the Global Survey on Youth and COVID-19 conducted by the Youth team of the International Labour Organization (ILO) in 2020, aimed to capture the immediate effects of the pandemic on the lives of young people (aged 18–29) with regards to employment, education, mental well-being, rights and social activism, the impact of the pandemic on young people is systematic, deep and disproportionate. It has been particularly hard on young women and younger youth in lower-income countries. Of the young people who were either studying or combining study and work before the onset of the crisis, three-quarters experienced school closures, yet not all were able to transition into online and distance learning (ILO, 2020).

The pandemic is also inflicting a heavy toll on young workers, destroying their employment and undermining their career prospects. One in six young people (17%) who were employed before the outbreak, stopped working altogether, most notably younger workers aged 18–24, and those in clerical support, services, sales, and crafts and related trades. Working hours among employed youth fell by nearly a quarter (i.e., by an average of 2 h a day) and two out of five young people (42%) reported a reduction in their income (ILO, 2020).

The chapter will address four broad questions. First, who are those left behind? Second, why are they left behind? Third, what methods and mechanisms exist to reach and involve them? And fourth, what types of strategies and policies that national authorities develop might be appropriate in order to leave no one behind?

The purpose of the 2030 Agenda is to realize the commitment to achievement of SDGs and to leaving no one behind. Succeeding in achieving the purpose of SDGs requires national authorities to empower youth as global leaders and engage them in realization of SDGs by creating an enabling environment that promotes innovation and entrepreneurship. Fostering innovation and youth entrepreneurship calls for multi-pronged strategies, implementation and involvement at all levels including government, industry, political, social and as well as educational sectors.

The chapter will examine the implications of 'ensuring no one is left behind' for the implementation of the 2030 Agenda. It will briefly discuss the connections between the commitment to leave no one behind and three related strategies for achievement of the SDGs: innovation, youth, and entrepreneurship. The chapter then reviews some of the concepts and methods used to identify those left behind, as well as some of the methods that are used to reach them in practice. Finally, the chapter highlights examples of development strategies that Chinese government has used in the achievement of sustainable development goals.

No One Is Left Behind: SDGs and Taoism's Wisdom

> The new agenda is a universal,
> integrated and transformative vision for a better world...
> An agenda for shared prosperity, peace and partnership.
> Above all, it pledges to leave no one behind.
> – Ban Ki-Moon, former UN Secretary-General

The United Nations declares in the Agenda "*As we embark on this great collective journey, we pledge that no one will be left behind. Recognizing that the dignity of the human person is fundamental, we wish to see the goals and targets met for all nations and peoples and for all segments of society. And we will endeavour to reach the furthest behind first*" (The United Nations, 2015). The pledge to leave no one behind is a fundamental guiding principle for its implementation. The pledge of the Agenda embraces the Taoism's wisdom. In Tao Te Ching, Laozi says,

> Make the best use of anyone, no one is left behind.
> Make the most use of anything, nothing is left to waste.
> – Laozi, Tao Te Ching, Ch. 27

Laozi was concerned not only about people, but about the planet, not only about human resources, but about natural resources. It embodies the core and guiding principles of sustainable development for the modern leaders to uphold. It provides a shared roadmap to build a world that is inclusive, fair, sustainable, stable and prosperous.

"Ensuring no one is left behind" encompasses multiple meanings. For some, it will mean focusing action on disadvantaged groups of society, for example, people living in poverty, women, indigenous people, youth, older people, and persons with disabilities, migrants, or people in conflict and post-conflicts situations. Others will focus on reducing inequalities between countries, including focusing action on countries at the lowest stages of development or facing challenging circumstances. It means that decades years from now, when the current and the next generations together assess the implementation of the 2030 Agenda, a key measure of success will be the extent to which it has allowed every single person to thrive, regardless of gender, race, age, religion, place of residence, or any other factor. The call to leave no one behind has been heeded—many organizations have already started to work on the implications of this principle for the delivery of the 2030 Agenda for Sustainable Development.

In this chapter, '*Ensuring no one is left behind*' will focus on the youth. At the conceptual and practical levels, the chapter will address four broad questions. Figure 18.1 shows the framework of the core concepts and relationships of the concepts. The purpose of the SDGs is to realize the commitment of leaving no one behind. Succeeding in achieving the purpose of SDGs requires national authorities to engage and empower youth in SDGs, particularly to create an enabling environment that promotes innovation and youth entrepreneurship. Fostering innovation and youth entrepreneurship calls for multi-pronged strategies, implementation and involvement at all levels including government, industry, political, social and as

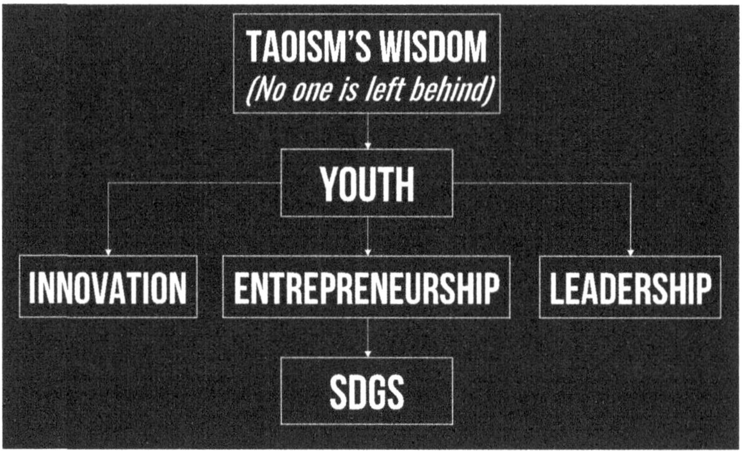

Fig. 18.1 Framework of Taoism's wisdom, youth and SDGs

well as educational sectors. The chapter will examine the implications of 'ensuring no one is left behind' for the implementation of the 2030 Agenda. It will briefly discuss the connections between the commitment to leave no one behind and three related strategies for achievement of the SDGs: innovation, entrepreneurship and leadership. The chapter then reviews some of the concepts and methods used to identify those left behind, as well as some of the methods that are used to reach them in practice. Finally, the chapter highlights examples of development policies that Chinese government has developed in the achievement of SDGs.

Why Youth Matters? The Challenges and Drivers of Economic Growth

> The working youth is critical to our future.
> The economy depends on you.
> With your hard work and efforts at improving your skills,
> you can make ours one of the most prosperous nations in the world.
> – Nelson Mandela
> Former President of South Africa

The pledge to leave no one behind places a focus on youth, women and girls, persons with disabilities, indigenous people and other vulnerable groups who continue to see their potential undermined by poverty and exclusion. Ensuring that these commitments are translated into effective action requires a precise understanding of target populations.

The chapter will shed light on the particular situations of young peoples. According to UN data, the world today is home to 1.8 billion people between the ages of 10 and 24. Close to 90% of them live in developing countries, where they

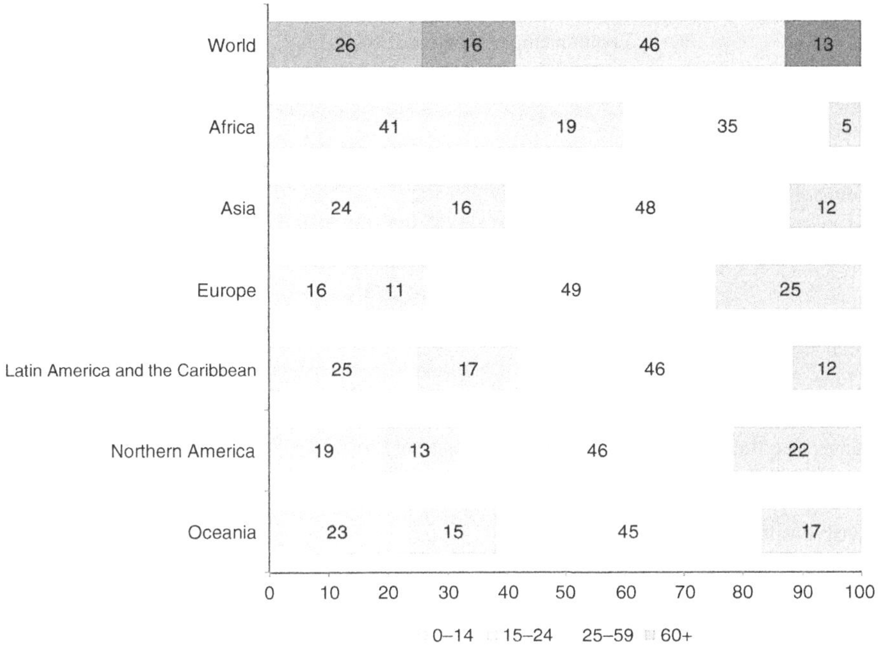

Fig. 18.2 Percentage of population in broad age groups for the world and by region, 2017. Source: United Nations, Department of Economic and Social Affairs, Population Division (2017). World Population Prospects: The 2017 Revision. New York: United Nations

make up a large proportion of the population. Their numbers are expected to grow—between 2015 and 2030 alone, about 1.9 billion young people are projected to turn 15 years old. Populations in many regions are still comparatively young. In Africa, children under age 15 account for 41% of the population in 2017 and young persons aged 15–24 account for an additional 19% (Fig. 18.2). Latin America and the Caribbean, and Asia, which have experienced greater declines in fertility, have smaller percentages of children (25 and 24%, respectively) but similar percentages of youth (17 and 16%, respectively). In total, these three regions are home to 1.8 billion children and 1.1 billion young persons in 2017.

Therefore, providing these generations of children and youth with health care, education, and employment opportunities, including in the poorest countries and groups, will be critical for the successful implementation of the 2030 Agenda for Sustainable Development. Because young people want to and already contribute to the resilience of their communities, proposing innovative solutions, driving social progress and inspiring political change. They are also agents of change, mobilizing to advance the Sustainable Development Goals to improve the lives of people and the health of the planet. However, the benefits of development are not equally shared by the youth.

Young people are over-represented among the direct and indirect victims of violence. Some 200,000 homicides each year—43% of all homicides globally—

Table 18.1 Youth unemployment 2007–2017

	Youth unemployment rate, 2007–17 (percentages)				Unemployed youth, 2015–17 (millions)		
	2007–14	2015	2016	2017	2015	2016	2017
World		12.9	13.1	13.1	70.5	71.0	71.0
Developed countries		15.0	14.5	14.3	10.2	9.8	9.6
Emerging countries		13.3	13.6	13.7	52.9	53.5	53.5
Developing countries		9.4	9.5	9.4	7.4	7.7	7.9
	Youth working poverty rate, 2007–17 (percentages)				Youth working poverty, 2015–17 (millions)		
	2007–14	2015	2016	2017	2015	2016	2017
Total emerging and developing		38.4	37.7	36.9	159.9	156.0	152.2
Emerging countries		31.2	30.2	29.3	107.3	102.7	98.4
Developing countries		73.3	72.2	71.0	52.6	53.3	53.8

Source: The ILO (2016), World Employment and Social Outlook

involve children and adults aged 10–29 years. Young men have the highest risk of becoming homicide victims and the highest rates, by far, of being suspected homicide perpetrators (The United Nations, 2016). Children are among those most affected by human trafficking and, in several regions, they make up the majority of trafficking victims. In sub-Saharan Africa and South-Eastern Asia, children comprise 65% and 57%, respectively, of total human trafficking victims (The United Nations, 2017b). In addition, the youth is also facing the tough employment. The International Labour Organization (ILO) estimates that the global youth unemployment rate is expected to reach 13.1% in 2016 and remain at that level through to 2017 (up from 12.9% in 2015). The ILO's World Employment and Social Outlook 2016, Trends for Youth report shows that as a result, the global number of unemployed youth is set to rise by half a million this year to reach 71 million (Table 18.1)—the first such increase in 3 years (ILO, 2016). Of greater concern is the share and number of young people, often in emerging and developing countries, who live in extreme or moderate poverty despite having a job. In fact, 156 million or 37.7% of working youth are in extreme or moderate poverty (compared to 26% of working adults).

In the case of China, in 2017, the estimated youth unemployment rate in China was at 10.8% (see Fig. 18.3) (Statista, 2017). It is much higher than the average rate of developing countries, and extremely higher than the average rate of 4% of total unemployment in China.

The youth employment is becoming one of the top priorities of Chinese government. To address the big challenge, Chinese central authorities released a detailed 10-year youth development plan in 2017, vowing better education, employment and healthcare for the nation's youth. China has formulated the Medium and Long-Term Youth Development Program (2016–2025), which sets a general goal of establishing a "youth development policy system and work mechanism" by 2020 and improving the system by 2025. It requires expanding areas of employment for young people and fully leveraging fiscal, financial, tax, subsidy and other policy tools to support them in finding various forms of employment through multiple channels or starting

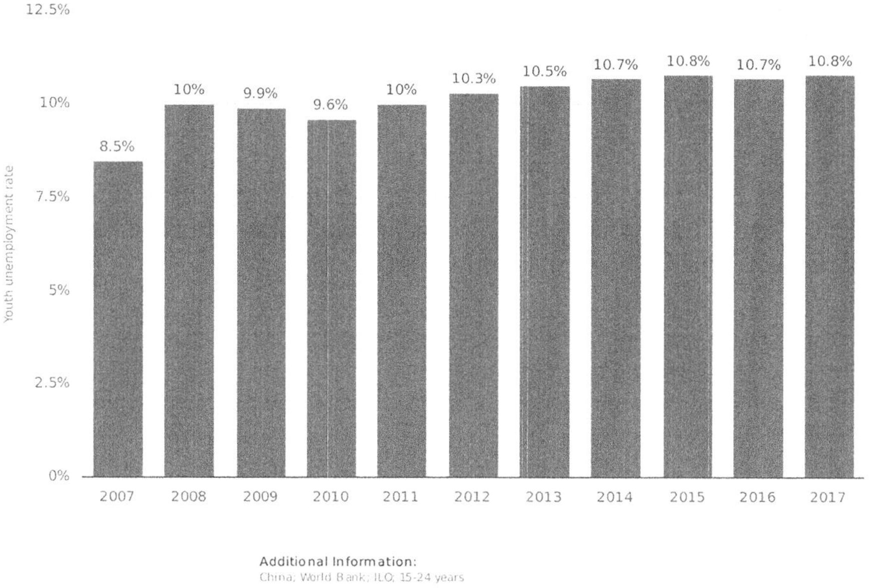

Fig. 18.3 China: youth unemployment rate from 2007 to 2017. Source: World Bank

their own businesses. Specifically, the plan sets educational goals of an average 13.5 years of education for the newly added labor force and a gross higher education enrollment rate of over 50% within 10 years (China, 2017).

Young people on one hand are facing incredible challenges, and on the other, they are main drivers of economic growth. They can take a lead in driving SDGs in a bid to promote inclusive and sustainable economic growth. The international community and national authorities cannot achieve their missions and goals without partnering with young people. We must ensure they are not only heard but understood, not only engaged but empowered, and not only supporting but leading to be full-fledged partners in the work of international community and national authorities to build a better world for all, as they are both beneficial and partners. Therefore, if we provide young people with the necessary skills and opportunities needed to reach their potential, young people will be able to be a driving force for supporting development and contributing to peace and security. Youth-led organizations need to be encouraged and empowered to participate in translating the 2030 Agenda into local, national and regional policy. They play a significant role in the implementation, monitoring and review of the Agenda as well as in holding governments accountable. With political commitment and adequate resources, young people have the potential to make the most effective transformation of the world into a better place for all.

The United Nations launched in 2018 the new initiative of Generation Unlimited. Generation Unlimited (GenU) is a global multi-sector partnership to meet the urgent need for expanded education, training and employment opportunities for young people, aged 10–24, on an unprecedented scale. Despite the challenges that exist—or perhaps because of them!—Leaders around the world are responding positively to GenU's mission and asking how they can help. Politicians, CEOs, foundation heads and civic leaders are recognizing that forging innovative collaborations with young people at the center is the best way forward.

Why Youth Entrepreneurs Matters? The Change-Makers of Society and Driving Force of SDGs

In China, people have a saying "young people is the hope of a nation, and the future of the world." This statement stands true in every sense. When a country has a healthy youth population, you will find the country making headway in terms of overall development and progress. A country with high aging population and lower youth population has many problems to content with that can slow its growth. Because young people are critical thinkers. They involve making sense of personal experiences and asking questions about the world around you. They have the capacity to identify and challenge existing power structures and barriers to change, and to expose contradictions and biases. Young people are change-makers. They also have the power to act and mobilize others. Youth activism is on the rise the world over, bolstered by broader connectivity and access to social media. Young people are innovators. They often have direct knowledge of and insights into issues that are not accessible to adults. They best understand the problems they face and can offer new ideas and alternative solutions. Young people are communicators. Outside the international development sector, few people are aware that world leaders have come to a historic, far-reaching agreement to improve the lives of people and the planet by 2030. Young people can be partners in communicating the development agenda to their peers and communities at the local level, as well as across countries and regions. And finally, young people are leaders. When they are empowered with the knowledge of their rights and equipped with leadership skills, young people can drive change in their communities and countries. As young leaders of tomorrow, it is pivotal that youth are informed and engaged with the global vision for the future. Over the next 15 years, youth will not only directly experience the outcome of SDGs and plans, but will also be the key driver for their successful implementation. For this reason, it is vital to raise awareness about the recently adopted 17 SDGs and the 2030 Agenda for Sustainable Development among youth, build a platform for discussion, and create the conditions for active engagement (UNESCAP, 2017).

As we discussed preceding section, one of the major challenges faced by China and other countries in the world today is to do with youth unemployment. The current global youth population is estimated to be at 1.2 billion aged 15–24 years, of which 620 million are employable and ninety percent of this population live in developing countries. Countries like China have an increasing youth population and the rate of unemployment too is rising rapidly. As per ILO's prediction approximately 660 million youth will be seeking employment by 2015. The youth unemployment is higher measuring up to 50–60% in Asia (MSG, 2018). Chinese authorities and governments in other countries have focused on looking at framework and strategies to creating new jobs and increasing employment rates. In this context, fostering youth entrepreneurship has gained importance on the global and national policy agendas as a way to expand employment and earning opportunities. Youth entrepreneurship can help sustain growing economies; integrate youth into the workforce besides leading to overall development of society and is being recognized as a promising alternative and is being actively promoted by various agencies.

Entrepreneurship has become a key focus of research over the past three decades. With the focus on entrepreneurship and its potential for economic development and job creation, the recognition of entrepreneurs as having an important role in the economy has emerged. Entrepreneurship is widely acknowledged as a driver of sustainable economic growth as entrepreneurs create new businesses, drive and shape innovation, speed up structural changes in the economy, and introduce new competition—thereby contributing to productivity. Entrepreneurship also drives job creation and hence entrepreneurship is a critical contributor to economic growth that is inclusive and reduces poverty. The Global Entrepreneurship Monitor (GEM) defines entrepreneurship as "any attempt at new business or new venture creation, such as self-employment, a new business organization, or the expansion of an existing business, by an individual, a team of individuals, or an established business (Bosma et al., 2012)".

In low-and middle-income countries, self-employment is the dominant form of entrepreneurship and accounts for an important share of youth employment. According to the Global Entrepreneurship Monitor (GEM), a significant proportion of the youth population aged 18–24 were nascent entrepreneurs or owners-managers of a new business in 2016—about 10% in Asia and Oceania, 15% in Africa and 17% in Latin America and the Caribbean. For many people in these regions, including youth, entrepreneurial activity is the sole entry point into the labour market and the only way out of poverty. In sub-Saharan Africa, for example, approximately one third of all youth with a new or nascent business were pushed towards entrepreneurship out of necessity. Often this involved small-scale self-employed subsistence activities, in farming or outside the agricultural sector (OECD, 2017).

Therefore, it is important for the international community and national authorities to actively engage youth in sustainable development efforts through fostering entrepreneurship is central to achieving sustainable, inclusive and stable societies by the target date, and to averting the worst threats and challenges to sustainable development, including the impacts of climate change, unemployment, poverty, gender inequality, conflict, and migration. The study shows that youth entrepreneurship has many great advantages in contribution to social progress and environmental sustainability. For instance, young entrepreneurship is an option to create employment for the youth; young entrepreneurs are more likely to hire fellow youths; young entrepreneurs are particularly responsive to new economic opportunities and trends; young people are active in high growth sectors; young people with entrepreneurial skills are better employees; young people are more innovative and often create new forms of independent work; young people who are self-employed have higher "life satisfaction" (African Economic Outlook, 2013); entrepreneurship offers unemployed or discouraged youth an opportunity to build sustainable livelihoods and a chance to integrate themselves into society(The United Nations, 2013); entrepreneurial experience and/or education help youth develop new skills that can be applied to other challenges in life. Non-cognitive skills, such as opportunity recognition, innovation, critical thinking, resilience, decision-making, teamwork, and leadership will benefit all youth whether or not they intend to become or continue as entrepreneurs (GEM, 2013).

Why Social Innovation Matters? The Engine of Social Change

Traditionally when we talk about innovation, we immediately think of technical innovation, service innovation, organizational innovation, etc. However, these innovations alone have proven to be insufficient to address the pressing challenges of today such as climate change, resource depletion, economic deprivation, poverty alleviation, increased migration and improved life quality. We need a brand new innovation to address these problems, and to enable transitions to more sustainable solutions. Social innovations are new strategies, concepts, ideas and organizations that aim to meet social needs resulting from working conditions, education, community development, and health. From the academic perspective, social innovation is defined as a novel solution to a social problem that is more effective, efficient, sustainable, or just than existing solutions and for which the value created accrues primarily to society as a whole rather than private individuals.

Social Innovation happens in the process of innovation, and it also happens in new work and new forms of cooperation, especially those that work towards a sustainable society. The Centre for Social Innovation at the Stanford Graduate School of Business defines social innovation as "the process of inventing, securing support for, and implementing novel solutions to social needs and problems." OECD defines it as concerning conceptual, process or product change, organisational change and changes in financing, and dealing with new relationships with stakeholders and territories. From the European perspective, social innovations are defined as new ideas that meet social needs, create social relationships and form new collaborations. These innovations can be products, services or models addressing unmet needs more effectively. The World Economic Forum's Global Agenda Council on Social Innovation, an advisory body comprised of leading practitioners, thought leaders and academics, defines social innovation as "the application of innovative, practical, sustainable, market-based approaches to benefit society in general, and low-income or underserved populations in particular". Social innovation means being more strategic, more ambitious and more collaborative in how access and opportunity can be provided for billions of low-income people to participate in the global economy.

Social innovation often emerges through companies that seek more than pure profits or when non-profit foundations find more secure funding models. In other words, social innovation can be achieved through hybrid organizations that combine aspects of non-profits and for-profits to achieve social impact. Therefore, an important aspect of social innovation is to discover new organizational models that have social concerns, but also have sustainable revenue generation.

Business cannot succeed in ecologies and societies that fail. Social innovators are invited to go into training to become regenerative practitioners. They need to go to the very heart of the markets and align new revenue opportunities with a value-generating capability that make both people and the rest of the natural world stronger, more vibrant, and more resilient. Social innovators' ecological and economic decisions should coincide with ecosystem boundaries. Using natural resources efficiently within the system in regenerative loops is both profitable and better for the environment, on which all business is dependent. The carbon-intensive waste economy concentrated in narrow bands of the population has had its day. Business models that harness environmental performance are engines of competitive advantage. Innovation should balance new sustainable consumption and production patterns with protection of terrestrial ecosystems.

Social Innovation, Social Entrepreneurship and SDGs

Social Innovation and Social Entrepreneurship

We understand from the preceding section that the purpose of social innovation is to look for new ideas and methods of solving social and environmental problems. It is also the effective ways to meet the ambitious challenges, like the SDG 2030 Agenda. The main driver for social innovation is the need to address unmet social needs. Most social innovations are initiated through entrepreneurial activities from the bottom up, by organizations and actors with roots in civil society and the third sector (such as cooperatives, associations and foundations). One of the most exciting sectors of social innovation today are a group of social entrepreneurship start-up companies that have sustainable business models and apply emerging technologies to achieve social impact. The social entrepreneurship companies attempt to tackle problems from scratch to develop approaches that might be difficult to implement in more established organizations. The commonality that can be found in all these social innovation approaches is a desire to find new organizational models to achieve social impact. We need bolder and more ambitious efforts to achieve the SDG 2030 Agenda. And we can look for novel solutions among the various practitioners of social innovation around the world.

Social entrepreneurs can pursue social innovation opportunities which SDGs will create, particularly in the social and environmental areas. The opportunities can be grouped into four broad clusters such as building future markets, strengthening supply chains, investing in talent and leveraging finance (WEF, 2016). Each cluster offers a starting point for entrepreneurs and companies to look for social innovation opportunities most relevant to them. Specific opportunities will be driven by multiple factors including a company's operating environment, geographic footprint, product portfolio, supplier base and raw material dependencies, and talent models. For example, market-facing companies from sectors such as healthcare or consumer goods have embraced business growth through innovations in products, services or distribution channels targeting underserved consumers. Companies heavily reliant on supply chains, including from food, agriculture or textiles, have pursued strategies that secure raw material supply, increase product quality and engage customers, while companies in professional services or IT focus on building future talent pools and enhancing employee loyalty.

Companies that successfully pursue social innovation as an opportunity for developing new markets typically innovate in three specific ways. First, they design products and services that respond to the unique needs and behaviours of low-income customers. This can include developing new products and services or adapting existing product lines for their needs (e.g., food brands fortifying existing products with micronutrients to address malnutrition). Second, the products and services must offer strong value for money despite—or because of—low purchasing power, necessitating the design of cost-effective products. Third, products must be made accessible across large geographies with poor infrastructure, which requires thinking creatively about distribution channels.

There are three major strategic benefits for social innovation in a corporate supply chain. The first motivation is to ensure the stability of access to raw materials. Many supply chains, particularly those in the agriculture, food and consumer goods industries, are laced with intermediaries, all of whom take a share of the price paid by the consumer. Unless small suppliers can increase productivity or volumes, households may abandon crops that have become unviable, threatening the supply of raw materials. Extreme weather is another driver of supply volatility. Diversification of and investment into a supplier base can create direct and trusted relationships with farmers, which help maintain stability in supplies and prices in the face of extreme weather events. The second strategic benefit revolves around improving the quality of raw materials, which supports a company's ability to achieve a price premium while strengthening consumer loyalty. A third motivation is reputation and proactively responding to changing consumer preferences. An increasing number of consumers are willing to pay a premium for products sourced through socially responsible supply chains.

Increasing levels of diversity in the workforce can present a significant social innovation opportunity. Seeking a more diverse workforce both increases the size of the recruiting pool and can introduce new capabilities into an organization. Many companies have realized the opportunity this can bring—according to the "2011 Fostering Innovation through a Diverse Workforce survey" by Forbes, 85% of companies agree talent diversification results in more innovative product generation ideas. Firms have recognized that "new" talent pools (other examples might be immigrants, the long-term unemployed and the disabled) can bring new strengths and perspectives to their team. However, to successfully tap into these groups, firms need to assess how existing hiring approaches and work procedures will need to be adapted. Firms have approached the issue by searching for allies who share the same mission and are willing to enter into partnerships. Governments or educational institutions—or even competitors—are often willing to co-invest or bring in their expertise and teaching infrastructure. At the same time, companies can play an active role by (co-)designing the curricula, bringing in their practical experiences and ensuring a targeted skill development that matches the demands of business.

Finance can be a key tool for a company to engage in social innovation. Companies have helped grow social enterprises by managing impact investment funds or incubators. In addition to generating financial returns, such investments can offer a pipeline of ideas to support a company's innovation agenda and can become future partners, or even future customers. To benefit the most from its impact investments, a company should invest in start-ups that are strongly aligned with the company's business strategy or operating in adjacent markets. Targeted investments into social entrepreneurs can generate new business opportunities for the company.

Social Innovation and Sustainable Development

The UN now acknowledges that social innovation approaches are needed as mainstream tools for delivering sustainable development, alongside large-scale public and private funding. Today, the role of bottom-up social innovation in designing and delivering public services to income-poor and marginalized people in a gender sensitive manner, especially when based on local acceptance and advocacy campaigns, is seen as an important issue in achieving the SDGs by 2030. In reality, social innovation and sustainable development go hand-in-hand. For example, the United Nations Social Development Network is supporting Asia-Pacific countries' use of social innovation to tackle ageing population and gender inequality (The United Nations, 2017a). In India, building a mass social movement around the lack of basic utilities and services, through the mobilization of opinion and advocacy across as many groups and interests as possible, can help change the behaviour and attitudes of both citizens and service providers to issues like public health. The potential benefits of public-civil partnerships in northern Ghana, where the former provides the framework and expertise and the latter provides community activism, knowledge and resources, is a core issue addressed in the high impact 'School for Life' basic education initiative in rural areas. In 2001, a bottom-up social innovation was launched in Brazil's dry Northeast by a network of civil society institutions and small farmers working to promote co-existence and local empowerment. One million cisterns were built for capturing rainwater to provide rural families with healthy drinking water year-round, regardless of when the rains come. This was undertaken in partnership with the government and the private sector, but retained its strong focus on ensuring the democratization of access to water in order to ease the lives of the poor and especially women whose task it normally is to obtain water for family use. The experimental cistern was designed to capture rainwater, and is easy to build at low cost, using local knowledge and support from local authorities, universities and companies for technical assistance. The result is not only good quality drinking water but also the empowerment of family farmers, women and local organizations, as well as their capacity to influence public policy.

Social innovation is thus increasingly recognized as an important component of the new innovation framework necessary for sustainable development. In addition to most developed countries, it is starting to become embedded and recognized in many developing countries and emerging economies. It helps to meet social needs (for example for an education or health service) in a new way that also involves collaboration with, and the empowerment of, the service user or beneficiary. It works with them rather than just doing something to them as passive recipients, also developing their own capabilities around and ownership of the service, and thereby transforming their social relations and improving their access to power and resources.

SDGs Create Business Opportunities for Youth Entrepreneurs

The SDGs provide all businesses with a new lens through which to translate the world's needs and ambitions into business solutions. These solutions will enable companies to better manage their risks, anticipate consumer demand, build positions in growth markets, secure access to needed resources, and strengthen their supply chains, while moving the world towards a sustainable and inclusive development path (The United Nations, 2017a, 2017b).

According to a report by the Business & Sustainable Development Commission, the SDGs could generate US$12 trillion in business savings and revenue across four sectors by 2030 (see Fig. 18.4) (BSDC, 2017a): energy, cities, food and agriculture, and health and well-being. It points out the 60 biggest market opportunities related to delivering the SDGs, such as sustainable aquaculture and mine rehabilitation. The report also estimates the creation of 380 million new jobs linked to these four sectors in the next 10 or 15 years due to alignment of business strategy to the SDGs.

Business leaders and entrepreneurs can unlock new market opportunities worth US$5 trillion and generate 230 million jobs in Asia by 2030 through sustainable business models, according to Better Business, Better World Asia, a new report released today by the Business & Sustainable Development Commission (BSDC). The research also shows that, instead of being a constraint to growth, companies pursuing strategies aligned with the Global Goals could open economic opportunities across 60 "hot spots" worth up to US$12 trillion and increase employment by up to 380 million jobs globally by 2030. Asia represents 40% of the global value, and nearly two-thirds of total jobs. In terms of the impact of SDGs on business in Asia and China, BSDC estimated in its 2017 Report, SDGs will generate US$5 trillion of

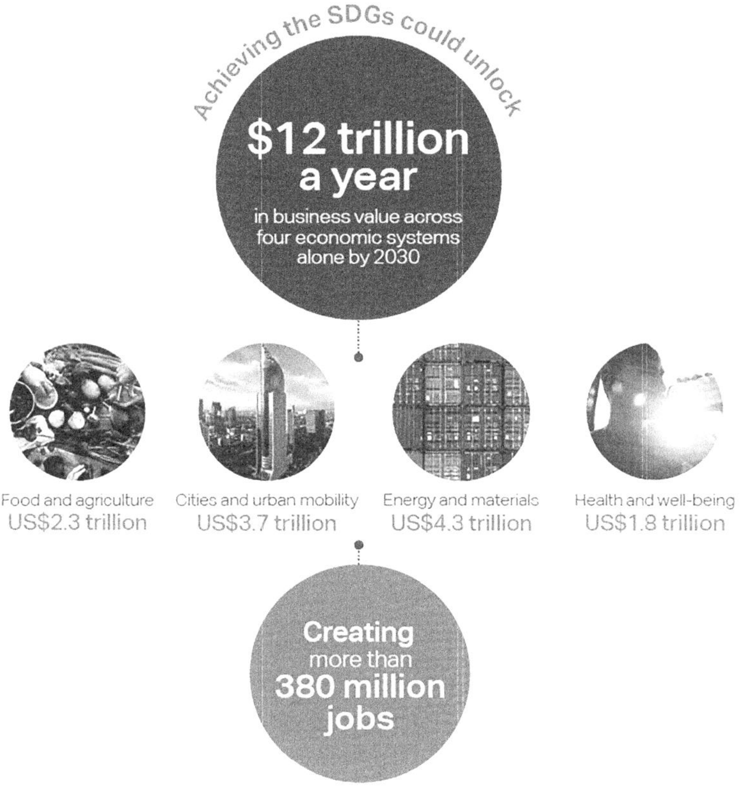

Fig. 18.4 Business opportunity and SDGs. Source: Better Business, Better World, Business & Sustainable Development Commission, 2017

economic value across four key systems: food & agriculture: US$1 trillion for food & agriculture; US$1.5 trillion for cities, US$1.9 trillion for energy & minerals, and US$670 billion for Health & Well-being (BSDC, 2017b) . Of the total value for Asia, around US$2.3 trillion could be found in China alone, US$1.1 trillion in India, US$1.1 trillion in developing and emerging Asia, and US$0.7 trillion in developed Asia, which include Australia, New Zealand, Japan, and South Korea. The estimated value of US$5 trillion is conservative. Additional value could be released from other sectors, including information communication technologies (ICT), education, and consumer goods. Globally, these sectors could add a further 66% to the global value of US$12 trillion. Pricing in environmental costs such as climate change could increase the 'real' size of the prize by a further 40%. And making progress on the single global goal of gender equality in countries in Asia where women are not strongly engaged in the economy is likely to add an additional 30 percent to the economic growth of these countries. According to the report, 230 million jobs could be generated through SDGs-aligned business models in Asia, however, these jobs

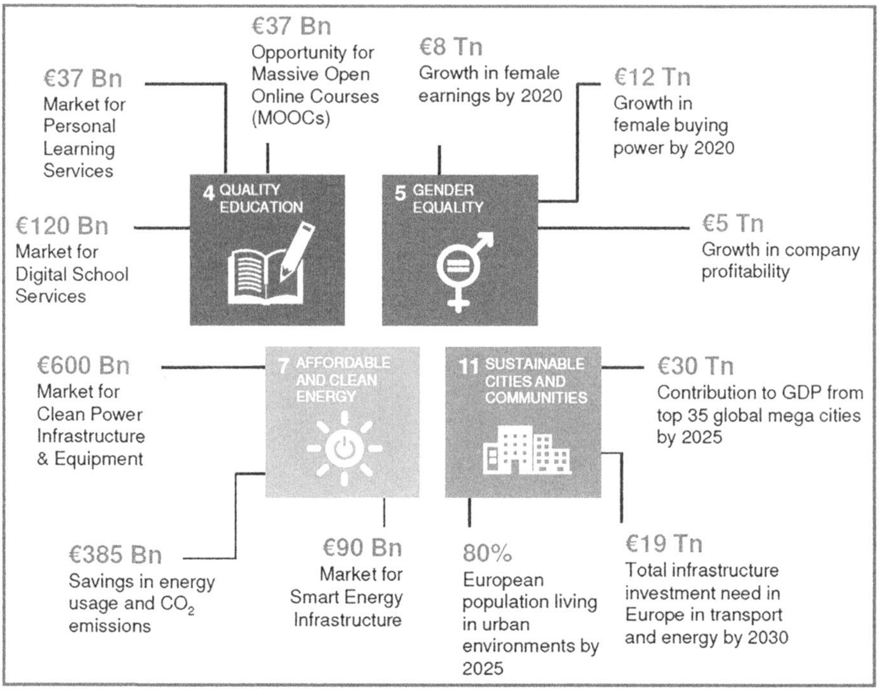

Fig. 18.5 Economic business opportunities from selected SDGs. Source: Frost & Sullivan and GlobeScan (2017), The Sustainable Development Goals (SDGs): The Value for Europe. Whitepaper

will only meet Global Goals targets if they provide decent work that creates sufficient reward and development opportunities for workers.

It is obvious that on one hand, SDG creates enormous opportunities for business, on the other; it demands strategies for tackling urgent environmental and social challenges so that market value can be successfully unlocked. Aligning these strategies with the Global Goals is not just good for society and the environment, but makes strategic business sense.

If we want to identify the impact of the specific SDGs on business, we can take a look at the study which was undertaken by Frost & Sullivan and GlobeScan on behalf of CSR Europe. The study demonstrates that while the SDGs have already been embraced by many business leaders, middle-management remains disconnected from their narrative. The study warns that while progress has been made, collaborative efforts must be reinforced in order to meet the UN 2030 Agenda.

The SDGs not only provide a common language for the private and public sector to communicate, they also offer Europe a critical opportunity to foster sustainable and inclusive growth and secure trust in Europe. Figure 18.5 showcases the market value that four sustainable development goals will generate in the future: *SDG4:*

Quality Education, SDG 5: Gender Equality, SDG 7: Affordable and Clean Energy, SDG 11: Sustainable Cities and Communities (Frost & Sullivan, 2017).

Education is always an important area that influence business. 'Education for all' has been a global campaign since 2000 when UNESCO set in motion the movement with over 160 countries pledging to achieve six education related goals by 2015. Two years have passed since the desired timeline and sadly only a third of the countries have achieved six goals with many still struggling to provide basic education. 58 million children are out of school and over 100 million without a primary education. In addition to the problem of access, the quality of education has also suffered with poor teacher-student ratios (1–47 in Pakistan) and low conversion rates to higher education (30% dropout from secondary school globally).

It is believed that a more unexpected and consequently untapped source of growth is the so called 'gender dividend'. This is the growing body of evidence that by addressing female consumers and harnessing the power of females within private industry, businesses will yield significant returns. Equality and empowerment for women and girls is not just the right thing to do but essential to achieve our most promising and sustainable future. By 2025, women will change the workforce landscape with an average participation rate of more than 40%—an additional 250 million women workers. This will close the gender gap in labour participation rates by 25%, which, in turn, will have a huge economic impact across both developing and developed nations. Equal male and female employment rates would boost the economy of European nations by 5–9%.

Energy is a key enabler of economic growth, a driver of industrial output and business, and also a crucial ingredient to bringing progress in sectors such as transportation and healthcare. Energy is also a critical factor in guaranteeing access to clean water, sanitation and education in developing countries, as well as bringing essentials such as warmth, light and safety to people's homes. In essence, the security and efficiency of energy is one of the most essential components of improving the lives of individuals while also securing a sustainable and dynamic future for society.

Providing for smart and sustainable solutions is vital for cities. Urban migration along with city expansion is resulting in resources becoming scarce. Frost & Sullivan estimates project that, by 2025, the global urban population is expected to breach the 4.6 billion mark, which will roughly account for 58% of the total population.

Youth Leadership Development: GYLA of the Youth, by the Youth and for the Youth

> All our hopes for a better world rest on young people. The world is home to the largest generation of young people. Sustainable development, human rights, peace and security can only be achieved if we empower these young people as leaders.
>
> – António Guterres, UN Secretary-General

> We must not, in trying to think about how
> we can make a big difference, ignore the small daily differences
> we can make which, over time,
> add up to the big differences that we often cannot foresee.
> – Marian Wright Edelman

Young people have the potential to drive significant social change and promote the Sustainable Development Goals. However, they are faced with several challenges that make it difficult for them to become change-makers without the proper resources and support. Despite widespread stereotypes about unmotivated and unskilled youth, particularly in developing countries, it has been demonstrated that they tend to be "better educated and more connected to global knowledge relative to older ages." This indicates that it is not the lack of skills, but rather of available opportunities, that prevents them from becoming change-makers and leaders in their communities.

As I introduced at the beginning of this book, Global Youth Leadership Academy (GYLA) shares the purpose and vision of the United Nations on youth development and engagement in the Agenda for Sustainable Development. GYLA is a solid, positive step to foster youth inclusion in social change and engagement in SDGs. The UN Youth Strategy has prioritized promoting the civic and political engagement of youth, noting that the UN must leverage its capacity in order to promote youth participation in public affairs at all levels. Young change-makers are identified and supported in this program and closer collaboration is fostered among the government, civil society, and private sector through this initiative. GYLA equips and transforms the lives of young people by providing the interlinks of SDGs and institutional changes.

We understand that youth development is a process that prepares young people to navigate adolescence and realize their potential as an adult. An important aspect of youth development is leadership potential. GYLA defines youth leadership as young people empowered to inspire and mobilise themselves and others towards a common purpose, in response to personal and/or social issues and challenges, to effect positive change. Based on this definition, GYLA's mission is to inspire and empower youth as future leaders and change makers for global engagement in social change and sustainable development goals.

In recent years, GYLA has closely collaborated with many United Nations agencies, such as ILO, UNIDO, WHO, UNTCAD, UNEF, FAO, WMO, etc. to develop and offer innovative learning and training programs for young people. For this purpose of youth empowerment and engagement, GYLA focuses on developing youth's ability to analyse their own strengths and weaknesses, set personal and vocational goals, and have the self-esteem, confidence, motivation, and abilities to carry them out including the ability to establish support networks in order to fully participate in community life and effect positive social change and the ability to guide or direct others on a course of action, influence the opinions and behaviours of others and serve as a role model. While GYLA programs meet basic physical, developmental, and social needs, GYLA seeks to position youth as leaders in their community, to take positions of leadership in companies, organizations and international community. Through GYLA programs, young people gain the skills and knowledge to lead civic engagement, education reform, and community organizing activities.

We are aware that nowadays, the nature and meaning of leadership is changing in response to a dramatically changing society, and the rise of complex challenges. Leadership is increasingly seen as situational and as an inherently collaborative, social and relational activity. Because of this, GYLA integrates in her curricula the social and emotional skills or competencies that foster and build interpersonal relationships—such as relationship management and communication, self-discipline, flexibility, creativity, and emotional intelligence. GYLA endeavours to offer in terms of helping build up young people's leadership skills and capacities in order to make positive contributions to their communities, alongside building their employability skills.

GYLA provides young people with the opportunity to develop and exercise leadership that can have benefits for the individual young person, their peer group and society more broadly. The emotional and social skills that enable effective leadership have broader significance beyond their potential to prepare young people to take on formal leadership roles; these skills are crucial to young people's successful transition to adulthood. Additionally, youth leadership can serve as a vehicle for tackling pressing social challenges and catalysing positive social change.

GYLA launched in 2016 to build the most global dynamic network working at the intersection of youth, leadership, innovation, entrepreneurship and sustainable development. GYLA has run seven successful learning and training programs and, as of end of 2020, has worked with over 1000 youth participants. GYLA participants have launched and established successful small social and green businesses, received recognition and awards for their innovative solutions, and presented their ideas at renowned universities and global platforms like the International Youth Forum.

As GYLA has been successful and influential across the China, attracting immense talent and diverse skill sets, the plan for the next few years is to scale up and extend the reach to over 10,000 young people and 1000 youth-serving organizations. In order to do so GYLA is working on introducing a number of tools, platforms and ideas that will enhance the collective knowledge and bring people together on national, regional and global levels:

- Exploring new mechanisms of support, beyond the traditional approaches, to advance youth development solutions. GYLA will develop a new platform that will encourage networking opportunities to explore forward thinking, analyze emerging trends and foresee upcoming developments. The platform will facilitate exchange of expertise, building collective knowledge and offering collaboration opportunities that will cross borders of countries as well as thematic areas. In addition, the platform will help provide and facilitate global networking opportunities, conferences and forums to extend reach to show case youth projects and prototypes.
- Experimenting to strengthen the design of solutions and learn through experimentation. GYLA is determined to support (a) strategic thinkers that can

collectively tackle a tough challenge, (b) crafty experimenters that are constantly looking for ways to test what they're working on, so they can better understand how it works and how to improve it and (c) systems thinkers to design solutions that take into account the different parts of a society to be connected and impact each other. GYLA would mobilize the means required to implement this agenda based on a spirit of strengthened global solidarity. GYLA aims to establish a grants scheme that would offer financial and technical support to young innovators and change makers.

- Expanding knowledge by institutionalizing the GYLA approach. To enhance the collective knowledge and build the capacity of its participants, GYLA has launched and will expand the online Learning Facility that will host more materials, guides and manuals that GYLA participants can access. A new curriculum on topics and solutions identified during the first 5 years of the learning activities will be developed. In the era of technological advancement and virtual conduct of business, the curriculum will contain learning materials on digital literacy with demand-driven thematic courses and training. These skills are vital for participants' development solutions to succeed and reach a wider audience.

GYLA believes that investing in expanding knowledge, networking and resources will facilitate the scale up process and support participants in becoming global leaders in innovation, solution mapping and change-makers and a force for change across the region. Once taken to the new heights GYLA has the potential to revolutionize the way youth can contribute to the development, peace and stability in their communities and around the globe.

Sustainability of GYLA

Since its inception 6 years ago, GYLA has been designed and implemented with the goal of becoming a sustainable model that relies on high quality interventions, and on the enthusiasm, passion and dedication of the program participants themselves. The youth participants are part of every phase of the program, with their responsibilities increasing over the 6 years from recipients in the first and second editions of GYLA programs to serving as dream team, organizers and implementers in the third and fourth edition of GYLA programs. This approach has helped not only establish a cadre of innovative and engaged youth, but youth who are actively taking part in supporting the development of their incoming peers.

Sustainability is also envisioned through reliance on an online platform that in the long-run will be a low-cost and high-impact initiative operated and managed by the youth-serving organizations themselves. For the establishment of the hubs, the program leverages on the facilities and resources of its partners which include youth serving organizations, ministries and councils, and incubators. These hosting organizations will be provided with the knowledge and know-how to independently operate them as well as to connect and collaborate with the other hubs in the world.

In considering the global level, GYLA programs consists of technical and hands-on sessions, complemented by the participation of inspirational speakers who share experiences on how to develop youth talent, launch sustainable social/green enterprises and initiatives, and become agents of change. Experts and speakers from the United Nations agencies, national/regional partners, and private sector/academic institutions, in addition to entrepreneurs, innovators, and activists, facilitate sessions.

Conclusions

GYLA is in every way a platform and instrument for our participants, partners and communities as well as for the UN agencies. GYLA has successfully piloted a rapidly growing programme for youth that has already made its marks on the world. Therefore, we know that if taken to new heights this programme has the potential to revolutionize the way youth can contribute to peace and sustainability in their communities and across the globe. GYLA will work closely with the UN agencies and global academic institutions to identify and engage national youth focused organizations, based on a rigorous selection process using specific criteria to ensure that we build upon the lessons learned from past years. We will continue to select youth who have demonstrated professional experience and knowledge in supporting youth in development and have a strong proven record, with quantifiable results, of making an impact on the youth in their communities.

We will also ensure that the individuals participating in the program have an extensive reach in the number of young people involved in their programmes. We are continuing to strike new ground with our strong, demonstrable connection to Agenda 2030. We understand the exchange of familiarity with social innovation methodologies, especially systems thinking and design thinking with participants and them with us. In lessons learned we understand there must be a willingness and commitment to collaborate with the UN agencies and national governments as well as to have capacity (people, time, resources) to commit to GYLA international activities.

The Young Leaders for SDGs: The United Nations Initiative

Since September 2016, the Office of the UN Secretary-General's Envoy on Youth has organized three editions of global award of the Young Leaders for the Sustainable Development Goals. Every 2 years, 17 young change-makers are recognized for their leadership and contribution to a more sustainable world.

The Young Leaders Initiative is powered by the Office of the UN Secretary-General's Envoy on Youth and is part of the Global Youth Partnership for Sustainable Development Goals, launched in 2015 and housed in the Envoy's Office. From food to fashion to finance, the Young Leaders for the SDGs, aged 19–30 years old, come from many different backgrounds, represent every region in the world and inspire all of us to achieve the goals. The Young Leaders for the SDGs are recognized for their leadership and contribution to a more sustainable world. The Young Leaders for the SDGs support one or more of the following:

- *Advocate for the Goals, in ways most accessible and relatable to young people across different contexts;*
- *Promote innovative ways of engaging their audiences and peers in the advocacy and realization of the Goals;*
- *Contribute to a brain trust of young leaders supporting the UN and partners for key moments and initiatives related to the Goals.*

The 17 Young Leaders have been recognized for their leadership and contribution to the achievement of the 2030 Agenda for Sustainable Development, which includes a set of 17 Goals to end poverty, fight inequality and injustice, and tackle climate change by 2030.

As a community of supporting young people for social change, GYLA also works with the UN agencies to support efforts to engage young people in the realization of the SDGs and will have opportunities to engage in UN and partner-led projects. For example, in recent years, GYLA has empowered young people by providing learning programs on social innovation and social entrepreneurship to encourage young people to start up their own social and green enterprises. GYLA has seen some of the successful social and green young entrepreneurs who graduated from GYLA programs, and made great contributions to sustainable development goals.

The flagship initiative of the Office of the Secretary-General's Envoy on Youth comes against a backdrop of increasing efforts by the UN to engage young people in its efforts to achieve the SDGs. In 2016, 17 Young Leaders were selected from over 18,000 nominations from 186 different countries. I want to introduce one of the 17 young leaders to illustrate how these young global citizens have transformed their communities, and made immense contributions to peace, development and the achievement of the Sustainable Development Goals.

Vincent Loka, 23-year-old from Indonesia, is one of the three founding partners of WateROAM, a social enterprise developing water filtration solutions that bring rapid access to clean drinking water in disaster-hit locations. One such solution is Fieldtrade Lite, a product that fits easily into a backpack and can filter dirty river water within minutes.

"We are committed to bringing clean water to people everywhere," says Vincent, which is why he and two co-founders, all in their early twenties, launched WateROAM—a water innovation enterprise championing the vision of a world without prolonged thirst. WateROAM is developing water filtration solutions that bring about the quickest access to clean drinking water at disaster-hit locations, and helping to promote social change in rural areas. "I lead the engineering team to develop filtration systems that are simple, affordable, durable and portable," says Vincent. "We realized that these four pillars are critical when it comes to getting water solutions to the people on the ground." One of these solutions, otherwise known as Fieldtrade Lite, fits easily into a backpack and can filter dirty river water within minutes.

The impact has been significant. In 2015 alone, WateROAM's filtration systems provided drinkable water for thousands of the victims of the earthquake in Nepal, Cyclone Pam in Vanuatu and the floods in Myanmar. "WateROAM" also supplies the filters to non-profit organizations that deliver them as part of their disaster-relief work. Vincent and his team are committed to continuing this work to achieve Sustainable Development Goal 6 on clean water and sanitation.

References

African Economic Outlook. (2013). *Who are the working youth in Africa?*

Bosma, N., Wennekers, S., & Amorós (2012). The global entrepreneurship monitor global report.

BSDC. (2017a). *Better business, better world.*

BSDC. (2017b). *Better business, better world: sustainable business opportunities in Asia.*

China. (2017). *China's progress report on implementation of the 2030 agenda for sustainable development, August 2017.*

Frost & Sullivan, GlobeScan. (2017). *The Sustainable Development Goals (SDGs): The value for Europe.* Whitepaper.

GEM. (2013). *Generation entrepreneur: The state of global youth entrepreneurship.*

ILO. (2016). *The world employment and social outlook.*

ILO. (2020). *Youth & COVID-19: Impacts on jobs, education, rights and mental well-being.* ILO.

MSG. (2018, December 16). *Youth entrepreneurship.* Retrieved July 11, 2019, from https://www.managementstudyguide.com/youth-entrepreneurship.htm

OECD. (2017). *Unlocking the potential of youth entrepreneurship in developing countries: From subsistence to performance.*

Statista. (2017). *China: Youth unemployment rate from 2007 to 2017*. https://www.statista.com/statistics/811935/youth-unemployment-rate-in-china/
The United Nations. (2013). *Opportunities and constraints to youth entrepreneurship*.
The United Nations. (2015). *Transforming our world: The 2030 Agenda for Sustainable Development*.
The United Nations. (2016). *The sustainable development goals report*. https://unstats.un.org/sdgs/report/2016/leaving-no-one-behind.
The United Nations. (2017a, 15 December 2018). *Asia-Pacific countries use social innovation to face ageing population and gender inequality*. Retrieved December 15, 2019, from http://unsdn.org/2017/03/20/asia-pacific-countries-use-socialinnovation-to-face-ageing-population-and-gender-inequality/
The United Nations. (2017b). *World population prospects*.
UNESCAP. (2017). *UN and SDGs: A handbook for youth*.
WEF. (2016). *Social innovaiton: A guide to achieving corporate and societal value*.

Chapter 19
The Chinese Way for Realization of SDGs

The Chinese Way Demystified

I discussed the role of youth, entrepreneurship, and social innovation that play in achieving the UN 2030 Agenda, and in the meantime, I also showcased the great business opportunities that SDGs will create for private sectors and youth entrepreneurs. I will concentrate on the Chinese way and its relationship with the achievement of SDGs in this chapter.

I have the impression of whenever we talk about China, and whatever we touch on China, we immediately think of the Chinese way. What is the Chinese way? Let's look at it from the perspective of life and culture. Min Ding and Jie Xu (2014) explored the Chinese Way and culture through the examination of the nine core concepts that best represent the Chinese way of life: *doctrine of mean, tribalism, hierarchicalism, polymorphism, usefulism, emotionalism, wealthism, effortlessism, and cynicism* (Min Ding and Jie Xu 2014). Doctrine of Mean (DoM) is fundamental to the Chinese way of life. It requires people not go to extremes and instead strive to be in the middle. Finding equilibrium is not the same as finding the mean, and most certainly, finding the mean should not be the objective. On social issues, DoM is reflected in a collective desire to seek a middle ground solution when there is a difference of opinion on a particular topic.

At the core of tribalism is the "*us versus them*" mentality. As long as one's own tribe can survive, another tribe's fortune or misery is inconsequential. People behave differently when they are within a circle than when they are outside a circle. Within a tribe (circle), one exhibits dedication, loyalty, and sacrifice, but the opposite is likely true towards people outside the tribe. One trusts people within the same tribe, but not outsiders. Within the tribe, collectivism reigns supreme; but outside the tribe, the Chinese are quite individualistic—even more so than their American counterparts. Tribalism also impacts how the Chinese view other countries. The guiding principle of Chinese foreign policy—non-interference—can be traced back to tribalism, where one is not supposed to interfere with other tribes' internal affairs and vice versa.

L. Zu, *Responsible and Sustainable Business*,
https://doi.org/10.1007/978-3-030-91117-1_19

Polymorphism in China takes two forms: across individuals and within an individual. Polymorphism across individuals is essentially the heterogeneity that exists among the Chinese. Polymorphism within an individual is more complex, yet integral to the Chinese way of life. In essence, the Chinese are taught and expected to behave differently in different situations, and they do not consistently follow the same principles in all contexts (Min Ding 2014). The author claims that understanding of Chinese Way can equip international business students, scholars, and practitioners with a deep understanding of a society that is a major player in global business today and offers a foundation for successful business interactions with Chinese companies, organizations, and people.

The Chinese Way of Life (CWoL) is a little different from the Chinese Way of Governance (CWoG). For the purpose of this chapter, particularly for the SDGs, I will focus on the second way. I interpret CWoG as the processes of interaction and decision-making among the actors involved in a collective problem that led to the creation, reinforcement, or reproduction of social norms and institutions in China, it combines the top-down and bottom-up approach. These strategic approaches lead to increased insight, effective project management, and clear lines of communication across a company or a project. Top-down approach starts with the big picture. It breaks down from there into smaller segments. The top-down approach relies on the higher authority figures to determine larger goals that will filter down to the tasks of lower-level employees. In comparison, the bottom-up style of communication features a decision-making process that gives the entire people a voice in company goals. Each task remains fluid as employees achieve their goals. Therefore, I believe that CWoG is effective, efficient and productive. Let's take a look at the role of CWoG played in the achievement of SDGs.

The Chinese Way for the UN 2030 Agenda: The Top-Down Approach

In September 2015, Mr. Jinping Xi, President of China, attended the United Nations Sustainable Development Summit and joined other leaders in endorsing the 2030 Agenda for Sustainable Development. As the largest developing countries in the world, China has always place development as the first priority. According to the 13th Five-Year Plan approved in 2016, it defines the development concept featuring innovative, coordinated, green, open, and shared development. China will pursue innovative development and improve the quality and efficiency of development in the future. Coordinated development will be promoted to form a balanced structure of development. China has developed the strategies and taken measures to implement the 2030 Agenda in accordance with national conditions and respective characteristics. For example, the Chinese way of the seven approaches were developed: *synergy of strategies, institutional guarantee, social mobilization, resource input, risk management, international cooperation, and oversight and review* (China 2016).

Synergy of Strategies aims at integrating the 2030 Agenda into China's mid-and-long term development strategies and creating synergy and complementarity between international agenda and domestic strategies. The focus in this synergy includes the following three aspects:

First, integrating the 17 SDGs and 169 targets into China's overall development planning and break down, incorporate, or link them in specialized plans. The China's 13th Five-Year Plan commits to the "active implementation of the 2030 Agenda for Sustainable Development". Government departments of China have turned the SDGs into specific tasks in the economic, social and environmental areas. In the economic field, the Chinese government has formulated the National Outline for Innovation-Driven Development Strategy, the National Sustainable Agricultural Development Plan (2015–2030), and the National Outline for Information Technology Development Strategy and. In the social field, it has published the Decision of the Communist Party of China (CPC) Central Committee and the State Council on Winning the Tough Battle in Poverty Reduction and the Healthy China Outline (2030). In the environmental field, it has prepared the China Biodiversity Conservation Strategy and Plan of Action (2011–2030) and the National Climate Change Program (2014–2020). Second, bringing the development objectives of local governments in line with the 2030 Agenda. Based on the Outline of the 13th Five-Year Plan, the 31 provinces, autonomous regions and municipalities directly under the central government in China have formulated their own five-year plans, and the cities and counties have completed their road maps and annual plans. In this way, the central and local governments have created synergy for the implementation of the 2030 Agenda. Third, pushing multilateral mechanisms to formulate action plan for the 2030 Agenda to create synergy at international level. China plays a leading role in facilitating the G20 to draw up action plan on implementation of the 2030 Agenda. China also initiated the "Belt and Road" strategy for assisting other countries in the implementation of the 2030 Agenda. And China intends to support the concerted efforts that regional commissions and specialized agencies of the United Nations have made to formulate actions plans for the goals and targets that fall within their respective regions or fields.

The second approach is institutional guarantee. It refers to the institutions, mechanisms and policies that will support the implementation of the 2030 Agenda and it includes the four aspects: first, promoting targeted reforms to establish an institutional framework for the implementation of the 2030 Agenda. The Chinese government will step up the improvement of institutions and systems to ensure that the market plays the decisive role in resource allocation and the government better plays its role, and remove all institutional barriers to scientific development, and to provide institutional impetus for the implementation of the 2030 Agenda. China will also advance the construction of innovation demonstration zones for the implementation of the 2030 Agenda to accumulate best practices. Second, the rule of law must be improved to provide legal guarantee for the implementation of the 2030 Agenda. China will step up the legislative work to improve the market economic system, develop democratic political system, foster advanced socialist culture, innovate on social governance, safe- guard citizens' rights and enhance people's livelihood, safeguard national security, protect the environment and improve government functions. It will also take efforts to build a comprehensive, scientific, effective and law-based government administration system. Third, ensuring to provide policy guarantee for the 2030 Agenda. The Chinese government will establish a comprehensive policy system, which is led by national policies and supported by specialized policies and local policies, with emphasis on the ten aspects: eliminating poverty and hunger, maintaining economic growth, advancing industrialization, improving social security and social services, safeguarding equity and justice, strengthening environmental protection, addressing the climate change, enhancing energy and resource efficiency, improving national governance and promoting international cooperation. Fourth, the responsibilities and accountability for governments must be articulated at all levels. China will not only enhance the horizontal cross-region and inter-agency coordination, but also establish a vertical implementation mechanism linking the central, local and grassroots levels. China's domestic inter-agency coordination mechanism comprised of 43 government departments has been established for the implementation of the 2030 Agenda, and its local governments will set up corresponding working mechanisms to ensure smooth implementation.

The third approach is social mobilization. Effective implementation of the 2030 Agenda requires better understanding, recognition and participation of people in SDGs, particularly, focusing on the three aspects: First, enhancing the sense of responsibility in participating in the implementation. Adhering to the principle of putting people first, China will implement the 2030 Agenda by the people and for the people. China will help its people fully appreciate the personal and public interests in the implementation of the 2030 Agenda and enhance their initiative and sense of responsibility in the implementation. Second, extensive use of the media for social mobilization. China will make the 2030 Agenda more accessible to people and create an enabling environment for the implementation via social media and public campaigns. Third, promoting public participation. China will engage non-governmental groups, the private sector and individuals especially the youth in training courses, networking and management activities related to the 2030 Agenda, to help them realize the importance of coordinated economic, social and environmental sustainability and build a broad- based social consensus on the 2030 Agenda. Governments at all levels will play their due role in coordination, mobilization, implementation and supervision to form the social synergy for the Agenda.

In alignment with the strategies, China proposed nine key areas as the top priorities in the implementation of the 2030 Agenda (China 2016).

- *Goal 1 and 2: Eradicating poverty and hunger through targeted measures to alleviate and eliminate poverty, and enhancing agricultural production capacities and food security.*
- *Goal 8: Implementing innovation-driven development strategies and generating momentum for sustainable, healthy and stable economic growth.*

- *Goal 9 Advancing industrialization to inject impetus to coordinated development between urban and rural areas and among the three dimensions of sustainable development.*
- *Goal 10 Improving social security and social services to ensure equal access to basic public services.*
- *Goal 16 Safeguarding equity and social justice to improve people's well-being and promoting all-round human development.*
- *Goal 14–15 Protecting the environment and building protective barriers for eco-security.*
- *Goal 13 Addressing climate change actively and integrating climate change response into national development strategies.*
- *Goal 7 Promoting efficient utilization of resources and sustainable energy.*
- *Goal 16 Improving national governance and ensuring economic and social development in line with the rule of law.*

Committing to delivering all 17 goals, China has identified several top priorities within the agenda: sustainable consumption and production, health and education, equality, employment, and migration. Implementing the 2030 Agenda is a systemic project. Chinese authorities are also determined to provide sound support from five dimensions:

- *Strengthening capacity building of governments to improve institution building, increase public resources, and generate internal growth momentum.*
- *Creating an enabling international environment for development, building a balanced, win-win and inclusive multilateral trading system and improving economic governance.*
- *Engaging with all stakeholders, and working towards a more equitable and balanced partnership for development.*
- *Promoting coordination mechanism and incorporating development policy into macroeconomic policy coordination.*
- *Improving evaluation and assessment of performance by conducting regular reviews of implementation progress while review of national implementation would be done according to respective national conditions and the principle of voluntary action.*

The year of 2016 is the first year of implementing the 2030 Agenda for Sustainable Development. China has made great efforts in its implementation, linking the 2030 Agenda with domestic mid-and-long term development strategies. The domestic coordination mechanism for the implementation, comprised of 43 government departments, has been established to guarantee the implementation. Great efforts has been be made to publicize the 2030 Agenda nationwide in order to mobilize domestic resources, raise public awareness, and creating favourable social environment for the implementation. China will also strengthen inter-sector policy coordination, review and revise relevant laws and regulations to provide policy and legislative guarantee for the implementation. In the next 5 years, China is determined to lift all the 55.75 million rural residents living below the current poverty line out of poverty, and to double its GDP and people's per capita income of 2010. China has already released the Position Paper on the Implementation of the 2030 Agenda for Sustainable Development, which reflects China's views on the principles, priorities, policies and progress made in the implementation of the 2030 agenda. China will also issue its national plan of implementing the 2030 Agenda this year and share its development experience with other countries.

The Chinese Way for Innovation and Entrepreneurship: The Bottom-up Approach

Creativity and innovation are drivers of economic growth as China looks to young entrepreneurs to steer it away from an investment-led model. Over the past two decades, entrepreneurship in China has grown at an exponential rate. It is bringing forth disruptive changes not only to China but increasingly also to the rest of the world. As economic growth slows and the property sector cools, China is relying on more people, especially young people, to be creative and innovative enough to turn their ideas into economic benefit. The government hopes young entrepreneurs will help transform China from productivity-driven into innovation-driven economy. Innovation and entrepreneurship is always the driving force of economic growth in China. The future growth in China can come from innovation, not just in the use of technology but through imaginative ways of managing businesses and processes. Capturing these gains would make China a principal contributor to global growth (Daniel Ren 2015).

Mass entrepreneurship and innovation is the leading agenda of China's national economic strategy. It has been an effective driver for both economic growth and the consistent transition between traditional and new growth engines. It has also significantly contributed to the creation of new jobs and the increase in incomes. China issued a policy to boost mass entrepreneurship and innovation in 2015, and adopted a guideline in 2017 to further enhance the support for innovation and entrepreneurship. The purpose of the policy is to intensify structural reform, boost efforts to implement the strategy of pursuing innovation-driven development, and removed all institutional obstacles which impede mass entrepreneurship and innovation. The government is determined to innovate its institutional mechanisms to facilitate mass entrepreneurship and innovation. It aims at creating a better environment for fair competition, deepening business system reforms, strengthening intellectual property protection and establishing a mechanism for the training and hiring of talented professionals; related government bodies are optimizing their financial policies to support mass entrepreneurship and innovation. China will also strengthen financial support policies, inclusive funding measures and more government purchasing in the near future. Statistics of the State Administration for Industry and Commerce show that the country saw the registration of more than 13 million new enterprises between March 2014 and February 2017, 94.6 percent of which are in the private sector, adding an average of 15,600 new enterprises on a daily basis in the first five months of this year, giving employment a major boost (Xu Wei 2017).

Social entrepreneurs and social enterprises have been also growing in China over past years. The consensus about social enterprise is that this new type of organization, possessing both social purpose and business traits, and combining innovation with entrepreneurship, can play an important role in poverty alleviation. It can also enhance participation and capacity building for vulnerable and disadvantaged groups, establishing social capital and ensuring sustainable development. More and more NGO leaders and intellectuals believe that social enterprise will be a remedy for many social problems and unmet social needs, and a boost for social sector development in China. As a result, hundreds of social enterprises have emerged in the last eight years. The findings of SEFORÏS research in 2015 show that Chinese social entrepreneurial activities span a wide variety of fields, but the majority of these activities fall in to three broad categories: Education, (21%), Community and Social Services (21%), and Business Services for SMEs (29%). It also found that over 75% of social entrepreneurs are under 39 years old (Ding 2017).

Social enterprise in its current form is a new phenomenon in China. But as an old Chinese saying goes: a little spark may kindle a great fire. Many social enterprises are rising stars with great potential due to their unique positioning and innovative approach to tackling societal challenges, and satisfying unmet social needs, especially from underprivileged groups in China.

References

China. (2016). *China's national plan on implementation of the 2030 agenda for sustainable development.*

Ding, L. (2017). *How China's social enterprises can prosper alongside the Country's state-run businesses.*https://www.weforum.org/agenda/2017/06/how-china-s-social-enterprises-can-prosper-alongside-the-country-s-state-run-businesses/

Min Ding, J. X. (2014). *The Chinese way.*

Daniel Ren. (2015, 3 March 2015). *China looks to young entrepreneurs to drive its innovation economy.* Retrieved 22 December 2018 from https://www.scmp.com/news/china/article/1727961/chinas-young-entrepreneurs-drive-its-innovation-economy

Xu Wei. (2017, 12 July 2017). *China to further promote innovation and entrepreneurship.* Retrieved December 20, 2018, from http://english.gov.cn/premier/news/2017/07/12/content_281475723086902.htm

Chapter 20
Conclusion

The SDGs set out the UN agenda for people, planet and prosperity, achieving a prosperous, inclusive and sustainable society for all by 2030. Only can purpose and vision of the Agenda be achieved if people's mindset is changed and people's trust in today's capitalism is restored. The former Secretary-General, Ban Ki-Moon once said, "*The SDGs represent the change we need to restore people's trust in the global economy. The SDGs represent an enormous opportunity to make our economy work for dignity for all, prosperity for all and a better planet for all. . . . The SDGs aim to end poverty in all its forms everywhere, ensuring people live in dignity and prosperity while protecting the planet.*"

Creating a prosperous, inclusive and sustainable society where everyone can live in dignity and prosperity is always a great challenge and a long way to go. The challenge is that how we are able to create a new economic system and model that unleashes innovation and entrepreneurship potential in young people as a creative force, and particularly, empower young people as leaders and engage them in achievement of SDGs. We believe that it might be the most important responsibility for the United Nations to shoulder to strengthen and increase commitments at the global, regional and national level so that young people's needs can be met, help them realize their rights, and recognize their positive contributions as agents of change. Because "*All our hopes for a better world rest on young people. The world is home to the largest generation of young people. Sustainable development, human rights, peace and security can only be achieved if we empower these young people as leaders*".

Young people of today are the ones who will lead the world in creating the new civilization we desperately need. They are already hard at work, looking for ideas and an action agenda. Once they know what they want, they can achieve it much more easily than it could have been done thirty years back. Today's youth are remarkably well equipped for any big task. Better educated than any generation in history, they are highly diverse and globally connected. Today's youth have only a blurred picture of what kind of world they want. However, they realize that both the academic world and the political world have failed to give them a road map to the

L. Zu, *Responsible and Sustainable Business*,
https://doi.org/10.1007/978-3-030-91117-1_20

better world they want, nor have they provided the tools they need to design a road map of their own (Muhammad Yunus 2017).

In September 2018, the United Nations launched Youth 2030: The United Nations Youth Strategy at a high-level event of the 73rd session of the General Assembly. We have observed the momentum of great progress that young people have made in transforming the economic and social systems in the last decade. Thousands of people and organizations have already embraced the new economic model through their own social action groups in the world, launching innovative social businesses designed to serve human needs rather than accumulate wealth. They are bringing solar energy to millions of homes in Bangladesh; turning thousands of unemployed young people into entrepreneurs through equity investments; financing female-owned businesses in cities across the United States; bringing mobility, shelter, and other services to the rural poor in France; and creating a global support network to help young entrepreneurs launch their start-ups (Muhammad Yunus 2017).

I never forget wisdom of Peter Drucker, the founder of modern management style when we discuss innovation and entrepreneurship. His famous quote for his thoughts on entrepreneurship is "*The entrepreneur always searches for change, responds to it, and exploits it as an opportunity*." The implication is obvious, international community and national authorities should ensure to empower young people as leaders, innovators and entrepreneurs for social change in their communities, and society as a whole. Specifically, young entrepreneurs should be on the look for change that the UN 2030 Agenda may bring about, and respond to SDGs, take advantage of SDGs and exploit SDGs as the opportunity, and make the most of it.

Realization of SDGs requires young people to start businesses that are more social and ecological. Social entrepreneurship provides viable and innovative solutions to social and environmental issues at the local, national and regional levels. It can also showcase the benefits and value of social business to policymakers and other relevant stakeholders, the ecosystem will be strengthened, and young social entrepreneurs will be able to trigger social transformation in their communities, and thereby contribute to sustainable development.

As we already discussed in this book, to achieve the UN 2030 Agenda, SDGs and each target must be translated into action plan at country level. As the largest developing country in the world, China has always given top priority to development. China attaches great importance to the 2030 Agenda. For example, the UN 2030 Agenda has been closely integrated in domestic mid-and-long term development strategies of the 13th Five-Year Plan. The Chinese authority also recognizes that achievement of SDGs largely relies on innovation and youth entrepreneurs in the future. Since 2015, Chinese authority has encouraged young people to engage in mass entrepreneurship and innovation campaign. The strategy of mass entrepreneurship and innovation not only boosts employment, social innovation, and the development of industries, but also transform economic development mode from efficiency-driven economy, which exhibits scale-intensity as a major driver of development, to the innovation-driven stage of development, which is characterized by their production of new and unique goods and services that are created via sophisticated, and often pioneering, methods.

Reference

Muhammad Yunus. (2017). *A world of three zeros: The new economics of zero poverty, zero unemployment, and zero net carbon emissions.*

The manufacturer's authorised representative in the EU is Springer Nature Customer Service Centre GmbH, Europaplatz 3, 69115 Heidelberg, Germany. If you have any concerns regarding our products, please contact ProductSafety@springernature.com

Printed and bound by CPI Group (UK) Ltd, Croydon, CR0 4YY

30/09/2026

02225497-0017